Administrative Assistant's & Secretary's HANDBOOK

Second Edition

Administrative Assistant's & Secretary's HANDBOOK

Second Edition

James Stroman
Kevin Wilson
Jennifer Wauson

AMERICAN MANAGEMENT ASSOCIATION
New York • Atlanta • Brussels • Chicago • Mexico City • San Francisco
Shanghai • Tokyo • Toronto • Washington, D.C.

Special discounts on bulk quantities of AMACOM books are available to corporations, professional associations, and other organizations. For details, contact Special Sales Department, AMACOM, a division of American Management Association, 1601 Broadway, New York, NY 10019.
Tel: 212-903-8316. Fax: 212-903-8083.
E-mail: specialsls@amanet.org
Website: www.amacombooks.org/go/specialsales
To view all AMACOM titles go to: www.amacombooks.org

This publication is designed to provide accurate and authoritative information in regard to the subject matter covered. It is sold with the understanding that the publisher is not engaged in rendering legal, accounting, or other professional service. If legal advice or other expert assistance is required, the services of a competent professional person should be sought.

Library of Congress Cataloging-in-Publication Data

Stroman, James.
    Administrative assistant's & secretary's handbook / by James Stroman,
Kevin Wilson, Jennifer Wauson.—2nd ed.
        p.   cm.
    Includes bibliographical references (p.) and index.
    ISBN-10: 0-8144-0784-6
    ISBN-13: 978-0-8144-0784-4
    1. Secretaries—Handbooks, manuals, etc.   2. Office practice—Handbooks,
manuals, etc.   I. Title: Administrative assistant's and secretary's handbook.
II. Wilson, K. (Kevin). 1958–   III. Wauson, Jennifer.   IV. Title.
HF5547.5 .A247   2004
651.3—dc21

                                                        2003010063

Various names used by companies to distinguish their software and other products can be claimed as trademarks. AMACOM uses such names throughout this book for editorial purposes only, with no intention of trademark violation. All such software or product names are in initial capital letters. Individual companies should be contacted for complete information regarding trademarks and registration. A list of these companies appears on pg. vi of this book.

Printing number

10   9   8   7   6

Special thanks to Linda Wauson

. . . a corporate rock star.

Contents

21. Multimedia and Presentation Software   **260**

22. Office Ergonomics   **280**

23. Glossary of Computer Terms   **289**

BUSINESS DOCUMENTS   311

24. The Business Letter   **313**

25. Other Written Communications 338

26. Forms of Address 349

27. Legal Documents and Terms 363

SECTION FOUR

LANGUAGE USAGE 377

28. Grammar 379

29. Language Usage and Style 403

SECTION FIVE

FINANCIAL ACTIVITIES   479

SECTION SIX

CAREER ADVANCEMENT   525

40. Your Future   527

Index   535

Preface

One of the most important positions in any company is that of administrative assistant, also referred to as executive secretary, private secretary, personal secretary, or office administrator. The job requires versatility, skill, precision, efficiency, and a constant willingness to increase one's knowledge.

Being a top-notch administrative assistant in the business or the professional world is a satisfying and rewarding career in itself. It also provides, for those who want it, an excellent opportunity for advancement.

This handbook covers the many aspects of an administrative assistant's job: from opening the mail to handling bookkeeping, from making travel arrangements to operating computers. It's both an ideal how-to book for newcomers and a handy reminder for veterans; a compact, yet comprehensive, all-purpose business reference that provides the information you need quickly and concisely.

We hope that the *Administrative Assistant's & Secretary's Handbook* will sharpen your interpretation of this exciting vocation and provide you with everything you need to become a valued, competent, indispensable assistant on your way up the wonderful ladder of success.

James Stroman
Kevin Wilson
Jennifer Wauson

GENERAL PROCEDURES

SECTION ONE

A good administrative
assistant can be an
indispensable part of
any team.
*Photo by Jennifer Wauson.
Digital photography courtesy
of Kyocera Optics.*

Overview for the New Administrative Assistant

Why Are You Needed?

As an administrative assistant, you are hired to relieve your busy employer of a great deal of work, especially the details of office procedure and other matters that do not require your employer's personal involvement. You'll act as a liaison between your boss and the rest of the company. Sometimes you'll act as a buffer. Depending on the size of the company, you may also be called on to perform tasks normally outside the secretarial role in sales, banking, billing, payroll, accounting, advertising, public relations, purchasing, and more. Everything you do for your employer must duplicate as closely as possible what he or she would do if not absorbed in work that couldn't be delegated.

Every business person dreams of having the perfect administrative assistant, and every administrative assistant dreams of having the perfect boss. Hopefully you and your boss will become so well adjusted to each other that you'll work as a team, each trusting the other to carry part of the load in harmony.

What Do Employers Want?

It's helpful to know what an employer expects of a "perfect administrative assistant" so that you can present yourself at your best during both the job interview and those critical first weeks on the job. Here are a few of the most important qualities:

- *Punctuality.* An employer wants an administrative assistant who is consistently punctual and always on hand during office hours. An administrative assistant who continually arrives even a few minutes late or who is ill frequently can cause havoc in a busy office. The employer knows from experience that such an administrative assistant may not be truly interested in the work. This person will be passed over or terminated in favor of someone with greater respect for the job, an administrative assistant who is always punctual and always there when needed.

FIGURE 1-1. An administrative assistant makes copies.
Photo by Kevin Wilson.

During an interview, the employer may try to see where your attention is focused, asking such questions as how many sick days you used on your previous jobs, how many outside activities you engage in, and so on. Previous sick days can and will be checked, so don't lie. If you have many outside interests, mention only those that in some way contribute to your job, such as night courses or professional associations. You don't want to give the impression that you're "too busy" to work.

- *Dependability.* An employer considers the applicant's disposition and personality, trying to judge whether he or she is dependable. For example, would the candidate rush home at precisely five o'clock despite an office crisis, or take enough responsibility to volunteer to remain after hours if an emergency arises?

- *Ability to learn.* An employer wants to know the extent of the applicant's education—not only formal programs and degrees, but also self-instruction and single courses. This information indicates the applicant's willingness and capacity for learning. For example, an employer may hope that you know the specific computer software the company already uses but not be too concerned if you aren't familiar with it, if you show the potential to learn quickly.

■ *Willingness to follow instructions.* An employer wants a candidate who follows instructions carefully and willingly. Of course, a good administrative assistant will soon take initiative and perform certain tasks differently to save time or improve results. But the administrative assistant who always demands complete control may ultimately become unwilling to follow instructions, debating or questioning every one of the boss's directives. Though intelligent input from an administrative assistant is prized, an employer usually prefers not to argue points that he or she has already decided. There are more important matters than explaining all the reasons for pursuing a particular policy. Therefore, the employer looks for an administrative assistant who will execute a decision no matter how many alternatives may seem obvious, or no matter what a former boss did in the same situation. In other words, the employer wants someone whose personality will be an asset rather than a handicap.

■ *Loyalty and confidentiality.* Although these qualities are impossible to discover during an interview alone, every boss wants his or her administrative assistant to possess them. In an office, there is nothing more unwelcome than the "human sieve" who constantly chatters about every conversation heard, spreads idle rumors like wildfire, and must constantly be screened from confidential projects and information. No matter how efficient, how educated, and how experienced that administrative assistant is, his or her employment will be short-lived.

■ *And something else.* A keen employer wants more in a prospective administrative assistant than these general qualifications. During an extended interview, the employer will be looking for quick-wittedness, flexibility, commitment to work, a certain quality and level of conversation, and a sense of courtesy. This last attribute is essential in establishing cordial relations with clients and fellow employees.

Interview Tips

During your interview, it is wise to be as relaxed as possible despite a natural tendency to be nervous. Appear on time, of course, and be well groomed and neatly dressed; otherwise the appointment may be cancelled at the receptionist's desk.

If you try too hard to sell yourself, you'll make a poor impression. Allow the employer to form his or her own first impression. After all, he or she knows what kind of administrative assistant is needed and, in addition, may prefer to work with a certain type of person. If you're not what the employer wants, it's wiser for both of you that another applicant be chosen.

If you receive a job offer, the salary may be less than what you think you're worth. There's often a discrepancy between what we'd like to make and what we can make. Job applicants fresh from school, in particular, may feel this way until they become more familiar with what the market is actually paying. Before refusing a position on the basis of salary alone, first be sure you know what the salaries are for comparable secretarial and administrative assistant positions in your area and for someone with your education and experience. Then, find out whether you'll be eligible for a raise after a short period of probation. Finally, consider whether the position has opportunities for increased responsibility and advancement. While it may not seem true to you right now as a job applicant, a big salary is rarely more important than professional satisfaction.

Your Apprenticeship

Even if you are already well experienced, once you have a new position, you must be prepared to serve an apprenticeship with your new employer. Your past experience may be useful only in that it has taught you to learn quickly and to evaluate new situations. At your new office, there may be a different method for almost every daily procedure, even for distributing and opening the mail. No doubt, there will be a filing system you haven't used elsewhere. You may be asked to use letter formats, paragraphing, punctuation, and abbreviations that were vetoed by a previous employer.

You may also discover that your new boss has an extensive vocabulary with many words you'll need to learn, or just the reverse—a poor vocabulary that needs your assistance. Will your new boss wish you to type a letter exactly as dictated, or do you have permission to "add to and take from?" Or will the boss furnish only the essentials of what he or she wishes to convey and request that you put the letter together in proper form?

Your need to be flexible extends to the computer system in the new office. You may find many differences between the hardware and software you used in school or at a past job and what you must use now. Even an updated version of the same software package may have a different user interface and functions. You need to familiarize yourself with the new computer and software, even if it means staying after work to read the manual and to experiment.

Stimulated by your brand-new environment and your past experience, you may find yourself coming up with dozens of ideas and suggestions within your first few weeks on the job. Remember that when you do have a suggestion to offer, it may very well have been made before and rejected for excellent reasons. When one of your ideas is refused, don't take it personally. Soon, after you're more familiar with the company and its operations, you'll be able to make a better suggestion. At the same time, don't be reluctant to give input freely when the boss asks for it.

A new employee's overeagerness to offer advice, recommend changes, and carry over methods from old jobs may just disguise a need to be recognized for his or her capability. In this situation, the best way to prove yourself is to do your best, learn quickly, follow instructions accurately and intelligently, and co-operate with fellow employees. Show consideration for others beyond the call of duty. A little extra giving will cost you absolutely nothing and will bring huge dividends in trust and friendship among your coworkers and your employer.

Daily Routine

Your Office

Office conditions for administrative assistants vary. Your employer may be an entrepreneur working from a small office or even from home. You may find yourself in a law firm, a doctor's office, a sales office, a warehouse front office, a retail business, or a service business. Your company may have branches in several states or even several countries. The general activity of the business—selling, servicing, or perhaps manufacturing—may be located in the same area where you're expected to perform your job, or it may be far removed from where you work. And all these conditions may change over time as the company does.

Your Workstation

The location and conditions of where you do your day-to-day work can be critical to how effectively you perform. Look first at how your workstation is placed physically within the entire office setup. Is there a reason that your desk is where it is? Analyze the traffic patterns around and through your workspace. Do coworkers have to pass through it to get from one operation to another? Study your own work patterns. How often do you go back and forth to the filing cabinets each day? How far away from your desk are they? Do other workers share these files? Is there a more efficient way to organize the office?

You may find it helpful to draw a sketch of your office and try out alternative arrangements on paper before you make suggestions to your employer. Each proposed change must consider two questions: 1.) Will you work more effectively in a different office layout? 2.) Will your proposed changes affect another worker's effectiveness?

Whether or not you have input on the physical placement of your workstation, your desk and immediate workspace are yours to organize in a way that makes you comfortable and allows you to be as productive as possible. Your immediate workspace may include a desk, chairs, files, bookshelves, credenza, and portable tables. As you arrange these items, plan a layout that considers your work habits as well as the travel patterns for yourself, other employees, and clients.

Here are just a few factors to consider:

■ *Desk chair.* Your chair should help promote good posture and back support, and it should be adjustable so you will not tire quickly. If possible, try to obtain an ergonomically designed chair.

■ *Lighting.* Proper lighting is highly important in any office. Your work area should have sufficient lighting to avoid causing you eyestrain and headaches yet be positioned to minimize glare on your computer monitor.

■ *Desk.* Your desk should be large enough to hold the office supplies and equipment you work with most often and to provide a clear area on which to work. Keep your most often-used supplies and equipment, such as telephone, memo pad, in and out box, and stapler, within easy reach when you are seated at your desk. Any reference books that you use frequently should also be easy to reach, as well as a desk organizer. A desk organizer with slots is useful to store various work-in-progress folders so they can be quickly found when needed.

■ *Supplies.* In your own desk, keep enough frequently used supplies to last for a week. At the beginning of each week, restock your supply. Neatly arrange these materials in drawer organizers, small boxes, or other containers. Store ink pads upside down.

■ *Computer or typewriter.* Your computer or typewriter should be on a surface apart from your desk, preferably its own desk or table. In any case, you should be able to fit your legs under this surface comfortably as you work. Power cords should be kept out of the way, so you will not inadvertently disconnect them with your feet. Multiple power cables can be connected together with twist-ties. Besides a computer, keyboard, monitor, and printer, your computer workstation will most likely also be equipped with a mouse, a good-quality mouse pad for extra traction, a modem or network card for communications and file sharing, a hard disk drive, an external storage drive, diskette or CD-ROM files, a diskette or CD-ROM storage system, and software reference manuals. Other useful accessories to help organize and protect this equipment include plastic dust covers for both the computer and keyboard when not in use, a computer fan to prevent overheating, an antiglare monitor cover to reduce eyestrain, and acoustical hoods for printers. All expensive office equipment such as memory typewriters and computers should be equipped with a surge protector.

If you work for a small company, you may have to arrange all these elements so they can also be used by fellow employees without interfering with your other work.

Office Supplies

Depending on the size of the company and your own responsibilities, you may have to order office supplies for yourself, your department, or the entire business. You can purchase supplies at an office supply store, either in person or by ordering over the phone, fax, or by mail from an office supply catalog. You can also use office supply Web sites such as Staples.com, Officemax.com, or OfficeDepot.com to order online. Purchases can be shipped or delivered.

When determining an order, do not overestimate your need. A multiple-item discount is not always useful, because certain items cannot be stored too long. Keep an inventory of your supplies and when you use them. A logbook is a useful way to keep a record of supply consumption.

In addition to everyday supplies like pens, pencils, staples, paper clips, and file folders, some items may need special consideration. For example, fax paper, computer printer toner or ink cartridges, computer diskettes, copier replacement cartridges or toner, and copier paper must each be ordered with your exact office equipment in mind.

Office supplies should be kept in a supply cabinet, shelf, or file cabinet. If coworkers have access to these supplies, consider labeling the shelves to help stay organized. Keep the supply storage area orderly and clean. Items that you use most often should be stored at eye level, where they will be easy to see and reach. Those that might spill should be kept on the bottom shelf. Try to keep the label from the original packaging attached to the supplies; the information will be helpful when reordering the item. For the same reason, keep opened reams of copier and office paper inside the wrapper leaving the label on one end. There are many different types and weights of office paper, and some are better suited for certain applications than others. For example, most copiers work best with 20-pound uncoated paper stock. Saving the label will help ensure you have the right product for the job.

The following is a list of common office supplies listed by type.

Audiovisual Supplies and Equipment

- Audiovisual equipment and accessories
- Binding equipment and supplies
- Business presentation tools and supplies
- Graphic arts and drafting supplies
- Laminating equipment and supplies
- Message boards, signs, and lettering
- Wall boards

Basic Supplies and Labels

- Adhesives and tape dispensers
- Cash boxes, coin handling, and key control
- Clips, pushpins, fasteners, and rubber bands

- Correction fluid and tape
- Labels
- Mailroom supplies
- Message pads, memo books, and Post-It Notes™
- Paper punches and trimmers
- Safes and security items
- Stamps and stamp pads
- Staplers and staples
- Name tags and tickets

Breakroom and Safety

- Beverage dispensers
- Breakroom appliances
- Coffee and hot beverages
- Cold beverages
- Cups, plates, and utensils
- First aid supplies
- Safety products
- Snacks
- Time clocks

Business Cases

- Attaché cases
- Backpacks
- Briefcases
- Business card holders and accessories
- Catalog and sample cases
- Computer and multi-use cases
- Portfolios
- Ringfolios and pad holders
- Travel accessories

Calendars and Planners

- Address books
- Appointment books
- Calendars
- Organizer books
- Organizer book refills and accessories
- Telephone books, address books
- Wall planners

Cleaning Supplies

- Air fresheners
- Bathroom cleaners
- Brooms and dustpans
- Brushes and dusters
- Floor and carpet cleaners
- General office cleaners
- Glass cleaners
- Mops and buckets
- Soap and hand cleaners
- Sponges and squeegees
- Trash cans and liners
- Vacuums

Custom Printing

- Business cards
- Business and human resource forms
- Business stationery
- Custom stamps
- Engraved products
- Envelopes
- Labels
- Specialty imprints

Filing, Binding, and Storage

- Binder accessories
- Binders
- Boxes
- Catalog racks
- Dividers for binders
- Files
- Index cards
- Index tabs
- Portfolios
- Reference systems
- Report covers
- Sheet protectors
- Tabs

Hardware

- Air purifiers
- Batteries
- Extension cords
- Fans
- Handtrucks
- Heaters
- Key control
- Ladders and stools
- Light bulbs
- Tools
- Utility cabinets

Organizers and Desk Accessories

- Bookends
- Cord and cable management
- Desk pads and blotters
- Desktop collections
- Desktop and drawer organizers
- Desktop sorters
- Desk trays
- Desktop, wall, and floor literature holders
- Hanging wall files
- Partition organizers
- Surface protectors

Paper, Forms, and Envelopes

- Blank certificates
- Business forms
- Card products
- Clipboards
- Document covers
- Envelopes
- Notebooks
- Paper
- Paper rolls
- Photo and specialty paper
- Recordkeeping
- Seals
- Tax forms
- Writing pads

Pens, Pencils and Markers

- Erasers
- Highlighters
- Markers

- Pencils
- Pencil sharpeners
- Pens

Printer and Fax Supplies

- Inkjet cartridges and supplies
- Laser toner cartridges and supplies

- Printer ribbons
- Thermal printer supplies

Restroom Paper Goods

- Bathroom tissue
- Facial tissue
- Napkins and dispensers

- Paper towels and dispensers
- Wipes and towelettes

Reference Works

Every office should have a minimum number of reference works and other sources of information. These are invaluable in writing, taking dictation, and transcribing, and will help you improve your work by enlarging your knowledge of the subjects covered in correspondence or in reports. By telephoning a specific question to the reference department of the local public library, you can often obtain the information you need or gather advice on how it may be found, but try to anticipate problems by having good reference books in the office.

The book you will consult most often will be an abridged dictionary, and it should be on your desk. There are a number of good dictionaries. The one recommended here is *Webster's New Collegiate Dictionary* because it contains most of the information an administrative assistant requires for daily work: spelling, syllabication, pronunciation, meaning, usage, derivation, and even synonyms in many cases. Occasionally, the *Dictionary of American Synonyms* and *Roget's Thesaurus,* may also be of value, though in a busy office, there is seldom time to consult these works.

If you do most of your work on a computer, you may elect to use a software dictionary. These programs can be installed on your computer and allow you to look up word spellings, definitions, synonyms, and antonyms with the click of a mouse. If you have an Internet connection that is always on, you can use an online dictionary. Dictionary.com is an excellent online resource that allows you to look up words from within a word-processing document by typing a special combination of keys on the keyboard.

If your employer has a literary bent and inserts quotations in dictation now and then, a copy of *Bartlett's Familiar Quotations* will help prevent misquotations.

You should also have a world atlas. In addition, try to have *World Almanac and Book of Facts* and a good single-volume encyclopedia. A copy of *Who's Who* will simplify your search for the addresses of people with whom your employer might correspond (or, again, you could call the reference librarian). A *Directory of Directors*, a *Directory of Merchants and Manufacturers*, and similar books appear annually. Ask the reference librarian at your local public library to advise you which are best for your purpose.

If you have an Internet connection, you'll find many reference works available online.

Work Planning

The first thing to do when you arrive at the office every day should be to air the rooms and regulate the heat or air conditioning (unless it's set on a permanent basis by building maintenance). Then arrange your desk for maximum efficiency, and replenish your supplies. Prepare your notebook and pencils for taking phone messages or to be ready if your employer gives you a task that requires taking notes.

Consult your desk calendar or your computer's calendar to be sure you're aware of all you must do during the day. Check your list of recurring matters: appointments, meetings, payroll dates, bill payments, and tax or insurance deadlines. Give your employer a reminder list of appointments and other activities, and prepare any material from the files he or she will need.

As part of your normal daily routine, try to order your activities in the most productive way. When you have to leave your desk to run an errand, for example, do other errands at the same time. Whenever possible, use the telephone instead of delivering a message in person (unless, of course, your employer asks you to do so). You may also use e-mail.

If you have tasks that involve mailing or shipping, plan them with pickup and delivery times in mind. Maintain a daily "to-do" list on paper or in your computer, and check off each item as it is accomplished. When new projects come in, try to complete them as quickly as possible. Prioritize your work. If you have several ongoing projects, and a new one comes in, ask your employer which one has the highest priority.

Each evening before you leave the office, make a list of what you need to do the following workday. Then put away all of your work and work-in-progress files, either in your desk drawers or in a filing cabinet. Work that is especially sensitive, such as client lists or accounting records, should be put away in a locked file cabinet.

Your regular routine includes keeping your work area clean. Clean out your desk drawers periodically. Your computer, typewriter, and other office equipment should be cleaned using a slightly damp towel. Compressed air in a can is useful for blowing dust off your computer keyboard and monitor screen. Disk-drive cleaning kits use a special diskette to clean the internal working parts.

In addition to maintaining your immediate area, schedule regular servicing for all office equipment as part of a preventive maintenance program. Do not wait for equipment to break down in the middle of a big project with a firm deadline. Here, the old adage is so important: an ounce of prevention is worth a pound of cure.

Finally, always be thinking of ways you can improve your own performance and the efficiency of the office. Look for problems, and try to find ways to solve them. An orderly, smoothly running business has a greater chance for success, and your company's success will help ensure your own.

Dictation

Besides storing notebooks and pens in your own desk, keep a notebook, pencil, and pen in an inconspicuous place in your boss's office so you'll always be ready to take dictation, even if you've just looked in to announce a caller or deliver a message. You will save your boss valuable time, since you won't have to retreat to your own desk for supplies.

Each day, when you begin dictation, first write the date at the top of the notebook page. When the dictation is over, write the date once more at the end, and draw a line across the page. Though there may be several dictation periods each day, you will find this notation helpful, if only in times of emergency, for you will be able to refer to your notes rapidly should questions arise.

When you take dictation from more than one person, keep separate notebooks with the name of each person on the outside in a prominent place. If you are asked a question about one of the letters, you will be able to reply without

FIGURE 2-1. An assistant discusses the day's activities with her manager.
Photo by Jennifer Wauson. Digital photography courtesy of Kyocera Optics.

hesitation, especially if you've remembered to write the date before and after each session of dictation.

During regular dictation, your employer will often include faxes, telegrams, or other communications that should be sent out promptly, though he or she may continue dictating for an hour or more before you can take care of them. In such an event, immediately after taking the dictation of the fax, telegram, or urgent letter, turn down the page in your notebook so that you can find the material as soon as you reach your desk. Occasionally your employer may dictate a remark that you cannot hear distinctly. It's imperative that you ask your boss to repeat the statement before continuing. Accuracy is more important than an unwillingness to interrupt, and your employer will respect you the more.

When the dictation contains names of correspondents, companies, and products that are unfamiliar to you, ask if these names are in the files or whether there are explanatory papers you should have. Ask this before you close that bit of dictation, and plan to refer to those papers before transcribing your notes.

✦ Transcription

Ideally, your shorthand is so reliable you can count on reading it even after the lapse of years. Just the same, sometimes it is not. When the material you've taken in shorthand is an unfamiliar subject, and you have to wait until the next workday before transcribing, take the time before leaving the office to scan your notes and check that they will be comprehensible later. A few minutes now may save an hour of puzzling later.

While transcribing your notes, always allow yourself to doubt a spelling now and then rather than hastily type what may be incorrect. When you have the slightest doubt, refer to the dictionary. If the word is one of those demons that you seemingly first have to know how to spell before you can even look it up, ask for help. Usually, at least one person in the office will welcome your inquiry. Computers, of course, have dictionaries built into them to check for spelling or typographical errors, but not every word is in every spell-check program. Be careful when you are correcting what you think is an error on your employer's part. Check a dictionary or a book on language usage, as it may be you who is mistaken.

An employer who is intelligent, well read, and well traveled will have an extensive vocabulary that he or she will naturally use in dictation. Take every opportunity to improve your own vocabulary, day by day adding to your knowledge of language. When dictation contains a word unfamiliar to you, place a large question mark on the page, and when the particular fax or letter is finished, ask your boss—without embarrassment—to spell the word for you. This shows that you want to learn and make your employer's vocabulary your vocabulary.

After transcription of your notes, be sure to read over what you've typed. If there is even one error, it's better for you to find it rather than another person. With computers and word processors, correction can be made in a second, and you can produce a perfect, well-spaced, and balanced page.

Dictation Machines

In many offices, administrative assistants do not take dictation or use shorthand. Instead, the employer uses a dictation machine. These machines save you the double job of taking dictation before transcribing the letter. While the employer is dictating into the machine, you can finish other tasks that would otherwise have to be neglected. In addition, some employers have difficulty dictating to another person but can speak into a machine with ease; therefore, their dictation is actually easier to comprehend this way.

Portable dictating machines fit into an attaché case, purse, or even a pocket, enabling the boss to get dictation done at home or while traveling. In many cases, a small audio tape recorder is used. The tape is delivered or dropped off with you to transcribe when convenient. Transcription machines are usually larger than the recorder and include earphones and a foot pedal for conveniently pausing the tape.

In addition to tape-based recorders, a variety of digital models are available. The digital versions connect to a computer in order to transfer the audio file for transcription. Specialized software is available that allows an administrative assistant to listen to the audio files on the computer for transcription. Some systems include a foot pedal that connects to the computer for pausing the audio playback.

FIGURE 2-2. A manager dictates into a tape-based recorder.

Photo by Jennifer Wauson. Digital photography courtesy of Kyocera Optics.

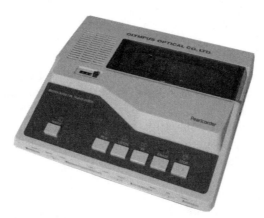

FIGURE 2-3. A transcription machine.
Photo by Jennifer Wauson.
Digital photography courtesy of Kyocera Optics.

If your boss has noted on the tape that there are several corrections to make, take the time to listen before you type. You may save yourself a second typing this way, especially if your employer failed to mark the end of the letter, or if you want to estimate its length before you begin. In such a situation, perhaps you'll prefer to do a rough draft instead of merely listening. Using a rough draft is also a good idea when you begin to transcribe for a new dictator, because your ear may have to accustom itself to the voice. A rough draft is simple to do using a computer or word processor, with corrections made quickly and effortlessly.

Your Employer's Office

Some employers consider their offices sacred ground that is not to be touched; others appreciate having their assistants dust and straighten up. You'll soon learn your own boss's preferences. If he or she doesn't mind, start by stacking the files being consulted and replacing in the cabinet those already consulted. Ask, however, before removing papers or documents from your boss's desk, especially those you have noticed there for quite some time. Discretion is always necessary. You must not overstep your role by touching or mentioning papers that your employer considers personal or private. In addition, many employers maintain their own unique filing system atop their desks and will advise their administrative assistant not to touch those stacks unless absolutely necessary. One such necessity may be if the boss telephones from out of the office and asks you to retrieve a letter or document from atop the desk. If this happens, turn the stack to the side at the point you found the letter, so that you can later replace it exactly where it was.

When you make appointments for your employer, record them on both the boss's calendar and your own. Be sure to remind the employer of these appointments—even though they're clearly on the calendar—so that he or she won't schedule too much work, for example, on the morning of a conference.

The Intangibles

Besides performing the usual office duties, all administrative assistants en-counter many situations that are a test of character, judgment, and memory. The administrative assistant must know exactly what the employer wants kept confidential. In some instances, your employer may frankly explain when something is not for public consumption, but do not assume otherwise if he or she says nothing. When someone asks you about a confidential matter, it should never be necessary to lie. A graceful "I couldn't say," is sufficient, especially in response to those who understand and respect your position.

An administrative assistant must exercise self-control every moment, even when courtesy is strained. While on the job, you are not living your personal life but rather representing your employer. Because of this, you cannot suc-cumb to mood swings or to criticism of those around you. You must always think before speaking and keep yourself open like an impersonal channel for the fulfillment of your role as administrative assistant. Think of how a diplo-mat must act while representing his or her country in a foreign land.

A great many little matters between an administrative assistant and his or her boss will be left unmentioned between them. In a good working relation-ship, a type of telepathy develops between employer and administrative assis-tant. Their understanding of each other contributes to their mutual success.

Telephone Usage

Telephone Manners

Administrative assistants must have a pleasing telephone personality and a well-modulated voice that conveys dignity and courtesy. Because you are not seen by the person at the other end of the line, you are judged—and more important, your employer is judged—by your telephone manners. Show interest in what is being said. Reply in clear tones, never raising your voice. Be a good listener, and know what the other person at the other end of the line is saying to you.

When the telephone rings, answer it as quickly as possible. At all times, have a memo pad and pen near the telephone. If it's necessary to delay for some reason, make a polite request such as, "Please wait a moment while I check the record for you." If you must spend some time finding the desired information, offer to call back. If the caller prefers to hold the line, put the line on hold rather than setting the telephone receiver down on your desktop.

For the sake of out-of-town visitors who may call you to ask directions, keep a map of the area on a nearby wall or in a desk drawer. You can provide extra courtesy by plotting their trip from the airport or freeway.

Taking and Transferring Calls

If there is no switchboard, state the name of your company and your own name when answering an incoming call: "The Brown Company, Ms. Robertson speaking." If the business is large enough to have several departments, and the operator has already answered the call before ringing your extension, state your department and your name: "Accounting Department, Ms. Robertson speaking." If there is no department, and a call is referred to you, give only your name: "Ms. Robertson speaking."

Answering a Colleague's Telephone
When answering a colleague's extension, state the colleague's name and your own: "Ms. Scott's office, Ms. Robertson speaking." If the person called is un-

available, ask if the caller wishes to hold the line, leave a message, or call back. If the preference is to hold, go back on the line at short intervals to explain the delay, asking if the caller wishes to leave a message. (See the next section on taking messages.) Be sure that the person called receives the message as soon as he or she returns.

Transferring a Call

If you can take care of the matter yourself, do not transfer the call. If you must, first tell the caller: "Mr. Jack Phillips is in charge of insurance, and I am sure he will advise you promptly. I'll transfer you." If the transfer must be made through an operator, always provide full information so that the caller doesn't need to be questioned again: "I have Mr. Black on the line. Please connect him with Mr. Phillips in the insurance department." Or, if the caller has not identified himself: "Please transfer this call to Mr. Phillips in the insurance department." If you do not know to whom the call should be directed, advise the caller: "I'll have the proper person call you back in just a few minutes."

Handling Your Boss's Calls

When answering your employer's telephone, you may sometimes discover that the caller's assistant has placed the call. In that case, say: "Thank you. Just a moment, please." Then announce the call. Your boss will pick up the telephone and wait until the person calling is connected. Never ask the calling administrative assistant to put his or her employer on the line first, unless your employer is a high-ranking personage requiring special consideration. When one business person calls another, both should be treated equally.

When you place a call for your boss, you naturally expect the assistant of the person called to put his or her employer on the line before you connect your own. If you are calling Mr. Fisk, and the assistant answers, say: "Is Mr. Fisk there, please, for Ms. Barrett of the Barrett Company?" If Mr. Fisk's assistant knows the proper response, he or she will put Mr. Fisk on the line. Then you say to your employer: "Mr. Fisk is on the line, Ms. Barrett." If Mr. Fisk's assistant is not cooperative, continue to speak courteously. Return to your boss, and explain that the other administrative assistant insists that Ms. Barrett go on the line before Mr. Fisk will be connected.

Taking Messages

Many companies do not have a central switchboard with an operator or a computerized voice mail system. In this case, the administrative assistant will be asked to answer incoming calls and place outgoing calls. It's useful for the assistant to keep an accurate written record of both, particularly incoming calls when the employer is not in the office. You should record the caller's name, telephone number, purpose of call, and any message.

When a caller has a message to leave for your employer or another employee, take the message verbatim. Write it exactly as stated, taking time and being patient with the caller. If you don't understand what the caller is saying, ask to have it repeated. The message may be very important to your employer, and a single word omitted or out of place could make a significant difference in the meaning. If you are unfamiliar with the caller's name, ask for the spelling. Make sure you note whom the message is for.

All office supply stores have telephone message slips to make this record keeping easy (Figure 3-1 shows a typical message slip). Some message slips come in booklets with carbon copies. The original can be placed on the employer's desk, while a copy is maintained in the booklet, perhaps for later use or reference when the original might have been destroyed.

A major advantage of using printed telephone message slips rather than blank scraps of paper is that you are more likely to take a complete message by filling in the printed form. A telephone message slip has lines for the name of the person being called, the date and time of the incoming call, the name of the person calling, the name of that person's company or organization, if given, the caller's telephone number, and the message, if any. The last line of the slip is for your initials as the taker of the message. By placing your initials at the end, you will be advising yourself as well as your employer that the information is complete and accurate.

To: _____	Urgent ☐
Date: _____ Time: _____	A.M./ P.M.

WHILE YOU WERE OUT

From: _____

Of: _____

Phone: _____
       Area Code   Number   Ext

☐ Telephoned   ☐ Please call

☐ Came to see you   ☐ Wants to see you

☐ Returned your call   ☐ Will call again

Message: _____

_____

_____

_____

_____

Message taken by: _____

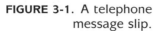

FIGURE 3-1. A telephone message slip.

Screening Calls

Although many employees answer their own telephone, you'll be expected at one time or another to screen the boss's incoming calls. In this case, you become the judge as to whether your boss should be disturbed.

When screening calls, be extremely tactful, so the caller will not be affronted. You want to be able to meet the caller face-to-face the next day without feeling embarrassed about the way you treated him or her over the telephone. A simple question—"May I tell Mr. Jones who's calling?"—should encourage the caller to give a name without hesitation. If the caller refuses, explain that your employer is unable to accept a call without knowing whom it's from, and suggest that a letter be written.

Many callers will ask for your employer by name and will tell you the question they need answered. You then need to confer with your boss to know if screening should be done or the call put through immediately.

Protecting Your Employer

Don't be overly zealous in trying to "protect" your employer by screening calls when not specifically asked to do so. When a business is just getting underway, for example, many executives welcome all calls and don't want the adminis-

FIGURE 3-2. An administrative assistant takes a message from a caller.

Photo by Linda Wauson. Digital photography courtesy of Kyocera Optics.

trative assistant to screen any potential clients. If that is the case, then simply say to the caller: "Thank you. I will connect you with Mr. Jones." Then, on your intercom telephone, tell Mr. Jones the name of the person calling.

If you answer the telephone for all of the employees in the company, and a caller does not request a specific person, inquire as to the nature of the call, so you can transfer it to the proper department or employee. When you realize what the caller's needs are, you could say: "Ms. Johnson in our accounting department should be able to assist you with this. I will transfer your call to her."

Courtesy

All callers should be treated with great respect and a patient tone of voice. If another call comes in while you're speaking, ask the first caller to hold the line, answer the second call, ask if the second caller can hold for a moment, saying you are on another line, and then return to the first. Never keep a caller waiting or on hold for any length of time. When you return to the line, thank the caller for holding. Keep in mind that his or her time is valuable.

Never put one line on hold without informing the caller, not even when two or more incoming calls arrive simultaneously, and two or more lines are ringing. Many callers will hang up when this happens, and your employer could very well miss a much-needed business call. You've no doubt experienced this yourself as a caller and will always retain negative thoughts concerning that company. Always have the courtesy to say, "Hello. Can you hold a moment, please?" Then wait until the caller answers yes or no. It is frustrating for a caller to be asked, "Can you hold a moment, please?" and then be cut off before the caller has had a chance to say no.

Telephone Etiquette Tips

The following checklist will assist you in practicing good telephone etiquette and performing your telephone answering responsibilities in a professional manner.

1. When you take a call, turn away from your computer, desk, and other work. Don't allow distractions to take your attention away from the caller.

2. Always have something available to write with.

3. Answer calls by the second or third ring.

4. Smile when you answer your calls. Even though the caller can't see it, they'll hear the smile in your voice.

5. Use a "telephone voice" in which you control your volume and speed. Speak clearly.

6. Be enthusiastic and respectful.

7. Greet the caller, and identify yourself, your business, and your department.

8. Ask the caller, "To whom am I speaking?"

9. Ask your caller, "How may I help you?"

10. Avoid unnecessary jargon and acronyms in your conversations.

11. Use the caller's name in your conversation.

12. Practice good listening skills.

13. If there is a problem, be concerned, empathetic, and apologetic.

14. Thank your caller for calling. Ask them to call again.

15. Never eat, drink, or chew gum while you are on a call.

Often-Used Numbers

Your employer no doubt will use certain personal telephone numbers regularly. You will soon memorize many of them without effort, but it's useful to keep a short alphabetical list of these numbers close to the telephone for quick consultation. The list might include numbers for the boss's spouse's workplace, schools his or her children attend, stores the boss and family frequent, as well as their country or health clubs, plus the boss's physician, dentist, mechanic, accountant, and personal friends. Most office telephones can be programmed to dial frequently called numbers automatically, saving you time and effort. Some computers also have this function and can dial frequently used numbers quickly and efficiently.

On any directory that you make up, the telephone numbers opposite each name should contain the area codes, if that person is not in your immediate area. For long-distance areas, also note the time differentials between other cities and your own to avoid disturbing people at awkward times. Some assistants leave their directory fitted beneath the desk blotter or taped to a pull-out shelf of the desk. Others like to keep their desks uncluttered. Still others prefer to keep the boss's personal numbers confidential.

Telephone Companies

Many offices have both a company that provides telephone equipment and a company that provides telephone service. The telephone equipment company is responsible for the functionality of the telephones, fax machines, and computer data lines, as well as voice mail systems. You should contact the telephone equipment company if you are experiencing problems with the telephone hardware.

Your telephone service provider may include a local service provider and a long distance provider. For many telephone users, one of the Regional Bell Operating Companies (RBOCs) provides local service. These companies include: Verizon, Bell Atlantic, Bell South, Ameritech, Quest, Southwestern Bell, and PacTel. In addition, many traditional long distance companies such as Sprint, MCI, and AT&T are providing local service. Many traditional cable television companies are also providing local service.

The same confusing mixture of companies also provides long distance service. Deregulation of telephone services has opened the local service and long distance markets to anyone and everyone. Normally, your company will select a long distance provider. Any time you make a long distance call, the long distance provider will provide the service and charge your account. You can use special dialing codes to have calls billed to particular long distance service providers.

Local calls are those that are made within your local calling area. For some callers, this means within your area code; however, there are limitations in some large cities where area codes have been divided into zones.

Some offices now rely on cellular telephones that include nationwide long distance and roaming without additional charges.

Domestic Long Distance Calls

There are a variety of domestic long distance services available, ranging from direct dialing to calling cards.

Domestic Direct Dialing

When you are willing to speak with anyone who may answer, dial the number yourself. Charges for the call begin as soon as an answer is heard, including an answering machine. Long distance calls within your area code are usually dialed as 1 + seven-digit number; however, many telephone service providers now require dialing the area code. In fact, in many large cities, you must dial the area code to make a local call. Long distance calls outside your area code are dialed as 1 + area code + seven-digit number.

Domestic Operator Assisted Calls

You will need an operator's assistance if you wish to make a person-to-person call or a collect call, or to bill a call to another telephone number. For calls within your area code, dial 0 + seven-digit number. For long distance calls, dial 0 + area code + seven-digit number.

You can make a person-to-person call when you want to speak only to a specific individual. Charges for a person-to-person call do not begin to accrue until the person called answers. This service is more expensive than a direct-dialed call. To make this call, say to the operator: "I wish to make a person-to-person call to Mr. Sullivan at 212-555-7900."

If you expect the person on the other end to pay for the call, say: "This is a collect call. My name is Miss Scott for the Brown Company." If you are willing to speak to a second person if the first person is unavailable, give this information to the operator before he or she places the call. If you have reason to believe that the person called may be at another telephone number or in another city, explain that as well: "If Mr. Greene is not at 555-1860, please try 555-8430."

When billing a call to a third number, the operator will usually need to confirm the billing by calling the third number and speaking with someone au-

3 ■ TELEPHONE USGAE

thorized to approve the call. Normally, third-party billing is only necessary when you are traveling and do not have access to a calling card.

Calling Cards

Calling cards are credit cards issued by a telephone company for use in making long distance calls. To place a call using a calling card, you usually dial a toll-free access number, wait for a computer tone, then enter your calling card number followed by your password, wait for another computer tone or message, then dial the area code + seven-digit number you wish to call.

Calls made on a calling card are billed to your long distance service provider. Calls are billed by the minute. However, most companies also include a surcharge for each call you place.

Domestic Information

For telephone number information within your area code, dial 411. For long distance information dial 1 + area code + 555-1212. See Table 3.1 for a list of domestic area codes.

TABLE 3-1	Domestic Area Codes by Geographic Region		
Region	**Area Code**	**Region**	**Area Code**
Alabama	205	California	213
Alabama	251	California	310
Alabama	256	California	323
Alabama	334	California	408
Alaska	907	California	415
Alberta	403	California	510
Alberta	780	California	530
Anguilla	264	California	559
Antigua/Barbuda	268	California	562
Arizona	480	California	619
Arizona	520	California	626
Arizona	602	California	650
Arizona	623	California	661
Arizona	928	California	707
Arkansas	479	California	714
Arkansas	501	California	760
Arkansas	870	California	805
Bahamas	242	California	818
Barbados	246	California	831
Bermuda	441	California	858
British Columbia	250	California	909
British Columbia	604	California	916
British Columbia	778	California	925
British Virgin Islands	284	California	949
California	209	Cayman Islands	345

Region	Area Code	Region	Area Code
Commonwealth of the Northern Mariana Islands	670	Illinois	815
		Illinois	847
Colorado	303	Indiana	219
Colorado	719	Indiana	260
Colorado	720	Indiana	317
Colorado	970	Indiana	574
Connecticut	203	Indiana	765
Connecticut	860	Indiana	812
Delaware	302	Iowa	319
District of Columbia	202	Iowa	515
Dominica	767	Iowa	563
Dominican Republic	809	Iowa	641
Florida	239	Iowa	712
Florida	305	Jamaica	876
Florida	321	Kansas	316
Florida	352	Kansas	620
Florida	386	Kansas	785
Florida	407	Kansas	913
Florida	561	Kentucky	270
Florida	727	Kentucky	502
Florida	754	Kentucky	606
Florida	772	Kentucky	859
Florida	786	Louisiana	225
Florida	813	Louisiana	318
Florida	850	Louisiana	337
Florida	863	Louisiana	504
Florida	904	Louisiana	985
Florida	941	Maine	207
Florida	954	Manitoba	204
Georgia	229	Maryland	240
Georgia	404	Maryland	301
Georgia	478	Maryland	410
Georgia	678	Maryland	443
Georgia	706	Massachusetts	339
Georgia	770	Massachusetts	351
Georgia	912	Massachusetts	413
Grenada	473	Massachusetts	508
Guam	671	Massachusetts	617
Hawaii	808	Massachusetts	774
Idaho	208	Massachusetts	781
Illinois	217	Massachusetts	857
Illinois	224	Massachusetts	978
Illinois	309	Michigan	231
Illinois	312	Michigan	248
Illinois	618	Michigan	269
Illinois	630	Michigan	313
Illinois	708	Michigan	517
Illinois	773	Michigan	586
		Michigan	616

(continued)

Region	Area Code	Region	Area Code
Michigan	734	New York	315
Michigan	810	New York	347
Michigan	906	New York	516
Michigan	947	New York	518
Michigan	989	New York	585
Minnesota	218	New York	607
Minnesota	320	New York	631
Minnesota	507	New York	646
Minnesota	612	New York	716
Minnesota	651	New York	718
Minnesota	763	New York	845
Minnesota	952	New York	914
Mississippi	228	New York	917
Mississippi	601	Newfoundland	709
Mississippi	662	North Carolina	252
Missouri	314	North Carolina	336
Missouri	417	North Carolina	704
Missouri	573	North Carolina	828
Missouri	636	North Carolina	910
Missouri	660	North Carolina	919
Missouri	816	North Carolina	980
Montana	406	North Dakota	701
Montserrat	664	Nova Scotia	902
North American		Ohio	216
Numbering Plan area	456	Ohio	234
North American		Ohio	330
Numbering Plan area	880	Ohio	419
North American		Ohio	440
Numbering Plan area	881	Ohio	513
North American		Ohio	567
Numbering Plan area	882	Ohio	614
Nebraska	308	Ohio	740
Nebraska	402	Ohio	937
Nevada	702	Oklahoma	405
Nevada	775	Oklahoma	580
New Brunswick	506	Oklahoma	918
New Hampshire	603	Ontario	289
New Jersey	201	Ontario	416
New Jersey	551	Ontario	519
New Jersey	609	Ontario	613
New Jersey	732	Ontario	647
New Jersey	848	Ontario	705
New Jersey	856	Ontario	807
New Jersey	862	Ontario	905
New Jersey	908	Oregon	503
New Jersey	973	Oregon	541
New Mexico	505	Oregon	971
New York	212	Pennsylvania	215

Region	Area Code	Region	Area Code
Pennsylvania	267	Texas	682
Pennsylvania	412	Texas	713
Pennsylvania	484	Texas	806
Pennsylvania	570	Texas	817
Pennsylvania	610	Texas	830
Pennsylvania	717	Texas	832
Pennsylvania	724	Texas	903
Pennsylvania	814	Texas	915
Pennsylvania	878	Texas	936
Puerto Rico	787	Texas	940
Puerto Rico	939	Texas	956
Quebec	418	Texas	972
Quebec	450	Texas	979
Quebec	514	Trinidad and Tobago	868
Quebec	819	Turks and Caicos Islands	649
Rhode Island	401	US Virgin Islands	340
Saskatchewan	306	Utah	435
South Carolina	803	Utah	801
South Carolina	843	Vermont	802
South Carolina	864	Virginia	276
South Dakota	605	Virginia	434
St. Kitts and Nevis	869	Virginia	540
St. Lucia	758	Virginia	571
St. Vincent and		Virginia	703
Grenadines	784	Virginia	757
Tennessee	423	Virginia	804
Tennessee	615	Washington	206
Tennessee	731	Washington	253
Tennessee	865	Washington	360
Tennessee	901	Washington	425
Tennessee	931	Washington	509
Texas	210	West Virginia	304
Texas	214	Wisconsin	262
Texas	254	Wisconsin	414
Texas	281	Wisconsin	608
Texas	361	Wisconsin	715
Texas	409	Wisconsin	920
Texas	469	Wyoming	307
Texas	512	Yukon, NW Territories	867

International Long Distance Calls

You can place 1 + area code + seven-digit number direct dial calls to the United States, Canada, Bermuda, Puerto Rico, and most of the Caribbean islands. Other international calls may be dialed directly by dialing the following:

■ International call dial prefix 011

- Country code—every country has a two or three digit country code (see the list that follow in Table 3.2.)

- City code—most major international cities have a city code that is one to five digits

- Local telephone number—local numbers vary in length

TABLE 3-2	International Country Codes		
Country Name	**Country Code**	**Country Name**	**Country Code**
Afghanistan	93	China (People's Republic of)	86
Albania	355	Christmas Island	618
Algeria	213	Cocos-Keeling Islands	61
American Samoa	684	Colombia	57
Andorra	376	Comoros	269
Angola	244	Congo	242
Antarctica	672	Cook Islands	682
Argentina	54	Costa Rica	506
Armenia	374	Croatia	385
Aruba	297	Cuba	53
Ascension Island	247	Curaçao	599
Australia	61	Cyprus	357
Austria	43	Czech Republic	420
Azerbaijan	994	Denmark	45
Bahrain	973	Diego Garcia	246
Bangladesh	880	Djibouti	253
Belarus	375	East Timor	670
Belgium	32	Easter Island	56
Belize	501	Ecuador	593
Benin	229	Egypt	20
Bhutan	975	El Salvador	503
Bolivia	591	EMSAT (mobile satellite service)	88213
Bosnia & Herzegovina	387	Equatorial Guinea	240
Botswana	267	Eritrea	291
Brazil	55	Estonia	372
Brunei	673	Ethiopia	251
Bulgaria	359	Faeroe Islands	298
Burkina Faso	226	Falkland Islands	500
Burundi	257	Fiji Islands	679
Cambodia	855	Finland	358
Cameroon	237	France	33
Cape Verde Islands	238	French Antilles	596
Central African Republic	236	French Guiana	594
Chad	235	French Polynesia	689
Chatham Island (New Zealand)	64	Gabon	241
Chile	56		

Country Name	Country Code	Country Name	Country Code
Gambia	220	Liberia	231
Georgia	995	Libya	218
Germany	49	Liechtenstein	423
Ghana	233	Lithuania	370
Gibraltar	350	Luxembourg	352
Global Mobile Satellite		Macau	853
System (GMSS)	881	Macedonia	
Greece	30	(formerly Yugoslav Republic)	389
Greenland	299	Madagascar	261
Guadeloupe	590	Malawi	265
Guantanamo Bay	5399	Malaysia	60
Guatemala	502	Maldives	960
Guinea-Bissau	245	Mali Republic	223
Guinea (PRP)	224	Malta	356
Guyana	592	Marshall Islands	692
Haiti	509	Martinique	596
Honduras	504	Mauritania	222
Hong Kong	852	Mauritius	230
Hungary	36	Mayotte Island	269
Iceland	354	Mexico	52
India	91	Micronesia (Federal States of)	691
Indonesia	62	Moldova	373
Inmarsat		Monaco	377
(Atlantic Ocean, East)	871	Mongolia	976
Inmarsat		Morocco	212
(Atlantic Ocean, West)	874	Mozambique	258
Inmarsat (Indian Ocean)	873	Myanmar	95
Inmarsat (Pacific Ocean)	872	Namibia	264
Inmarsat SNAC	870	Nauru	674
Iran	98	Nepal	977
Iraq	964	Netherlands	31
Ireland	353	Netherlands Antilles	599
Israel	972	New Caledonia	687
Italy	39	New Zealand	64
Ivory Coast (Côte d'Ivoire)	225	Nicaragua	505
Japan	81	Niger	227
Jordan	962	Nigeria	234
Kazakhstan	7	Niue	683
Kenya	254	Norfolk Island	672
Kiribati	686	Norway	47
Korea (North)	850	Oman	968
Korea (South)	82	Pakistan	92
Kuwait	965	Palau	680
Kyrgyz Republic	996	Palestine	970
Laos	856	Panama	507
Latvia	371	Papua New Guinea	675
Lebanon	961	Paraguay	595
Lesotho	266	Peru	51

(continued)

Country Name	Country Code	Country Name	Country Code
Philippines	63	Tajikistan	992
Poland	48	Tanzania	255
Portugal	351	Thailand	66
Qatar	974	Thuraya (mobile satellite service)	88216
Réunion Island	262	Togo	228
Romania	40	Tokelau	690
Russia	7	Tonga Islands	676
Rwanda	250	Tunisia	216
St. Helena	290	Turkey	90
St. Pierre and Miquelon	508	Turkmenistan	993
San Marino	378	Tuvalu	688
São Tomé and Principe	239	Uganda	256
Saudi Arabia	966	Ukraine	380
Senegal	221	United Arab Emirates	971
Serbia	381	United Kingdom	44
Seychelles Islands	248	United States of America	1
Sierra Leone	232	Universal Personal Telecommunications (UPT)	878
Singapore	65	Uruguay	598
Slovak Republic	421	Uzbekistan	998
Slovenia	386	Vanuatu	678
Solomon Islands	677	Vatican City	39
Somalia	252	Venezuela	58
South Africa	27	Vietnam	84
Spain	34	Wake Island	808
Sri Lanka	94	Wallis and Futuna Islands	681
Sudan	249	Western Samoa	685
Suriname	597	Yemen	967
Swaziland	268	Yugoslavia	381
Sweden	46	Zambia	260
Switzerland	41	Zanzibar	255
Syria	963	Zimbabwe	263
Taiwan	886		

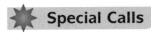

Special Calls

Calls can be made to ship, airplanes, and trains.

Ship-to-Shore Calls

You may call a ship at sea if the ship has facilities for receiving the call. Most ships do. Ask for the ship-to-shore operator.

Air-to-Ground and Ground-to-Air Calls

Many airlines provide air-to-ground and ground-to-air calls while a plane is in flight. Many planes are equipped with telephones that require the use of credit cards when placing a call from air to ground. When placing a call from ground to air, tell the long distance operator the name of the person being called, the airline (e.g., American or Delta), the flight number, the destination of the flight, and the passenger's seat number, if known.

Calls to Trains

For a message to be delivered to someone on a train, give the person's name, train number or name of train, direction the train is traveling, car and reservation number, if known, station, city and state, and arrival date and time. Say also that the message is to be delivered in care of the conductor of the train. For example:

> Mr. Philip W. Wade
> Care of the Conductor
> AMTRAK, Westbound
> Car 9, Bedroom 22
> Due at LaSalle Station
> Chicago, Illinois
> December 1, 5:30 p.m.

Telegram Airport Delivery

When calling in a telegram to be sent to an airport for delivery to a plane passenger, provide the person's name, airline, flight number, direction of travel, airport destination, city and state, and arrival date and time. For example:

> Ms. Janet Harrold
> A Passenger
> American Airlines, Flight 88, Northbound
> Due at Chicago, Illinois—O'Hare Airport
> May 5, 1:20 p.m.

Voice Mail Etiquette

The goal of voice mail etiquette is to improve communications without being inconsiderate. With voice mail, there are two sides to the communication: callers and callees. Each should follow certain guidelines.

Callers frequently become upset with "bad" voice mail systems; however, they fail to pay attention to the fact that sometimes they are "bad" callers. The following are some things for callers to consider when encountering voice mail:

■ Leave a clear concise message with a phone number.

■ Provide a good time to return the call.

■ Unless you have indicated that it is an emergency or a problem with an extreme time deadline, do not assume the person checks voice mail regularly—you should assume a call back will not be immediate.

■ Remember that sometimes voice messages are lost somewhere in the system—a person may accidentally delete a message.

- Use voice mail as a way of informing a person that other communications are waiting or coming, since voice mail users frequently check voice mail more often than e-mail or the fax machine.

- Never leave confidential, inflammatory, or embarrassing messages on a voice mail message.

If your office has voice mail available, you should observe the following guidelines:

- Keep your greeting short.

- Tell people how and when they can reach you.

- Update your message frequently to inform people of your schedule, especially if you cannot return messages quickly.

- Keep your message friendly, but don't forget professionalism.

- If you use voice mail, check it frequently throughout the day.

- Return calls in a timely manner—don't use voice mail as a way to avoid interaction.

- Encourage your callers to leave detailed messages—you may be able to leave the answer on their voice mail without a two-way conversation.

- Respect the confidentiality of any messages you receive—treat all voice mail messages the same way you would treat any private conversation.

Answering Services

If your company uses an answering service, always let the service know when you come into the office in the morning and when you are leaving in the evening. Many services will allow you to forward your telephone calls to the service, or they will answer your calls automatically if you do not pick up after a set number of rings. Always leave the answering service a number where your employer can be reached in case of an emergency.

Mail Services and Shipping

✦ Beyond a Letter and a Stamp

Mail is an important method of communication between a company and the outside business world. The daily processing of mail is usually handled by the administrative assistant. This may include sorting the mail and distributing it to the proper departments or individuals. It may also include opening the employer's mail, prioritizing it, and gathering the necessary preliminary information needed to answer specific requests or problems.

Sending out business mail involves much more than a letter and a stamp, even when those letters are sent by the hundreds of thousands. There are larger documents and packages to be mailed, varying timetables to be met, and destinations ranging from next door to around the world. Dozens of work-saving, timesaving, and money-saving strategies can help move the mail more efficiently

A competent assistant should become acquainted with these profit-boosting moves, from the best physical ways to prepare the mail to the advantages of one mail service over another. He or she should also keep abreast of United States Postal Service (USPS) rules and regulations and methods of moving the mail. Neither you nor the company may need all this information at the present, but companies constantly change and grow. The assistant who can fulfill a company's new mailing needs—or who knows where to get the information quickly—is invaluable.

✦ Addressing for Success

A company is judged by the way its letters are composed and spaced on the pages and even by the manner in which its envelopes are addressed. All of this does more than simply create a good impression. It affects whether the mail is even delivered in a timely fashion.

The USPS relies on computerized mail processing machines—optical character readers (OCRs) and bar-code sorters (BCSs)—designed to increase the speed, efficiency, and accuracy of processing mail while keeping postal operating costs down. Consistently accurate delivery, faster mail turnaround, and greater profits are just some of the ways your company can benefit from these state-of-the-art systems.

This high-speed equipment is programmed to "read" and sort up to 36,000 pieces of mail per hour. That's 10 pieces every second. But if your company's mail is not technically compatible, these sophisticated machines will not be able to sort it. Your mail will have to be sorted by hand, and the company will miss the related benefits of the equipment.

Two factors determine whether mail is considered technically compatible: (1) mail that is "machineable" or, in other words, the right size and shape to speed with ease through the equipment, and (2) mail that is electronically "readable" or capable of being read, coded, and sorted by the equipment.

The following is a list of the most common addressing problems:

- Not enough contrast
- Script type font used
- Address not visible through window
- Address slants
- Serif type font
- Using upper and lower-case letters versus all capital letters
- Characters touch
- Logo behind delivery address line
- Information below delivery address line

How Your Company Can Receive the Benefits

There are a variety of issues related to successful mail delivery, such as the size of your letters, address information and location, bar code area, the use of windowed envelopes and print quality.

Size

Begin by making sure that your letter mail is the proper size. Envelopes and cards with dimensions that fall between the minimums and maximums listed in Table 4-1 below will speed through the machines without a hitch.

Envelopes or cards smaller than the minimums will not be delivered. Letter mail larger than the maximums may be mailed, but it must bypass the OCR

TABLE 4-1	Size Requirements for Envelopes and Cards	
Dimensions	**Minimum (inches)**	**Maximum (inches)**
Height	3 1/2	6 1/8
Length	5	11 1/2
Thickness	0.007	3/16
		(card stock not to exceed .0095)

and be processed through slower and less efficient manual or mechanized methods. It may also be subject to a surcharge, even though the postage is correct for the weight.

Address Location

The OCR looks for the address within an imaginary rectangle on each mail piece called the OCR read area (Figure 4-1). Make some quick measurements of your company's envelope stationery. The OCR will not have trouble finding the delivery address if it's located within the following boundaries:

SIDES OF THE RECTANGLE: 1/2 inch in from the right and left edges
BOTTOM OF THE RECTANGLE: 5/8 inch up from the bottom edge
TOP OF THE RECTANGLE: 2 3/4 inches up from the bottom edge

To provide the OCR with the information needed for the finest sort, put all the lines of the address within the above area. If that is not possible, it will still help to place as many address lines in the OCR read area as you can. **A WORD OF CAUTION:** Make sure no portion of the return address appears in the read area.

Lines of the Address

The OCR cannot rearrange address information that is out of proper sequence. Make sure addresses are complete, including apartment or suite numbers and proper delivery designations (e.g., street, road, avenue). Often there will be, in a single city, streets with the same name—for example, Hanford Street, Hanford Court, Hanford Lane, and Hanford Avenue—so always use the proper designation.

Two-letter state abbreviations (listed in Table 4-2) should always be used, because the OCR recognizes them at a glance. Do not place a period after each initial of the abbreviation—that is, use AR instead of A.R.

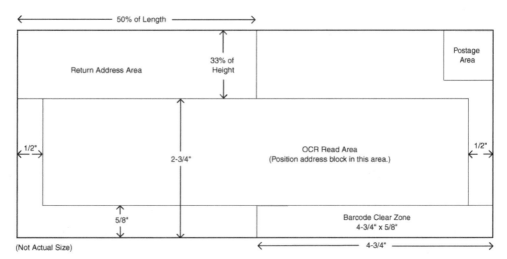

FIGURE 4-1. Diagram of OCR read area.
Courtesy of the United States Post Office.

TABLE 4-2	Two-Letter Postal Abbreviations for States, Territories, and the District of Columbia

Abbr.	Name	Abbr.	Name
AL	Alabama	NE	Nebraska
AK	Alaska	NV	Nevada
AS	American Samoa	NH	New Hampshire
AZ	Arizona	NJ	New Jersey
AR	Arkansas	NM	New Mexico
CA	California	NY	New York
CO	Colorado	NC	North Carolina
CT	Connecticut	ND	North Dakota
DE	Delaware	MP	Northern Mariana Islands
DC	District of Columbia	OH	Ohio
FM	Federated States of Micronesia	OK	Oklahoma
FL	Florida	OR	Oregon
GA	Georgia	PA	Pennsylvania
GU	Guam	PR	Puerto Rico
HI	Hawaii	RI	Rhode Island
ID	Idaho	SC	South Carolina
IL	Illinois	SD	South Dakota
IN	Indiana	TN	Tennessee
IA	Iowa	TX	Texas
KS	Kansas	UT	Utah
KY	Kentucky	VT	Vermont
LA	Louisiana	VA	Virginia
ME	Maine	VI	Virgin Islands, U.S.
MH	Marshall Islands	WA	Washington
MD	Maryland	WV	West Virginia
MA	Massachusetts	WI	Wisconsin
MI	Michigan	WY	Wyoming
MN	Minnesota	AA	Armed Forces, the Americas
MS	Mississippi	AE	Armed Forces, Europe
MO	Missouri	AP	Armed Forces, Pacific
MT	Montana		

Table 4-3 shows common abbreviations that may be used with addresses. Do not use periods at the end of the abbreviation; instead use all upper-case letters.

Foreign Addresses

Foreign mailings should have the country name printed in capital letters as the only information on the bottom line. The postal delivery zone, if any, should be included with the city, not after the country. For example:

Mr. Thomas Clark
117 Russell Drive
London WIP6HQ
ENGLAND

TABLE 4-3	**Common Abbreviations Used with Addresses**				
Abbr.	**Word**	**Abbr.**	**Word**	**Abbr.**	**Word**
AVE	Avenue	MTN	Mountain	WAY	Way
BLVD	Boulevard	PKWY	Parkway	APT	Apartment
CTR	Center	PL	Place	RM	Room
CIR	Circle	PLZ	Plaza	STE	Suite
CT	Court	RDG	Ridge	N	North
DR	Drive	RD	Road	E	East
EXPY	Expressway	SQ	Square	S	South
HTS	Heights	ST	Street	W	West
HWY	Highway	STA	Station	NE	Northeast
IS	Island	TER	Terrace	NW	Northwest
JCT	Junction	TRL	Trail	SE	Southeast
LK	Lake	TPKE	Turnpike	SW	Southwest
LN	Lane	VLY	Valley		

Non-Address Information

Extraneous (non-address) printing that appears in or near the OCR read area could cause the piece of mail to be rejected. To ensure that the equipment locates and reads only the delivery address, non-address information (advertising copy, company logos, etc.) that must appear in the read area should be positioned above the delivery address line. In other words, the space below and on either side of the delivery address line within the read area should be clear of all printing and other markings not actually part of the address. Positioning such information as far away from the address as possible also helps.

Bar-Code Area

After reading an address, the OCR will print the appropriate bar code on the bottom of the piece of mail. Then, by reading the code, bar-code sorters quickly route each envelope and card to its destination. But BCSs recognize only bar codes and will reject mail that has some other type of printing where the bar code goes. Make sure the bar code area (see Figure 4-1) remains free of all markings.

Window Envelopes

If your company uses window envelopes, be certain that the entire address is always visible, even during full movement of the insert. If part of the address is hidden, the OCR will reject the envelope and send it off for manual or mechanized processing.

Address Characters

The OCR will read most typewritten and other machine-printed addresses (see Figure 4-2). It cannot read type styles such as script, italic, and highly stylized characters. It also has trouble deciphering dot-matrix print if the dots that form each character are not touching each other. Among the best typeface designs to choose from are those known as sans serif.

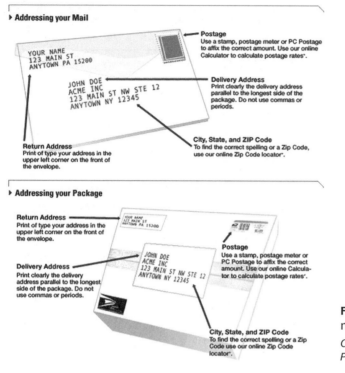

FIGURE 4-2. Addressing your mail and packages.

Courtesy of the United States Post Office.

Print Quality and Color

Print quality is of great importance to the OCR. It quickly reads clear sharp print but may not be able to distinguish characters that are faded, broken, or smudged. Black ink on a white background is best. Although certain color combinations are acceptable, the OCR cannot read the address if there is not enough contrast between the ink and paper. Keep the ink as dark as possible and the background as light as possible.

Spacing

Spacing between characters, words, and address lines is equally important. The OCR must see a clear vertical space between each character and each word, or it will not know where one ends and the next one begins. For similar reasons, it needs a clear horizontal space between each line of the address.

 Postal Automation: Encoding for Business Mailers

Even if an address is sharply imprinted and speeds through the OCR, the letter itself won't be deliverable if the information in the address is incorrect. If your company maintains its address list on computer, the postal service can help you here too. Suppose your company has an in-house list of its best customers. The Postal Business Center for your area may be able to help you clean up your list and add valuable ZIP+4 (5-digit zip code plus 4-digit addendum) and carrier route information. This is accomplished using downloadable software tools available from the USPS Web site at www.usps.com.

The postal service provides this service for your company because the benefits are mutual: for your company, more accurate and readable addresses, which provides faster sorting of mail and fewer undeliverable pieces (undeliverable Third Class Mail is money thrown away), and for the USPS, more efficient moving of the mail, saving it money, which can then be passed on to customers by holding the line on rates.

To clean up your list, here is what you can do:

1. Standardize your address list, making sure cities match the zip codes on the list.

2. Change all characters to uppercase for increased readability by automation equipment.

3. Correct minor misspellings, and add missing directions and suffixes.

4. Validate or correct each five-digit zip code.

5. Add the extra digits of ZIP + 4 codes.

6. Ask the USPS for a report on any address that cannot be coded. For example, you'll discover which address needs an apartment or suite number to be complete or which address does not exist as given.

Metering

What's the next step after addressing your company's mail with the most accurate address information? Putting on postage, of course, so you can get the mail on its way. Many small companies stamp their short letters and save longer correspondence and packages for a trip to the post office. Your company can save both time and money by investing in its own postage meter instead.

A postage meter (see Figure 4-3) offers savings for every office, not just larger ones with a heavy flow of outgoing mail. A postage meter ensures that your office does not overpay postage or underestimate it, which results in the embarrassing situation of mail arriving at clients' offices marked "postage due." It takes much less time to put metered postage on mail than it does to apply stamps, helping make more efficient use of staff time. In addition, your business correspondence moves more quickly once it leaves your office, since the post office does not have to spend time canceling and postmarking the mail.

A postage meter prints postage directly onto your mail pieces (or onto a meter tape, which you apply to your mail piece), and provides a convenient way to pay for postage and track postage costs for your business or organization. You can send out any class of mail (except periodicals) in any quantity at any rate with the same postage meter.

Some mailers use metered postage because they believe that it adds a more personal touch. A postage meter is also great to have around the office for all of your mailing needs.

Postage meters come in all sizes. Very large mailers have big, specialized meters that fold, stuff, weigh, and meter postage onto envelopes. Some meters are small and require each mail piece to be hand-fed. That can take time. A me-

FIGURE 4-3. An administrative assistant runs mail through a postage meter.
Photo by Jennifer Wauson. Digital photography courtesy of Kyocera Optics.

ter manufacturer can help you decide which meter is right for your mailing needs.

If you already have a postage meter, and you're starting to do bulk mailing, using your meter is a smart choice. However, although you can use the same postage meter for all of your mail, you must apply for a permit to use the meter for bulk mailings. In addition, there are special markings required for bulk mailings. These can be applied with your meter stamp, thus saving you an extra step.

Postage meters and personal computer postage systems (PC Postage) generate indicia imprinted on or affixed to a mailpiece as evidence of prepayment of postage for bulk or business reply mailings. This method of postage payment may be used on any class of mail except periodicals. PC Postage systems access a personal computer to print postage indicia. Postage meters and PC Postage systems are available only by lease from an authorized provider. The USPS holds the provider responsible for the control, operation, maintenance, and replacement of their products. No one other than the provider may use a postage meter or PC Postage system without a valid USPS postage meter license and a rental agreement with the provider. See Table 4-4.

Postal Authorization

To obtain a postage meter license, submit a completed Form 3601-A, Application for a Postage Meter License, to the post office where your company

TABLE 4-4	USPS-Authorized Postage Meter and PC Postage System Providers	
Company	**Telephone Number**	**Web Address**
Hasler Inc.	800-243-6275	www.haslerinc.com
Francotyp-Postalia Inc.	800-341-6052	www.fp-usa.com
Neopost	800-624-7892	www.neopostinc.com
Pitney Bowes Inc.	800-322-8000	www.pitneybowes.com
PSI Systems Envelope Manager	800-576-3279	www.envmgr.com
Stamps.com	888-434-0055	www.stamps.com

will deposit its metered mail. To obtain the meter itself, you may lease one from an authorized manufacturer (Table 4-4), who will install it. The post office will then, on request, set it for the amount of postage you wish to purchase. You may purchase postage for the meter at the same post office where the company has its meter license. If you will be using the meter for bulk rate postage, you also need to order a "Bulk Rate" or "Nonprofit Organization" slug that is inserted into the meter.

Guidelines for Using a Postage Meter

While a postage meter can make any business more cost efficient, properly using it is vital.

Your *meter manufacturer* will give you instructions on how to operate the meter and how to refill it with postage. Most of the newest systems connect directly to a telephone line, allowing you to order postage and charge it to an account.

Until you presort your mail, you may not know how much postage you owe on each piece. Some mailers meter all of their pieces at the lowest rate they qualify for and then pay the difference when they bring their mail to the post office. When using this method, you may meter your mail only at the lowest of the rates you qualify for. You cannot randomly pick a number and meter your mail at that rate. The first time you do a mailing, the business mail entry unit clerk at the post office can help you fill out your postage statement to calculate how much postage you still owe.

If you know up front which pieces qualify for which rate, you can go ahead and meter them at the correct postage rate.

There are requirements for what appears in your meter imprint. Your meter manufacturer will help you comply with these requirements:

1. Postage amount
2. Meter number
3. City and state of the post office where you hold your permit
4. Rate marking (PRSRT STD, NONPROFIT ORG, PRSRT FIRST-CLASS).

First Class Mail (single-piece and presorted) *must* show the date the mail is deposited with the Postal Service. If you are using meter tapes, you *must* show the month and year. No date is required for metered bulk mailings if the meter impression is placed directly on the mailing piece (Figure 4-4). If a date is shown, it must be the actual date of the mailing. Meter tape must show the month and year but not the day of the mailing

Metered presorted and discount-rate mail must be brought to the post office where you hold your permit. Metered presorted and discount-rate mail *cannot* be dropped in a collection box or given to a carrier.

Use special postage meter fluorescent ink. Properly prepared metered mail should bypass the post office's facer/canceler machine. If metered mail inadvertently passes through the machine, fluorescent ink (known as 'hot" ink in the trade) will speed the process. Use the ink provided by the meter manufacturer.

As small a thing as facing all metered envelopes up and in the same direction speeds your company's mail on its way. If the post office does not have to turn pieces over to read the address before distributing each to the proper sorting area, a costly step has been saved. Package five or more pieces of metered mail securely with rubber bands, and it will be handled more efficiently. Your post office will provide you with rubber bands for this purpose at no charge.

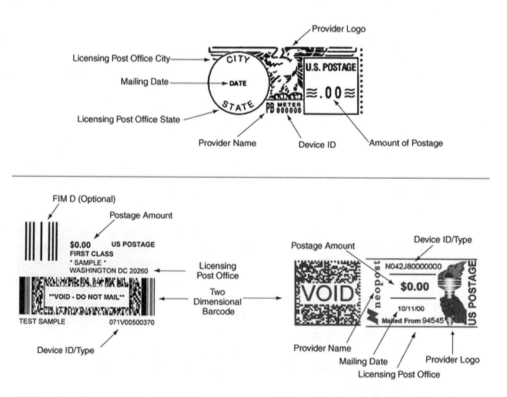

Information-Based Indicia with FIM
(without fluorescent ink)

Information-Based Indicia without FIM
(with fluorescent ink)

FIGURE 4-4. Examples of metered mail.
Courtesy of the United States Post Office.

When preparing large volumes of letter-metered mail, place it in trays secured from the post office. This method creates a cleaner environment for your employees and your mail, and it helps direct the mail to the appropriate sorting equipment, thus speeding up the process.

If your meter's printing or recording mechanism is faulty, contact your local post office and meter manufacturer for instructions.

Postage Statement

When preparing your mail, use the "postage affixed" postage statement, since you've already put some postage (but maybe not all of it) on your mail piece. The postage statement will help you figure out how much postage is due when you drop off your mail.

After you fill out your postage statement, you'll know how much postage, if any, you still owe. You can pay the difference with a meter strip affixed to your postage statement through an advance deposit account or at the Post Office.

Here is an example for calculating how much postage is owed: If you have 150 pieces that qualify for the Standard Mail 3/5 rate and 50 pieces that qualify for the Standard Mail basic rate, you can meter all 200 pieces at the 3/5 rate (the lower of the two) and pay the additional postage for the 50 basic rate pieces when you bring in your mail.

✸ Packaging

Much of the mail you'll be asked to send out as an administrative assistant will consist of letters and documents. But even with a mailroom on the premises, you may have to prepare and send out the occasional package yourself. For a package to arrive in good condition at its destination, it's important to observe four basic principles in packaging your shipments.

1. *Use a corrugated container.* These "cardboard boxes" come in a variety of strengths and weights. Primarily there are three basic types: singlewall, doublewall, and triplewall containers. You can tell the difference by examining the sides of the box and noticing the number of layers. Singlewall containers have two outside liners and a wavy corrugated medium in the middle. Doublewall boxes have two wavy corrugated layers in the middle separated by a third liner. A triplewall box has three corrugated layers and a total of four liners.

Select a box that is large enough to allow some room around the contents in every direction. This will allow the contents to be safe from punctures, tears, or rips on the corners or side of the box that may occur in transit. Boxes are available from many shipping supply companies, as well as mailing and packaging chain stores. Make sure that the box will support the weight of your shipment. Every box has a stamp printed on it specifying the maximum weight it will support. Doublewall and triplewall containers are stronger than most singlewall boxes. It is not a good idea to reuse shipping containers unless they are in good shape and will not be supporting much weight. Moisture and other shipping conditions tend to lessen the strength of corrugated containers.

To see whether a box is strong enough for mailing your item, look for the manufacturer's strength certification on the bottom of the box. The first and last measurements are the most important to you. "BURSTING TEST" shows you (in pounds per square inch) how well the fiberboard can resist rupture or breaking. "GROSS WT LT" shows you (in pounds) how much weight the box can hold.

You can choose a box by grade if necessary. Once you know the load type (easy or difficult), weight, and size of your item, you can use Table 4-5 to determine the necessary grade.

2. *Protect the contents.* Use wadded-up newsprint, crumpled brown grocery bags, air bubble pack, foam peanuts, or shredded paper. Depending on the contents of the package, it may be a good idea to wrap the contents in plastic as well to keep the packing material from sticking to the contents or getting inside. The packing material should be placed on the bottom, all four sides, and the top to provide several inches of protection between the contents and the sides of the box.

3. *Close the box securely.* Most shipping companies, including the USPS, will not accept boxes tied with string, nor should you use masking tape or regular cellophane tape; neither has enough strength to keep the box closed. Instead, use carton-sealing tape, pressure-sensitive place tape, water-activated paper tape, or water-activated reinforced tape. Generally, apply three strips of tape to the top and the bottom. One strip should seal the box, and the other two strips should seal the sides.

4. *Use the proper labeling.* Make sure you include a zip code. As an added precaution you may want to include the addressee's telephone number. Your company's return address is also important. You never know if the recipient has moved or is out of town and cannot receive your shipment. In some cases, your shipment can be held at the destination, but there are time limits on this. It's also a good idea to pack a copy of the label with all of the identifying information inside the box, so that if the outside label is damaged or removed, the shipper can determine the destination by opening the box. When applying your labels to the package, always place them on the top of the package away from seams or box edges. Apply several strips of clear carton sealing tape over the label to prevent it from falling off.

TABLE 4-5	Box Grade Requirements

Maximum Weight of Box and Contents

Easy and Average Loads (pounds)	Difficult Loads (pounds)	Maximum Length Plus Girth (inches)	Box Grade
20	—	67	125
40	20	100	175
65	40	108	200
70	65	108	275
—	70	108	350
—	70	130	350

You should write both addresses in waterproof ink (or type them on a label), using letters that can be easily read from 30 inches away (arm's length). Ten- to 12-point type is a good size for computer-printed labels. The address format preferred by the Postal Service uses uppercase letters and has a uniform left margin in the address block. For example:

LUIS ENSOR
23 MAPLE CT APT 4
ANYTOWN, CA 99887–7665

On the outside of your parcel, you should put special markings like those listed below. They let postal employees know the nature of the parcel's contents. However, do not assume that the markings in themselves will keep your parcel from getting damaged.

- Mark "Fragile" on parcels that contain breakable items.
- Mark "Perishable" on parcels that contain food or other items that can decay or spoil.
- Mark "Do Not Bend" on parcels that contain photographs, artwork, or similar items, but only if they are protected with a stiffener like fiberboard.

You should put these special markings in three places: above the address, below the postage, and on the back or bottom of your parcel. If you prefer, ask a post office window clerk to rubber stamp your parcel with these markings.

For odd-shaped or extremely fragile objects, it's best to check with the shipping service for advice on how to package the item and the best way to send it.

Hazardous and Illegal Items

Except as permitted by mailing standards, it is illegal to send through the U.S. mail any article, composition, or material that can kill or injure a person, obstruct mail service, or damage property. Harmful matter includes, but is not limited to:

- All kinds of poison or matter containing poison
- All snakes, turtles, spiders, poisonous animals (except scorpions), poisonous insects, and poisonous reptiles
- All disease germs or scabs
- All explosives, flammable material, and mechanical, chemical, or other devices or compositions that can catch fire or explode

There are also legal restrictions on who may mail the following items and how they must be prepared for mailing:

- Firearms, knives, and sharp instruments
- Drugs and narcotics
- Other controlled substances as defined by federal law and related federal regulations

- Live scorpions
- Locksmithing devices
- Vehicle master keys

Certain potentially harmful or dangerous articles and substances may be mailed if special packaging and labeling requirements are met. Contact your local postmaster for details, ask for Publication 2, *Packaging for Mailing,* or visit the US Postal Service website at www.usps.com.

Important US Postal Service Mail Services

Most of your company's mail probably goes out and comes in via the US Post Office. The following information touches only the high points of the many services it offers, so that you'll know they are available when needed. A complete and separate brochure is available on each subject mentioned. USPS services change from time to time, so it's useful to call or visit a local post office occasionally. In addition, the USPS maintains a Marketing and Communications Office in large metropolitan areas to advise the public of such services and answer questions by telephone or in person.

Should you experience a problem with any mail service, complete a Consumer Service Card, Form 4314 (Figure 4-5), available from letter carriers and at all post offices. Detailing your problem will help your postmaster respond. You may also advise the postmaster of a problem by calling your local post office.

The Consumer Advocate represents consumers at the top management level in the postal service. If your problem cannot be solved by your local post office, write to the Consumer Advocate at:

Consumer Advocate
U.S. Postal Service, Room 5821
475 L'Enfant Plaza West SW
Washington, DC 20260–2200

Following is a brief description of the major mail services provided by the USPS.

Express Mail

Express Mail is the US Postal Service's fastest service. It offers guaranteed delivery service 365 days a year, including weekends and holidays. The USPS also offers Express Mail International Service to nearly 175 countries and territories, and is the only provider offering Express Mail Military Service at domestic prices to select Army Post Office (APO) and Fleet Post Office (FPO) addresses.

For a minimum fee, important letters, documents, and merchandise may be sent Express Mail. A full postage refund is made for all domestic shipments delivered later than the guaranteed commitment for that particular service.

1 PRINT FIRMLY   2 REMOVE TOP COPY FOR CUSTOMER RECORD   3 FILL IN ADDRESS BLANK   4 MAIL
(do not separate remaining copies)   ON BACK OF LAST CARD   (postage free)

U.S. POSTAL SERVICE CONSUMER SERVICE CARD

| Name | | Date *(Mo., Day, Yr.)* | No. M 13 238 969 |
| Address *(Apt./Suite No., No. and Street, City)* | State | ZIP Code | Customer Phone *(8 a.m.-5 p.m.)* |

Is This
☐ Information Request   ☐ Suggestion   ☐ Problem   ☐ Compliment

Did It Involve	If This Is A Problem With A Specific Mailing, Please Complete The Following:		This Section Is For USPS Use Only
Delay			Recording Employee Name
Nonreceipt			
Damage	**Was It**	**Was Mailing**	Date Customer Contacted	Customer Contacted By
Misdelivery	Letter	First-Class	
Improperly Returned	Package	Special Delivery	USPS Action
Change of Address	Newspaper/ Magazine	Certified	
Vending Equipment		Registered	
Window Services	Advertisement	Insured	
Personnel	Electronic Transmission	Express Mail	
Other		Other	

Please Give Essential Facts *(If this involves a change of address problem, please include previous address.)*

PS Form 4314-C, July 1991   THANK YOU. You will be contacted soon by your Post Office.   CUSTOMER COPY - 1

FIGURE 4-5. USPS Consumer Service Card, Form 4314.
Courtesy of the United States Post Office.

To use Express Mail Next Day Service, you can take your shipment to any designated Express Mail post office, generally by 5 p.m.; deposit it in an Express Mail collection box; call for on-demand pickup; or hand it to your letter carrier. Your local post office can give you specific Express Mail acceptance times for your area. Depending upon the destination, your mailing will be delivered to the addressee either by noon or by 3 p.m. the next day. Express Mail post-office-to-post-office service can also be picked up at the destination post office by 10 a.m. the next day. If you require expedited delivery but are not sure that your correspondents will physically be at the delivery address to accept and sign for the mail, you may exercise the Waiver of Signature option at the time of mailing.

The U.S. Postal Service may not be able to reach some destinations overnight, and in this case, they provide guaranteed second-day delivery service. You can get on-demand pickup and information on the delivery status of your mailing by calling 1-800-222-1811.

Express Mail is convenient to use. USPS provides you with mailing containers (envelopes, boxes, and tubes) and the necessary mailing labels (see Figure 4-6) at no charge. Customers often find the two-pound flat-rate envelope convenient to use. Any amount of material that fits into it may be mailed in this special flat-rate envelope, and the rate of postage is the rate charged for a two-pound piece of Express Mail, regardless of the weight of the material in the envelope. Merchandise is automatically insured up to $500 against loss or damage, and for a nominal fee, additional insurance can be purchased up to $5,000. However, the Waiver of Signature option cannot be used when additional insurance above $500 is purchased.

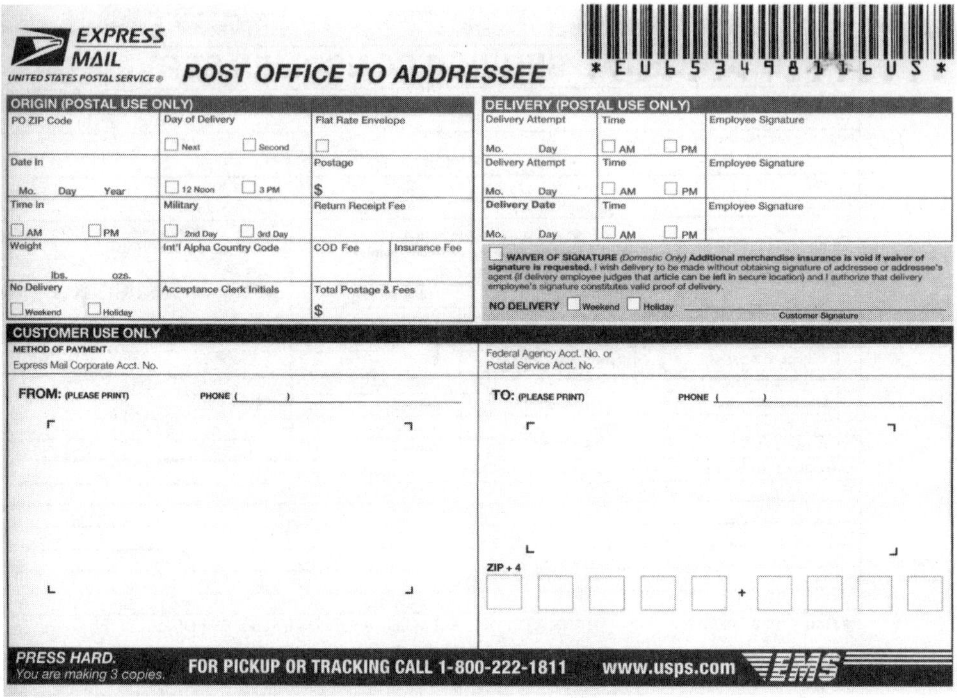
EXPRESS MAIL
UNITED STATES POSTAL SERVICE®
POST OFFICE TO ADDRESSEE
* E U 6 5 3 4 9 8 1 1 6 U S *

ORIGIN (POSTAL USE ONLY)
PO ZIP Code | Day of Delivery: Next, Second | Flat Rate Envelope
Date In: Mo. Day Year | 12 Noon, 3 PM | Postage $
Time In: AM, PM | Military: 2nd Day, 3rd Day | Return Receipt Fee
Weight: lbs. ozs. | Int'l Alpha Country Code | COD Fee | Insurance Fee
No Delivery: Weekend, Holiday | Acceptance Clerk Initials | Total Postage & Fees $

DELIVERY (POSTAL USE ONLY)
Delivery Attempt: Mo. Day | Time: AM, PM | Employee Signature
Delivery Attempt: Mo. Day | Time: AM, PM | Employee Signature
Delivery Date: Mo. Day | Time: AM, PM | Employee Signature
WAIVER OF SIGNATURE (Domestic Only) Additional merchandise insurance is void if waiver of signature is requested. I wish delivery to be made without obtaining signature of addressee or addressee's agent (if delivery employee judges that article can be left in secure location) and I authorize that delivery employee's signature constitutes valid proof of delivery.
NO DELIVERY: Weekend, Holiday — Customer Signature

CUSTOMER USE ONLY
METHOD OF PAYMENT
Express Mail Corporate Acct. No.
Federal Agency Acct. No. or Postal Service Acct. No.
FROM: (PLEASE PRINT) PHONE ( )
TO: (PLEASE PRINT) PHONE ( )
ZIP + 4

PRESS HARD. You are making 3 copies.
FOR PICKUP OR TRACKING CALL 1-800-222-1811 www.usps.com EMS

FIGURE 4-6. Express Mail label.

Courtesy of the United States Post Office.

Express Mail services also include Express Mail Custom Designed Service, Express Mail International Service, Express Mail Military Service, and Express Mail Drop Shipment and Reshipment Services. You can pay for Express Mail with stamps or postage meter strips or through an Express Mail Corporate Account. Also, in some cities, credit and debit cards may be used. Contact your post office for details and rate information.

Priority Mail

When the overnight speed of Express Mail is not needed, but preferential handling is desired, use Priority Mail. Priority Mail offers expedited delivery at the least expensive rate in the industry. The maximum weight for Priority Mail is 70 pounds, and the maximum size is 108 inches in length and girth combined. You also have the option of sending mail weighing less than 13 ounces as Priority Mail.

For proper handling, Priority Mail should be well identified. Your local post office will provide Priority Mail stickers, labels (see Figure 4-7), envelopes, and boxes at no extra charge. For larger quantities (usually 50), you can also order over the phone (1-800-222-1811) or via the Internet (www.supplies.usps.gov). You will find the post office's special flat-rate envelope convenient to use. Any amount of material that fits into the envelope may be mailed at the regular two-pound rate regardless of the weight of the material in the flat-rate envelope.

Priority Mail Dropship or Reship Service is also available. Check with your local Postal Business Center for more information. Priority Mail can be in-

FIGURE 4-7. Priority Mail label.
Courtesy of the United States Post Office.

sured, registered, certified, or sent Collect on Delivery (COD) for an additional charge, including delivery and signature confirmation.

First Class Mail

Use First Class Mail for sending letters, postcards, stamped cards, greeting cards, personal notes, checks, and money orders. All mail weighing over 13 ounces sent as First Class Mail will be handled as Priority Mail.

Additional services such as certificates of mailing and certified, registered, COD, and restricted delivery can be purchased for First Class Mail. Insurance can also be purchased; however, insured articles mailed at the First Class Mail rate must contain only merchandise or material not required to be sent as First Class Mail.

All First Class Mail receives prompt handling and transportation. If your First-Class Mail is not letter size, make sure to mark it "First Class" or use a large green diamond-bordered First Class Mail envelope. First Class Mail is generally delivered overnight to locally designated cities, and within two days to locally designated states. Delivery by the third day can be expected for remaining outlying areas.

First Class Mail in mailings of 500 pieces or more qualifies for a postage rate discount if the mailer presorts and prepares the mail according to specific requirements. There is also a discount rate for properly presorted postcards. Pieces that cannot be presorted and prepared as required are residual mail and are paid at the full first class letter or postcard rate.

CARRIER ROUTE PRESORT FIRST CLASS MAIL

The postal service offers a rate with a greater discount for each piece of qualifying First Class Mail sorted to a carrier route. The geographical density of a mailing eligible for the carrier route rate is greater than for regular presort First Class Mail. For example, there must be ten or more pieces going to a specific carrier route to be eligible for the carrier route rate.

ZIP + 4 CODING AND/OR BAR CODING YOUR MAIL

First Class Mail presorters may qualify for additional rate discounts if they add ZIP+4 codes to their addresses and/or use bar codes on their outgoing mail. Details are available at all post offices.

REQUIREMENTS FOR PRESORTING DISCOUNTS

To qualify for presorting discounts, your company must fulfill all of the following basic requirements:

■ All pieces must be in the same processing category (all letters, all flats, etc.)

■ There must be a minimum of 500 pieces per mailing.

■ An annual presort First Class Mailing fee must be paid once each 12-month period at each post office of mailing by any person or organization entering mail at a presort first class rate; this same fee also allows the person or organization to enter mail at the carrier route first class and ZIP+4 bar-coded rates.

■ The correct zip code must be on each piece.

■ The weight may not exceed 11 ounces.

■ Postage must be paid by postage meter stamps, precanceled adhesive stamps, or permit imprint.

■ Each piece must be endorsed (on the postage meter or stamp) "Presorted First Class." Precanceled stamps preprinted with the endorsement may also be used. (See Figure 4-8.)

RULES FOR PRESORTING

Here are the basic rules for presorting (see Figure 4-9). If your company qualifies for the presorting discount, make sure the mailroom has a copy of these instructions:

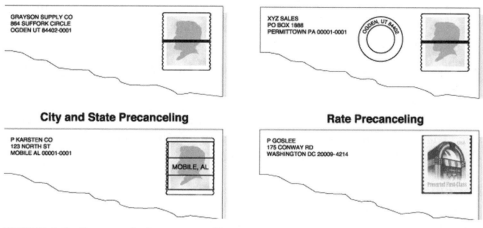

FIGURE 4-8. Precanceled stamp mailings.

Courtesy of the United States Post Office.

- Ten or more pieces to the same first five digits of the zip code—for example, 75214—must be grouped together and banded with rubber bands.

- Fifty or more pieces to the same first three digits of the zip code—for example, 752—must be grouped together and banded with rubber bands.

- Mail that cannot be separated as above is referred to as residual mail—it can be counted toward the 500-piece minimum volume requirement but does not qualify for the lower presort postage rate.

- Accurately label each tray or sack of presorted mail for proper postal handling.

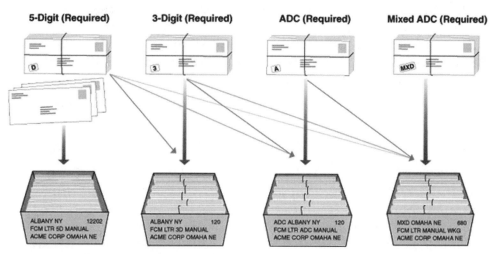

FIGURE 4-9. Sorting bulk mail.

Courtesy of the United States Post Office.

- Accompany each mailing with a properly completed Form 3602-R, Statement of Mailing with Permit Imprints (for a permit imprint mailing), or a Form 3602PC, Statement of Mailing Bulk Rates (for a metered or precanceled stamps mailing), available at all post offices.

- Deliver the mail to a bulk mail acceptance unit during normal operating hours.

In certain circumstances, the postal service will provide customer mail collection. The collection must be part of an existing collection service for another class of mail. Call your post office for details.

Periodicals

Only publishers and registered news agents approved for periodicals mailing privileges may mail at the Periodicals rates of postage. First Class Mail rates must be paid for magazines and newspapers mailed by the general public.

Standard Mail (A)

Standard Mail (A) is used primarily by retailers, catalogers, and other advertisers to promote their products and services. Advertising by mail allows advertisers to reach existing customers or to target new customers by sending messages to specific neighborhoods or to certain demographic groups that are likely to be interested in their products. Standard Mail (A) also allows advertisers to convey a significant amount of information about their products and to measure the effectiveness of their advertisements. Churches and other eligible nonprofit organizations may apply to take advantage of the attractive nonprofit rates for their large mailings.

The minimum volume needed for using either regular or nonprofit Standard Mail (A) rates is 200 pieces or 50 pounds per mailing. The pieces must each weigh less than 16 ounces and be prepared in a manner that allows for efficient handling.

Most people enjoy receiving information in the mail about subjects that interest them or products and services they may need or want. Some consumers, however, would like to receive less advertising mail at home. Mail Preference Service (MPS), a service of the Direct Marketing Association, is designed to assist in decreasing the amount of national nonprofit or commercial mail you receive. You may register with the name removal file by writing to:

Mail Preference Service
Direct Marketing Association
P.O. Box 9008
Farmingdale, NY 11735–9008

Standard Mail (B)

Use Standard Mail (B) service for parcels weighing one pound or more. If you enclose or attach First Class Mail, you must usually pay additional postage for the enclosure or attachment. (Ask your postmaster about incidental First Class Mail attachments or enclosures that do not require separate payment of First

Class Mail postage.) You can purchase insurance to cover the value of articles mailed as Standard Mail (B). (For details, see Insurance, pp. 59–60.) Parcel Post mailed within the continental United States may weigh up to 70 pounds and measure up to 130 inches in length and girth combined. Your post office also has information about lower local mailing rates and special mailing rates for books, catalogs, and international mailings.

The U.S. Postal Service's delivery goal for parcel delivery is two to nine days, depending on distance. For faster delivery of parcels, use Priority Mail or Express Mail.

Forwarding First Class Mail and Other Mail

First Class Mail is forwarded at no charge for one year. Second Class Mail, including magazines and newspapers, is forwarded at no charge for 60 days from the effective date of a change-of-address order. All post offices have information about holding mail, temporary changes of address, and forwarding and return of other classes of mail.

Other Special Mail Services

In addition to the services already outlined, USPS offers a wide variety of other options to provide customers maximum convenience and to give individual pieces of mail special handling or protection.

Any piece traveling by one of these special services must be so labeled. The appropriate marking (registered, insured, certified, etc.) should be placed above the delivery address and to the right of the return address.

Post Office Box and Caller Services

Post office box and caller services are available at many post offices for an annual fee. Post office box delivery is a secure and private means of getting your mail any time the post office lobby is open. With post offices conveniently located near most businesses, you can get a jump on your day by picking up your company's mail at a post office box in the morning.

Caller (pickup) service, available when post office retail windows are open, is for customers who receive a large volume of mail or those who need a box number address when no boxes are available. Call your post office for more information.

Passport Applications

You can apply for a passport at more than 1,200 postal facilities nationwide. State Department regulations require that each applicant present two recent photographs (two inches by two inches), valid identification, and a certified copy of his or her birth certificate, along with the appropriate fee when applying for a new passport. The passport fee may be paid in cash, by check, or by money order. For additional information, call the Department of State information line nearest you or your local post office.

Money Orders

Because you should *never send cash through the mail,* money orders are a safe way to send money when checks cannot be used. The special color-blend Benjamin Franklin watermark, metal security thread, and twice imprinting of the dollar amount are incorporated security features. You can buy domestic and international money orders at all post offices in amounts up to $700. Military money orders can be purchased on U.S. military ships and foreign bases.

If your money order is lost or stolen, present your customer receipt, and the money order can be replaced. For a small fee, you can obtain a copy of a money order for up to two years after the date it is paid for.

Mailgram

A Mailgram™ (a registered trademark of Western Union Corporation) is an electronic message service offered by Western Union that provides next-day postal service delivery for messages sent to any address in the United States or Canada. The messages are transmitted for delivery with the next business day's mail.

Mailgrams are often used for short messages when you need to get someone's attention. For instance, if a company or individual is extremely late in paying a bill and is ignoring your other written correspondence, a Mailgram might help get their attention. Mailgrams are also useful as a way to get the attention of a potential client. While they are delivered with the regular mail, the Mailgram stands out and looks important.

Mailgram messages may be sent by calling Western Union and dictating your message to the operator, or you can use your office telex or TWX. For more information, call Western Union Telegraph Company. In Hawaii, call your local post office for information on how to send a message. In Alaska, call Alascom, Inc., for Mailgram service.

Address Changes

Before moving from one location to another, each company or individual should obtain from the local post office a Mover's Guide. The guide includes instructions for submitting a change of address using a toll-free telephone number or by accessing the Address Change section of the USPS Web site at www.usps.com.

It's best to notify the post office several weeks in advance of the move to keep the mail coming without interruption. Be sure the effective date of the change is on the notification form (see Figure 4-10). Your complete new address on the notification form should include directions (North, East, South, West), if applicable, the correct suffix (Street, Avenue, Road, Circle), suite number, rural route number, box number, and correct zip code or ZIP+4 code, if known—all essential to proper addressing and fast delivery of your mail.

Collection Delivery (COD) Service

Use COD service when your company wants to collect for merchandise and postage when the merchandise is delivered. COD service may be used for mer-

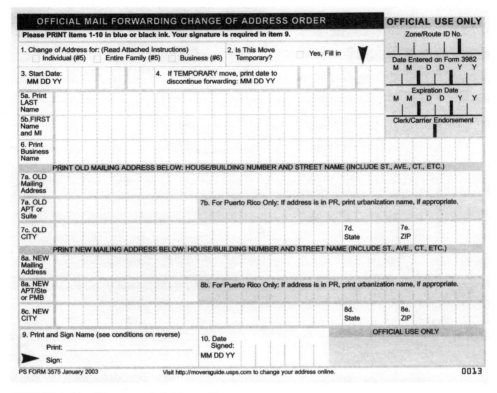

FIGURE 4-10. Change of Address Form.

Courtesy of the United States Post Office.

chandise sent by First Class Mail, Express Mail, Priority Mail, Third or Fourth Class Mail, or registered mail. The merchandise must have been ordered by the addressee. The fee charged for this service includes insurance protection against loss or damage, although the service is limited to items valued at a maximum of $600. (For further details, see Insurance, pp. 59–60.) COD service is not available for international mail.

Merchandise Return Service

Merchandise return service is available to authorized parties through a special permit. The service enables one of your company's customers to return a parcel and have the postage paid by you. Under this arrangement, the company provides the customer with instructions and a special label to attach to the parcel if it must be returned. The customer applies the label to the parcel and deposits it at a post office or in a mailbox. Unless the label is provided, the customer must pay the required postage charges.

Certified Mail

Certified Mail service (Form 3800; see Figure 4-11) provides the mailer with a receipt and a record of the delivery of the item mailed from the post office from which it is delivered. No record is kept at the post office at which the item is mailed. Certified Mail is handled in the ordinary mail and is not covered by in-

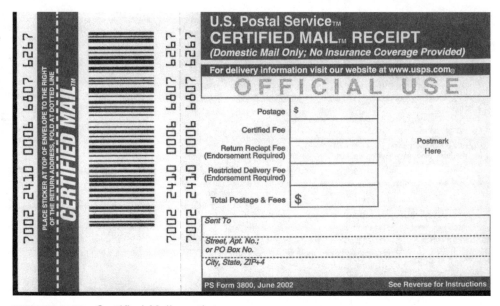

FIGURE 4-11. Certified Mail receipt.
Courtesy of the United States Post Office.

surance. The matter mailed usually has no intrinsic value, with the sender wishing only to be sure that it has been sent to the correct point of receipt. If the item mailed does have intrinsic value, it should be sent via registered mail (see p. 60), *not* certified mail.

Certified Mail may be sent special delivery if additional postage is paid. An additional fee is also charged if delivery is restricted (only to the person named in the address) or if a return receipt is requested by the mailer.

Certificate of Mailing

At a fee somewhat lower than that for certified mail, a certificate of mailing will furnish evidence of mailing only. No receipt is obtained upon delivery of mail to the addressee. The fee does not insure the article against loss or damage to the item mailed.

Return Receipt

When the sender wants evidence that the mail was delivered, he or she should request a return receipt at the time the article is mailed. A return receipt can be purchased for mail that is sent COD or by Express Mail or for mail that is insured for more than $50 or is registered or certified. It identifies the article by number, the signer, and date of delivery. For an additional fee, the sender can get the addressee's correct address of delivery or can request restricted delivery service (see below).

Return receipt for merchandise service—another form of return receipt service, which provides a mailing receipt, return receipt, and record of delivery—is available for merchandise sent at First Class, Priority, Third Class, and Fourth Class rates of postage.

Restricted Delivery

Restricted delivery means that the sender's mail is delivered only to the addressee or to someone authorized in writing to receive mail for the addressee. Restricted delivery is offered in connection with return receipt service and is available only for Registered Mail, Certified Mail, COD mail, and mail insured for more than $50.

Restricted delivery mail addressed to officials of government agencies, members of the legislative and judicial branches of federal and state government, members of the diplomatic corps, minors, and individuals under guardianship can be delivered to an agent without written authorization from the addressee.

Insurance

Protection against loss or damage to packages with contents valued in any amount up to $5,000 is available (Figure 4-12). The fee is based on the amount of insurance desired. Insurance can be purchased for Third and Fourth Class Mail, as well as for Third and Fourth Class matter that is mailed at the Priority Mail or First-Class Mail rate. Insurance coverage up to $25,000 can be purchased on registered mail, the most secure service offered by the postal service. For articles insured for more than $50, a receipt of delivery is signed by the recipient and filed at the delivery post office.

Do not over-insure your packages, since the amount of insurance coverage for loss will be the actual value less depreciation. No payments are made for sentimental losses or for any expenses incurred as a result of the loss. For example, if you send a package containing a three-year-old computer that was originally purchased for $2,500, its actual value (due to depreciation) might

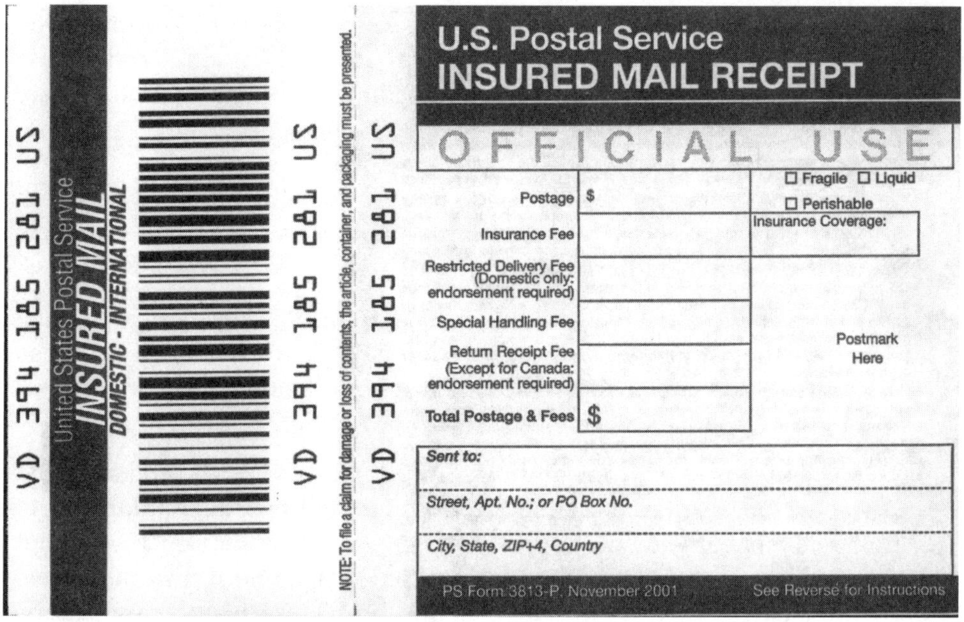
VD 394 185 281 US
United States Postal Service
INSURED MAIL
DOMESTIC - INTERNATIONAL
VD 394 185 281 US
NOTE: To file a claim for damage or loss of contents, the article, container, and packaging must be presented.
VD 394 185 281 US

U.S. Postal Service
INSURED MAIL RECEIPT

OFFICIAL USE

Postage	$	☐ Fragile ☐ Liquid ☐ Perishable
Insurance Fee		Insurance Coverage:
Restricted Delivery Fee (Domestic only: endorsement required)		
Special Handling Fee		Postmark Here
Return Receipt Fee (Except for Canada: endorsement required)		
Total Postage & Fees	$	

Sent to:

Street, Apt. No.; or PO Box No.

City, State, ZIP+4, Country

PS Form 3813-P, November 2001 See Reverse for Instructions

FIGURE 4-12. Insurance receipt.
Courtesy of the United States Post Office.

only be $800. Even if you insured the computer for $2,500, if it were damaged or lost, the insurance would only pay the current value of $800.

Registered Mail

The most secure option offered by the post office is registered mail. Registered articles are placed under tight security from the point of mailing to the delivery office, providing added protection for valuable and important mail. Insurance may be purchased on domestic registered mail up to $25,000 at the option of the mailer. Return receipt and restricted delivery services are available for additional fees. Registered mail to Canada is subject to a $1,000 indemnity limit. For all other foreign countries, the indemnity is currently $32.35. First Class or Priority Mail postage is required on domestic registered mail.

There are special packaging requirements for registered mail. For example, you can't send a soft-sided package or put tape over the edges or reinforce an old box with tape. The box must be able to accept a postage ink stamp, and ink will not stay on slick tape surfaces.

Special Handling

Special handling service is required for parcels whose unusual contents require additional care in transit and handling. Note: Special handling is not required for those parcels sent by First Class Mail, Express Mail, or Priority Mail. Examples of such contents include live poultry or bees. Special handling is available for Standard Mail only, including insured and COD mail. This service provides preferential handling to the extent practical in dispatch and transportation.

Special handling service is not necessary for sending ordinary parcels, even when they contain fragile items. Breakable items will receive adequate protection if they are packed with sufficient cushioning and clearly marked "FRAGILE." Use registered mail for valuable or irreplaceable items.

Stamp Services

The U.S. Postal Service has made it more convenient than ever to buy stamps. Whether you use one of their shop-at-home services or buy stamps where you work or shop, you have these options:

- *At retail establishments.* Look for the STAMPS TO GO logo at places where you shop. In cooperation with the USPS, many businesses offer stamps at post office prices. Ask the cashier at your local grocery or convenience store if that store is a STAMPS TO GO outlet.

- *Stamps by mail.* You can buy stamps, stamped cards, and stamped envelopes through the mail by completing Form 3227, Stamps by Mail, available at your post office or from your letter carrier. Just fill out the order form, enclose a check or money order, and return the envelope to the carrier or drop it in a collection box. There is no service charge, and you should receive your order within three to five business days.

■ *Stamps by phone.* Stamps are as close as your telephone. Call 1-800-STAMP24 (1-800-782-6724) 24 hours a day, 7 days a week, to place your order. Visa, MasterCard, American Express, and Discover credit cards are accepted. Your stamps are delivered within three to five business days. No minimum order is required, but there is a service charge based on the total cost of the order.

■ *Self-service vending equipment.* Self-service vending equipment, providing stamps and stamped products such as stamped cards and stamped envelopes, is available at many locations throughout the country. The conveniently located equipment enables you to access basic postal services around the clock. Some locations include postal scales that provide rate information for mailing packages. Selected self-service vending machines can accept currency up to $20 bills and dispense a variety of products such as 100-stamp coils, Express Mail stamps, envelopes, stamp booklets, and even stamped cards, all at face value. If you experience a loss because of an equipment malfunction, you will be reimbursed upon request at the local post office or by completing a consumer service card.

Information on the Internet

A wealth of information is available at your fingertips when you visit the US Postal Service's Web site at www.usps.gov. You can look up ZIP+4 codes, track your Express Mail, get information on the latest postal rates, and find answers to frequently asked questions.

If you keep exploring, you can find postal news releases and learn about the history of the Postal Service. The Inspection Service has included information on consumer fraud and other crimes, and information about the history of the Inspection Service. The Web site is continually changing. Visit often for new postal information. You can also make inquiries and request additional information. Figure 4-13 shows the United States Postal Service Web site.

International Mail

Getting Mail from Abroad

All mail originating from foreign countries and U.S. overseas territories, other than the Commonwealth of Puerto Rico, is subject to U.S. Customs Service examination upon entering the United States. Many imported goods are subject to the payment of U.S. Customs duty. When dutiable merchandise enters the United States by mail, the amount due is determined by the Customs Service but is collected by the Postal Service. When the duty is collected on behalf of the Customs Service, the Postal Service also collects a customs clearance and delivery fee on each dutiable item. This fee offsets the cost of collection and remittance.

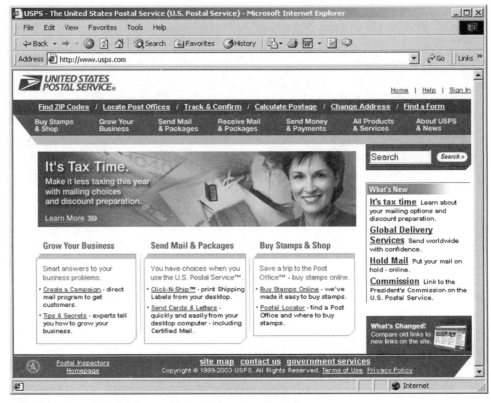

FIGURE 4-13. United States Postal Service Web Site.
Courtesy of the United States Post Office.

For customs information, please write to:

United States Customs Service
Treasury Department
1301 Constitution Ave NW
Washington, DC 20229–0001

Sending Mail Abroad

The principal classes of international mail are as follows:

- Express Mail International Service (EMS): For mailing high-priority or other urgently needed items including merchandise. Express Mail International Service can be sent to nearly 200 countries and territories around the world—the delivery target is two to three days.

- Global Priority Mail: For mailing urgent items weighing up to four pounds including merchandise. Global Priority Mail can be sent to more than 30 countries around the world.

- Aerogrammes: Air letter sheets that can be folded and sealed to form an envelope.

■ Letters, postcards, and letter packages: Personal handwritten or typewritten communications as well as other items that are paid for at letter class rates.

■ Printed Matter: Includes books, sheet music, publishers' periodicals, and regular printed matter (i.e., advertising mail, catalogs, and directories).

■ Small Packets: For light-weight merchandise, commercial samples, or documents other than personal correspondence.

■ Parcel Post: For shipping heavier merchandise and printed matter.

All printed matter items, small packets, and parcel post packages may be sent either airmail or surface mail. Check with your local post office for specific information about the mail service in the country to which you are mailing.

Customs

Customs forms are required when you send dutiable letter packages, small packets, printed matter, and parcels to international destinations. The specific customs form is governed by the type of mail, the weight of the item, and the regulations of the destination country.

Individual countries may restrict or prohibit certain articles. Articles that are prohibited by the destination country are nonmailable. Articles that are restricted are subject to the import requirements of that country. Specific information about restrictions and prohibitions for individual countries and about the forms required for mailing is listed in the International Mail Manual, available at your local post office or online at www.usps.gov.

Special Services

Registry service, with a very limited level of indemnity protection, is available for letter mail, small packets, and all printed matter. (For details, see Registered Mail, p. 60.) Insured parcel post service is also available to many countries.

Recorded delivery service, like domestic Certified Mail service, is intended for letters, documents, and items of little or no value. It is an appropriate service if you want the assurance of knowing that a record of delivery exists in the event an inquiry is necessary. For an added fee, you can purchase a return receipt at the time of mailing. Note: Publication 51, International Postal Rates and Fees, is available at all post offices or online. This booklet contains general mailing information and current postal rates and fees for postal services from the United States to foreign countries.

Parcels and Publications Sent to Military Bases

Parcel airlift (PAL) mail and space-available mail (SAM) are only for personal parcels and publications mailed to military personnel overseas at the Standard Mail rates.

Packages up to 30 pounds and 60 inches in combined length and girth may be sent by PAL. This mail is flown to a military mail dispatch center, where it is sent overseas on a space-available basis by air transportation. You pay the regular parcel post rate, depending on weight, plus a small fee for the air service to the military mail dispatch center. Parcels of any class marked SAM that weigh up to 15 pounds and are not more than 60 inches in combined length and girth also are airlifted overseas on a space-available basis to military post offices. However, this mail is transported by surface within the United States to a military mail dispatch center. There is no additional fee for space-available mail.

Express Mail Military Service (EMMS) is available for sending urgent letters, documents, and packages to select overseas military APO and FPO addresses. The U.S. Postal Service delivers to more than 300 military post offices. Postage for EMMS is the same as domestic Express Mail.

Alternatives to the USPS

Although documents, letters, and advertisements are usually shipped through the USPS, it is likely that your company will also use an alternative form of service, for example, United Parcel Service or air express transportation companies like Federal Express (FedEx) or Airborne Express. Many airlines have an air-freight express service that can transport a package from one city to another the same day. In addition, there are trucking freight shippers, and even couriers that can deliver packages in town the same day. Here's a quick overview of these delivery options.

United Parcel Service

Many business use United Parcel Service (UPS) for shipping parcels and freight. UPS offers both overnight delivery as well as a standard ground service. Shipping costs vary depending on weight and shipping distance.

You can ship packages with UPS by visiting a UPS office or by calling UPS and scheduling a pickup. You can also use the UPS Web site at www.ups.com to print a shipping label and schedule a pickup. There are also many local UPS pickup stations at print shops and office supply stores as well as mail and packaging shops. If you ship a lot of packages, you can schedule regular weekday pickups.

UPS services include next-day delivery, second-day delivery, three-day delivery, and standard ground service. In addition to domestic shipping services, UPS offers a variety of international delivery services including next-flight-out delivery to more than 180 countries.

UPS offers delivery tracking and delivery confirmation services for all ground and air shipments. You can track your packages online at www.ups.com.

FedEx

FedEx Express and FedEx Ground offer a wide variety of package shipping services ranging from overnight letters to ground freight. You can set up an account for FedEx by calling 1–800–GoFedEx (1–800–463–3339) or by visiting the Web site at fedex.com.

FedEx services include:

- FedEx Express (U.S.)—for fast reliable, time-definite delivery.

- FedEx Express International—for shipping to more than 210 countries door-to-door by specific delivery times.

- FedEx Express Freight (U.S.)—for time-definite delivery of packages that weigh between 151 lbs. and 2,200 lbs.

- FedEx Express International Freight—for time-definite delivery of high-volume international shipments in 1 to 5 business days to major global markets.

- FedEx Ground (U.S.)—for cost-effective, day-definite delivery for business-to-business packages.

- FedEx Ground International—for door-to-door delivery in 3 to 7 days from the U.S. to Canada and Puerto Rico.

- FedEx Home Delivery—for business-to-residence deliveries at extended hours, competitive ground rates, and delivery backed by a money-back guarantee.

To ship a package with FedEx, follow these steps:

1. Pack your shipment in FedEx packaging or your own packaging. Shipping supplies, such as overnight letter envelopes, boxes, and shipping forms, can be ordered or picked up from one of many conveniently located FedEx locations.

2. Log-on to the fedex.com Web site and select a service.

3. Create a shipping label by filling out the name, address, and phone number of the recipient. You can print a shipping label on your laser or ink-jet printer.

4. Drop off your package at the nearest self-service FedEx® Drop Box, staffed service center, FedEx Authorized ShipCenter®, or select Post Office locations around the country. You can locate one of the more than 48,000 drop-off locations using the fedex.com Web site. In addition to dropping off your package, you can schedule a pickup. No pre-qualification is needed for a FedEx pickup; however, there is a small surcharge added to the shipping cost.

The FedEx® Ship Manager at fedex.com allows you to prepare shipments, schedule pickups, and track the delivery of your packages. Up to 2,000 names and addresses can be stored in the online Address Book, so you don't have to retype recurring shipment information. Each shipment also includes a tracking number. FedEx Ship Manager can send you an e-mail to notify you when a package is shipped and when it is delivered. You can use the tracking feature to check the status of your shipments. If the shipment has already arrived, you can even see who signed for it. You can track packages by your own reference number, your shipment tracking number, an e-mail address, or—for Ground—a purchase order or invoice number.

FedEx shipping rates are affordable and can be obtained for a particular shipment from the FedEx Ship Manager at fedex.com.

✦ Airborne Express

Airborne Express is an overnight document and package shipping service that offers a variety of services. You can call 1-800-AIRBORNE to set up an account or visit their Web site at www.airborne.com.

With AirborneExchange at www.airborne.com, you can process your US and international shipments online. Shipments prepared online are subject to a discount. The online site also allows you to:

- Prepare and print shipping labels and international documentation.
- View a cost and service estimate before sending your shipment.
- Send an e-mail to the recipient with the air bill number and a link for tracking.
- Track, view, edit, and void shipments.
- Schedule pickups.
- Store frequently used contacts in your personal address book.
- View reports on the most recent 90 days of shipping history.
- Find drop box locations and Airborne Express shipping centers.

Airborne offers a wide array of options for domestic shipments, including:

- Same Day Delivery by Sky Courier, for urgent delivery on the next available flight.
- 10:30 Urgent AM, for guaranteed delivery by 10:30 a.m.
- Overnight Express, for delivery by noon the next business day.
- Next Afternoon Service, for delivery of shipments up to five pounds by 3 p.m. the next business day.
- Second Day Service, for delivery by 5:00 p.m. on the second business day.
- Ground Delivery Service, for guaranteed delivery within 1 to 5 business days.
- Airborne@home, for residential delivery for high-volume shippers.
- Saturday delivery.
- Hold for pickup service.

Airborne Express also delivers to more than 200 countries. Airborne's international services include:

- Next Flight Out by Sky Courier, for international delivery on the next flight out.
- International Air Express, for door-to-door delivery of documents and packages weighing up to 70 pounds within 1 to 4 business days including customs clearance.

- International Air Freight, for delivery of shipments of any size, door-to-door, door-to-airport, or airport-to-airport.
- Ocean Freight, for large cargo shipments.

Other Shipping Services

Air Freight

For special situations, such as large packages or packages that must be delivered to another city the same day, air freight services are available from many airlines and specialty air freight companies. Some have special offices at the airport for same-day shipments. These shipments must usually be dropped off at the freight office and picked up at the destination freight office. The fees are much higher than other next-day air and two-day air shipments.

Bus Freight

Most passenger bus lines provide a freight service, often useful for moving packages to small towns that are not served by other shipping services. Packages are taken along with passenger baggage and unloaded at the bus station at the intended destination. The recipient must pick up the package at the station.

Trucking Freight

For large shipments and heavy or bulky packages, there are many trucking companies that specialize in hauling freight. These companies will load the shipment at your place of business, transport it to the destination, and unload it for a fee that is usually competitive. Depending on what you are shipping and where it is going, coast-to-coast shipping can take anywhere from 7 to 21 days.

Courier Services

If you need to ship a package across town within a few hours, your best bet is a courier service. These companies operate in most large towns and cities and provide pickup and delivery within a few hours. The prices for these services vary depending on the distance traveled and the weight and size of the package. Most of the time, the charge is paid in advance by the sender. Courier services are bonded against theft or damage.

For documents and other small items, many taxi companies also provide a courier-type service. Check your telephone book for courier services or taxi services.

Travel Arrangements

✴ Today's Business Traveler

In today's competitive market, companies routinely buy and sell products and services both across the country and around the world. Because of this, business-related travel is common to every type and every size of company.

A small business just getting under way may have interest in local markets only; however, as the business grows and expands, a larger domestic market and, possibly, international markets will be of greater interest. Thus, as a business grows, and an owner's needs increase, your administrative duties will include keeping abreast of how to handle your employer's travel needs quickly and efficiently, no matter how far he or she goes.

Even if you work for a larger company that has an in-house travel department, it's useful to know the following procedures to troubleshoot for your boss when needed.

✴ Getting the Trip Underway

Your main purpose in making travel arrangements is to get your boss to his or her destination and back home again as smoothly as possible. Other considerations may be speed and cost. If you are a new administrative assistant or new to a particular office, see what the policies and precedents for making travel arrangements are. You may find helpful information in the files, there may even be a step-by-step procedures manual to consult, or you may find a special intranet Web page that contains travel information. If such information is not readily available, ask your boss whether to use a travel agency or to make the arrangements without an agent.

Whether you're going to do it yourself or are collecting information for the travel agent, be sure to determine the following basics:

- What is the purpose of the trip?

- What are the desired departure and return times and dates?

- What is the point-by-point itinerary?

- Will the boss be traveling alone, or will other staff members or family members be traveling along?

- What type of transportation does your boss desire? What is the best means of transportation available to that particular destination? If you're not sure, a travel agent may help you with some of this information even if arrangements are ultimately not made through the agency.

- What is the lodging facility closest to the activities of the trip? If your boss's appointments are scattered throughout the city, perhaps a downtown hotel or an airport hotel or motel would be preferred.

If your employer travels frequently, it might be wise to secure a copy of the *Official Airline Guide* (OAG) available in both domestic and international editions. It is obtainable from:

OAG
3025 Highland Parkway
Suite 200
Downers Grove, Illinois 60515-5561
USA
TEL: 630-515-5300
FAX: 630-515-5301
E-MAIL: custsvc@oag.com

OAG
6303 Blue Lagoon Drive
Suite 120
Miami, Florida 33126
USA
TEL: 305-265-2700
FAZ: 305-265-2701
E-MAIL: custsvc@oag.com

OAG
1215 Jefferson Davis Highway
Suite 303
Arlington, VA 22202
USA
TEL: 703-414-5372
FAX: 703-414-5381
E-MAIL: govt@oag.com

You can also view the OAG on the Web at www.oag.com.

Another useful guide provides a complete description of many hotels and motels throughout the United States as well as their toll-free 800 numbers. This is the *American Hotel and Motel Red Book*. It can be ordered from:

American Hotel & Lodging Association
1201 New York Avenue, NW, #600
Washington, DC 20005–3931
TEL: 202-289-3100
FAX: 202-289-3199
E-MAIL: info@ahla.com

You can also view this information on the Web at www.ahma.com.

If you make arrangements on your own, this guide lets you call hotels toll free to make reservations directly. Even if you do use an agency, the publication might still be valuable, because it provides information concerning each hotel and motel, including room rates, which will help you select a hotel best suited to your employer's needs and desires.

Doing It Yourself

Many employers ask administrative assistants to arrange travel services and not use a travel agent. If this is the case, first have your boss confirm basic departure and return times and dates, and then proceed to make the reservations.

Hotel Reservations

If the meeting is in a major city, make the lodging reservations without delay, because city hotels are often fully booked weeks in advance. State your employer's name, office or home address, telephone number, type of accommodation preferred (single room, two-bedroom suite, etc.), plus your own name as the contact person. Ask for written confirmation, which your boss should carry when traveling in case he or she arrives only to be told that no such reservation exists.

Some hotels also make airport shuttle or limousine reservations. If your boss needs either of these, make a reservation now. Have the date and the exact time of day the shuttle or limousine is needed, and give that information to the hotel reservation person. Again, ask for written confirmation to be mailed, faxed, or e-mailed to you with the room reservation information.

Hotels hold room reservations only until a specific deadline, typically 6 p.m. You can extend the reservation beyond that time limit by guaranteeing payment whether or not the boss arrives. To do this, you must give the hotel reservation person a credit card number. Remember that if the boss should change his or her mind about making the trip or staying at that hotel, the room charge will have to be paid anyway, since you've guaranteed arrival. However, most hotels and motels will allow you to cancel a guaranteed reservation without charge if you cancel before 6:00 p.m. on the day of arrival.

What if you aren't able to make a reservation in the hotel of your boss's choice? You may be able to use a travel agency for this service alone. Large travel agencies often have a number of hotel and motel rooms blocked and held exclusively for them, a practice especially common at conventions. Select an agency that's very large, perhaps choosing on the basis of telephone classified ads if you don't have a personal recommendation. Call, and explain your problem. The travel agent will usually be eager to assist you, with the hope you'll eventually become a regular client.

All of this presumes you know which hotel to choose. If your boss is traveling to a city he or she has never visited before or is going to a convention that does not recommend a particular hotel, investigate your choices using the *Hotel and Motel Red Book.* You may also write to the convention bureau or chamber of commerce in that city or secure a local newspaper. Much valuable information can be obtained from these sources. If your boss has a favorite hotel chain, you can call the national reservations center for the chain and find out if they have a hotel in the city your boss will be visiting. You can then make reservations using the national reservations center.

Transportation Reservations

Airline

Call the preferred airline's reservation office by consulting your telephone directory for a toll-free 800 number. If you're unable to find one, call 800 telephone information: 800-555-1212.

As soon as you're in touch with the airline, you can instantly make a reservation and usually secure a preferred seat and/or car reservations as well. Advise the reservations agent of the company's or employer's credit card number and whether the ticket and reservations information should be electronic, mailed, or held for pickup.

The following is a list of major airlines:

- Aer Lingus
- Aeromexico
- Air Canada
- Air China
- Air France
- Air Jamaica
- Air New Zealand
- AirTran Airways
- Alaska Airlines
- Alitalia
- All Nippon Airways
- America West
- American Airlines
- Asiana Airlines
- ATA
- Austrian Airlines
- BMI British Midland

- British Airways
- Cathay Pacific
- China Airlines
- Continental
- Delta
- El Al
- EVA Airways
- Finnair
- Frontier Airlines
- Hawaiian Airlines
- Iberia
- Icelandair
- Japan Airlines
- KLM
- Korean Air
- Lan Chile
- LOT (Polish Airlines)

- Lufthansa
- Malaysia Airlines
- Mexicana
- Midwest Express
- Northwest
- Qantas Airways
- SAS
- Southwest Airlines

- Spirit Airlines
- Sun Country Airlines
- Swiss International Air Lines
- Thai Air International
- United
- US Airways
- Virgin Atlantic

Electronic Tickets

Electronic tickets, or e-tickets, allow travel without a paper ticket. An e-ticket confirms your airline ticket purchase without requiring a paper record. The only record of an e-ticket sale is in electronic form in the airline's computer system.

When flying on an e-ticket, airport security and airline check-in locations require you to provide a government-issued photo ID, such as a driver's license, along with one of the following documents indicating a flight departure for the current date:

- An e-ticket receipt (including ticket number)
- An itinerary (including ticket number)
- A boarding pass

This information is required in order to enter the secured area beyond the security screening checkpoint. Passengers who do not need to check baggage and already have an approved document (outlined above) may proceed through the security checkpoint directly to the departure gate. The printed documentation you present at the airport must include your airline ticket numbers. Ticket numbers are displayed on your itinerary as well as your e-ticket receipt.

Some employers require paper receipts for business travel expense reports. Some companies accept printouts of confirmation e-mails, but check your company's policy to find out what is acceptable documentation.

Train

In days gone by, rail travel was the way to go, with comfortable Pullman compartments and dining cars with fine food graciously served. But today, with time being money, more and more executives prefer air travel. Still, there are executives who either prefer not to fly or genuinely enjoy leisurely travel such as that provided by Amtrak. Railway travel is usually done when there is adequate time and easy access to rail terminals.

If your employer prefers rail travel, obtain a schedule for Amtrak trains as well as for commuter lines and connecting lines from the nearest rail station. A call to Amtrak will answer your questions.

Automobile

Call the preferred car rental company's reservation office by consulting your telephone directory for a toll-free 800 number. If you're unable to find one, call 800 telephone information: 800-555-1212. Many car rental companies have frequent renter programs that speed up the rental process both when making reservations and when picking up a car. Check with your employer to find out which car rental company is preferred, and whether or not he or she has a frequent renter membership. The following is a list of the major car rental companies:

- Advantage
- Alamo
- Avis
- Budget
- Dollar

- Enterprise
- Hertz
- National
- Payless
- Thrifty

Car rentals are handled much the same way as hotel reservations. You'll need to provide a credit card in order to guarantee the reservation. You will need to know the following in order to make a car rental reservation:

- City
- Specific rental location in the city

- Car pick-up time
- Car drop-off time
- Car class

Check with your employer to determine the car class. A variety of car classes are available for rental including:

- Economy
- Compact
- Midsize
- Standard
- Full size

- Premium
- Luxury
- Convertible
- Mini-van
- Sports utility vehicle

Using a Web-Based Travel Service

You can book travel yourself using a Web-based travel service such as Expedia.com. Expedia.com will allow you to make both personal and business travel reservations for airlines, hotels, car rentals, cruises, and other vacation packages.

With a Web-based travel service, you can create a traveler profile for your employer, so that his or her personal preferences regarding airline seats, hotels, car rental agencies, hotel rooms, and so forth are stored for all future trips. You can also instantly create an itinerary that can be printed on your computer's printer. In addition, you can print maps and driving directions.

Using a Travel Agency

A good travel agency is invaluable to the busy secretary. Few other outside services provide more time-saving help. A competent agency can provide a host of services. It can: recommend hotels and make reservations; make airline, ship, and rail reservations; take advantage of special fares you may not be aware of; issue tickets; make car rental reservations; assist in securing passports and visas; provide tickets to shows, the theater, sporting events, or a special event occurring in one or more of the cities on the itinerary; and mail all these tickets and reservation information directly to you.

Usually, travel agencies do not charge your company a fee for making these reservations since their commissions are paid directly by the hotels; however, some do add a small surcharge to airline tickets. A charge may also be made for rail reservations, unless the reservation is part of a prearranged package tour. Refunds for any unused tickets can also be obtained by the agency. In addition, a travel agency can often help solve problems that occur during your employer's stay. Even small agencies often have a toll-free 800 number, making it convenient for either you or the boss to call from anywhere.

After you've compiled an itinerary for your boss and know his or her exact travel needs and desires, a telephone call to a travel agency may be all that's needed. This will save you an incredible amount of time from the moment your employer leaves home or the office to the time of return.

Finding a Reputable Agent

To find a reputable travel agent, ask administrative assistants in other companies or your own company for a recommendation, or obtain a list of agencies from this professional organization:

> American Society of Travel Agents
> 1101 King Street, Ste. 200
> Alexandria, VA 22314
> TEL: 703-739-2782
> FAX: 703-684-8319

Many good and reputable agents do not belong to this society, so do not discount a recommended agency simply because it's not a member. If you need still further sources of agencies, consult your classified telephone directory. If you wish, ask if the agency can give you the name of one or more business clients as references.

Once you've found a good travel agent, use that same person whenever possible every time your employer travels. The agent will soon become familiar with your boss's travel habits and travel needs, making it easier to arrange trips. A rapport between you and that agent will be to your employer's advantage and perhaps to your own when vacation time comes for you.

Making the Arrangements

To establish a good relationship between you, your employer, and your travel agent, always have all the facts ready when you call. If you're not sure what your employer needs, you cannot expect the agent to know. But once you do have complete information, the agent can begin to find the best schedules, the best fares, and the best hotels and hotel rates. The facts you should have ready for the agent include:

- Your name and the traveler's name
- The traveler's office address and office telephone number
- Date and time of departure and date and time of return
- The traveler's preferences: Specific carrier, if desired; general time of departure, such as early morning or evening; general time of return; and type of service desired, such as first-class, coach, smoking, or nonsmoking
- The traveler's home telephone number
- The traveler's frequent flyer number
- Your home telephone number (in case an emergency should arise, such as a change in return-flight time or a return-flight cancellation, and the boss needs to be notified while away)

Quickly and efficiently, a good travel agent will provide you with confirmation of your reservations, the advised check-in time, the travel time, and estimated time of arrival. These services may be paid for with a credit card. The airline tickets and reservation confirmation forms can be picked up by you or mailed, as you wish.

The Itinerary

An itinerary—that is, a written travel agenda—is useful to both the executive and the administrative assistant who remains in the office. Quick reference to it can be made when questions arise. Perhaps the executive has forgotten the address or time for an appointment, or perhaps the administrative assistant, faced with a sudden emergency, needs to know exactly where the employer can be contacted.

Before preparing the written itinerary, confer with your boss, making notes of all activities on the trip. Show your employer a draft of the written schedule, so that changes can be made or forgotten items added. Once the itinerary has been completed, it can be typed on small pocket-size cards or on plain paper. Figure 5-1 contains a sample itinerary.

Before-the-Trip-Checklist

Before leaving on a trip, you should confirm the following:

- Airline tickets and frequent flyer number
- Lodging information and confirmation number
- Car rental information and confirmation number
- Money or travelers' checks
- Passport, visa, driver's license, or international driving permit'
- Itinerary
- Destination contact names, addresses, and phone numbers

Philip Smith

Itinerary

Monday, June 1 (Dallas to New York)

8:00 AM   Leave Dallas residence by limousine for airport. (Limousine reservation attached.)

9:00 AM   Leave DFW Airport on American Airlines Flight 122, Seat 1B. Includes lunch. (Ticket attached.)

12:40 AM   Arrive New York, JFK Airport. Limousine to Americana Hotel. (Limousine reservation attached.)

2:30 PM   Don Daley, President of Bryant Industries, will provide car for trip to his office, Empire State Building, 34th Street and Fifth Avenue, Suite 1000. (Bryant Industries file in briefcase.)

Tuesday, June 2

9:00 AM   Appointment with Henderson, Smith & Jackson, Empire State Building, Suite 8000.

10:30 AM   Appointment with Mary Louise Henderson. (Henderson, Smith & Jackson file in briefcase.)

2:00 PM   Appointment with August Terrell, your hotel; meet in lobby. (Terrell Corporation file in briefcase.)

7:00 PM   Dinner, Don Daley's home. (5203 Legendary Lane, New York; Telephone 212-555-6120.)

Wednesday, June 3

7:45 AM   Leave hotel by limousine for airport. (Reservation attached.)

9:45 AM   Leave JFK Airport on American Airlines Flight 292, Seat 12A. Includes breakfast. (Ticket attached.)

11:05 AM   Arrive Dallas. Limousine to office. (Limousine reservation attached.)

FIGURE 5-1. Sample itinerary.

- Meeting agendas
- Speeches, reports, and presentations
- Computer and modem

⭐ International Travel

If the boss's trip involves international travel, make plans well in advance because of the many details involved. He or she should be aware of both U.S. requirements regarding foreign travel and the requirements of the country or countries to be visited. There are many conditions imposed on business travelers that are different from those imposed on tourists.

For assistance in arranging an international business trip, you can contact:

U.S. Department of Commerce
1401 Constitution Avenue
Washington, DC 20230

You can also visit the US Department of Commerce on the Web at www.commerce.gov.

For International Travel, Always Use a Travel Agent

Even if you do not use a travel agency to arrange domestic business trips, it's highly recommended that a reliable agency be used for international travel. To select a travel agency, solicit recommendations from coworkers or friends, consult the classified section of your telephone directory, or look for advertisements in the newspaper that indicate an agency is not only well versed in foreign travel rules and regulations but also specializes in individual itineraries rather than package tours.

The agency will handle all of the complicated details involved in foreign travel. Its expertise will be invaluable to you, and at little or no cost to your company since the travel agent's fee will be paid by the hotels.

The agency will handle all arrangements for transportation, lodging, car rentals, even sightseeing excursions. It will furnish accurate information as to documents needed for each particular country—passport, health certificates, police certificates, visas, and so forth—and exactly how to obtain each. The agency will handle all checks or arrange for letters of credit, as your employer prefers, and will even secure a small amount of currency in the denominations of the country visited so that the boss won't arrive with US currency only.

Visas and Passports

Most U.S. citizens need a passport to leave the United States and to reenter it. A passport is not required by US law for travel to North America, South America, Central America, or adjacent islands (except for Cuba). Nevertheless, citizenship documentation is required (a birth certificate will do), and the traveler should always carry personal identification, such as a driver's license.

In addition to a passport, many countries require a visa to enter. Usually, the visa must be obtained in advance and can't be purchased at the border or point of entry. Visas are issued by the individual embassies and consulates of various countries. Sometimes there is a small fee charged, while other countries issue visas for free. Since the requirements can and do change often, even if you have obtained a visa in advance of a trip, double-check before you leave to make sure the visa is still valid.

To find out more about passports and visas, use the telephone directory, or call telephone information. Some telephone directories list the numbers under "United States Government, Passport Information" or "Government Offices, County—Passport Acceptance Office." Call the county in which the prospective traveler lives.

If a passport is needed, apply at a passport agent's office or go to a clerk of a federal court, a clerk of a state court of record, a judge or clerk of a probate court, or a designated postal clerk.

Passport agencies are located in the following cities:

Boston Passport Agency
Thomas P. O'Neill Federal Building
10 Causeway Street
Suite 247
Boston, MA 02222-1094

Charleston Passport Agency
1269 Holland Street
Charleston, SC 29405

Chicago Passport Agency
Kluczynski Federal Building
230 S. Dearborn Street
18th Floor
Chicago, IL 60604-1564

Connecticut Passport Agency
50 Washington Street
Norwalk, CT 06854

Honolulu Passport Agency
Prince Kuhio Federal Building
300 Ala Moana Blvd.
Suite 1-330
Honolulu, HI 96850

Houston Passport Agency
Mickey Leland Federal Building
1919 Smith Street
Suite 1400
Houston, TX 77002-8049

Los Angeles Passport Agency
Federal Building
11000 Wilshire Blvd.
Suite 1000
Los Angeles, CA 90024-3615

Miami Passport Agency
Claude Pepper Federal Office Building
51 SW First Avenue
3rd Floor
Miami, FL 33130-1680

National Passport Center
31 Rochester Avenue
Portsmouth, NH 03801-2900

New Orleans Passport Agency
One Canal Place (corner of Canal and North Peters Streets)
365 Canal Street, Suite 1300
New Orleans, LA 70130-6508

New York Passport Agency
376 Hudson Street
New York, NY 10014

Philadelphia Passport Agency
U.S. Custom House
200 Chestnut Street
Room 103
Philadelphia, PA 19106-2970

San Francisco Passport Agency
95 Hawthorne Street
5th Floor
San Francisco, CA 94105–3901

Seattle Passport Agency
Henry Jackson Federal Building
915 Second Avenue
Suite 992
Seattle, WA 98174–1091

Washington Passport Agency
1111 19th Street, N.W.
Washington, D.C. 20524

Special Issuance Agency
1111 19th Street, N.W.
Suite 200
Washington, D.C. 20036

Required Immunizations and Vaccinations

Anyone traveling to a foreign country must have up-to-date information concerning required immunizations. The U.S. Department of Health has information on required immunizations for travelers available by calling 877-FYI-TRIP. You can also visit them on the Web at www.cdc.gov/travel.

Customs

When returning from foreign countries, the traveler must declare certain items acquired abroad to determine whether a tax is owed. Travelers returning home to the United States are allowed certain exemptions, which help cover the inevitable souvenirs. Articles totaling $800 (fair retail value in the country where purchased) are duty free, except for cigarettes, cigars, and liquor.

Be aware: Travelers should not try to understate the value of an article or misrepresent the nature of any article. To do so could result in the seizure and forfeiture of the item, and the tax will still be assessed. If a traveler has doubt as to whether to declare an item, he or she should declare it and then ask the customs inspector about it. Complete and detailed information concerning customs regulations are available by visiting www.customs.ustreas.gov/travel/travel.htm or by writing:

U.S. Customs Service
1300 Pennsylvania Ave., N.W.
Washington, D.C. 20229

Languages Spoken in Foreign Countries

The average businessperson will sometimes be aware of the language spoken in some countries of the world but not in others. Table 5-1 indicates the official language(s) spoken in certain countries.

TABLE 5-1	Countries and Their Official Language(s).		
Country	**Official Language(s)**	**Country**	**Official Language(s)**
Afghanistan	Afghan, Persian, Pashto	Indonesia	Indonesian
		Iran	Persian
Algeria	Arabic	Iraq	Arabic
Angola	Portuguese	Ireland	English, Gaelic
Argentina	Spanish	Israel	Arabic, Hebrew
Australia	English	Italy	Italian
Bahamas	English	Ivory Coast	French
Bahrain	Arabic	Jamaica	English
Barbados	English	Japan	Japanese
Belgium	Dutch, French, German	Jordan	Arabic
		Kenya	English, Swahili
Belize	English	Korea	Korean
Bermuda	English	Kuwait	Arabic
Bolivia	Spanish	Lebanon	Arabic
Bosnia and Herzegovina	Bosnian	Lesotho	English, Sesotho
		Liberia	English
Botswana	English	Libya	Arabic
Brazil	Portuguese	Macedonia	Macedonian, Albanian
Bulgaria	Bulgarian	Madagascar	French, Malagasy
Canada	English, French	Malawi	English
Chad	French	Malaysia	Malay
Chile	Spanish	Mali	French
China	Chinese (Mandarin)	Malta	English, Maltese
Colombia	Spanish	Mauritania	Arabic, French
Congo	French	Mexico	Spanish
Croatia	Croatian	Monaco	French
Cuba	Spanish	Morocco	Arabic
Denmark	Danish	Mozambique	Portuguese
Dominica	English	Myanmar	Burmese
Dominican Republic	Spanish	Nepal	Nepali
		Netherlands, The	Dutch
Ecuador	Spanish	New Zealand	English
Egypt	Arabic	Nicaragua	Spanish
El Salvador	Spanish	Nigeria	English
England	English	Norway	Norwegian
Ethiopia	Amharic	Oman	Arabic
Fiji	English	Pakistan	Urdu
Finland	Finnish, Swedish	Panama	Spanish
France	French	Paraguay	Spanish
Germany	German	Peru	Spanish, Quechua
Ghana	English	Philippines	English, Philipino, Spanish
Great Britain	English		
Greece	Greek	Poland	Polish
Grenada	English	Portugal	Portuguese
Guatemala	Spanish	Spain	Spanish
Guyana	English	Trinidad and Tobago	English
Haiti	French		
Honduras	Spanish	Tunisia	Arabic
Iceland	Icelandic	Turkey	Turkish
India	English, Hindi		

✦ Time Zones

A variety of useful time-zone-related information is available on the Web at www.timeanddate.com. The following is a list of time zone abbreviations:

- **Standard**
  - **UTC**   Coordinated Universal Time, civil time, the one most often used by "ordinary" people
  - **UT**   Universal Time, based on the Earth's rotation, often used in Astronomy
  - **TAI**   International Atomic Time, based on atomic clocks

- **European**
  - **GMT**   Greenwich Mean Time, as UTC
  - **BST**   British Summer Time, as UTC + 1 hour
  - **IST**   Irish Summer Time, as UTC + 1 hour
  - **WET**   Western Europe Time, as UTC
  - **WEST**   Western Europe Summer Time, as UTC + 1 hour
  - **CET**   Central Europe Time, as UTC + 1
  - **CEST**   Central Europe Summer Time, as UTC + 2
  - **EET**   Eastern Europe Time, as UTC + 2
  - **EEST**   Eastern Europe Summer Time, as UTC + 3
  - **MSK**   Moscow Time, as UTC + 3
  - **MSD**   Moscow Summer Time, as UTC + 4

- **U.S. and Canada**
  - **AST**   Atlantic Standard Time, as UTC – 4 hours
  - **ADT**   Atlantic Daylight Time, as UTC – 3 hours
  - **EST**   Eastern Standard Time, as UTC – 5 hours
  - **EDT**   Eastern Daylight Saving Time, as UTC – 4 hours
  - **ET**   Eastern Time, either as EST or EDT, depending on place and time of year
  - **CST**   Central Standard Time, as UTC – 6 hours
  - **CDT**   Central Daylight Saving Time, as UTC – 5 hours
  - **CT**   Central Time, either as CST or CDT, depending on place and time of year
  - **MST**   Mountain Standard Time, as UTC – 7 hours
  - **MDT**   Mountain Daylight Saving Time, as UTC – 6 hours
  - **MT**   Mountain Time, either as MST or MDT, depending on place and time of year
  - **PST**   Pacific Standard Time, as UTC – 8 hours
  - **PDT**   Pacific Daylight Saving Time, as UTC – 7 hours

5 ▪ TRAVEL ARRANGEMENTS

- **PT** Pacific Time, either as PST or PDT, depending on place and time of year
- **HST** Hawaiian Standard Time, as UTC − 10 hours
- **AKST** Alaska Standard Time, as UTC − 9 hours
- **AKDT** Alaska Standard Daylight Saving Time, as UTC − 8 hours

- **Australia**
  - **AEDT** Australian Eastern Daylight Time, as UTC + 11 hours
  - **ACST** Australian Central Standard Time, as UTC + 9.5 hours
  - **ACDT** Australian Central Daylight Time, as UTC + 10.5 hours
  - **AWST** Australian Western Standard Time, as UTC + 8 hours

Time Zone Time Differences

Table 5-2 shows the time differences between countries and various time zones in the United States.

TABLE 5-2	Time Zone Time Differences				
Country	GMT	USA Eastern	USA Central	USA Mountain	USA Pacific
A					
Afghanistan	+4.5 H	+9.5 H	+10.5 H	+11.5 H	+12.5 H
Albania	+1.0 H	+6.0 H	+7.0 H	+8.0 H	+9.0 H
Algeria	+1.0 H	+6.0 H	+7.0 H	+8.0 H	+9.0 H
American Samoa	−11.0 H	−6.0 H	−5.0 H	−4.0 H	−3.0 H
Andorra	+1.0 H	+6.0 H	+7.0 H	+8.0 H	+9.0 H
Angola	+1.0 H	+6.0 H	+7.0 H	+8.0 H	+9.0 H
Antarctica	−2.0 H	+3.0 H	+4.0 H	+5.0 H	+6.0 H
Antigua and Barbuda	−4.0 H	+1.0 H	+2.0 H	+3.0 H	+4.0 H
Argentina	−3.0 H	+2.0 H	+3.0 H	+4.0 H	+5.0 H
Armenia	+4.0 H	+9.0 H	+10.0 H	+11.0 H	+12.0 H
Aruba	−4.0 H	+1.0 H	+2.0 H	+3.0 H	+4.0 H
Ascension	+0.0 H	+5.0 H	+6.0 H	+7.0 H	+8.0 H
Australia North	+9.5 H	+14.5 H	+15.5 H	+16.5 H	+17.5 H
Australia South	+10.0 H	+15.0 H	+16.0 H	+17.0 H	+18.0 H
Australia West	+8.0 H	+13.0 H	+14.0 H	+15.0 H	+16.0 H
Australia East	+10.0 H	+15.0 H	+16.0 H	+17.0 H	+18.0 H
Austria	+1.0 H	+6.0 H	+7.0 H	+8.0 H	+9.0 H
Azerbaijan	+3.0 H	+8.0 H	+9.0 H	+10.0 H	+11.0 H
B					
Bahamas	−5.0 H	+0.0 H	+1.0 H	+2.0 H	+3.0 H
Bahrain	+3.0 H	+8.0 H	+9.0 H	+10.0 H	+11.0 H
Bangladesh	+6.0 H	+11.0 H	+12.0 H	+13.0 H	+14.0 H
Barbados	−4.0 H	+1.0 H	+2.0 H	+3.0 H	+4.0 H
Belarus	+2.0 H	+7.0 H	+8.0 H	+9.0 H	+10.0 H
Belgium	+1.0 H	+6.0 H	+7.0 H	+8.0 H	+9.0 H

Country	GMT	USA Eastern	USA Central	USA Mountain	USA Pacific
Belize	− 6.0 H	− 1.0 H	+ 0.0 H	+ 1.0 H	+ 2.0 H
Benin	+ 1.0 H	+ 6.0 H	+ 7.0 H	+ 8.0 H	+ 9.0 H
Bermuda	− 4.0 H	+ 1.0 H	+ 2.0 H	+ 3.0 H	+ 4.0 H
Bhutan	+ 6.0 H	+ 11.0 H	+ 12.0 H	+ 13.0 H	+ 14.0 H
Bolivia	− 4.0 H	+ 1.0 H	+ 2.0 H	+ 3.0 H	+ 4.0 H
Bosnia and Herzegovina	+ 1.0 H	+ 6.0 H	+ 7.0 H	+ 8.0 H	+ 9.0 H
Botswana	+ 2.0 H	+ 7.0 H	+ 8.0 H	+ 9.0 H	+ 10.0 H
Brazil West	− 4.0 H	+ 1.0 H	+ 2.0 H	+ 3.0 H	+ 4.0 H
Brazil East	− 3.0 H	+ 2.0 H	+ 3.0 H	+ 4.0 H	+ 5.0 H
British Virgin Islands	− 4.0 H	+ 1.0 H	+ 2.0 H	+ 3.0 H	+ 4.0 H
Brunei	+ 8.0 H	+ 13.0 H	+ 14.0 H	+ 15.0 H	+ 16.0 H
Bulgaria	+ 2.0 H	+ 7.0 H	+ 8.0 H	+ 9.0 H	+ 10.0 H
Burkina Faso	+ 0.0 H	+ 5.0 H	+ 6.0 H	+ 7.0 H	+ 8.0 H
Burundi	+ 2.0 H	+ 7.0 H	+ 8.0 H	+ 9.0 H	+ 10.0 H
C					
Cambodia	+ 7.0 H	+ 12.0 H	+ 13.0 H	+ 14.0 H	+ 15.0 H
Cameroon	+ 1.0 H	+ 6.0 H	+ 7.0 H	+ 8.0 H	+ 9.0 H
Canada Central	− 6.0 H	− 1.0 H	+ 0.0 H	+ 1.0 H	+ 2.0 H
Canada Eastern	− 5.0 H	+ 0.0 H	+ 1.0 H	+ 2.0 H	+ 3.0 H
Canada Mountain	− 7.0 H	− 2.0 H	− 1.0 H	+ 0.0 H	+ 1.0 H
Canada Pacific	− 8.0 H	− 3.0 H	− 2.0 H	− 1.0 H	+ 0.0 H
Canada Newfoundland	− 3.5 H	+ 1.5 H	+ 2.5 H	+ 3.5 H	+ 4.5 H
Cape Verde	− 1.0 H	+ 4.0 H	+ 5.0 H	+ 6.0 H	+ 7.0 H
Cayman Islands	− 5.0 H	+ 0.0 H	+ 1.0 H	+ 2.0 H	+ 3.0 H
Central African Republic	+ 1.0 H	+ 6.0 H	+ 7.0 H	+ 8.0 H	+ 9.0 H
Chad Republic	+ 1.0 H	+ 6.0 H	+ 7.0 H	+ 8.0 H	+ 9.0 H
Chile	− 4.0 H	+ 1.0 H	+ 2.0 H	+ 3.0 H	+ 4.0 H
China, People's Republic of	+ 8.0 H	+ 13.0 H	+ 14.0 H	+ 15.0 H	+ 16.0 H
Christmas Islands	− 10.0 H	− 5.0 H	− 4.0 H	− 3.0 H	− 2.0 H
Colombia	− 5.0 H	+ 0.0 H	+ 1.0 H	+ 2.0 H	+ 3.0 H
Congo	+ 1.0 H	+ 6.0 H	+ 7.0 H	+ 8.0 H	+ 9.0 H
Cook Islands	− 10.0 H	− 5.0 H	− 4.0 H	− 3.0 H	− 2.0 H
Costa Rica	− 6.0 H	− 1.0 H	+ 0.0 H	+ 1.0 H	+ 2.0 H
Croatia	+ 1.0 H	+ 6.0 H	+ 7.0 H	+ 8.0 H	+ 9.0 H
Cuba	− 5.0 H	+ 0.0 H	+ 1.0 H	+ 2.0 H	+ 3.0 H
Cyprus	+ 2.0 H	+ 7.0 H	+ 8.0 H	+ 9.0 H	+ 10.0 H
Czech Republic	+ 1.0 H	+ 6.0 H	+ 7.0 H	+ 8.0 H	+ 9.0 H
D					
Denmark	+ 1.0 H	+ 6.0 H	+ 7.0 H	+ 8.0 H	+ 9.0 H
Djibouti	+ 3.0 H	+ 8.0 H	+ 9.0 H	+ 10.0 H	+ 11.0 H
Dominica	− 4.0 H	+ 1.0 H	+ 2.0 H	+ 3.0 H	+ 4.0 H
Dominican Republic	− 4.0 H	+ 1.0 H	+ 2.0 H	+ 3.0 H	+ 4.0 H
E					
Ecuador	− 5.0 H	+ 0.0 H	+ 1.0 H	+ 2.0 H	+ 3.0 H
Egypt	+ 2.0 H	+ 7.0 H	+ 8.0 H	+ 9.0 H	+ 10.0 H
El Salvador	− 6.0 H	− 1.0 H	+ 0.0 H	+ 1.0 H	+ 2.0 H

5 ■ TRAVEL ARRANGEMENTS

(continued)

Country	GMT	USA Eastern	USA Central	USA Mountain	USA Pacific
Equatorial Guinea	+1.0 H	+6.0 H	+7.0 H	+8.0 H	+9.0 H
Eritrea	+3.0 H	+8.0 H	+9.0 H	+10.0 H	+11.0 H
Estonia	+2.0 H	+7.0 H	+8.0 H	+9.0 H	+10.0 H
Ethiopia	+3.0 H	+8.0 H	+9.0 H	+10.0 H	+11.0 H
F					
Faeroe Islands	+0.0 H	+5.0 H	+6.0 H	+7.0 H	+8.0 H
Falkland Islands	−4.0 H	+1.0 H	+2.0 H	+3.0 H	+4.0 H
Fiji Islands	+12.0 H	+17.0 H	+18.0 H	+19.0 H	+20.0 H
Finland	+2.0 H	+7.0 H	+8.0 H	+9.0 H	+10.0 H
France	+1.0 H	+6.0 H	+7.0 H	+8.0 H	+9.0 H
French Antilles (Martinique)	−3.0 H	+2.0 H	+3.0 H	+4.0 H	+5.0 H
French Guinea	−3.0 H	+2.0 H	+3.0 H	+4.0 H	+5.0 H
French Polynesia	−10.0 H	−5.0 H	−4.0 H	−3.0 H	−2.0 H
G					
Gabon Republic	+1.0 H	+6.0 H	+7.0 H	+8.0 H	+9.0 H
Gambia	+0.0 H	+5.0 H	+6.0 H	+7.0 H	+8.0 H
Georgia	+4.0 H	+9.0 H	+10.0 H	+11.0 H	+12.0 H
Germany	+1.0 H	+6.0 H	+7.0 H	+8.0 H	+9.0 H
Ghana	+0.0 H	+5.0 H	+6.0 H	+7.0 H	+8.0 H
Gibraltar	+1.0 H	+6.0 H	+7.0 H	+8.0 H	+9.0 H
Greece	+2.0 H	+7.0 H	+8.0 H	+9.0 H	+10.0 H
Greenland	−3.0 H	+2.0 H	+3.0 H	+4.0 H	+5.0 H
Grenada	−4.0 H	+1.0 H	+2.0 H	+3.0 H	+4.0 H
Guadeloupe	−4.0 H	+1.0 H	+2.0 H	+3.0 H	+4.0 H
Guam	+10.0 H	+15.0 H	+16.0 H	+17.0 H	+18.0 H
Guatemala	−6.0 H	−1.0 H	+0.0 H	+1.0 H	+2.0 H
Guinea-Bissau	+0.0 H	+5.0 H	+6.0 H	+7.0 H	+8.0 H
Guinea	+0.0 H	+5.0 H	+6.0 H	+7.0 H	+8.0 H
Guyana	−3.0 H	+2.0 H	+3.0 H	+4.0 H	+5.0 H
H					
Haiti	−5.0 H	+0.0 H	+1.0 H	+2.0 H	+3.0 H
Honduras	−6.0 H	−1.0 H	+0.0 H	+1.0 H	+2.0 H
Hong Kong	+8.0 H	+13.0 H	+14.0 H	+15.0 H	+16.0 H
Hungary	+1.0 H	+6.0 H	+7.0 H	+8.0 H	+9.0 H
I					
Iceland	+0.0 H	+5.0 H	+6.0 H	+7.0 H	+8.0 H
India	+5.5 H	+10.5 H	+11.5 H	+12.5 H	+13.5 H
Indonesia Central	+8.0 H	+13.0 H	+14.0 H	+15.0 H	+16.0 H
Indonesia East	+9.0 H	+14.0 H	+15.0 H	+16.0 H	+17.0 H
Indonesia West	+7.0 H	+12.0 H	+13.0 H	+14.0 H	+15.0 H
Iran	+3.5 H	+8.5 H	+9.5 H	+10.5 H	+11.5 H
Iraq	+3.0 H	+8.0 H	+9.0 H	+10.0 H	+11.0 H
Ireland	+0.0 H	+5.0 H	+6.0 H	+7.0 H	+8.0 H
Israel	+2.0 H	+7.0 H	+8.0 H	+9.0 H	+10.0 H
Italy	+1.0 H	+6.0 H	+7.0 H	+8.0 H	+9.0 H

Country	GMT	USA Eastern	USA Central	USA Mountain	USA Pacific
J					
Jamaica	−5.0 H	+0.0 H	+1.0 H	+2.0 H	+3.0 H
Japan	+9.0 H	+14.0 H	+15.0 H	+16.0 H	+17.0 H
Jordan	+2.0 H	+7.0 H	+8.0 H	+9.0 H	+10.0 H
K					
Kazakhstan	+6.0 H	+11.0 H	+12.0 H	+13.0 H	+14.0 H
Kenya	+3.0 H	+8.0 H	+9.0 H	+10.0 H	+11.0 H
Kiribati	+12.0 H	+17.0 H	+18.0 H	+19.0 H	+20.0 H
Korea, North	+9.0 H	+14.0 H	+15.0 H	+16.0 H	+17.0 H
Korea, South	+9.0 H	+14.0 H	+15.0 H	+16.0 H	+17.0 H
Kuwait	+3.0 H	+8.0 H	+9.0 H	+10.0 H	+11.0 H
Kyrgyzstan	+5.0 H	+10.0 H	+11.0 H	+12.0 H	+13.0 H
L					
Laos	+7.0 H	+12.0 H	+13.0 H	+14.0 H	+15.0 H
Latvia	+2.0 H	+7.0 H	+8.0 H	+9.0 H	+10.0 H
Lebanon	+2.0 H	+7.0 H	+8.0 H	+9.0 H	+10.0 H
Lesotho	+2.0 H	+7.0 H	+8.0 H	+9.0 H	+10.0 H
Liberia	+0.0 H	+5.0 H	+6.0 H	+7.0 H	+8.0 H
Libya	+2.0 H	+7.0 H	+8.0 H	+9.0 H	+10.0 H
Liechtenstein	+1.0 H	+6.0 H	+7.0 H	+8.0 H	+9.0 H
Lithuania	+2.0 H	+7.0 H	+8.0 H	+9.0 H	+10.0 H
Luxembourg	+1.0 H	+6.0 H	+7.0 H	+8.0 H	+9.0 H
M					
Macedonia	+1.0 H	+6.0 H	+7.0 H	+8.0 H	+9.0 H
Madagascar	+3.0 H	+8.0 H	+9.0 H	+10.0 H	+11.0 H
Malawi	+2.0 H	+7.0 H	+8.0 H	+9.0 H	+10.0 H
Malaysia	+8.0 H	+13.0 H	+14.0 H	+15.0 H	+16.0 H
Maldives	+5.0 H	+10.0 H	+11.0 H	+12.0 H	+13.0 H
Mali Republic	+0.0 H	+5.0 H	+6.0 H	+7.0 H	+8.0 H
Malta	+1.0 H	+6.0 H	+7.0 H	+8.0 H	+9.0 H
Marshall Islands	+12.0 H	+17.0 H	+18.0 H	+19.0 H	+20.0 H
Mauritania	+0.0 H	+5.0 H	+6.0 H	+7.0 H	+8.0 H
Mauritius	+4.0 H	+9.0 H	+10.0 H	+11.0 H	+12.0 H
Mayotte	+3.0 H	+8.0 H	+9.0 H	+10.0 H	+11.0 H
Mexico Central	−6.0 H	−1.0 H	+0.0 H	+1.0 H	+2.0 H
Mexico East	−5.0 H	+0.0 H	+1.0 H	+2.0 H	+3.0 H
Mexico West	−7.0 H	−2.0 H	−1.0 H	+0.0 H	+1.0 H
Moldova	+2.0 H	+7.0 H	+8.0 H	+9.0 H	+10.0 H
Monaco	+1.0 H	+6.0 H	+7.0 H	+8.0 H	+9.0 H
Mongolia	+8.0 H	+13.0 H	+14.0 H	+15.0 H	+16.0 H
Morocco	+0.0 H	+5.0 H	+6.0 H	+7.0 H	+8.0 H
Mozambique	+2.0 H	+7.0 H	+8.0 H	+9.0 H	+10.0 H
Myanmar	+6.5 H	+11.5 H	+12.5 H	+13.5 H	+14.5 H
N					
Namibia	+1.0 H	+6.0 H	+7.0 H	+8.0 H	+9.0 H
Nauru	+12.0 H	+17.0 H	+18.0 H	+19.0 H	+20.0 H

(continued)

5 ■ TRAVEL ARRANGEMENTS

Country	GMT	USA Eastern	USA Central	USA Mountain	USA Pacific
Nepal	+5.5 H	+10.5 H	+11.5 H	+12.5 H	+13.5 H
Netherlands, The	+1.0 H	+6.0 H	+7.0 H	+8.0 H	+9.0 H
Netherlands Antilles	−4.0 H	+1.0 H	+2.0 H	+3.0 H	+4.0 H
New Caledonia	+11.0 H	+16.0 H	+17.0 H	+18.0 H	+19.0 H
New Zealand	+12.0 H	+17.0 H	+18.0 H	+19.0 H	+20.0 H
Nicaragua	−6.0 H	−1.0 H	+0.0 H	+1.0 H	+2.0 H
Nigeria	+1.0 H	+6.0 H	+7.0 H	+8.0 H	+9.0 H
Niger Republic	+1.0 H	+6.0 H	+7.0 H	+8.0 H	+9.0 H
Norfolk Island	+11.5 H	+16.5 H	+17.5 H	+18.5 H	+19.5 H
Norway	+1.0 H	+6.0 H	+7.0 H	+8.0 H	+9.0 H
O					
Oman	+4.0 H	+9.0 H	+10.0 H	+11.0 H	+12.0 H
P					
Pakistan	+5.0 H	+10.0 H	+11.0 H	+12.0 H	+13.0 H
Palau	+9.0 H	+14.0 H	+15.0 H	+16.0 H	+17.0 H
Panama, Republic Of	−5.0 H	+0.0 H	+1.0 H	+2.0 H	+3.0 H
Papua New Guinea	+10.0 H	+15.0 H	+16.0 H	+17.0 H	+18.0 H
Paraguay	−4.0 H	+1.0 H	+2.0 H	+3.0 H	+4.0 H
Peru	−5.0 H	+0.0 H	+1.0 H	+2.0 H	+3.0 H
Philippines	+8.0 H	+13.0 H	+14.0 H	+15.0 H	+16.0 H
Poland	+1.0 H	+6.0 H	+7.0 H	+8.0 H	+9.0 H
Portugal	+1.0 H	+6.0 H	+7.0 H	+8.0 H	+9.0 H
Puerto Rico	−4.0 H	+1.0 H	+2.0 H	+3.0 H	+4.0 H
Q					
Qatar	+3.0 H	+8.0 H	+9.0 H	+10.0 H	+11.0 H
R					
Reunion Island	+4.0 H	+9.0 H	+10.0 H	+11.0 H	+12.0 H
Romania	+2.0 H	+7.0 H	+8.0 H	+9.0 H	+10.0 H
Russia Central 1	+4.0 H	+9.0 H	+10.0 H	+11.0 H	+12.0 H
Russia Central 2	+7.0 H	+12.0 H	+13.0 H	+14.0 H	+15.0 H
Russia East	+11.0 H	+16.0 H	+17.0 H	+18.0 H	+19.0 H
Russia West	+2.0 H	+7.0 H	+8.0 H	+9.0 H	+10.0 H
Rwanda	+2.0 H	+7.0 H	+8.0 H	+9.0 H	+10.0 H
S					
Saba	−4.0 H	+1.0 H	+2.0 H	+3.0 H	+4.0 H
St. Lucia	−4.0 H	+1.0 H	+2.0 H	+3.0 H	+4.0 H
St. Maarteen	−4.0 H	+1.0 H	+2.0 H	+3.0 H	+4.0 H
St. Pierre and Miquelon	−3.0 H	+2.0 H	+3.0 H	+4.0 H	+5.0 H
St. Thomas	−4.0 H	+1.0 H	+2.0 H	+3.0 H	+4.0 H
St. Vincent	−4.0 H	+1.0 H	+2.0 H	+3.0 H	+4.0 H
Samoa	−11.0 H	−6.0 H	−5.0 H	−4.0 H	−3.0 H
San Marino	+1.0 H	+6.0 H	+7.0 H	+8.0 H	+9.0 H
Sao Tome	+0.0 H	+5.0 H	+6.0 H	+7.0 H	+8.0 H
Saudi Arabia	+3.0 H	+8.0 H	+9.0 H	+10.0 H	+11.0 H

Country	GMT	USA Eastern	USA Central	USA Mountain	USA Pacific
Senegal	+0.0 H	+5.0 H	+6.0 H	+7.0 H	+8.0 H
Seychelles Islands	+4.0 H	+9.0 H	+10.0 H	+11.0 H	+12.0 H
Sierra Leone	+0.0 H	+5.0 H	+6.0 H	+7.0 H	+8.0 H
Singapore	+8.0 H	+13.0 H	+14.0 H	+15.0 H	+16.0 H
Slovakia	+1.0 H	+6.0 H	+7.0 H	+8.0 H	+9.0 H
Slovenia	+1.0 H	+6.0 H	+7.0 H	+8.0 H	+9.0 H
Solomon Islands	+11.0 H	+16.0 H	+17.0 H	+18.0 H	+19.0 H
Somalia	+3.0 H	+8.0 H	+9.0 H	+10.0 H	+11.0 H
South Africa	+2.0 H	+7.0 H	+8.0 H	+9.0 H	+10.0 H
Spain	+1.0 H	+6.0 H	+7.0 H	+8.0 H	+9.0 H
Sri Lanka	+5.5 H	+10.5 H	+11.5 H	+12.5 H	+13.5 H
Sudan	+2.0 H	+7.0 H	+8.0 H	+9.0 H	+10.0 H
Suriname	−3.0 H	+2.0 H	+3.0 H	+4.0 H	+5.0 H
Swaziland	+2.0 H	+7.0 H	+8.0 H	+9.0 H	+10.0 H
Sweden	+1.0 H	+6.0 H	+7.0 H	+8.0 H	+9.0 H
Switzerland	+1.0 H	+6.0 H	+7.0 H	+8.0 H	+9.0 H
Syria	+2.0 H	+7.0 H	+8.0 H	+9.0 H	+10.0 H
T					
Taiwan	+8.0 H	+13.0 H	+14.0 H	+15.0 H	+16.0 H
Tajikistan	+6.0 H	+11.0 H	+12.0 H	+13.0 H	+14.0 H
Tanzania	+3.0 H	+8.0 H	+9.0 H	+10.0 H	+11.0 H
Thailand	+7.0 H	+12.0 H	+13.0 H	+14.0 H	+15.0 H
Togo	+0.0 H	+5.0 H	+6.0 H	+7.0 H	+8.0 H
Tonga Islands	+13.0 H	+18.0 H	+19.0 H	+20.0 H	+21.0 H
Trinidad and Tobago	−4.0 H	+1.0 H	+2.0 H	+3.0 H	+4.0 H
Tunisia	+1.0 H	+6.0 H	+7.0 H	+8.0 H	+9.0 H
Turkey	+2.0 H	+7.0 H	+8.0 H	+9.0 H	+10.0 H
Turkmenistan	+5.0 H	+10.0 H	+11.0 H	+12.0 H	+13.0 H
Turks and Caicos	−5.0 H	+0.0 H	+1.0 H	+2.0 H	+3.0 H
Tuvalu	+12.0 H	+17.0 H	+18.0 H	+19.0 H	+20.0 H
U					
Uganda	+3.0 H	+8.0 H	+9.0 H	+10.0 H	+11.0 H
Ukraine	+2.0 H	+7.0 H	+8.0 H	+9.0 H	+10.0 H
United Arab Emirates	+4.0 H	+9.0 H	+10.0 H	+11.0 H	+12.0 H
United Kingdom	+0.0 H	+5.0 H	+6.0 H	+7.0 H	+8.0 H
Uruguay	−3.0 H	+2.0 H	+3.0 H	+4.0 H	+5.0 H
USA Alaska	−9.0 H	−4.0 H	−3.0 H	−2.0 H	−1.0 H
USA Central	−6.0 H	−1.0 H	+0.0 H	+1.0 H	+2.0 H
USA Eastern	−5.0 H	+0.0 H	+1.0 H	+2.0 H	+3.0 H
USA Hawaii	−10.0 H	−5.0 H	−4.0 H	−3.0 H	−2.0 H
USA Mountain	−7.0 H	−2.0 H	−1.0 H	+0.0 H	+1.0 H
USA Pacific	−8.0 H	−3.0 H	−2.0 H	−1.0 H	+0.0 H
Uzbekistan	+5.0 H	+10.0 H	+11.0 H	+12.0 H	+13.0 H
V					
Vanuatu	+11.0 H	+16.0 H	+17.0 H	+18.0 H	+19.0 H
Vatican City	+1.0 H	+6.0 H	+7.0 H	+8.0 H	+9.0 H

5 ■ TRAVEL ARRANGEMENTS

(continued)

Country	GMT	USA Eastern	USA Central	USA Mountain	USA Pacific
Venezuela	− 4.0 H	+ 1.0 H	+ 2.0 H	+ 3.0 H	+ 4.0 H
Vietnam	+ 7.0 H	+ 12.0 H	+ 13.0 H	+ 14.0 H	+ 15.0 H
W					
Wallis and Futuna Islands	+ 12.0 H	+ 17.0 H	+ 18.0 H	+ 19.0 H	+ 20.0 H
Y					
Yemen	+ 3.0 H	+ 8.0 H	+ 9.0 H	+ 10.0 H	+ 11.0 H
Yugoslavia	+ 1.0 H	+ 6.0 H	+ 7.0 H	+ 8.0 H	+ 9.0 H
Z					
Zaire	+ 2.0 H	+ 7.0 H	+ 8.0 H	+ 9.0 H	+ 10.0 H
Zambia	+ 2.0 H	+ 7.0 H	+ 8.0 H	+ 9.0 H	+ 10.0 H
Zimbabwe	+ 2.0 H	+ 7.0 H	+ 8.0 H	+ 9.0 H	+ 10.0 H

International Currencies

The following is a list of countries and their currencies.

- Afghanistan: Afghani
- Albania: Lek
- Algeria: Dinar
- Andorra: French Franc
- Argentina: Peso
- Armenia: Dram
- Australia: Dollar
- Austria: Schilling
- Azerbaijan: Manat
- Azores: Portuguese Escudo
- Bahamas: Dollar
- Bahrain: Dinar
- Bangladesh: Taka
- Barbados: Dollar
- Belarus: Ruble
- Belize: Dollar
- Bermuda: British Pound
- Bhutan: Negultrum
- Bosnia and Herzegovina: Dinar
- Botswana: Pula
- Brazil: Cruzeiro
- Bulgaria: Lev
- Cambodia: Riel
- Cameroon: CFA Franc
- Canada: Dollar
- Chad: CFA Franc
- Chile: Peso
- China: Yuan
- Columbia: Peso
- Congo: CFA Franc
- Costa Rica: Colon
- Croatia: Kuna
- Cuba: Peso
- Czech Republic: Koruna
- Denmark: Krone
- Ecuador: Sucre
- Egypt: Pound
- El Salvador: Colon
- Ethiopia: Birr
- Europe: Euro
- Finland: Markka
- French Guiana: French Franc
- Gabon: CFA Franc
- Gambia: Dalasi

5 ■ TRAVEL ARRANGEMENTS

- Georgia: Ruble
- Ghana: Cedi
- Greece: Drachma
- Grenada: East Caribbean Dollar
- Guadeloupe: French Franc
- Guatemala: Quetzal
- Guinea: Franc
- Guyana: Dollar
- Haiti: Gourde
- Honduras: Lempira
- Hong Kong: Dollar
- Hungary: Forint
- Iceland: Krona
- India: Rupee
- Indonesia: Rupaih
- Iran: Rial
- Iraq: Dinar
- Ireland: Pound
- Israel: New Shekel
- Jamaica: Dollar
- Japan: Yen
- Jordan: Dinar
- Kazakhstan: Ruble
- Kenya: Shilling
- Kuwait: Dinar
- Kyrgyzstan: Som
- Laos: Kip
- Latvia: Ruble
- Lebanon: Pound
- Lesotho: Loti
- Liberia: Dollar
- Libya: Dinar
- Liechtenstein: Swiss Franc
- Lithuania: Litas
- Luxembourg: Franc
- Macedonia: Denar
- Madagascar: Franc
- Malaysia: Ringgit

- Maldives: Rufiyaa
- Mexico: Peso
- Mongolia: Tugrik
- Morocco: Dirham
- Mozambique: Metical
- Myanmar: Kyat
- Namibia: Dollar
- Nepal: Rupee
- New Zealand: Dollar
- Nicaragua: Cordoba
- Niger: CFA Franc
- Nigeria: Naira
- North Korea: Won
- Norway: Kroner
- Oman: Rial
- Pakistan: Rupee
- Panama: Balboa
- Paraguay: Guarani
- Peru: Sol
- Philippines: Peso
- Poland: Zloty
- Qatar: Rial
- Romania: Leu
- Russia: Ruble
- Rwanda: Franc
- Saudi Arabia: Riyal
- Senegal: CFA Franc
- Sierra Leone: Leone
- Singapore: Dollar
- Slovenia: Tolar
- Somalia: Shilling
- South Africa: Rand
- South Korea: Won
- Sri Lanka: Rupee
- Sudan: Dinar
- Suriname: Guilden
- Swaziland: Lilangeni
- Sweden: Krona

5 ■ TRAVEL ARRANGEMENTS

- Switzerland: Franc
- Syria: Pound
- Taiwan: Dollar
- Tajikistan: Ruble
- Tanzania: Shilling
- Thailand: Baht
- Togo: CFA Franc
- Tonga: Pa'anga
- Trinidad and Tobago: Dollar
- Tunisia: Dinar
- Turkey: Lira
- Turkmenistan: Manat
- Uganda: Shilling

- Ukraine: Karbovanets
- United Arab Emirates: Dirham
- United Kingdom: Pound
- Uruguay: Peso
- Uzbekistan: Ruble
- Venezuela: Bolivar
- Vietnam: Dong
- Yemen: Dinar/Rial
- Zaire: Zaire
- Zambia: Kwacha
- Zimbabwe: Dollar

Meetings

✦ Anatomy of a Meeting

Whether we like it or not, meetings are a regular and time consuming part of business life. Because meetings require planning, coordination, and documentation, they are a major job responsibility for most administrative assistants.

The assistant's job includes sending invitations to in-house meetings, finding time in the schedules of meeting attendees, and selecting meeting times and locations. A thoughtful administrative assistant is careful to avoid scheduling meetings for early Monday morning or late Friday afternoon.

Some executive meetings are scheduled weekly. Despite their being routine, the administrative assistant must still schedule the meetings, send invitations, and reminders. This also involves creating meeting agendas that include the names of everyone attending the meeting, the date, time, and meeting location, as well as any advanced preparation required of the attendees.

Sometimes a meeting will be called with a moment's notice. When this happens, the assistant will need to coordinate the meeting by calling the attendees on the phone, seeing them in person, or using an e-mail scheduling program such as Microsoft Outlook.

Types of Corporate Meetings

Every corporation holds an annual meeting of stockholders for the election of directors. During the year, it may also hold other meetings when the stockholders' consent is required for some proposed action, such as an increase or decrease in capital stock, an amendment of the corporate charter, or a merger.

Annual stockholder meetings have special legal requirements for when meeting notices must be sent. Printed notices are sent along with proxy voting forms and a return address, postal paid envelope.

As an administrative assistant, your duties include preparing notices of the meeting as well as a proxy form to be used in case a stockholder cannot attend. This proxy gives another person the right to vote for the stockholder. These must be sent to everyone concerned, in accordance with the bylaws of the group. In most cases, these notices must be sent out 3 to 4 weeks in advance.

You must arrange for a meeting place and confirm that it will be ready for use at the time specified. You'll also type and distribute the agenda. On the day of the meeting, place all pertinent papers in a folder with the corporate seal on the conference table at the chairperson's seat.

If you act as the recorder of the meeting, sit beside the chairperson in order to hear every word distinctly. If you have difficulty in hearing, signal the chairperson, who will then ask for a repetition of what has been said. Before the meeting, read all resolutions and reports to be presented. In addition, obtain the list of the persons attending (which you should have from distributing the agenda), and check the absentees ahead of time rather than write down names while the roll is being called. The greater your knowledge is of the meeting's purpose and the attendees, the easier recording will be.

Corporate director meetings are specified by the corporate bylaws. Most companies have quarterly or yearly director meetings. A written notice of these meetings is not required by law. An administrative assistant may be asked to contact directors via phone, letter, or e-mail to inform them of an upcoming meeting. The assistant will also be asked to track who is coming to the meeting and who has declined. A list of those attending the meeting should be created and made available at the meeting.

Other corporate meetings that are not regular events should be scheduled two weeks in advance. You should send out an invitation, agenda, and a follow-up reminder. The date, time, location, and subject should be clear in the invitation.

Outside meetings and conferences usually require printed invitations sent out as a mass mailing.

Double-check all the information on a proof of the invitation before it is printed. Confirm the date, week, day, time, room, location, and names of all the speakers. No one should have to telephone the sponsor to get information that was inadvertently omitted from the invitation.

Scheduling Meetings

Scheduling meetings is one of the most common tasks for administrative assistants. In the past, scheduling a meeting was a time-consuming task that involved hardcopy invitations sent as interoffice memos. Usually the telephone was the preferred method of confirming invitations. Today with computer technology and groupware software such as Microsoft Outlook or IBM Lotus Notes, the task of scheduling a meeting only requires a few mouse clicks.

Despite the advances in technology, scheduling a meeting is not as simple as it looks. There is a lot of judgment involved. Anytime you bring together a group of people, there are many factors to consider. You have to consider pecking order. Some members of the group are more important, so others must change their schedules to accommodate. Decisions about where a meeting is held can be important as well. Is the meeting room large enough and supplied with the right equipment? Can it be reserved for the entire meeting?

Common Problems When Scheduling a Meeting

The following are common problems that occur when scheduling a meeting:

1. The meeting is scheduled, and after everyone has been invited, you discover that some important participants can't attend. Another date has to be found. This can lead to a cycle of invitations and revisions.

2. You ask the participants about their availability for a meeting, but the available dates and times are so limited that no common date and time can be found.

3. A meeting is confirmed but then needs to be changed.

4. A meeting location is specified and then later changed in a subsequent meeting notice. Some of the attendees follow the original meeting notice and end up in the wrong room.

5. Repeated meeting notices and revisions are sent out, so that everyone is confused about meeting.

6. You use an Internet-based, meeting scheduling tool, but outside participants don't have the same software.

7. A work team uses an Internet system to schedule meetings, but eventually the team members get lazy about updating their schedules and begin to miss meetings.

8. A meeting is scheduled and confirmed, but the location is already booked.

9. No one sends a meeting reminder, and several attendees forget about the meeting.

10. You are invited to a meeting, but the meeting organizer didn't say what it is about, so you show up unprepared.

Scheduling Meetings Using Microsoft Outlook's Calendar

Microsoft Outlook is a desktop information management program. It allows you to send and receive e-mails, manage a list of contacts, organize your calendar and scheduling, and maintain a journal. Outlook also allows you to manage files and folders.

Depending on how your company uses Outlook, you may be able to use it to schedule your time. You can schedule appointments that do not involve other people or meeting rooms, and you can assign time blocks. When you are viewing your calendar in Outlook, if you click NEW on the toolbar, the New Appointment window opens. On this window, you can enter a subject, location, and start and end times for the appointment, as well as make the appointment an all day event. If the appointment conflicts with something else in your schedule, a message will appear informing you of the conflict. You can also set reminders for the appointment that will automatically alert you in advance of the upcoming appointment by an amount of time you choose. The reminder will appear as long as you have Outlook open on your computer. Figure 6-1 shows the New Appointment window in Microsoft Outlook.

You can also access and view other people's calendars and allow them to access and view yours. This option allows you to see when other team members have time available for meetings.

You can schedule meetings with Outlook in a manner very similar to the way you schedule appointments. The main difference is that a meeting is an appointment to which you invite other people and reserve resources. Resources are the things you typically need for a meeting, such as a conference room, overhead projector, white board, and so forth.

Although, in many cases, not everyone or all resources will be available for a meeting, Outlook allows you to view the availability of the meeting attendees and resources in order to determine a time that best fits everyone's schedule.

To schedule a meeting in Outlook, use the Meeting Planner to create and send meeting invitations and to reserve resources. The Meeting Planner allows you to invite attendees, view their availability, select a meeting location resource, and pick a time. You can enter the names of the people and resource directly into the All Attendees list, or you can use the INVITE OTHERS button. You can select individuals and resources from your Address Book to add to the All Attendees list. You can choose whether the person or resource is required

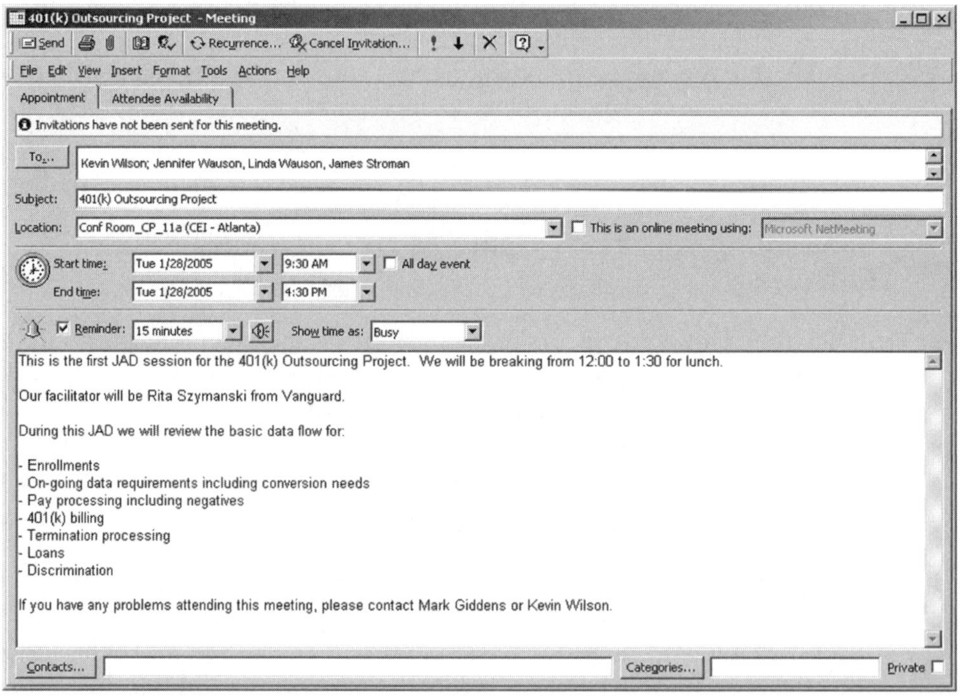

FIGURE 6-1. The New Appointment Window in Microsoft Outlook.

Screen shot reprinted by permission from Microsoft Corporation.

or optional. The All Attendees list displays each person and resource that will be attending and available for the meeting.

When you view the availability of your attendees and resources, the Meeting Planner shows you a time schedule with blue bars designating times when the person or resource is already scheduled for something else. If the time slot is blank, the attendee or resource is available. If you right-click any attendee's or resource's busy time slot in the planner, you will see more details. For example, if a conference room is already booked, you'll be able to see who booked it and for what meeting. To avoid scheduling conflicts, you can use the AUTOPICK tool to automatically locate the first time slot available for all specified attendees and resources. Figure 6-2 shows Microsoft Outlook's Meeting Planner with attendee availability data shown.

After the meeting notice is sent, meeting responses are delivered to your Inbox and can be tracked in the Appointment window.

As other users schedule meetings, you will receive meeting invitations in your Inbox. You can open the meeting invitation just as you would any e-mail message. You have the option of accepting, declining, or submitting a tentative response. When you click on one of the acceptance buttons, Outlook opens a message box in which you have the option of sending a response.

As soon as a meeting invitation is delivered and accepted, it is automatically added to your schedule.

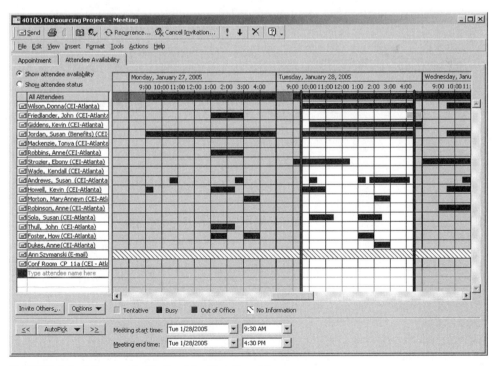

FIGURE 6-2. Microsoft Outlook's Meeting Planner.

Screen shot reprinted by permission from Microsoft Corporation.

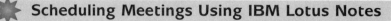

Scheduling Meetings Using IBM Lotus Notes

IBM Lotus Notes allows you to schedule meetings and view attendee availability with the same functionality as Microsoft Outlook. The main difference is in the overall look and feel of the software. You will find the same features with different names. Figure 6-3 shows an example of IBM's Lotus Notes calendar feature.

Meeting Agendas

The meeting agenda is like a roadmap for the meeting. It tells the participants what the plan is for the meeting, providing a sense of direction and purpose. A meeting agenda (see Figure 6-4) should include:

- Meeting start time and end time
- Meeting location
- Topic headings and topic detail for each heading
- How much time each topic discussion is expected to last
- Who will facilitate the discussion of a particular topic

FIGURE 6-3. IBM Lotus Notes Calendar Feature.

Screen captures © 2003 IBM Corporation. Used with permission of IBM. IBM Lotus SmartSuite and IBM Lotus Notes are registered trademarks of IBM.

Outsourcing Project
Meeting Agenda

Meeting Called By:	Session #:	Date:	Starting Time:
Mark Rivers		1/28/2006	9:30 a.m.

Location:	Dress Code (optional):		Ending Time:
Central Park Conference Room 11a			12:00 p.m.

Meeting Objective and Scope:			
JAD Session—The Big Picture.			

Time	Topic		Discussion Leader
9:30–9:35	Welcome and review agenda.		Mark Rivers
9:35–9:55	Basic data flow for enrollments.		Darlene Price
9:55–10:15	Ongoing data requirements including conversion needs.		Darlene Price
10:15–10:35	Basic data flow for pay processing including negatives.		Darlene Price
10:35–10:40	Break		
10:40–11:00	Basic data flow for 401(k) billing.		Darlene Price
11:00–11:20	Basic data flow for termination processing.		Darlene Price
11:20–11:40	Basic data flow for loans.		Darlene Price
11:40–11:55	Basic data flow for discrimination.		Darlene Price
11:55–12:00	Wrap-up		Mark Rivers

Facilitator:	Time Keeper:		Scribe:
Darlene Price			Debra Miller

Attendees:			
Anne Fried	Mark Rivers	Donna Morgan	Tonya Smith
Debra Miller	Sally Roberts	Susan Mullins	Ebony Hollings
Tanya Sanchez	Mary McKnight	Daphne Johnson	Mike Harper
Kevin Wilson	Kendall Williams	Rita Zezula	Darlene Price

6 ■ MEETINGS

FIGURE 6-4. Sample meeting agenda.

Agenda Wizard ☒

Start

Style

Details

Headings

Names

Topics

Minutes

Finish

Which style do you want for your agenda?

○ Bo_x_es   ● Modern   ○ _S_tandard

[?]   Cancel   < _B_ack   _N_ext >   _F_inish

FIGURE 6-5. The Agenda Wizard in Microsoft Word.

Screen shot reprinted by permission from Microsoft Corporation.

If you use word processing software such as Microsoft Word, you can use the Agenda Wizard to create an agenda. To access the Agenda Wizard, click the FILE MENU, then click NEW. On the New dialog, click the OTHER DOCUMENTS tab, then click the AGENDA WIZARD followed by the OK button. Figure 6-5 shows the Agenda Wizard in Microsoft Word.

The Agenda Wizard will ask you specific questions about the meeting, and when you are finished, it will create an agenda document. You can send the agenda as an attachment to a meeting invitation or print copies and bring them to the meeting.

Meeting Minutes

Meeting minutes are a record of what took place during a meeting. It allows the meeting attendees to review the meeting later to look for outstanding issues and action items. In some cases, such as stockholder and board-of-directors meetings, the minutes are required by law and are included in the corporate minute book.

While attending a meeting, you can make handwritten notes, type on a computer if the sound of the typing does not distract the meeting attendees, or use a recording device and transcribe the meeting later (see Conference Notes, p. 180). Regardless of which method you use, make sure that all of the essential elements of the meeting are noted: type of meeting, company name, date and time, facilitator, main topics, and time of adjournment.

Make a list of the expected attendees, or review the meeting agenda. As they enter the room, you can check them off the list. Optionally, you can pass around an attendance sheet for everyone to sign as the meeting begins.

If you prepare an outline in advance, based on the agenda, you will already have the main topics written down, and you can keep your notes organized.

If necessary, map out a seating arrangement for the meeting, and be prepared to introduce any unfamiliar people.

When you transcribe the minutes, you should write them up in formal language according to the following outline:

- Name of organization
- Name of body conducting meeting
- Date, hour, and location of meeting
- List of those present and those absent
- Reading of previous minutes and their approval or amendment
- Unfinished business
- New business
- Date of next meeting
- Time of adjournment
- Signature of recorder

Avoid the mistake of recording every single comment, but concentrate on getting the essence of the discussion by taking enough notes to summarize it later. Remember, minutes are a record of what happened at a meeting, not a record of everything that was said.

Always prepare ahead for meetings where you will take minutes. It's important that you understand the discussion without asking a lot of questions. Following the meeting, don't wait too long to write up the minutes. Always have a draft of the minutes approved by the meeting organizer or facilitator before distributing them to the attendees.

Figure 6-6 is an example of minutes for an organization.

Corporate Minutes

All corporations must document the minutes of shareholder and board-of-directors meetings. In fact, in many states, the absence of proper meeting minutes may be a liability for the corporation, especially in situations where the shareholders are also on the board of directors, or where there are close relationships between board members. All corporations in the United States are required to hold annual shareholder's meetings to elect directors. The bylaws of most corporations require the board of directors to have annual meetings.

**Minutes of Meeting of
the Historical Society of the University of Texas
Hotel Driscoll, Austin, Texas
May 1, 2006**

At the meeting of the Historical Society of the University of Texas at Austin, some 100 charter members being present, the Society was called to order at 1:05 p.m. by Mr. John R. Combs, Chairperson, who requested Mr. Warren T. Scaggs to serve as Temporary Secretary.

Mr. Combs dispensed with the reading of the minutes of the last meeting, because a copy had been previously distributed to all members.

A communication from the National Historical Society, read and accepted by the Society, dealt with the planting of redbud trees throughout America.

A communication from Miss Harriet Allen of New York City asked that the Society refrain from its normal pattern of conducting spring tours throughout the State of Texas. Several members, after the reading, expressed disagreement with the views given by Miss Allen.

There was no unfinished business.

New business was the election of officers for the remaining current year. The following nominations were announced by Mr. Warren T. Scaggs, Chairperson of the Nominating Committee:

President	Mrs. Rutherford Tinsdale
Secretary	Mr. Joseph Mapes
Treasurer	Mrs. Theodore R. Tollivar
Members of the Council	Ms. Louise Allen
	Mrs. Philip W. Crossman
	Mr. John Stobaugh
	Mrs. John C. McCann

After an unanswered call for nominations from the floor, it was moved by Mrs. William R. Metcalfe that the Secretary cast one ballot for officers nominated. The motion was seconded and carried, and the officers were declared elected.

The next meeting of the Historical Society of the University of Texas at Austin will be held on June 11 at the Hotel Driscoll in Austin, Texas, at 1:00 P.M.

After congratulations to the newly elected officers by the Chairperson, the Society adjourned at 3:25 p.m.

Warren T. Scaggs
Temporary Secretary

FIGURE 6-6. Minutes of a typical meeting.

At these corporate meetings the following actions will normally be approved by the board of directors:

- Election of officers of the corporation
- New business policies and plans
- Creation of committees and assignments
- Issuing and selling stock
- Approval of the sale, transfer, lease, or exchange of any corporate property or assets
- Approval of mergers and reorganizations
- Adoption of a pension, profit-sharing, or other employee benefit plans and stock-option plans
- Approval of corporate borrowing and loans
- Entering into joint ventures
- Designating corporate bank accounts and authorized signatures
- Changing an officer's compensation
- Entering into major contractual agreements

Small corporations have informal meetings where these matters are discussed. Large corporations have formal meetings. In both cases, the board of directors must pass a resolution to approve the action. Therefore, the meeting minutes are a record of the board's consent and the discussion surrounding the decision.

Resolutions
Formal resolutions may be made in one of these forms:

- WHEREAS it is necessary to . . . ; and
- WHEREAS conditions are such that . . . ; and
- Therefore be it
- RESOLVED, That . . . ; and be it
- RESOLVED further, That . . .

Note that the word *whereas* is in caps with no comma following it; the first word after it is not capitalized unless it is a proper name. The word *resolved* is also set in caps but is followed by a comma and a capital letter.

In formal resolutions, the facts are stated simply:

- . . . and the following resolution was unanimously adopted: RESOLVED, That . . . .

Office Meetings
Your boss may ask you to record in written form a meeting of various office personnel, perhaps department heads. Elaborate minutes are not required as long as the group is not a governing body within the company, such as the board of directors (Figure 6-7).

6 ▪ MEETINGS

Meeting of the United Way Committee
January 12, 2006

Attendance:

A meeting of the department managers was held in the office of John Smith, Executive Vice President, at 9 a.m. on January 12, 2006. Mr. Smith presided. Present were Martha Johnson, Philip Smith, Martin Allen, Raymond Martinez, Eloise Randolph, Anthony Guerrero, and Patricia Reese. James Augustine was absent.

Items Covered:

1. How the company can participate fully in the United Way campaign. Raymond Martinez reviewed last year's company goals and how these goals were reached. Anthony Guerrero suggested our goal for the present year be increased by 10 percent. Recommendations were made by each person present.
2. These suggestions and recommendations will be discussed and voted upon at the February 2 meeting of the committee.

Adjournment:

The meeting was adjourned at 10 a.m.

Martha Johnson, Recorder

FIGURE 6-7. Sample report of an office meeting.

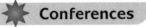 **Conferences**

Sometimes an administrative assistant will be asked to assist in the planning and coordinating of conferences for your company. This involves preparing for the event, carrying out your responsibilities during the conference, and follow up activities after it's over.

Planning for the Conference

The planning for a conference involves consideration of items related to the conference facilities and the speakers. As you plan for a conference, keep in mind the following:

▪ Booking the conference site
▪ Blocking reservations for hotel rooms, selection of room sizes, and price range

- Confirming auditorium sizes and breakout rooms
- Scheduling catering and beverage service
- Confirming smoking locations
- Inspecting facilities you haven't seen before
- Sending letters of invitations to speakers
- Following up with confirmation letters to the speakers and conference site personnel
- Obtaining background information, photos, and resumes of the speakers

Preparing Conference Materials

As the conference time approaches, you will need to confirm all necessary supporting materials: table and chair rentals, reports, financial statements, advertisements, meeting agendas, itineraries, and executive travel folders.

If it is your responsibility, you will need to make arrangements for printing packets, maps, tickets, and awards. You may also need to make arrangements for local tours and special outside events to entertain the speakers, attendees, and their spouses. Many times, family members accompany their spouses attending a conference, and any thoughtful conference organizer has made arrangements for shopping trips, outside restaurant gatherings, tickets to sporting events, museum tours, and other local attractions.

You will need to coordinate with the conference site to plan meals, refreshments, coffee breaks, and banquets. This should involve evaluating menus in advance and planning what will be served.

You may also be involved in pre-registration and registration. This requires organizing a filing system for those attendees who pre-register and having badges made. During the registration on the first day of the conference, you may be involved in staffing the registration desk. You should organize registration materials alphabetically. All conference materials should be assembled in packets with programs, brochures, reports, name tags, meal tickets, and so forth.

Confirm with the conference site any audio visual equipment or meeting supplies you may need. Breakout rooms will need chalkboards or whiteboards, easels with large pads of paper, and marker pens or chalk. Conference rooms may need lecterns, microphones, overhead projectors, video players, video projectors, projection screens, television monitors, and a public address system. Usually this involves filling out a reservation request form with the conference facility. Also make sure you order extra projector bulbs and extension cords.

If your conference involves international guests, you may need to make arrangements for a translation service.

Two weeks before the conference, you should mail all pre-work to attendees. You should also ship any supplies and conference materials to the conference site around this time.

If it is appropriate, you may need to arrange for press coverage by contacting media outlets, arranging for a photographer to take photos during the conference, and sending out press releases.

Finally, you'll need to coordinate any security concerns with conference location or security services. You may also need to coordinate parking with the conference location's parking attendants. You will need to provide both groups with a formal agenda listing event times, additional security protection needed, and parking requirements.

During the Conference

While the conference is underway, your duties may include checking meeting rooms and making sure all necessary materials are available. Confirm that lighting and heating are functioning, refreshments are available, audiovisual equipment is available and functioning, and that the room is clean.

As conference guests arrive, you should greet and welcome guests to the conference. Be a host, and introduce people, escort people who need directions, and be helpful where you can.

If you are asked to work the registration desk, you may need to provide statistics on who will attend the various events. Prepare lists of participants with names and addresses.

You may be asked to attend some meetings and take minutes, handle correspondence requests, or route incoming express shipments. You may also have to write and distribute a conference newsletter, coordinate messages between participants, or meet with media representatives and photographers.

After the Conference

At the end of each day during the conference, remove any surplus literature and conference packets from the meeting rooms. Inform the conference site staff regarding any catering items left in the meeting rooms. Make sure any audiovisual equipment is properly secured. Be sure to move and secure any other rental equipment. Any lost and found items should be taken to the conference site receptionist.

When you return to the office, you may need to complete follow-up reports or other conference-related mailings. You may need to send thank you letters to speakers or distribute meeting minutes.

Finally, you will need to calculate expenses and fill out expense reports. As a last step, update the meeting file with your notes. With everything fresh in your mind, write down what went well and what challenges you faced. If you have ideas on how to make improvements, put them down on paper in the file.

Conference Notes

If your employer asks you to report on all that is said in a conference, make place cards for the members of the group expected to meet. As they enter the room, direct them to sit where they have been assigned. Before your own seat, arrange tabs showing the names of the members in the same order as they are seated around the table so that you will know who is speaking at each given moment. This will enable you to take your notes in the form of a dramatic dialogue. Preface one remark with "Hansen" if the man whose name is Hansen has spoken; then preface the next remark with "Rosen" if the next voice has come from the seat you assigned to Mrs. Rosen, and so forth.

When you transcribe your notes, you can show the discussion in this dialogue form, if that's acceptable to your employer, or you can insert a full stage direction such as "Mr. Hansen replied:" or "The next speaker was Mrs. Rosen, who said . . ." In either case, open your transcription with a list of those present, giving the full name or initials and office held, if any, for each.

A recording device is usually used, but you should be ready if it's not available. It may be wise to take notes even when a recording device is used, because unless the meeting is held under strict discipline, there may be a jumble of voices. Your notes will help you decipher the recording.

Keeping Accurate Records

A Critical Duty

Keeping accurate records and maintaining an up-to-date filing system are important responsibilities for most administrative assistants. Any filing system ever conceived requires the person maintaining it to approach the duty with a sense of pride. He or she must be confident that any file can be retrieved quickly, perhaps even as the employer is speaking on the telephone.

Most firms today, even small businesses, store their letters and documents in their computers or word processing equipment and automatically maintain them there or on disk (see Chapter 12, Database Management). However, as administrative assistants know only too well, even with computers, the amount of paper correspondence and documents to be saved seems to grow daily.

Large companies often have a central file department where all papers are kept by competent file clerks. Other companies maintain files by division, and small companies may have only a few file cabinets for their entire operation. In these cases, it's the administrative assistant who is usually responsible for record keeping and maintenance. But no matter what your usual duties, you should be familiar with the various filing systems used in both small and large offices.

Getting Ready

It's often tempting, especially at the end of the day, simply to throw a file in its own folder. Don't. Filing is an important duty, no matter how tedious it seems. Instead of trying to get rid of that piece of paper as quickly as possible, approach it with these questions always in mind: Where could I easily find this tomorrow (or next week, or next year)? What's in this letter or document that would cause me to recall where I'm placing it in the file now?

Follow this checklist before you start to file:

■ Prepare the papers by separating personal correspondence from business correspondence and documents.

- Check all stapled papers to be sure that only papers belonging together have been stapled together.
- Remove all paper clips. They not only crowd the file but also can catch papers that should not have been clipped to them.
- Mend any torn papers with tape.
- Underline in bright pencil or with a highlighter the name or subject under which the paper is to be filed.

On the file folders, use staggered tabs or one-position tabs. The straight-line tab, all in the center or in the far right position on the edge of the folder, is often preferred.

When various sets of files are used, it's wise to tab each set with a different color label. For example: white for correspondence, blue for subject files, green for case files, and so forth. Each category then has its own color for quick recognition.

On labels, type the name of the folder on the first line beginning two or three spaces from the left edge. Use initial caps and lowercase letters, and abbreviate freely. Leave two spaces between name and any number.

Basic Filing Systems

Common or basic filing systems that might be used in a business office include the following: Alphabetical, subject, geographical, numeric, and combination subject (though the office would probably be a very large one with many technical files to utilize the last). About 90 percent of offices use the alphabetical system.

Two less-used systems are the decimal filing system and the group name system (sometimes called the phonetic filing system). The decimal system, based on the Dewey decimal classification system, is used primarily in libraries. The material being filed must be organized under ten or fewer main headings numbered 000 to 900. In turn, each main heading is divided into 10 or fewer subheadings numbered from 10 to 90 and preceded by the correct hundreds digit. Each subheading may then be subdivided into 10 or fewer further headings numbered from 1 to 9, preceded by the correct hundreds and tens digits.

The group name or phonetic system is used when there are a great many names involved, as in census surveys. Names that sound alike but are spelled differently are grouped together according to pronunciation rather than spelling: Allan, Allen, Allyn; Nielsen, Neilson, Nealson; Schneider, Snider, Snyder.

Alphabetical System
The alphabetical system is the most widely used filing method, because it's the most efficient and least complicated. Material is filed alphabetically according to name. No cross-indexing is necessary. A label should be typed for each name and applied to the tab on each folder.

Papers are placed in the folder in chronological order with the most current date in front. The folders are filed behind alphabet guides (obtainable in any office supply store). When there is heavy correspondence with one client, several folders may be needed to hold all current material. In this case, it's a good practice to separate the material into time periods: one folder for the year 2004, another for the year 2005, and another for 2006. If several projects have been handled for that customer, one folder may be labeled FLORIDA, another NORTH DAKOTA, another MICHIGAN, and so on.

If only the current year's files are kept handy (previous years' files are stored elsewhere), it's useful, for at least the first few weeks of the new year, to have the old year's files and the new year's files placed back to back or side by side. Of course, a different year will be on each file tab, perhaps a different color as well: red for 2004, for example, and yellow for 2005.

Subject System

This classification is used when papers are called for by subject, rather than by a person's or a company's name. Subject classification may be needed when dealing with, say, advertising, brand name products, or materials of all kinds.

You should be thoroughly familiar with the papers flowing through the office and across your desk before attempting to set up this kind of system. The list of subjects must be comprehensive, as simple as possible, and in alphabetical order or by number code. The alphabetical list is usually preferred so that a cross-index is not necessary. Papers in the subject folder are arranged chronologically, always with the latest date in front.

Subject Index

While an index of files is not required for a small filing system, it's imperative for large companies. And since most small businesses hope to grow, it's a good practice to maintain a filing system from the start. The subject index will prevent the filing of material under a new heading when a folder has already been set up for that subject, perhaps under a different title. It also permits a person other than the administrative assistant to trace information in the file.

An index card is made for each subject heading or subheading. Each subheading shows the main heading under which it is filed. Cross-reference cards are made if the subject is complex. The employer may indicate on the paper where he or she wants it to be filed, while the administrative assistant may have formerly filed that subject under another heading. A cross-reference enables both to find the paper later. The index cards are filed alphabetically.

How to Alphabetize for Filing and Indexing
INDIVIDUAL OR PERSONAL NAMES

The names of people are alphabetized by their surname. When surnames are the same, the position is naturally determined by the letters that follow:

- Smith, Mary B.
- Smith, Ned
- Smithson, John

When two or more similar names are of unequal length, file the shorter name first:

- Smith, M.
- Smith, Mary
- Smith, Mary C.
- Smith, Mary Charlene

Individual surnames with prefixes are alphabetized as each is written and are considered to be one word, whether or not they are written as one word:

- Mason, Tim
- McFarland, John
- Merrill, Jane
- Vane, K.
- Van Houton, Mae
- Vargas, Louise

A religious title or foreign title is alphabetized when it is followed by a first name only:

- Brother Thomas
- Burton, Francis (Rev.)
- Friar Tuck
- Queen Elizabeth
- Sister Mary Rose
- Tilton, Sarah (S.S.J.)

COMPANY OR BUSINESS NAMES

Words joined by a hyphen are treated as one word. However, if the hyphen is used instead of a comma in a business name, the individual parts of the name are treated as separate words, and therefore the name is indexed by the first word alone. The second name of the hyphenate is used only when needed, similar to a given name:

- Johnson, Samuel
- Johnson-Smith & Company
- Johnson, Steven
- Johnson, Victor

Whether a company name is composed of a compound word or is spelled as two words, it is alphabetized as if it were one word:

- New Deal Loan Company of America
- Newdeal Marine Works
- Suncity Shipbuilding Corporation
- Sun City Tannery

TABLE 7-1	Filing When Company Name Contains A Person's Name

Name	Filed As
American Petroleum Co.	American Petroleum Co.
Mary Brown Cafe	Brown, Mary Cafe
John Dillard Company	Dillard, John Company
Dillard Stores	Dillard Stores
Joyce Kilmer High School	Joyce Kilmer High School
May's Floral Center	May's Floral Center
John C. Wilson Realty	Wilson, John C. Realty
Wilson Realty Company	Wilson Realty Company

The exception is when a company name contains the full name of a person. In this case, alphabetize by using the surname, followed by first name, then middle initial or middle name if any. The exception is the names of schools. These are alphabetized as written, as are other organizations, businesses, or institutions. See Table 7-1.

Single letters used as words are treated as words and arranged alphabetically preceding word names:

- BB Shop
- BBB Service Company
- Bakery Heaven
- Brighton Clothes Company

When two or more similar company or business names are of unequal length, file the shorter name first:

- National Bank
- National Bank of Commerce
- Bronson Club
- Bronson Club of New York City

MISCELLANEOUS
Abbreviations are alphabetized as if spelled in full. See Table 7-2.

TABLE 7-2	Filing Abbreviations

Name	Filed As
St. Luke's Church	Saint Luke's Church
Jas. Smith	Smith, James
Chas. Williams	Williams, Charles

Designations following names are alphabetized according to natural order of age:

- Smith, James III
- Smith, James, 2d
- Smith, James, Jr.
- Smith, James, Sr.

Articles, prepositions, conjunctions, and the ampersand are disregarded in alphabetizing:

- Thomas & Anderson, Inc.
- Thomas, Brown R.
- Washington Bank, The
- Workshop for the Blind

When words end in *s*, the *s* is considered part of the name:

- Leon Neon and Light
- Leon's Art Supplies

If a name contains a number, do not put it in "numerical order" with other numbered names. Alphabetize it as if the number were spelled out:

- 1020 Building Corporation (one thousand twenty)
- 13 Park Avenue Studio (thirteen)
- 21 Club (twenty-one)

Titles are disregarded:

- Jones, R.L. (Dr.)
- Simms, Carlotta (Countess)
- Smith, Nancy (Miss)

Exception: If a firm name starts with a title, the title is considered to be the first word:

- Queen Mary Boat Company
- Sir John Thomas Cigar Company
- Viceroy of India Silk Company

File Cabinets

A standard file cabinet has four drawers that accommodate material written on 8½ inch by 11 inch typing or computer paper. An office with many legal-sized papers (8½ inch by 13 or 14 inches) will need a wider cabinet made specifically for these.

Your file cabinet should be near your desk, since you will go to it frequently throughout the workday. Label each drawer of the cabinet either horizontally (left to right) or vertically (top to bottom). If an alphabetical system is used, the top drawer might be labeled "A–G", the second drawer "H–M", and so forth.

Many secretarial desks have a built-in file drawer, handy for files used often so you can reach for them quickly without having to leave your desk to go to the larger cabinet.

OFFICE EQUIPMENT AND COMPUTERS

SECTION TWO

From administrative assistants to CEOs, modern office technology has revolutionized the way everyone works.
Photo by Kevin Wilson.

Office Machines

Typewriters

For years, electric typewriters accomplished much of what is now done with computers and word processors. For some applications, such as typing an address on an envelope or a mailing label, a typewriter is still the simplest office tool available, and now, the merging of electric typewriters with dedicated word processors has produced a machine that will do everything a sophisticated computer will do, and at much less expense.

Almost all models of electric typewriters have advanced word processing features built in. At the heart of them is a powerful microprocessor based on the technology found in early personal computers (PCs). Although this technology is outdated for today's PCs, it is perfectly capable of managing a word processing typewriter, allowing it to do everything from the ordinary to the truly extraordinary.

Here are a few of the many new features of today's electronic typewriters:

- Word erase for simple corrections
- Spell checkers, comparing every word you type with those in a built-in electronic dictionary
- Display screen
- Advanced revision features combined with an optional capacity for unlimited storage using diskettes
- Capacity to store and merge mail with telephone lists and other documents
- Background print feature to allow you to print documents while you create or revise other documents
- Ability to upgrade, one of the most useful features of all

Whether you're looking at an electronic typewriter as the sole typing tool for a small office or as a supplement to a larger office's PC, consider getting an upgradeable machine. Office needs change frequently, and what might not be quite right for you now could be a necessity in the near future. With upgradeability, you could move from a one-line display to 25 lines on the screen, or you could double your storage memory.

Because much of the correspondence and many of the documents you create tend to be repetitive, having a typewriter with some memory can greatly automate this task. For example, you can store commonly used addresses for typing envelopes or even a form letter, such as a "thank you" letter. These documents can be stored in the typewriter's memory or on a diskette. Later, you can recall and customize it for a particular person or company.

On a word processing typewriter (see Figure 8-1), you can automatically move to any position on the page and correct characters or whole words at a touch. The typewriter's cursor keys give you the same flexibility of movement on paper that you would have on a computer's display. The Word Tab and Line Find functions can be used in combination with the cursor keys. Whether you want to move across an area of blank space, jump from word to word, or locate your last line of typed text, there is a convenient way to do it.

To make your written letters and documents works of art, there are fast and easy ways to add interest and emphasis to a page: A bold function, automatic underlining, and so on. Both pitch and impression can be set to match ribbon and paper thickness automatically. A programmable paper feed function takes you to your customary top writing line and saves you the trouble of positioning the paper. On some advanced models, an adjustable keyboard lets you select from three typing positions the one that suits you best. Automatic correction cleanly removes or covers up typing errors. The Relocate feature automatically puts you back in position to continue typing after you make a correction. Alternate language keyboards allow you to type in many languages, such as French and Spanish.

In selecting the best typewriter for your office, you should consider the following word processing features:

- CRT display, with or without brightness and contrast adjustment
- Menu display, either text or icons
- PC compatibility, to allow for file data transfer with computers
- Keyboard type and design—number of keys, special keys

FIGURE 8-1. Word processing typewriter.

Photo by Jennifer Wauson.
Digital photography courtesy of Kyocera Optics.

- Memory—the amount in kilobytes (KB)
- Online help—the ability to get help via a CRT screen or display
- Double-column printing capability—prints two or more columns on the page
- Hyphenation—automatic insertion of hyphens
- Insert/delete/overwrite—special editing techniques
- Block moves/copy/delete—additional editing techniques
- Global search and replace, allowing replacement of words or phrases throughout the document
- Automatic word wrap—moves words that do not fit in the screen area down to the next line
- Headers and footers—automatic insertion of text at top or bottom of page (e.g., page numbers)
- Automatic page numbering—calculates and inserts page numbers
- Automatic pagination—determines where the page will break before you print
- Paper size adjustment—allows for different sizes of paper
- Save/retrieve documents—storage of documents in memory or diskette
- Grammar checking—looks for incorrect grammar usage
- Spell checker—looks for misspelled words
- Word count—automatic counting of the number of words in a document
- Redundancy check—looks for words typed twice in a row (usually part of a spell checker)
- Thesaurus—an online database of synonyms
- Paragraph/line indent—special function for indentation
- Decimal tab—keeps decimals lined up when printing a column of numbers
- Tab settings—insertion of tabs across the page
- Justification—centering, as well as right, left, and full justification
- Underlining—allows for underlining a word
- Bold typing—makes type darker for emphasis
- Super- and subscript—allows for typing special characters for formulas
- Line/word/letter correction—will remove typing mistakes

Copy Machines

Another essential office tool is the copy machine. Although the advent of word processing typewriters and personal computers has reduced reliance on copiers to some extent, because you can make additional paper copies by printing out duplicates, many documents that do not originate from your word processor or PC require copies.

Many small businesses use a local print shop for copies; however, considering the amount of time lost going back and forth to the shop and the convenience and relative cheapness of owning a personal copier, purchasing or leasing a copier for the business may be a good idea.

Copiers and laser printers function similarly (see Figure 8-2). They are often referred to as "nonimpact printing." Rather than have a hammer strike a ribbon to produce type on the page like a typewriter, copiers use a photographic process involving static electricity.

When you place a document to be copied inside a copy machine, a very strong light is projected on the original. The image of the original is then projected to an electrically sensitive rotating drum. The dark and light areas of the original affect the electric charge on the print drum. After being exposed to the original, the copier drum turns through a powder called *toner*, which sticks to the electrically charged areas. The drum then comes into contact with a fresh piece of copier paper, transferring the toner to the paper, thus creating a copy.

More advanced copiers magnify the projection of the light from the original to the copier drum, thus enlarging or reducing the size of the reproduction. Many copiers now use microprocessors to store images and to automate many of the functions such as sorting, collating, and making two-sided copies. With the use of multicolor toners, color copies can be produced. Other copiers have automatic document feeders, paper trays, sorters, and even built-in staplers. The choice of features makes for a wide range of prices.

FIGURE 8-2. Copy machine.

Photo courtesy of Kyocera Mita, all rights reserved.

How to Select a Copier

When selecting a new machine for your office, consider these six main factors:

- *Features.* What features do you really need?
- *Reliability.* How much reliability do you demand?
- *Cost.* What is the price of the copier, and are there any hidden costs?
- *Service/maintenance.* Who will maintain or repair your copier?
- *Warranty.* What does the warranty cover, and for how long?
- *Productivity.* Will this copier improve productivity in your office?

For some companies, even copiers stripped of all features are too large. These companies may want to consider the smallest of models, minicopiers, the most inexpensive way to acquire the convenience of a copy machine. Minicopiers are so small they don't even have paper trays and require the insertion of a single sheet of copier paper for each copy made. They use disposable toner cartridges (readily available at office supply stores) and replacement drums. They usually require little to no maintenance, and although it is possible to get paper jams just as in the larger machines, they are easily cleared.

One of the major drawbacks to minicopiers is the cost of the replacement cartridges. While a low-cost minicopier can be purchased for under $300, a replacement cartridge, good for anywhere from 1,000 to 5,000 copies depending on the model, can cost $75 or more. One alternative to purchasing a replacement cartridge is to have the cartridge refilled with toner. This is accomplished by a company that specializes in this service. The cost can be half the price of a new cartridge. You send your empty cartridge to one of these organizations, which evaluates and then refills it. Sometimes a cartridge cannot be refilled due to damage such as scratches on the copier drum.

8 ■ OFFICE MACHINES

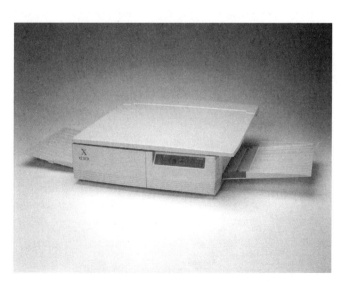

FIGURE 8-3. Minicopier.
Photo courtesy of Xerox Corporation, all rights reserved.

Calculators

Small electronic calculators have been around since the late 1960s and are now required in almost every business, large or small. They are useful for working with budgets, accounting, and other number-intensive business tasks. For larger projects, a spreadsheet on a personal computer is a better choice.

Calculators come in a variety of sizes and designs. Some have large LED (light-emitting diode) screens that can be used in dim light situations, and others use LCD (liquid-crystal display) screens that require good lighting to be seen. Some use solar power, while others use batteries or AC power from the wall outlet. Some are very small so they can be carried with you, while others are designed for desktop use. Some also have built-in printers (see Figure 8-4).

Besides being able to add, subtract, multiply, and divide, many calculators also have the ability to use fixed or floating-point decimals and have programmable function keys, memory keys, and special keys to perform square roots.

Many calculators are produced for specific applications. Here is a list of some of the many special-application calculators available:

- Scientific calculator
- Programmable calculator
- Graphing calculator

- Financial calculator
- Travel organizer
- Statistical calculator

Other Office Equipment

Additional office equipment found in today's businesses include:

- Binding systems
- Laminators

- Overhead projectors
- Paper shredders

FIGURE 8-4. Printing calculator.

Photo by Jennifer Wauson. Digital photography courtesy of Kyocera Optics.

Binding Systems

Binding systems (see Figure 8-5) are used to create professional-looking bound reports, presentations, and proposals. One of the most common systems is the plastic comb binding system. This is an ideal solution for binding standard letter-size documents in-house. The system includes a punch press that punches up to 20 sheets of 20-pound paper per punch and binds documents sheets with two-inch plastic binding combs. A paper guide and ruler are used to accurately align sheets.

Laminators

Laminators are often used to preserve photographs and to create quick reference cards, place mats, badges, and ID cards. A paper document is placed into a clear plastic lamination pouch and then run through the heated laminator, which seals the document in a protective hard plastic covering.

Overhead Projectors

Overhead projectors and video projectors are often used in meetings and presentations to large groups. With an overhead projector, presentation materials are copied or printed on clear plastic transparency pages called foils or transparencies. The transparencies are then placed on the light table of the overhead projector, and a powerful light passes through the transparency and projects

FIGURE 8-5. An administrative assistant uses a binding machine.

Photo by Jennifer Wauson. Digital photography courtesy of Kyocera Optics.

an image on a screen. The transparencies can be written on during a presentation for everyone in the meeting to see.

Video projectors are often used to display videos, television images, or computer data. With a video projector, presentation slides can be created using a program such as Microsoft PowerPoint. The slides are then displayed on a screen by the video projector. When the presenter wants to change slides, the mouse button is clicked or the space bar on the keyboard is pressed.

Paper Shredders

As a security measure to protect sensitive documents, paper shredders are used to destroy draft copies and old documents as an alternative to throwing them in the trash. Paper shredders vary in size from small models that fit on top of a trash can to large free-standing models.

Telecommunications Equipment

New developments in telecommunications equipment are changing the way all businesses, large and small, communicate. The telephone, computer, fax machine, cellular phone, and pager—each now plays a vital role in the success or failure of the company you work for. As a frequent user and a potential purchaser of such equipment for the company, you should be aware of all the latest features and benefits.

Telephones

Telephone service has come a long way since the late 1800s, when it was invented. In the early days, telephone service was primitive and selective. Not everyone had a telephone, nor could you call everyone or everywhere. Only towns that put up the poles and ran the wires had service, and even then, many people had to share a telephone line.

Today, telephone service is taken for granted. Businesses use voice mail and computerized answering machines to take messages, to network computers across town or across the country, and to send fax transmissions to offices around the world. Let's start with the basic business services that allow you to call across the street.

PBX

You may have seen in old movies a switchboard operator struggling with a tangle of wires and plugs. Today's larger businesses have replaced the switchboard operator with a PBX (private branch exchange) system. Ideal for a company with many employees and individual phone extensions, a PBX is a computerized telephone management system. It allows a single telephone number for a business to be accessed at the same time by numerous outside callers. As each call is received, it is automatically routed to the appropriate extension via a touch-tone phone or with the help of a receptionist or operator.

FIGURE 9-1. An administrative assistant uses the telephone.

Photo licensed by Digital Wisdom, all rights reserved.

Multi-Line Telephones

In a small business, a multi-line telephone system is often the preferred choice. This allows you to answer an incoming call from anywhere in the office and to route it to another telephone at the touch of a button. If one line is being used, you can access another line to make an outgoing call.

Other Business Telephones

A wide variety of other available business telephones combine telephone service with computer operations. Many of these more sophisticated telephones are equipped with special features, such as buttons and lights to designate different lines. More modern telephones use computer-like LED (light emitting diode) displays to designate and select lines as well as to indicate the number dialed. Others are programmable to store frequently called numbers in the telephone's memory. Some have speaker telephones built-in to free up one's hands while talking. Still others have automatic redialing, intercom capabilities, and built-in answering machines.

Voice Mail and Answering Machines

When you're away from your desk, and no one else can cover your telephone, it's important that you use an answering machine or computerized voice mail system. You don't want to miss critical calls for your boss or yourself. In addition, customers now expect the use of such devices, no matter what size company you work for.

Many different types of answering machines are available. Some use audiotapes to play an outgoing message and to record incoming messages. Others record messages digitally using built-in computer memory. Even the most inexpensive answering machine can automatically record the date and time of the call and allow the callee to retrieve messages from remote locations. This last is an essential feature to look for, especially if your boss is frequently away from the office. He or she doesn't have to wait to make contact with you to collect messages but can call in any time from home or on the road. By using a code combination from a touchtone telephone, the boss can listen to messages and even record a new outgoing message.

Computerized voice-mail systems, often used in larger companies, usually consist of a computer system along with a modem connected to the telephone line. These systems accept incoming calls and route them to various voice mail boxes for each employee. All messages are stored in the computer's memory or on a hard drive. The use of a touch-tone telephone is usually required to access voice-mail boxes and to leave and retrieve messages.

Special Telephone Services

Many telephone companies have a variety of special services that enhance the performance of your business telephone system, no matter which model you have. These services may vary from one part of the country to another. Here is a description of some of the more common services available:

- Call waiting is useful for individuals and for small businesses that have only one incoming telephone line. When you're on one call, you are alerted by a tone that another incoming call is waiting. If you wish, you can put the current call on hold and switch to answer the new incoming call.

- Select call waiting permits only the calls the user has programmed into the telephone to beep you in the call-waiting mode.

- Call forwarding allows you to redirect calls intended for your telephone to another telephone of your choice—ideal when you or your boss must spend extended time at another location.

- Select call forwarding enables you to program your telephone with a list of only those people you want to be able to contact you at the forwarding number.

- Three-way conferencing allows you to call more than one person at a time so that three or more people can participate in the same conversation.

- Caller ID shows you on a visual display the name and number of the person calling. Caller ID lets you use your telephone like a pocket pager, enabling you to decide whether to take the call, return it later, or ignore it.

- Busy number redial continues to dial a busy number automatically until the line is free. The telephone then alerts you when the line is ringing.

- Selective call acceptance allows you to program your telephone with a list of only those people you want to contact you. When a person on that list calls, the call rings through to your telephone. No other calls are allowed to get through.

- Voice message enables callers to leave a message which you retrieve later, just like an answering machine. Voice message is similar to voice mail; however, no special equipment is required at a user's location.

Long Distance Services

Since the break-up of AT&T, there have been many choices for long distance service. Besides AT&T, MCI, and Sprint, a host of smaller, regional long-distance companies market themselves to specific parts of the country. These services may or may not have their own long distance networks. In many cases, they purchase blocks of long distance time from a common telephone carrier and then resell that time to small businesses and individuals.

Toll-Free Numbers

One long distance service can benefit your company's customers: an 800 number, often called a "watts" line. As the owner of an 800 number, your company pays for all incoming long distance charges. A toll-free number is an expense, true, but it's more than just a convenience for your distant customers. It can be a selling point in whether your company makes the first sale at all.

Because of the demand for toll-free numbers, telephone companies have made a variety of other three-digit prefixes available, including 888, 878, 877, and 866.

900 Numbers

The 900 prefix is often associated with information lines that require the caller to pay a per-minute fee for the time on the call. This fee is charged to the caller's telephone bill and paid to the owner of the 900 number. Some small businesses involved in mail order have tried using 900 numbers, but often it is reserved for technical help, not for customers who want to order a product.

Teleconferences

One way to reduce travel costs associated with meetings is to use teleconferencing. Teleconferences can be scheduled in advance with a long distance carrier. With a reservation, you can link up different callers from around the country at the same time.

There are two basic ways to conduct a teleconference. In the first, each caller dials a special telephone number at a designated time and is connected to the group teleconference one by one. The second uses an operator, who calls and connects each individual to the teleconference. The cost of the teleconference includes a setup fee and an hourly fee for each caller along with the long distance charges for each individual.

Cellular Telephones

One of the most versatile ways your boss can communicate while away from the office is by using a cellular telephone. Cellular telephones use radio frequencies to communicate with a cellular telephone network consisting of various microwave radio towers spaced throughout a city or region. These are called cells. When a call is being made, the telephone first establishes a radio link with one of the cellular transmission towers. The cell then connects the telephone with the regular telephone system to make the call. Calls are received in much the same manner.

There are many different types of cellular phones. Some models include text messaging, small computer display screens, computer keyboards, and even digital cameras (see Figure 9-2). Various attachments allow a cellular telephone to be used inside a car. For example, power can be provided from the car's cigarette lighter, and an external antenna can be connected to increase the telephone's range. Many have a hands-free feature, which allows a speaker and microphone to be connected inside a car. Most cellular telephones also have memory for storing frequently called numbers.

Cellular Fees

Cellular service requires payment of a flat monthly fee plus a per-minute charge. Often, a telephone is provided as part of the basic package if your company agrees to a specific service contract of 1 to 3 years. Most cellular phone services include a home territory where calls can be made without long-distance charges. When a user ventures outside the home territory, the phone uses another cellular service provider's network. This is called roaming and involves additional charges. Some service packages include free nationwide roaming and long distance.

Special Services

Personal communications services combine the power of a cell phone with a two-way radio. The rates paid while using the radio service are different from those paid while using the cellular service. Most service plans include a certain number of credits for both types of phone usage.

Another innovation, cellular data services, combines the power of computer communications with a cellular modem. By having a cellular modem installed

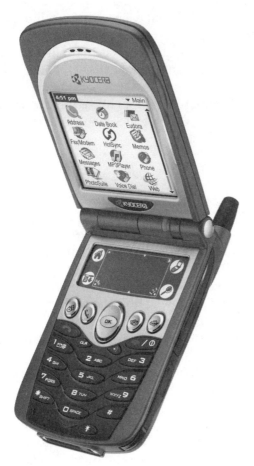

FIGURE 9-2. Cellular telephone with display screen.

Photo courtesy of Kyocera, all rights reserved.

inside a portable computer, you can connect your computer with various networks and databases while on the road.

Personal Data Assistants

Blurring the distinction between computer and cell phone are miniature computers called PDAs (personal data assistants) (see Figure 9-3). Many PDAs are also equipped with cellular modems for wireless communications.

Most PDAs do not use a traditional typewriter style keyboard for input. Instead, they use a touch screen and a pen interface to access various menu choices. To enter text information or graphics, simply write or draw on the small screen. Built-in handwriting recognition software translates handwriting into computer text so it can be stored in the PDAs memory or later transferred to an office computer.

Some of the most sophisticated PDAs can be used as a cell phone for making or receiving voice calls.

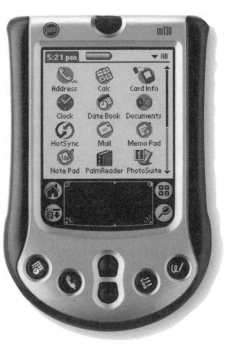

FIGURE 9-3. Personal Data Assistant.
Photo courtesy of Palm, Inc, all rights reserved.

Pagers

Pagers have become an important business communication tool. The caller dials the pager's telephone number and then enters his or her telephone number or even a voice message. The owner of the pager is then notified by the pager's beeping or vibrating, and information about the call is displayed on the LCD display screen. The owner of the pager can then go to the nearest telephone to return the call.

Pagers are very useful when your boss must be away from the office for extended periods of time. When there is an important call from a business associate or client, the pager can be used to pass on the caller's number. Most pagers function within the range of a city or a specific region. However, some systems, using satellite communications, can page a person anywhere in the country with just one call.

Facsimile Machines

While faxes are being replaced by e-mail, there are still millions of fax machines (Figure 9-4) in use, and millions more faxes are sent annually.

Today's facsimile machines are faster and more versatile than ever. There are even products available that tie your fax machine to your office telephone's voice messaging system. Those products make it as easy to check for fax messages when you're out of the office as it is to check for voice messages.

FIGURE 9-4. Fax machine.
Photo courtesy of Kyocera Mita, all rights reserved.

How to Select a Fax Machine

Selecting a machine begins with a clear understanding of how it is going to be used. Some of the factors to consider include:

- What type of documents will you send and receive?

- How many pages will each document have?

- How many locations will you send the same document to?

- Do you frequently send illustrations, photographs, or sketches?

- Are company employees often on the road? Would it be useful for them to be able to reroute fax messages to another fax machine? At any time of day or night?

- Does your company need more than one fax machine?

- Would it be more convenient and more efficient if employees could send and receive faxes right at their desks while at the same time transacting other business?

Low- and High-Volume Usage

Fax machines cost from several hundred dollars for basic no-frills machines up to thousands of dollars for more sophisticated models and plain-paper faxes. However, if you opt for a basic machine for the company or department, consider that usage often grows dramatically as employees become accustomed to the convenience of sending and receiving fax messages.

If you anticipate high usage, consider these factors:

- *Paper capacity.* Some fax machines use thermal paper, a glossy paper that comes in rolls ranging from 66 to 328 feet. Each foot equals approximately one page. Other fax machines can use regular office or copy paper and will hold from 25 to 500 sheets.

■ *Plain versus thermal paper.* Plain-paper fax machines cost more than those that use thermal paper and have more moving parts that can malfunction. Many users reconcile a preference for plain paper with the cost benefits of thermal fax machines by copying thermal fax messages on plain bond paper as they come in. But whatever your choice, use only the paper the manufacturer recommends. Improperly coated paper—usually the cheaper brands available—can damage your fax machine.

■ *Document feeder.* Document feeders can hold up to 50 pages at a time; however, approximately 60 percent of all fax messages transmitted today are three pages or less. If your company is small, or you're buying only for your own department, a 10-page document feeder may be adequate for most of your needs.

■ *Usage.* If your business sends or receives photos, illustrations, or graphics, consider purchasing a fax machine with grayscale (halftone) capability, which translates pictures into between eight and 64 shades of gray.

■ *Resolution.* Most faxes have a normal resolution (picture sharpness) appropriate for most business correspondence and simple line drawings. If your business requires a sharper image, higher resolutions are available. Remember, however, that the machines at both ends of the transmission must have that capability.

■ *Broadcasting.* If you send daily reports to satellite locations, broadcasting capability can be an important time saver. Broadcasting stores pages in the fax machine's memory for transmission to the locations you specify.

■ *Automatic dialing.* This is another time saver that lets you store frequently called fax numbers in the machine's memory bank. The numbers can be dialed at the touch of a button individually or in groups.

■ *Delayed send.* This money-saving feature lets you program a document for transmission at a specific time, for example, during off-peak hours, to take advantage of lower calling rates. It's also valuable to companies doing business overseas that want to schedule delivery during business hours in another time zone.

■ *Polling.* Polling lets your machine retrieve documents stored in another fax machine's memory. If collecting sales figures from branch offices is a routine part of your business day, polling lets you retrieve the data whenever it's convenient for you via their fax machines.

Fax Modems

In addition to dedicated fax machines, you should also know that there are fax modems (Figure 9-5) available for personal computer systems. A fax modem

FIGURE 9-5. A fax modem card for a personal computer.

Photo courtesy of Zoom, all rights reserved.

will connect your computer to the phone lines to send and receive data and allow your computer to send and receive faxes.

To send a fax, you first compose the document on the computer electronically. Then, without having to print out the document and take it to a fax machine, you access the software that comes with the fax modem and transmit the document just as a regular fax machine does. Incoming faxes are stored in your computer's memory like a graphic. You can read the fax using the software or print it out with your printer.

Computer Hardware

✸ Office Computers

Companies of all sizes routinely use personal or desktop computers in the office. Computers allow employees to be more productive by automating many repetitive tasks, such as word processing, billing, and filing. Even when an office has only one computer, the administrative assistant may be its most frequent user. You may also be the person who investigates the different types of hardware and software and recommends which PC the office should buy.

Computers available for business uses range from powerful mainframes and minicomputers to networked systems to the personal computers (PCs) many people have in their homes. For most small businesses, personal or desktop computers are often used. These come in a wide variety of different configurations in both IBM-compatible and Apple Macintosh operating systems.

When most people use a PC, what they really are using is a computer system. The computer itself may be no larger than a single integrated circuit chip soldered to a circuit board inside the computer's case. However, the user interfaces with a variety of other elements that together make up the computer system. These elements, called **peripheral devices,** include the keyboard, monitor, mouse, disk drives, and printer.

A true computer system usually consists of five elements:

- An input device, such as a keyboard or mouse, that allows you to communicate with the computer.

- An output device, such as a monitor or a printer, that allows the computer to communicate back with you.

- A processor that allows for the manipulation of your data. The central processing unit (CPU) is the brains of the computer system.

- A storage system, such as a floppy disk drive or hard disk drive, that allows you to save your work electronically.

- Software that provides instructions for the computer in the form of programs.

Hardware

How you can operate your computer and what type of work it can perform depend on how your system unit is equipped. From the outside, the system unit is just a case to house the electronic components. Most people refer to the system unit as "the computer" since it is the part of the system that handles all the processing jobs. There are a variety of different computer designs, such as the desktop system that sits on a desk, the floor-standing tower system, and the portable or laptop computer (see Figures 10-1 through 10-3).

All computers have a power switch on the system unit, located on the front of the case or on the back. Depending on which brand of computer you use, on the front there will also probably be **disk drives** mounted inside the system unit. One type of disk drive may be a $3\frac{1}{2}$-inch diskette drive. Another type of disk drive is a **hard disk** drive, which can be mounted inside the system unit or contained in its own case and connected via a cable. The hard disk drive (Figure 10-4) is capable of storing the same information as many floppy disks, depending on its size rating. In addition, most computers have a **CD-ROM** or **DVD-ROM** drive.

Each disk drive is given a letter, number, or name so that it's easy to load and save information to or from a particular drive location. On IBM-compatible computers, the first diskette drive is called drive A, the second diskette drive is called drive B, and the hard drive is called drive C. The CD-ROM or DVD-ROM drive would be called drive D. On Apple Macintosh computers, the drives are given names or labels.

PCs are usually designed to be expandable. For this reason, it's possible to remove the case should you need to get inside to install a new component. Many people are afraid to open the computer case; yet the more familiar you are with your computer, the better able you will be to troubleshoot little problems that arise from time to time. If you work for a small business, your boss is the person who probably bought the computer. Ask permission to open the case (or let the boss do so and look over his or her shoulder). Computer repairs and upgrades are simple skills to acquire; yet they are invaluable, especially in terms

FIGURE 10-1. Desktop computer system.

Photo (© 2003) IBM Corporation. Used with permission of IBM.

FIGURE 10-2. Tower computer configuration.

Photo (© 2003) IBM Corporation. Used with permission of IBM.

of time saved. Once a small company begins to rely on a computer to run its day to day business, the whole company can come to a screeching halt if the computer goes down.

Inside the system unit of a typical IBM compatible, you will see a metal box which is the computer's power supply. This **transformer** converts the power from the wall into electricity that can be used by the computer. You'll see the disk drives and hard disk drive that are mounted inside the case. And you'll see the **motherboard,** which occupies most of the inside of the computer. This large circuit board contains various chips and your processor. On the motherboard, you will see various slots for plug-in expansion boards. For example, if you want to use a monitor or a printer with your computer, you may need to plug an interface card into one of these slots so that the device can communicate with the computer.

Expansion boards are available for a variety of different purposes. They easily plug into the motherboard expansion slots so you can add a device such as a monitor or CD-ROM. There are several different types of expansion slots in your computer. Industry Standard Architecture (ISA) slots are for older 16-bit expansion boards. You can connect modems, disk drives, and video display adapters to the ISA slots. Peripheral Component Interconnect (PCI) slots are for newer, faster expansion boards. Most computer motherboards have three or four PCI

FIGURE 10-3. Laptop computer.

Photo (© 2003) IBM Corporation. Used with permission of IBM.

10 ▪ COMPUTER HARDWARE

FIGURE 10-4. A hard disk drive.
Photo (© 2003) IBM Corporation. Used with permission of IBM.

slots for connecting video display cards, modems, and other components. PCI cards and slots have "plug and play" capability. That means when you install one of these cards, your computer will automatically recognize the card the next time it starts up. The Accelerated Graphics Port (AGP) slot is reserved for high-performance graphic cards for connecting your monitor to the computer.

The expansion slots in the motherboard provide a common electronic signal called a **bus.** A bus allows electronic signals to be passed from one part of the PC to another. There are several different types of computer buses available in your PC. Since these are often described in the specifications when purchasing a computer, bus types include:

- System Bus—the pathway between the CPU and its memory.
- Backside Bus—the pathway between the CPU and its internal cache memory.
- Frontside Bus—the pathway between the CPU, main memory, and peripheral devices.
- Peripheral Bus—part of the frontside bus that includes the ISA, PCI, and AGP buses.
- SCSI Bus—a pathway that transports data between the Small Computer System Interface (SCSI) controller and SCSI devices such as hard drives and scanners.

Some expansion boards have a plug at one end where you can attach a device such as a disk drive or printer. These are called **ports.** Some ports are located on expansion boards, and some are connected directly to the motherboard. The two most common ports are the **parallel** port, used primarily for printers, and the **serial port,** used primarily to connect modems for telecommunications. Another useful port is the Universal Serial Bus (USB) port.

Looking at the back of a typical PC, you will see a parallel port for the printer, a serial port for the modem, another serial port for the mouse, and a video port for the monitor.

The term expansion board may appear to mean that all such boards are only options. However, there are several expansion boards found in almost all IBM-compatible models, such as the **display adapter** which converts the computer's instructions into pictures on your monitor screen.

Other key components in your computer are the **memory chips** and the *processor chip*. The amount of memory your computer has determines the amount of workspace available for data. For example, if you are working with a large word processing document or a large accounting program with a lot of data, you might eventually see messages on your monitor screen that the computer is running low or is out of memory. Most computers allow for upgrading the amount of memory. For most IBM compatibles and Apple Macintosh computers, you can add to the computer's memory by plugging in Random Access Memory (RAM) chips, which are what provides your computer's memory. RAM chips can be plugged into slots on the motherboard of your computer to increase system memory. Your computer will likely have between two and eight RAM slots. Adding two 128-megabyte (MB) RAM chips will increase your system memory to 256 MB. Figure 10-5 shows a typical motherboard with the processor, expansion slots, and RAM slots.

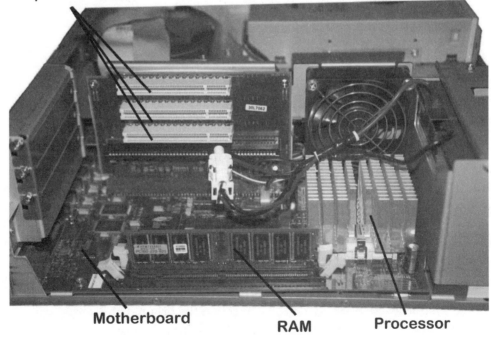

FIGURE 10-5. A computer system with the case removed to see the motherboard, processor, expansion slots, and RAM.

Photo by Kevin Wilson. Digital photography courtesy of Kyocera Optics.

Computer performance and speed are determined mainly by the type of processor chip included with your computer. In IBM-compatible computers the main processors are made by Intel, AMD, and Cyrix. Popular models include the Pentium, Celeron, K6, and Athlon.

Another performance enhancement enjoyed by many PC users is an internal **cache,** an extra bit of memory built into your processor that allows it to store certain instructions internally rather than using your computer's normal memory. This saves time and greatly increases speed. There are two different types of cache: L1 cache that is integrated with your processor and L2 cache which is installed as a group of memory chips on your motherboard.

Also important in evaluating speed and performance is the **clock speed** of your processor. Clock speed is the speed at which messages from the computer processor travel to other parts of the computer, such as the disk drives, hard drive, monitor, printer, and so on. Many early model PCs had clock speeds of 4 to 8 megahertz (MHz). Speeds ranging from 500 MHz up to several gigahertz are available.

The key point to remember when you're choosing a company computer is that better speed and performance usually translate into greater productivity. Therefore, an investment in a good computer system can help you do more in less time. In many cases, it isn't always necessary to replace the company's existing computer system. You may be able to add more memory and an add-on accelerator card that will equip your PC with the latest processor, math coprocessor, and internal cache. This would plug into one of the expansion slots on the motherboard of your PC.

Memory

Computer memory is often very confusing to new computer users, because it implies that the computer will remember your data automatically. However, if you create a document with a word processor but don't save it and then turn off your computer, that document will be lost. Unfortunately most computer users learn this lesson the hard way. Long-term storage of data is handled by the disk drives and hard disk drive, not by the computer's memory.

Your computer's memory is that area where programs and data are temporarily copied from a diskette or hard disk drive so that you can use them. Moving programs and data into memory is called **loading** or, on some systems, **opening.** It is just like taking a document out of a file cabinet and putting it on your desk. Unlike this analogy, however, when a computer loads a program or a document into memory, it only takes a copy—leaving the original intact on the disk. You can modify the original by saving your latest work with the same name as the original, or you can retain the original and keep a new version by saving the new version with a slightly different name.

Random access memory (RAM) is the area of memory where your programs and data are loaded. Memory is measured in terms of bits, bytes, kilobytes, megabytes, and gigabytes.

Electronically, the RAM in your computer is made up of lots of little electric switches that are turned on or off. For programming purposes, on is given a numerical value of 1, and off is given the numerical value of 0. Therefore, programs and data are represented as lots of 1s and 0s. Each character in the alphabet is represented by a special code made up of 1s and 0s. The same is true for numbers and graphics on your monitor. Some computers use a 16-bit system. That means that it takes a combination of 16 1s and 0s to form each character or graphic. Other more advanced graphics computers use 32-bit systems, and still other computers are using 64-bit systems.

Each group of eight 1s and 0s is called a **byte,** and 1,024 bytes equal a kilobyte, 1,024 kilobytes equal a megabyte, and a gigabyte is 1,000 megabytes.

Most computers are equipped with at least 64 megabytes of memory. However, this is usually not enough to handle today's modern operating systems and applications software. For many applications and operating systems, 128 MB is the recommended minimum, and 256 MB is common.

There are two different types of RAM: Main RAM and Video RAM. Main RAM is the type of RAM we've discussed so far. Video RAM is usually installed on the video display adapter and is used exclusively for handling graphics processing.

There are two types of Main RAM: Static RAM (SRAM) and Dynamic RAM (DRAM).

RAM chips are connected to larger circuit boards called memory modules that plug into your computer's motherboard. There are three different types of memory modules used: Single in-line memory modules (SIMMs), dual in-line memory modules (DIMMs), and rambus in-line memory module (RIMMs).

Another way some computers access even greater amounts of memory is to use **virtual memory.** Computers can use part of the computer's hard drive as if it were extra RAM. Virtual memory is slower than RAM memory and is used primarily when multiple programs are loaded and running at the same time. The program not being accessed by a user can be temporarily swapped to virtual memory.

Read-only memory (ROM) is another type of memory that is built into the computer and cannot be changed by programs. ROM chips contain a permanent set of instructions that support the overall operation of the computer. Essentially, they function automatically and require little attention from most computer users.

Input Devices

In order to use computers, you need some way to communicate with them. This process is known as **input.** There are many types of input devices. Probably the most common is a keyboard. By simply typing on a typewriter-like keyboard, information is sent to the computer for processing. In order to see what it is you have typed, most computers use a **monitor** or **video display.** As characters are typed on the keyboard, they appear on the monitor screen.

Among the most familiar devices for input are game controllers such as **joysticks.** These devices allow a game player to communicate information to a computer informing it of key decisions necessary to play a game. A similar device is a **mouse,** a hand controller that is used in some software applications and operating systems for a variety of different computers (see Figure 10-6). A mouse is used to select menu choices and to move a **cursor,** or pointer, around on the monitor screen. A mouse consists of a rubber ball inside a plastic housing. By moving the mouse over a surface such as a desktop or a mouse pad, the ball moves, providing input to the computer to move a pointer on the display screen. Similar to a mouse is a **track ball.** Many small portable computers use **touchpads,** since the operator may be using the computer where there is no desktop available for a mouse.

Another useful form of input designed originally for disabled individuals is **voice recognition.** Voice recognition and natural language speech systems interpret the human voice into signals that a computer can understand as input. Voice recognition systems are now popular and can be used to select menu items in software and, in some cases, even to create text for a word processing document or spreadsheet.

For graphic artists and designers and others who need to input precise drawings, a special drawing device called a **graphics tablet** is available. A graphics tablet consists of a plastic board containing a grid of fine electrical wires. A special drawing pen is used to draw. When the pen comes into contact with the grid of wires, information on the location of the pen is sent to the computer in order to create a graphics image on a monitor screen.

Another input tool used by graphic artists is the **scanner.** There are various models available. Some you hold in your hand; other desktop models operate much like a copy machine. With the desktop version, you place an original doc-

FIGURE 10-6. A mouse and trackball.

Photo by Jennifer Wauson. Digital photography courtesy of Kyocera Optics.

ument into the scanner, and the scanner copies an image of the document or graphic into the computer's memory. When the document is text, special optical character recognition software is often used. This software takes the images input from a scanner and compares them against various text styles in memory. It then translates the scanner image into text for your word processor.

Finally, **digital cameras** can be used to acquire digital images that can be transferred into a computer and used in desktop publishing applications. For more information about desktop publishing see Chapter 20.

Output Devices

When you work with a computer, most of your attention will be focused on output devices. This is where you can see the results of your work. The most common output devices found on computer systems are the monitor and the printer. Both output devices are available in many different models.

The Monitor

Monitors display information by painting the screen with tiny dots of color called **pixels.** Today there are several different types of monitors to fit various needs. There are flat screen liquid crystal display (LCD) monitors (as in Figure 10-7), and traditional cathode ray tube (CRT) monitors.

Monitors come in different screen sizes that are measured diagonally. The standard monitor size is 15-inches. However, 17-inch, 19-inch, and 21-inch monitors are available.

FIGURE 10-7. LCD monitor.
Photo (© 2003) IBM Corporation.
Used with permission of IBM.

The crispness of the monitor's picture is measured in dot pitch, refresh rate, and resolution. Dot pitch is the distance between pixels. The better the dot pitch, the better the monitor can display lines and curves. The refresh rate is the speed at which the monitor repaints the screen. Refresh rates are measured in Hertz (Hz). A low refresh rate will produce a noticeable flicker on the monitor. Resolution is the screen image size that can be displayed on the monitor as measured in horizontal and vertical pixels. Typical resolutions used include 640×480, 800×600, and 1024×768.

The Printer

Along with video display monitors, the other most popular form of output for a computer system is a **printer.** Printers produce a hardcopy paper version of what is on your display screen. There are several different types of printers available.

DAISY WHEEL PRINTERS

These old-style printers have a ring of typewriter-like keys that strike a moving inked ribbon to create text on a page. Finding one of these dinosaurs in your office would be rare.

DOT MATRIX PRINTERS

Dot matrix printers use a moveable print head with tiny pins that strike an inked ribbon to create a mark on the paper. Combinations of the tiny pins are used to create text. These inexpensive printers are often used in office shipping areas or as part of point-of-sale cash registers.

INK JET PRINTER

Ink jet printers produce letter-quality output by spraying ink through a series of tiny nozzles onto the paper to form each letter. Ink jet printers can print in black and white and in color. In fact, some ink jet printers can produce photographic-quality output that rivals traditional photographic film prints.

LASER PRINTER

Perhaps the most successful and popular method of producing letter-quality text is with a laser printer (see Figure 10-8). Although laser printers are more expensive than ink jet printers, their quality and speed have made them popular among all types of computer users. Laser printers function similarly to copy machines. A graphics image of the computer output is sent to the laser printer, which also has a computer processor. The laser printer then uses a laser to display an image on an electrically charged drum surface. Once the charged surface comes into contact with a powdered or liquid toner, the toner sticks in the image areas and falls off the non-image areas. When paper comes into contact with the drum, the toner is transferred to the paper, producing an image.

COLOR LASER PRINTING

Recent advances in color printing have resulted in laser printers that use multicolored toners for producing color output.

FIGURE 10-8. Laser printer.

Printer Performance

The performance of a printer is determined by its resolution, memory, and speed. Printer resolution is the sharpness of the image the printer can produce on paper. Resolution is measured in dots per inch (dpi). For draft quality text printing, a dpi setting of 300 is sufficient. For letter-quality printing, a dpi setting of 600 is good. For photographic-quality printing a resolution of 600 dpi or better is needed.

Dpi settings affect the speed of the printer. Most inkjet and laser printers can print three to six pages per minute, depending on the type of image. Photographic quality images may take much longer. Laser printers tend to be the fastest printers available.

Printer's have built-in memory that helps speed up the printing process. If you print large documents or documents with complex graphics, having additional printer memory will enhance printing speed.

Other Output Devices

Another device for reproducing computer output is a **pen plotter,** which draws the computer output using a group of multicolored pens (See Figure 10-9). This is often used in architectural and design offices. In addition, there are a variety of other devices for utilizing computer output, among them, your computer speakers or voice synthesizers for sound, modems for communications output, and electrical devices that are computer controlled.

Storage Devices

The ability to store, search for, and retrieve specific information from permanent data storage media is ideal for helping secretaries organize the department or company—and keep it organized. Using the computer's electronic filing system, you should see a great time savings for yourself as well as an increase in your productivity and efficiency in day-to-day business activities.

10 ■ COMPUTER HARDWARE

FIGURE 10-9. Plotter.
Photo courtesy of Kyocera Mita.

A computer stores your work in two areas: one temporary and one permanent. The temporary storage is your computer's memory, its RAM. We've already discussed computer memory, but it's important to remember that information stored in RAM is stored only as long as the computer is turned on.

The Hard Drive

The main permanent storage device is the computer's **hard drive** (sometimes called a **fixed disk**), which can be either internal (mounted inside the computer case) or external (in its own case connected to the computer via a cable). A hard drive is actually a stack of disks coated with a magnetic coating similar to audio- or videotape. Information is saved on a hard drive much the same way a song is recorded on audiotape. The computer's electronic signals are recorded on the magnetic hard drive disk, and when you want the information back, the hard drive "plays back" those signals. Saving information on a hard drive is called **writing** to the drive; playing information back is called **reading.** It is also possible to erase information on a drive; this is called **deleting.**

Disk storage capacity is measured in units called **bytes.** A byte is made up of 8 bits of information. A thousand bytes is a kilobyte, or K for short. A **megabyte** is 1024 K. One thousand megabytes is a **gigabyte.** Hard drives can store billions of bytes. Typically, hard drives store anywhere from 20 gigabytes—often called "gigs"—to several hundred gigabytes.

There are several different types of hard drives available for PCs. They include: IDE, ATA, and SCSI.

Diskette

Another form of permanent storage is a **diskette** (see Figure 10-10). A floppy disk, or diskette, is used in a diskette drive. The $3\frac{1}{2}''$ disk is housed inside a rigid case. Diskettes can store far less than hard drives. A $3\frac{1}{2}''$ diskette can store 1.44 MB of data. Improvements in disk drive storage capabilities have increased storage capacities up to 2.88 MB on some specially formatted $3\frac{1}{2}''$ diskettes, but this is still much less than the hard drive.

On a $3\frac{1}{2}''$ diskette is a sliding door that protects the read/write slot. There is also a small corner hole with a sliding piece of plastic. When the hole is open, your data are write-protected. When the hole is closed by the piece of plastic, you can write information on the disk and thus modify your existing data files.

Since the data and programs you use on floppy disks must be protected, an understanding of how to care for disks is very important. Here's a rundown of how to handle them:

■ Always keep disks so they'll be protected. For example, keep them away from food or drinks.

■ Always store disks upright in a closed container.

■ Avoid extreme temperatures and humidity.

■ Keep disks away from magnets, such as those in stereo speakers or the telephone.

■ Label your diskettes so you'll know what they contain.

■ Always insert diskettes label side up, with the read/write slot going into the disk drive first.

■ Never touch the exposed area of the disk behind the read/write slot cover.

■ Never insert or remove a diskette while the disk drive indicator light is on.

Tape Backup

One specialized storage medium is available solely for the purpose of making backups. Tape backup drives use a cartridge tape or 8-mm tape (similar to 8-mm

FIGURE 10-10. Diskette and CD-ROM.

Photo by Kevin Wilson.
Digital photography courtesy of
Kyocera Optics.

videotape) to back up your hard drive and all your data. A tape backup drive is much slower than a hard drive or even a floppy drive, so it's not very useful for normal day-to-day use as a storage medium. However, special software combined with a tape backup drive can automatically back up your data periodically so you'll also be protected in the event of hard drive failure.

Cartridge Drives

A cross between a floppy disk and a hard drive, **removable drives** are popular in many businesses. A removable cartridge drive acts like a hard drive, although it's somewhat slower in terms of reading and writing data; however, like a floppy disk, a removable cartridge can be taken from the drive and replaced with another. This offers great flexibility. When one cartridge is filled up, it can be replaced by another. It's like having a completely new hard drive. The removable cartridges are contained in a special housing that protects the sensitive media inside. Since these cartridges can store several gigabytes or more of programs and data, they must be handled very carefully and stored in a cool protected environment.

One of the most common cartridge drives is the Zip Drive from Iomega. Zip disks are about the size of a $3\frac{1}{2}''$ diskette, but can store several hundred megabytes. Another popular cartridge drive is the SuperDisk made by Imation Corporation. They are the same size as $3\frac{1}{2}''$ diskettes and can store over 100 MB of data.

CD-ROM and DVD-ROM

Another increasingly popular data storage medium is a **CD-ROM.** This system uses a compact disk to store computer data. Approximately 600 megabytes can be stored on one CD-ROM, the equivalent of more than 1,500 floppy disks. However, a CD-ROM does not allow you to modify and save data back on it. Thus you can read data from it but cannot write data to it.

If you have a CD-ROM drive that can create, or "burn" CDs, you can also use it for making backups of your data. These drives are often called CD Recordable (**CD-R**) or CD Read and Write (**CD-RW**) and can store approximately 600 megabytes of data.

Making the move from the entertainment center to the computer are **DVD-ROM** drives. These drives can store several gigabytes of data and are often used for viewing DVD movies on your computer.

DVD recordable (**DVD-R**) and DVD Read and Write (**DVD-RW**) drives are also available that can record DVD data disks that can store 4 to 9 gigabytes of data.

Laptop Computers

Many offices use small laptop computers in place of desktop computers to give employees mobility and flexibility when using their PCs. With a laptop, everything is combined into one unit: CPU, monitor, hard drive, CD-ROM, speakers, modem, network card, microphone, and diskette. Laptop computers can be upgraded with larger hard drives and additional RAM. You can connect them to printers, a phone line, an office network, or to an external monitor, keyboard, and mouse.

One nice feature of a laptop computer is the built-in battery. This battery will power the computer for several hours without being connected to a power outlet.

While you can connect an external mouse to a laptop computer, a variety of built-in pointing devices are available. Most laptops use a touchpad with buttons or a pointing stick positioned next to the G and H keys that resembles the eraser of a pencil.

When you are in the office, some laptops can be connected to a port replicator or docking station. When connected to one of these expansion units, you can use an external monitor, keyboard, and mouse just like a desktop computer system.

One feature unique to laptop computers is the PCMCIA card. These credit-card sized expansion cards are used for modems, network cards, and additional memory. They are connected to the PCMCIA slots in the side of the laptop. Most laptops can accept two of these cards.

Hand-Held Computers

Hand-held computers, often called **PDAs** (personal digital assistants) are rapidly taking the place of address books in many offices (see Figure 10-11). Many executives use these devices to take notes, store contact information, and to plan their schedules.

PDAs can be connected to your desktop computer using a cable or a wireless connection to download or upload information. In this way, a person can have portable access to much of the same information that is stored on their PC.

FIGURE 10-11. Handheld Computer.
Courtesy of Xerox Corporation. All rights reserved.

10 ■ COMPUTER HARDWARE

PDAs are normally pen-based computers. The user enters and accesses information using a stylus and a touch screen. The PDA will accept handwritten input and convert it to text. Optional small keyboards are also available.

Some of the most popular models of PDAs include the following:

- Palm from Palm, Inc.
- Treo from Handspring
- Jornada from Hewlett-Packard Corporation
- Clie from Sony Corporation

Maintaining Your Computer

For the most part, there is little you need to do to maintain your computer system. However, as for any machine, there are a few things you can do that will help your computer last longer and operate smoothly.

Cleaning Your Mouse

As your roll your mouse around over a mouse pad, it picks up lint and dust particles that eventually clog the little wheels and rollers inside. If you notice the mouse beginning to operate erratically, check the user manual for how to remove the roller ball. You can then clean the ball with a soft dry cloth and wipe the three sets of rollers inside the mouse. Normally, when a mouse is dirty, the rollers will be coated with a gunk that can be wiped off with a cloth, or scraped off using your fingernail.

ScanDisk

This is a utility that comes with your computer that can detect and fix hard disk errors that cause performance problems. ScanDisk can be run from within Microsoft Windows by opening the **My Computer** icon and right-clicking a hard drive icon. From the pop-up menu that appears, click **Properties.** On the Properties Dialog box, click the **Tools** tab and then click **Error Checking.**

Disk Defragmenter

As you use your computer, the files you save get divided and spread in different available spaces on your hard drive. The more spread out or fragmented they get, the more the performance of your computer is affected. The Disk Defragmenter Utility (see Figure 10-12) recombines files and resaves them in one continuous location. This reorganizes your hard drive and improves disk efficiency.

You can run Disk Defragmenter from within Microsoft Windows by opening the **My Computer** icon and right-clicking a hard drive icon. From the pop-up menu that appears, click **Properties.** On the Properties Dialog box, click the **Tools** tab and then click **Defragmentation.**

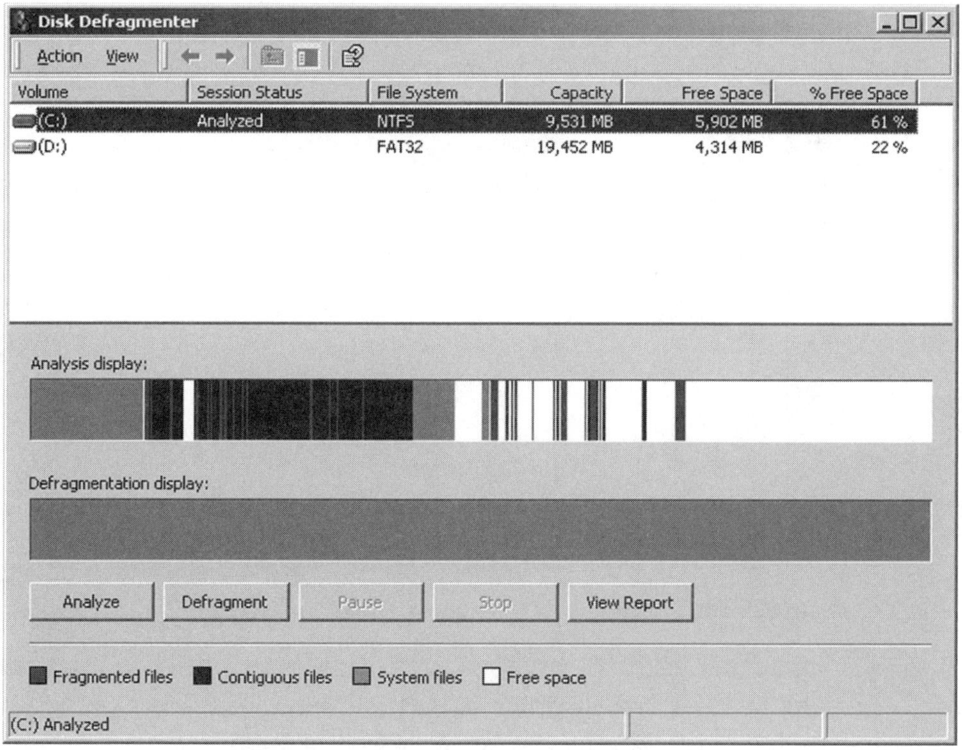

FIGURE 10-12. Disk Defragmenter in Microsoft Windows.

Screen shot reprinted by permission from Microsoft Corporation.

Disk Cleanup

As you work with various documents, print, view Web pages, and so forth, temporary information gets stored on your computer. These temporary files can grow in size and eventually squeeze out room for other things. It's a good idea to delete these files from time-to-time.

The Disk Cleanup Utility checks your computer for temporary files and eliminates them. You can access the Disk Cleanup Utility from within Microsoft Windows by clicking the **Start** button, then **Programs, Accessories, System Tools,** and **Disk Cleanup.**

Backup Your Data

When your hard drive fails, you could lose all your data. Since your hard drive is like a very large filing cabinet filled with important and often confidential data about the business you work for, protecting that information is very important. Therefore, you should backup your hard drive frequently by making copies of all data onto an external hard drive, a network drive, a backup tape, diskettes, or a CD-R, CD-RW, DVD-R, or DVD-RW.

You can schedule periodic backups and determine which files you want to backup by using the Backup Utility (Figure 10-13) provided with Microsoft

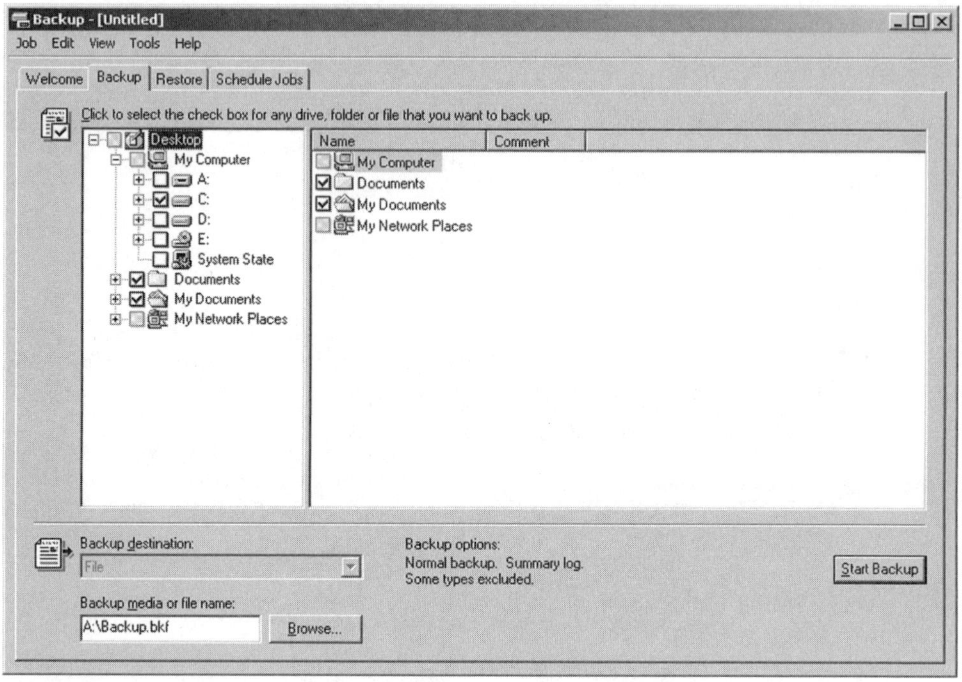

FIGURE 10-13. Microsoft Windows Backup Utility.

Screen shot reprinted by permission from Microsoft Corporation.

Windows. You can access the utility from within Microsoft Windows by opening the **My Computer** icon and right-clicking a hard drive icon. From the pop-up menu that appears, click **Properties.** On the Properties Dialog box, click the **Tools** tab, and then click **Backup.**

Computer Software

The BIOS

Unless you are a programmer and know how to write programming code that can communicate directly with the computer's hardware to perform a function, you need an operating system and software. But, even for a programmer to work, a basic set of software instructions must be installed. These basic instructions are the computer's Basic Input Output System (**BIOS**).

The BIOS is installed in a read-only memory (ROM) chip on the computer's motherboard. The BIOS is the first thing that loads when your computer is started. These basic instructions test the computer to make sure it is operating properly and then recognize the various components including the CPU, memory, keyboard, monitor, and so forth.

After your computer is up and running, the BIOS continues to act as an interface between the computer and the operating system. The BIOS interprets commands to access hard drives, display information to the monitor, accept keystrokes from the keyboard, and monitor system conditions such as temperature.

Fortunately, most computer users never have to interact with their computer's BIOS. The only time you may need to access and use the BIOS directly is when you install a new hard drive or set the date after installing a new battery. You can access the BIOS by pressing the DELETE key on the keyboard just after starting the computer.

Operating Systems

An operating system is the underlying software that allows other programs—such as word processors, databases, and spreadsheets—to operate with similar menu choices, processes, and functions. The operating system, sometimes called an OS, is a set of rules that other programs must follow. The operating system serves as an intermediary, handling communications between your software and the computer's hardware.

Microsoft Windows is the most widely used computer operating system. There are several alternative operating systems including:

- Apple OS for Macintosh
- Unix
- Linux

Because Microsoft Windows is by far the most commonly used operating system in business today, we'll spend the rest of this chapter discussing the features of Windows.

How Does Microsoft Windows Work?

Microsoft Windows is computer operating system software. It is the software that many computer manufacturers are installing on computers so that they do something more than act as a very expensive paperweight. As the operating system, Microsoft Windows provides instructions to the computer's "brain" for how to access disk drives, how to print, and even how to add 2 + 2. Think of the operating system as the interface between you and the computer components. Tell the operating system what you want to do, and it completes the task—if it is told in the proper way. So, your job is to learn how to "communicate" with the computer operating system.

Microsoft Windows has a graphical user interface (GUI). In simple terms, everything can be done with a point and click from a mouse. Graphics are used to create an understandable interface with the user. With Microsoft Windows, you can graphically see what you need to do and can accomplish it through the graphic interface. The secret is to know what you want to accomplish.

The Windows Desktop

The screen you see when you turn on your computer and Windows loads is the Windows Desktop. As you use Windows, you will be rearranging, removing, and placing items on the Desktop, just like a real desktop. The Desktop includes a variety of features such as:

- Desktop icons like My Computer
- The Taskbar
- The Start button

The Taskbar occupies the bottom edge of the Desktop by default. It can be moved to the top or either side, or it can be made to disappear and reappear when you need it.

In Figure 11-1, we see a typical Desktop after newly installing Windows. The Taskbar along the bottom contains the Start button on the left and the time on the right. The little speaker next to the time is for a pop-up volume control, indicating that this computer is equipped with an audio card. Open applications and folders are represented by buttons on the Taskbar at the bottom of the screen. These buttons come and go depending on which programs or folders

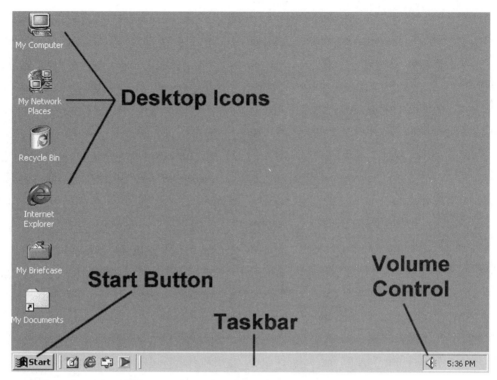

FIGURE 11-1. The Windows Desktop.

Screen shot reprinted by permission from Microsoft Corporation.

you have open at any given time. The icons on the left are for a number of folders and programs that are installed by default.

The Start Menu

The Start Menu is opened by clicking on the **Start** button at the left-hand end of the Taskbar. As an operating system, Windows presents an *interface* to you, the user. The job of the interface is to give you the means of commanding the computer to perform actions like launching programs, copying files, and activating a printer. Normally, once the operating system is started, you're supposed to know what to do next. Of course, new users often do not know what to do next, so Windows provides a clearly marked starting place, the Start button.

As a beginner, you will use the Start menu as home base for most operations you perform in Windows. Later, as you gain experience, you'll be creating folders and icons and will have the option of not using the Start menu as much. By the way, like most things in Windows, the Start menu may vary depending on certain programs and options that may be installed on your system. Also, the Start menu contains several options that have nothing to do with starting things. In fact, one command is Shut Down, the opposite of starting. Before we go any further, we'll need to mention two possibilities that may occur at any time, even though they may seem out of sequence at this point. The computer may be shut down, and individual programs, said to be "frozen" may be shut down.

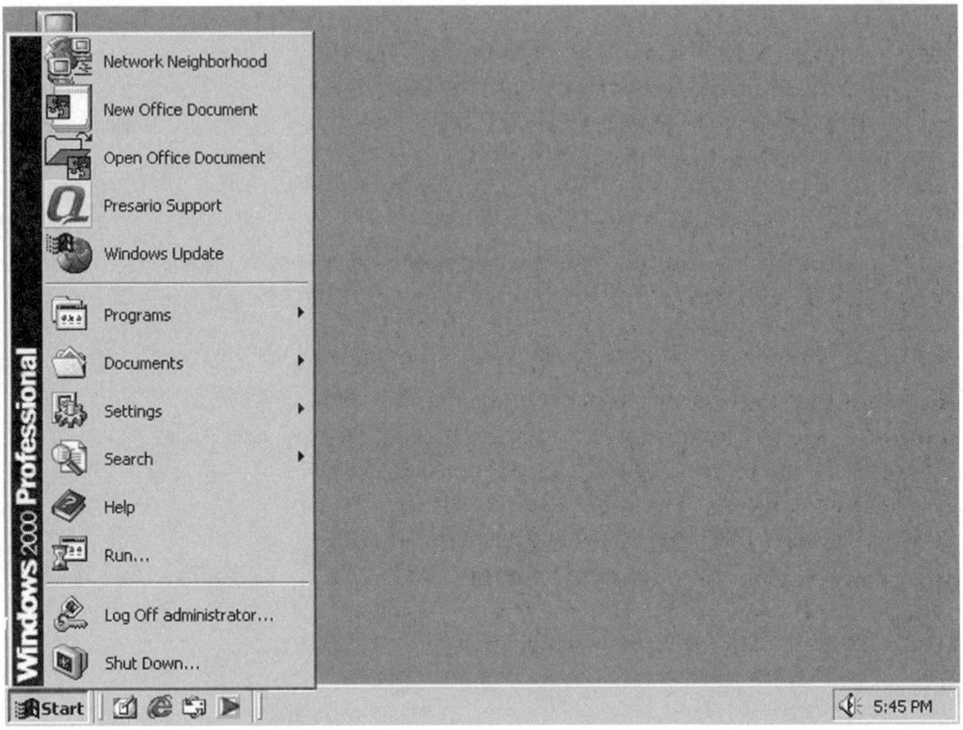

FIGURE 11-2. The Start Menu.

Screen shot reprinted by permission from Microsoft Corporation.

Shutting Down Windows

The bottom option on the Start menu is **Shut Down.** Although there is nothing to stop you from just switching off the computer, doing so without choosing the Shut Down procedure may result in lost data and corrupted files.

When you choose **Shut Down,** the screen dims and a new menu appears that gives you several options. Here you can click the **Yes** button to shut down, or make another selection first, *then* click **Yes.** If you choose to shut down, Windows will spend a few moments closing files, then will display a screen informing you that it is OK to turn off the power.

Closing a Frozen Program

If you have had any experience with personal computers, you will be familiar with the circumstance where the computer stops responding and becomes "frozen." Because Windows operates in *protected mode* with 32-bit applications (a technical term meaning that each 32-bit program can run independently of all other programs), it is often possible that the one program that is causing the problem can be closed, and others will continue to run normally.

Should your computer become frozen, you can press the CTRL + ALT + DEL keys simultaneously. When you do this, a list of tasks that are currently running will appear in a dialog box called Close Program.

From this task list, you can do one of four things: You can end the task (stop the program) that is causing the problem, perform a normal shut down, reboot (ie., restart) the computer immediately without a normal shut down, or cancel and return to where you left off. To end the task, you would make a guess at which program is causing the problem, select it from the list, then click **End Task.** If this does not un-freeze the computer, you can try a normal shut down by recalling the task list (by pressing CTRL + ALT + DEL again), then choosing **Shut Down.** If that doesn't work, you can press CTRL + ALT + DEL while the task list is displayed to force a system reset.

Starting a Program

The next option on the Start Menu that we'll look at is **Programs.** When the pointer is on Programs, a new menu appears to the right of the Start Menu.

As we'll discuss in more detail later, the little arrowheads to the right of some of the options means that another menu will appear when you point to that option. To start a program, you select it from the Programs Menu with your mouse and then click. The program will then load and appear on your screen.

Resizing a Window

If the program window occupies your entire screen with no part of the desktop background visible, it may be *maximized*. If your window is maximized, you'll see three buttons in the upper right corner of the window.

If the center button looks like Figure 11-3 (two small overlapping windows), your window is maximized. Each time you run a program, you'll notice that a new button appears on the Taskbar at the bottom of the screen. The button is labeled with the program name. When the Taskbar becomes crowded, the buttons are automatically made smaller to accommodate more of them. When the buttons are too small to show the program name, you can point to a button and wait a second or two, and the complete caption will appear in a little pop-up box.

To resize a window, you drag its border. You can do this my moving the mouse pointer to the border. When you are in the correct spot, the pointer will change to a two-headed arrow pointing left and right. You can then click and drag the window to a new size.

You can reshape both dimensions of a window by dragging the lower right corner. Position the mouse pointer over the corner until you see a diagonal sizing pointer. Then click and drag the mouse to change the dimensions. Some windows cannot be sized beyond certain limits. While using Windows, you'll frequently need to resize and move windows to arrange your desktop for efficiency.

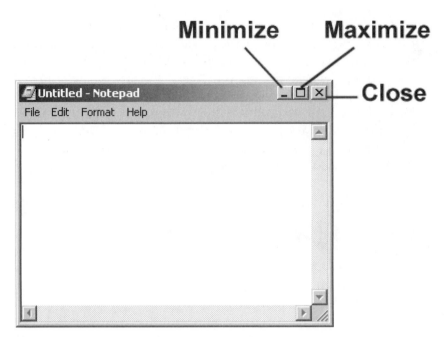

FIGURE 11-3. Minimize, Maximize, and Close Buttons.

Screen shot reprinted by permission from Microsoft Corporation.

Minimizing, Maximizing, Restoring, and Closing Windows

When you wish to get a window off the screen temporarily but have its program continue to run or its window instantly available, you can *minimize* it. To do this, you click the **Minimize** button in the top right corner of the screen (Figure 11-3). When you do this, you'll notice that the window appeared to zip down to the Taskbar. Technically, the window is still "open," so it appears on the Taskbar. To restore it, just click its button on the Taskbar.

If you need more space to work in an application window, you can *maximize* it to cover the entire screen. Just click the **Maximize** button in the top right corner of the window. If you maximize a window, the three buttons in the upper right corner of the window change. The Maximize button is replaced by a new button, called the Restore button. If you click the **Restore** button, the window returns it its original size.

When you wish to close a program or folder, you click the **Close** button in the upper right corner of the window. It is the button that is marked with an X.

Using Scroll Bars

When the material inside a window won't fit the current window size, scroll bars will automatically appear to allow you to move the view and reveal the rest of the space.

Within each scroll bar there is a scroll slider. At the ends of each scroll bar there are small arrow buttons. The length of the slider gives you some indication of the proportion of the whole that you are viewing. You use the scroll bars to move within the viewing space. To move a small increment at a time, you click on the arrow buttons at the ends of the scroll bars. You can also click and drag the slider up or down (or left or right on the horizontal scroll bar).

Using scroll bars is one of the basic techniques for using Windows. Scroll bars appear in windows, dialog boxes, and anywhere a screen display needs additional space for items.

Using Explorer to View Files and Folders

The program you use to manipulate files is called *Explorer*. You can start Explorer by clicking the **Start** button, then point to the Programs, and then click **Windows Explorer** near the bottom of the Programs Menu.

The window is divided into two panes (Figure 11-4). On the left is a tree diagram of disk drives and folders. On the right is a list of the files and folders contained within the selected folder in the tree. As you start the program, the selected folder is the current disk drive, Drive C. The address window shows **C:\.** On your computer this may be worded differently, because the screen shows the volume name of the hard disk.

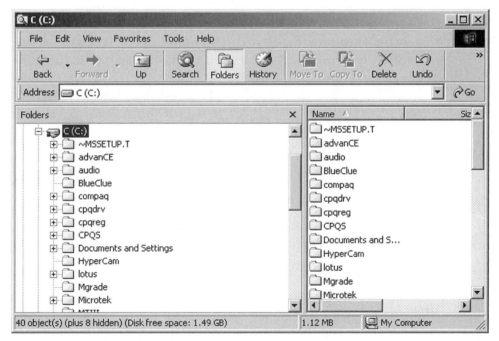

FIGURE 11-4. Windows Explorer.

Screen shot reprinted by permission from Microsoft Corporation.

11 ■ COMPUTER SOFTWARE

✳ Files and Folders

People talk about having information stored on their computers. The most common questions are where is the information stored, and how do you find it? Here are two definitions that you need to understand first.

File—A file is a document that has been created or an application that has been installed on the computer. Files are similar to piles of projects on your desk. They are the actual pieces with which you work.

Folder or Directory—A folder is a directory or the organizer for the files. Folders can be used to store all the pieces of a software package that are needed to run the software or to organize documents that are created. Folders organize files into logical groups. Folders can hold other folders. The first folder you come to is called the directory, and the folders inside the first folder are the sub-directories. The ultimate decision of how to organize a folder is up to you, since you will have to find and access files and folders for later use.

Placing a File in a Folder

To place a file in a folder, you only need to drag and drop it. When you drag the file, be sure to point to the icon, not the name of the file. Dragging by the name will work, but sometimes you'll try to drag a file that is already selected when you click it to drag it. If the file is already selected, clicking on the name switches to edit mode (so you can type a new name), and you can't drag it then. If you always drag the icon, you will avoid this potential pitfall. When you drag to the target folder, that folder will become highlighted when you are pointing at the correct spot.

Deleting a File or Folder

You use the same procedure to delete files and folders. When you delete a folder, all the files and other folders within it are also deleted. You can use one of three techniques to delete files or folders:

■ You can drag it to the Recycle Bin icon on your desktop.

■ You can open its context menu and click **Delete.**

■ You can select it and press the DELETE key on your keyboard.

✳ Windows Help

There are two types of help: the online help for Windows itself and the online help for the various applications running in Windows. Software manufacturers use the built-in facilities of Windows Help, so most applications have similar help features.

Table 11-1 lists ways you can call for help. Because applications differ, not all these methods are always available.

When you access Windows Help, you'll see three tabs along the top, labeled Contents, Index, and Find. Table 11-2 lists what they do. The most useful of these is the Index, since most often you know the topic you want help with.

TABLE 11-1	Windows Help
Help about Windows	Open Start Menu, click **Help.**
General help in an application	Open application's Help Menu.
Specific help about a current procedure	Press F1.
Help about a screen object	■ In some applications, click the **Toolbar Help** button, then click the object. ■ In some applications, press SHIFT + F1, then click the object. ■ In some applications (and Windows itself) dialog boxes have a question-mark button. Click it, then click the object in the box.
General help about a dialog box	Some dialog boxes have Help buttons. Also try F1.

Help from Applications

Applications have their own help systems. Usually, they use the same model as Windows, so they should look and behave in a familiar manner.

In many applications, pressing the F1 key while something is selected or while you are performing some function will give you help about the object or procedure. Since you often need help to *start* a procedure, you may find that selecting Help from the menu and using the search feature will be the most often-used technique.

Pop-Up Help

Some applications have automatic pop-up reminders to help you remember the functions of the various on-screen buttons. If you hold your mouse pointer over any of the buttons on a program's toolbar, a pop-up label appears, and a more detailed explanation is shown at the bottom of the window. Making the pointer remain still while pointing at an object is called *hovering* in some manuals. Many of the more recent Windows applications from different publishers use the pop-up help technique when you hover over a button.

Menus

Most applications and folder windows have menu bars. A menu bar is a list of menus. When you click the name of a menu it *drops down.* This is called *open-*

TABLE 11-2	Windows Help Features
Contents	Presents help like a book or outline with chapters, topics, and subtopics.
Index	Searches for key words in topics, like a book's index.
Find	Full text search for words within the entire help system including the body text of the help screens.

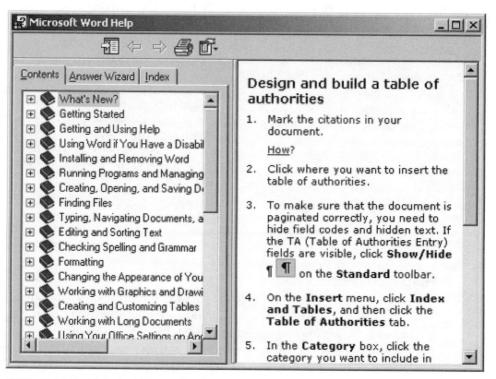

FIGURE 11-5. Help in Microsoft Word.

Screen shot reprinted by permission from Microsoft Corporation.

ing a menu or *pulling down* a menu. The most common menu choices include File, Edit, View, Tools, Window, and Help. In some menus, an arrowhead appears to the right of some of the listed options. This means that when you point to it, another menu will appear. Options that are followed by an ellipsis (three periods), will display a dialog box. Options with nothing after them will execute immediately.

Once a menu is opened, you can move to another menu with the mouse or with the left and right arrow keys. The same actions work vertically within each menu, so that you can point to an option with the mouse or use the up and down arrow keys to point to one.

You can close a menu without making a selection by clicking on the menu name again, clicking anywhere except on a menu option, or by pressing the ES-CAPE key (on the keyboard) twice.

Sometimes menus can be used to make settings, and the settings can be indicated on the menu. If you decide not to display, say, the Toolbar, you can click that item. The menu will close, and the Toolbar will disappear. The next time you open the View Menu, the Toolbar item will not be checked off.

Using Pop-up Context Menus

The right-hand mouse button is used often in Windows. Usually, it produces a pop-up menu that is sometimes called a context menu because it contains options appropriate for the specific object you are pointing to. Most applications use context menus, also.

Sometimes when a context menu appears, several of the options are grayed out. Grayed-out items do not work, because they are not appropriate for your current situation.

Objects on the Windows Desktop have their own context menus. If you point to any of the icons on the desktop and right click, a context menu appears.

Dialog Boxes

Often when you select an item from a menu, such as Print, a new small window will appear on the screen (Figure 11-6). These windows are called **Dialog Boxes.** Dialog boxes are used to adjust various settings. For example, with the Print Dialog Box, you can select the quality of the printing, the size of the paper, the number of copies, and so forth.

Within a Dialog Box you'll often use what are called **Radio Buttons.** Radio buttons are round, and the selected one has a dot in it. Radio buttons are always in groups of two or more, and one of them is always selected. When you select another one, the previously selected one is deselected, just like when you punch a station button on a car radio.

FIGURE 11-6. The Print Dialog in Microsoft Word.

Screen shot reprinted by permission from Microsoft Corporation.

11 ▪ COMPUTER SOFTWARE

Dialog boxes may also contain text entry boxes. When you click in one of these blanks, an insertion point (also called a cursor) will appear, indicating where the next character you type will appear. You can use this technique to edit the default value. By the way, typically in a numeric entry space, you will not be allowed to enter non-numbers.

To close a dialog box, you can choose one of the command buttons. Usually, you have a choice of **OK** and **Cancel.** Choosing OK closes the dialog box and accepts your entries. Cancel closes the dialog box but ignores any changes you made. If the dialog box also has a Close button in the upper right corner, it has the same effect as the Cancel button.

Saving Files

While working on a document, you'll want to save it frequently to prevent loss of any of your work. The first time you save a new document, you'll be prompted to give it a filename, and you'll need to select a folder in which to save it.

You can save by opening the File Menu and choosing **Save** or **Save As** (Figure 11-7). In an application such as Microsoft Word, you can click the **Save** button on the Toolbar. The first time you save an unnamed document, the Save As dialog box appears. Thereafter, each time you click the **Save** button, the document is saved immediately (no dialog box appears) under the same name. Should you wish to save it with a new name, you can open the File Menu and choose **Save As.**

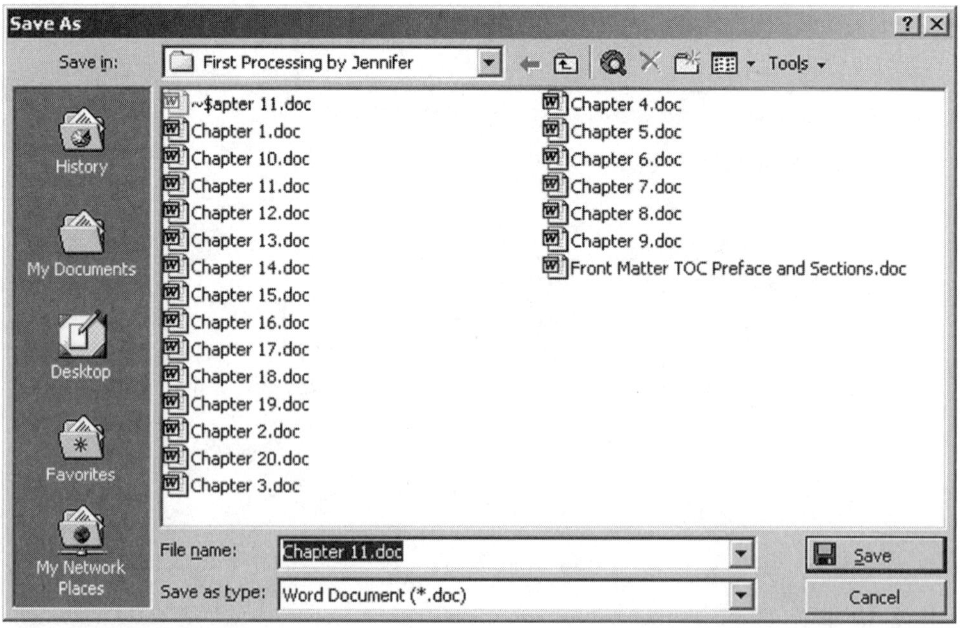

FIGURE 11-7. The Save As Dialog Box in Microsoft Word.

Screen shot reprinted by permission from Microsoft Corporation.

The Save As dialog box is called a **common dialog box** because Microsoft provides it as a tool that can be utilized by anyone writing programs for the Windows operating system. Most Microsoft programs and many applications from other companies use the common dialog boxes rather than design their own. This is a great advantage to users, since once they have learned the standard common dialog boxes, they will know how to perform the same function in many different programs.

The Save As and Open dialog boxes are very similar. They contain many of the features of the Explorer, including the ability to point to a drive and folder. In addition, the Save As and Open dialog boxes can be used for some file management tasks, such as deleting or renaming files and folders and creating new folders.

Whereas the basic function of the Open dialog box is to allow you to select or enter the name of the file you wish to open, the main function of the Save As dialog box is to allow you to choose where you wish to save a file and to give it a name of your choice.

The file is created on the disk. Once the file is saved the first time, you can continue to work on the document and save at intervals. When you click the **Save** button, the current version of the file will be saved immediately in the same folder and with the same filename, overwriting the previous version. This will happen without asking you for a filename.

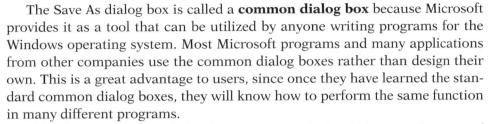 Printing Files

You can print a document by clicking the **File** Menu and then clicking **Print.** Many programs also have a print button on a toolbar. Sometimes this button will cause the Print dialog box to open, but many times, the toolbar button will make the document print one copy immediately to the currently selected printer without displaying the dialog box.

On the Print dialog box, you can choose which printer you wish to use, in case you have more than one such as you might on a network. You can also choose what portion of the document you want to print and the number of copies. Though this is the common dialog box for printing in Windows, other applications will often use different, though similar, boxes. Usually, they will offer additional options.

Windows will also allow you to print by dragging and dropping a file icon onto a printer icon.

Finding a File

The Find program is a very useful tool, so we're going to cover it in some detail here. You can start it several ways, but the most convenient way is the F3 key. When you press F3 on the keyboard, the Find dialog box appears. When you command Find to locate a file, it will begin searching from the folder or drive shown in the **Look in** blank. If you specify a folder as the starting point for the search, Windows will find it faster.

If you open a folder—either in Explorer or in its own window—then start Find with F3, that folder will be the Look in folder.

Here is an important note. The F3 key does not start Find unless the Desktop, Taskbar, a folder, or Explorer has the focus. In other words, if you are working in an application, that application's window will have the focus, and the F3 key will perform whatever function is assigned to it by the application. If the application does not use the F3 key, nothing will happen when you press it. If you want to start Find while working in an application, be sure to click the Desktop or the Taskbar first. Some applications, such as the Microsoft Office suite, have their own built-in Find-like features, so in actual practice, you will probably seldom use the Windows Find program while running an application.

Wildcard Searches

You can search for files by entering only part of the filename, or you can limit your search by using special symbols called wildcards (see Table 11-3). For example, you can find all files on drive C with *win* in the filename. A fairly long list of files should appear. The files can appear in several formats. The window containing the list of files acts exactly like a folder containing files or the Explorer. You can move and copy files, delete them, or work with them in the appropriate application. You can sort and reverse-sort the listed files by clicking on the column headers.

You can also use wildcards similar to those used in old DOS to search for files. Although your system may be set so that it does not show all the three-character extensions for the filenames, they are still used, even with long filenames. For instance, if you wish to display all the executable program files, you can use the wildcard *.exe. That tells Windows to find all files, regardless of name, with the extension "exe."

TABLE 11-3 Wildcards That Can Be Used With Find

Name	What will be searched for
*	All files and folders
.	All files and folders
*.	All files (not folders)
xyz	All files and folders with xyz in the name or extension
xyz	All files and folders with xyz in the name or extension
*.xyz	All files with the extension xyz
xyz.*	All files with the name xyz and any (or no) extension
?xyz	All files and folders where xyz is preceded by one or more characters
??xyz	All files and folders where xyz is preceded by at least two characters
x?yz	All files and folders where x is followed by one unknown character, then the letters y and z

Date Searches

Each time you create a file, the date and time are saved with the name. When the file is modified, the date and time are updated. Sometimes you might need to find a file whose name you do not remember, but you know you modified it in the last two or three days. The first place to look would be the Documents option on the Start Menu, since it remembers the last 15 files you modified. Failing that, you can have Find show you files in a certain date period.

Advanced Searches

Finally, you can find files and folders based on type, size, or even text contained in the file. When searching for text, you should be aware that such searches may take a while, so you should narrow the search as much as possible by specifying a specific folder, if possible, or other criteria such as date.

Shortcuts

Shortcuts are small files (with the extension .LNK) that "point" to other files, folders, and programs. When you open a shortcut, the object to which it points opens. This allows you to store objects in an appropriate place in the hierarchy of folders, but access them from another location, usually the Desktop or the Start Menu. So, for example, the Calculator program is stored in the Windows folder. It might just as easily be stored in some folder several layers deep. That might be the best place to keep it so that your computer is properly organized, but it makes it difficult to find when you want to use it. One solution to this problem is to place a shortcut on the Desktop. You can place a shortcut in any folder.

The Desktop itself is actually a folder. The rule is, when you drag a *program* (application) object to a folder, such as the Desktop, the default action is to create a *shortcut*. However, when you drag a *file* or *folder* to a folder, the default action is to *move* (if the folder is on the same drive), or *copy* (if the folder is on a different drive). Since this can get confusing for many people, we suggest that you always *right*-drag objects, then pick the action you want from the Menu.

How to Use Shortcuts

You should use shortcuts almost all the time. You can rename them all you want without affecting the original, and you can place copies in as many folders as you want. Almost all objects on the Desktop are shortcuts. You rarely place an original program, file, or folder on the Desktop.

Deleting Files, Folders, and Shortcuts

You can delete files, folders, and shortcuts by selecting them, then either dragging them to the Recycle Bin icon, pressing the DELETE key on your keyboard, or opening the right-click Context Menu and choosing **Delete.**

Recovering Deletions

If you wish to recover a file, you can do so by just dragging it out of the Recycle Bin window (see also Table 11-4). The Recycle Bin can be set so that once the files in the Recycle folder occupy a certain percentage of space on the drive, the oldest files will be automatically deleted permanently. You can also manually permanently delete files from the Recycle folder by selecting them in the Recycle Bin window and deleting them *again* using either the DELETE key or the **Delete** command from the Context Menu. You can also right-click the mouse on the **Recycle Bin** and click **Empty Recycle Menu** from the Context Menu.

The My Computer Icon

The drive icons are in the My Computer folder, which is placed in the upper left corner of the Desktop when a new copy of Windows is installed on the computer. If you prefer to use the drive icons for file management, rather than the Explorer, it is a good idea to place shortcuts on the Desktop.

Formatting Diskettes

Though diskette drives are not used as often as in the past, there will be times when you'll want to copy files to a diskette for backup purposes or to move them to another computer. Before a diskette can be used, it must be formatted. Most diskettes come already formatted, but sometimes they do not, or sometimes you might wish to format a diskette to refresh it and erase all the files and folders on it. To format a disk, do the following:

1. Place a diskette in the diskette drive.
2. Right-click the **Drive A** icon (shortcut) on your Desktop.
3. Click **Format.**

The Format dialog box allows you to perform a full format or a quick format. A full format is performed on new unformatted diskettes or disks that have some sort of data error. In this procedure, new tracks and sectors are laid out on the disk. A quick format is designed to erase the contents of a disk that has been previously formatted. Diskettes can be assigned *volume names*, also

TABLE 11-4	What Happens When You Delete an Object
Object	**What Happens When Deleted**
File	The file is moved to a special folder called **Recycle Bin.**
Folder	All files in the folder as well as files in subfolders, if any, are moved to the **Recycle Bin.** The folder(s) are erased when you select **Empty Trash.**
Shortcut	The shortcut is moved to the **Recycle Bin,** but not the object to which it points. It remains untouched.

known as a *label*. These are seldom used. Two options in the dialog box allow you to place system files on a diskette, which will make it possible to boot your computer from the diskette instead of the hard drive. This is seldom done, and if you need a system disk, a better method to create one is through the Control Panel's Add/Remove Programs icon, which we'll look at later.

Control Panel

The Control Panel contains a group of utility programs that allows you to make adjustments to your computer, the Windows operating system, and the drivers for hardware devices. Certain icons are added to the Control Panel when you install programs and features in Windows. The most commonly used utility programs are:

- Add/Remove
- Mouse
- Date/Time
- Printers
- Display

Add/Remove Programs

When you purchase a new program, you can run its installation program from the Add/Remove Programs icon. From this dialog box you can click the **Install** button to install a new program. It also shows a list of programs designed for

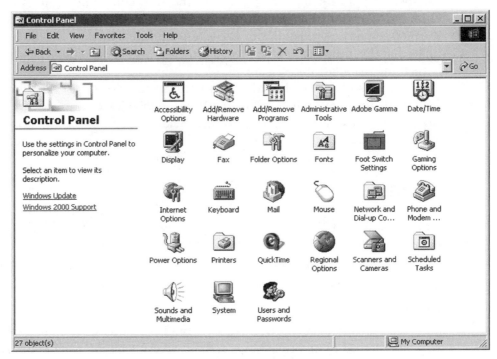

FIGURE 11-8. The Control Panel in Microsoft Windows.

Screen shot reprinted by permission from Microsoft Corporation.

11 ■ COMPUTER SOFTWARE

Windows that have been installed on your computer. If you wish to remove one of these programs, you can select it from the list. Windows will erase the program including all corollary files and undo any changes that were made to the system when the software was installed.

This option can be used to create a diskette that will boot your computer. This is recommended in case of a problem involving startup software or the hard disk drive. If you do not have such a diskette for your computer, you should create one and put it away for safe keeping. If your computer should fail to start some day, a technician may need the startup disk.

The Add/Remove Programs feature of the Control Panel provides a wizard for software installation. Once Add/Remove Programs is open, the wizard walks you through the installation process, step by step. The wizard looks for a disk with installation instructions in the (A:) drive. If the instructions are not found, the wizard then looks on the CD drive. If it does not find an installation program, you can browse to find it.

If you have software that needs to be installed, do the following:

1. Click the **Start Menu.**

2. Highlight **Settings.**

3. Click **Control Panel.**

4. Double-click the **Add/Remove Programs** icon.

5. Follow the instructions from the wizard for installation.

INSTALLATION FILE

Another method for installing is to use the Run command. You will need to know the name of the installation program. Usually, the installation program is called setup.exe or install.exe. The extension .exe following the file name signifies that the file is executable. Because these files are executable files, they will launch the installation software.

To install software with the Run command, select **Run** from the **Start** Menu. Locate the installation file by clicking **Browse.** Navigate your way to the drive that contains the installation disk or CD. Select the file with the .exe extension and click **Open.** Clicking **OK** will initiate the installation process and prompt you with the appropriate instructions to complete the task.

Date/Time

Your computer contains an internal clock and calendar. Incidentally, you can make this same dialog box appear by right-clicking the clock on the Taskbar. Date/Time allows the user to set the date and time on the computer's clock. The computer clock is used to label files as to the date and time they are created and modified.

Display

Your screen can be customized through the Display icon. This dialog box can also be accessed by right-clicking on the Desktop and choosing **Properties.**

The "background" is the surface of the Desktop. It can be set to a color and pattern, or you can make it display a graphic file. A graphic file displayed on the background is called **Wallpaper.** The Background tab allows you to set a pattern or choose a graphic file for wallpaper.

The Appearance tab has settings for color. A pattern overlays the background to add interest. Patterns do not change the basic color of the background, though one of the patterns—50% Gray—will darken whatever color is displayed.

Wallpaper graphics can be small, or fill the entire screen. If they are small, Windows gives you the option of repeating them to fill the entire screen. This is called **Tiling.** You can make your own wallpaper files in Windows Paint, if you like. Once you make the file, you just use the Browse button to tell Windows the name and location of the file.

Besides setting the colors of the standard parts of the Windows screen, you can set a number of other things, such as spacing of icons, the fonts used in title bars and menus, and so on. Once you have set your screen to the way you like it, you can just begin using Windows, and your settings will become the default. If you would like to change to other arrangements from time to time, you can save your settings as a **scheme** by giving it a name. Windows has a group of pre-set schemes, too.

SCREEN SAVER

Another popular feature is the Screen Saver. This is a screen that appears after a preset time period of no activity. The original purpose of screen savers was to prevent static images from burning in and damaging the monitor's screen. Modern monitors are rarely damaged by static images, but screen savers are a very popular way of personalizing computers, and most monitor manufacturers still recommend them.

SETTINGS

The Settings tab of the Display Dialog is where you can change the resolution of your monitor and the number of colors displayed. Typical resolutions are 640 × 480, 800 × 600, and 1,024 × 768. Color resolution ranges from 16 colors to 32 bit (true-color).

Mouse

You can modify the settings of your mouse to make it comfortable for yourself. When you run the Mouse Utility you will see four tabs on the dialog box. The first tab, Buttons, allows you to reverse the buttons. Left-handed users may prefer to have the buttons reversed. The left button takes on the actions of the right button, and vice versa. You can also set the double-click speed, and there is a little test area to check the different double-click settings.

You can choose different mouse pointers, including animated ones. You can also save your choices in a scheme, just as you can for the appearance options.

Printers

You may have one or more printer icons, each one representing a printer that is available to you, either connected to your computer or through a network. Though you will usually print while using an application, you can also drag a document file from the Explorer or a folder window and drop it on a printer icon. This will cause the document's associated application to start and print the document.

In most cases, a print job is **spooled** first, which means the output from the application is sent to a temporary disk file, then to the printer. This allows large print jobs to be transferred to the spool file quickly, allowing you to go on working while the document is printed from the spooler. If you print several jobs in rapid succession, they will form a queue, waiting for the printer to become available. Or, if you are attached to a network, several other people may be printing on the same printer, and all the documents will form a queue.

The printer icon in the Control Panel allows you to view the queue. The window that appears is where the print queue would be shown. On networks, unless you are the system administrator, you cannot rearrange or cancel print jobs except your own.

Applications Software

In addition to your computer's operating system, there are many other software programs available for particular applications. These programs, often called **applications software,** are your primary tools in a business computing environment. They are designed to accomplish specific tasks or applications such as word processing, database management, or accounting.

Most applications software comes with reference manuals and even special templates for the keyboard. Some have online help and tutorials to help you learn how to use them. Most applications software is contained on a CD-ROM. If your computer is equipped with a hard drive, you install the applications software on your hard drive to make it easier and faster to access. To install, you copy the program from the CD to the hard drive. The exact way you install an application is discussed in the first few pages of the program's user manual. The installation process will allow you to customize the software to your particular computer configuration. In this way, the software will know what type of printer you are using, what type of monitor, and where you want to save the data files it creates.

The following is a list of major types of applications software:

- Accounting
- Charting/graphing
- Clip art
- Communications
- Computer-aided design (CAD)
- Database management
- Desktop publishing
- Drawing
- Educational programs
- Electronic mail
- Integrated software
- Multimedia
- Music composition
- Optical character recognition
- Personal organizers
- Personal productivity
- Presentation graphics
- Programming tools

- Project managers
- Security
- Software emulators
- Software instruction
- Specialty printing

- Spreadsheets
- Statistics
- Virus detection
- Web browsers
- Word processing

Database Management

✳ Creating and Using a Database

Database management systems are efficient tools for organizing and processing large amounts of information, for example, your company's accounting
work, inventory customer records, and mailing lists. **Data** refers to individual
items of information such as a customer's name, address, or phone number. A
database is a collection of data, such as a mailing list. A **database management system** is computer software that allows you to store and manage the
data in your database.

Although the various database programs available are different, the key to
all of them is the way you organize your data. Let's say you want to keep a list
of the company's customers. You might start with their names, addresses, and
telephone numbers. With this list, you can easily look up telephone numbers
or print out mailing labels to send out a marketing newsletter. But what if you
wanted to know which customers purchased a particular product or service
from the company or how much they spent? To do this, you would have to keep
additional information about each customer.

✳ Fields, Records, and Files

To begin creating your database, you need to define its structure. Most database management systems provide a screen that prompts you through this procedure. "To define the structure," means to determine the **fields** that go into
your database. A field is a single category of information. Thus, the fields in an
address database might include customer name, street address, city, state, zip
code, and telephone number (Figure 12-1). Each of the fields needs to be defined individually and to be given a name. You must also tell the database
whether the field will contain text information or numbers and what the maximum number of characters per field is.

Once all of your fields are determined, the next step is to enter information
or data into your database. A record is a single entry of information. Thus, in
a mailing list database, a single record is one person's name, address, city, state,

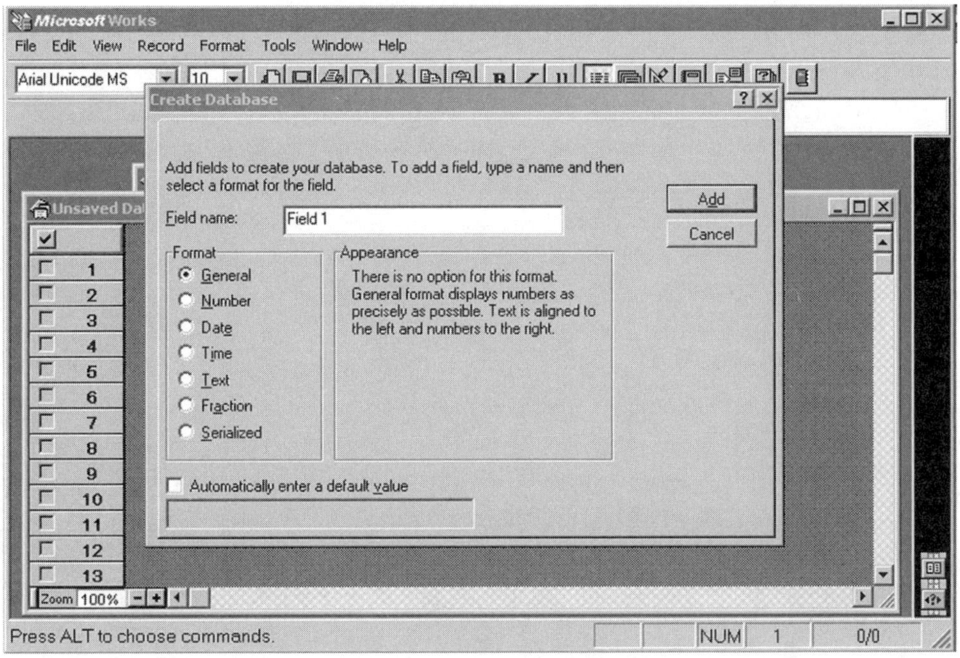

FIGURE 12-1. A database created using Microsoft Works.

Screen shot reprinted by permission from Microsoft Corporation.

and zip code (Figure 12-2). Most database management programs have enough room for thousands of records to be entered into the database, limited only by the amount of storage space available on your computer. You may view the data in your database by looking at individual records one at a time or by displaying a table showing your data arranged in rows and columns (Figure 12-3). To assist you in entering records, database management software programs provide a data entry form, although many programs allow you to design your own form. With the data entry display form on the screen, you only have to fill in the blanks. When one record is entered into the system, the program will display a new blank form.

Adding new records or updating previous records is relatively simple with most database programs. New records can be added to the end of your file of records. Changes to existing records can be made by accessing a record, erasing the current information, and then typing the update in its place.

Sorting and Searching

Sorting the Data

Once you've added some records, you can begin tapping the power of the database management software (Figure 12-4). One of the first things you may want to do is to sort the database. Indexing and sorting capabilities allow you to rearrange all the records in a meaningful order. Let's say you want to sort the records alphabetically by last name. In this case, the "last name" field would be

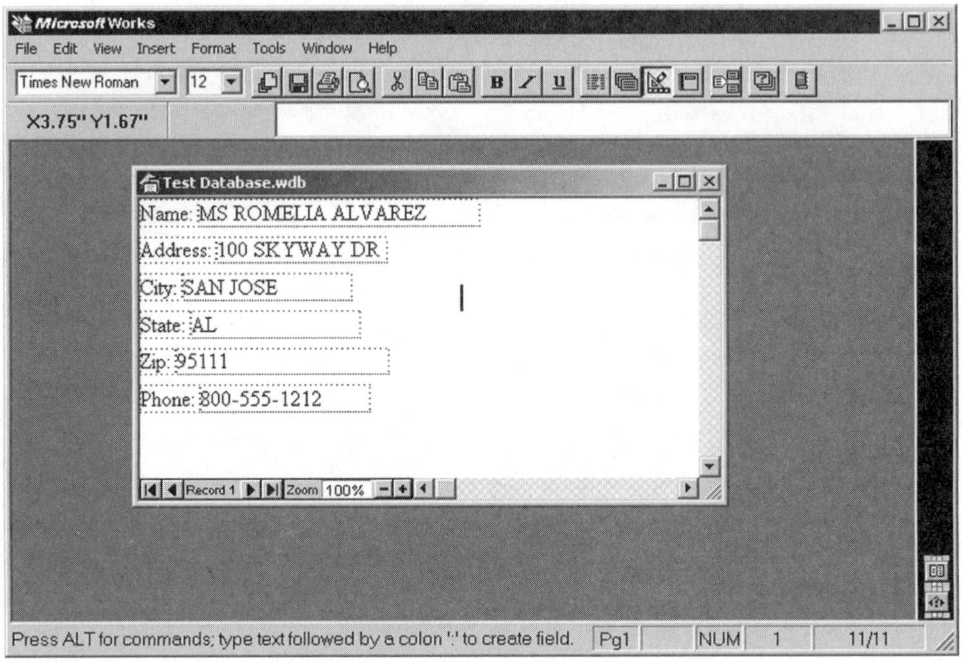

FIGURE 12-2. A record in a Microsoft Works database.
Screen shot reprinted by permission from Microsoft Corporation.

the key or primary field, the field that determines the sort order. The first name may be the secondary field, the field that determines the sort order in a case where two last names are identical.

Another use for your database is to extract information that meets a specific criterion, whether narrow or broad. You can choose simple criteria, such as displaying the address of a person named John Doe or locating the records for

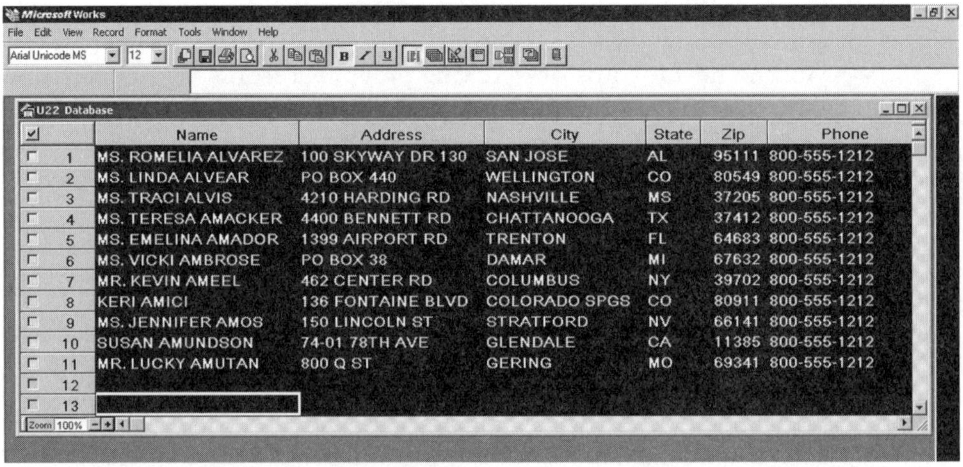

	Name	Address	City	State	Zip	Phone
1	MS. ROMELIA ALVAREZ	100 SKYWAY DR 130	SAN JOSE	AL	95111	800-555-1212
2	MS. LINDA ALVEAR	PO BOX 440	WELLINGTON	CO	80549	800-555-1212
3	MS. TRACI ALVIS	4210 HARDING RD	NASHVILLE	MS	37205	800-555-1212
4	MS. TERESA AMACKER	4400 BENNETT RD	CHATTANOOGA	TX	37412	800-555-1212
5	MS. EMELINA AMADOR	1399 AIRPORT RD	TRENTON	FL	64683	800-555-1212
6	MS. VICKI AMBROSE	PO BOX 38	DAMAR	MI	67632	800-555-1212
7	MR. KEVIN AMEEL	462 CENTER RD	COLUMBUS	NY	39702	800-555-1212
8	KERI AMICI	136 FONTAINE BLVD	COLORADO SPGS	CO	80911	800-555-1212
9	MS. JENNIFER AMOS	150 LINCOLN ST	STRATFORD	NV	66141	800-555-1212
10	SUSAN AMUNDSON	74-01 78TH AVE	GLENDALE	CA	11385	800-555-1212
11	MR. LUCKY AMUTAN	800 Q ST	GERING	MO	69341	800-555-1212
12						
13						

FIGURE 12-3. A table view of a database created in Microsoft Works.
Screen shot reprinted by permission from Microsoft Corporation.

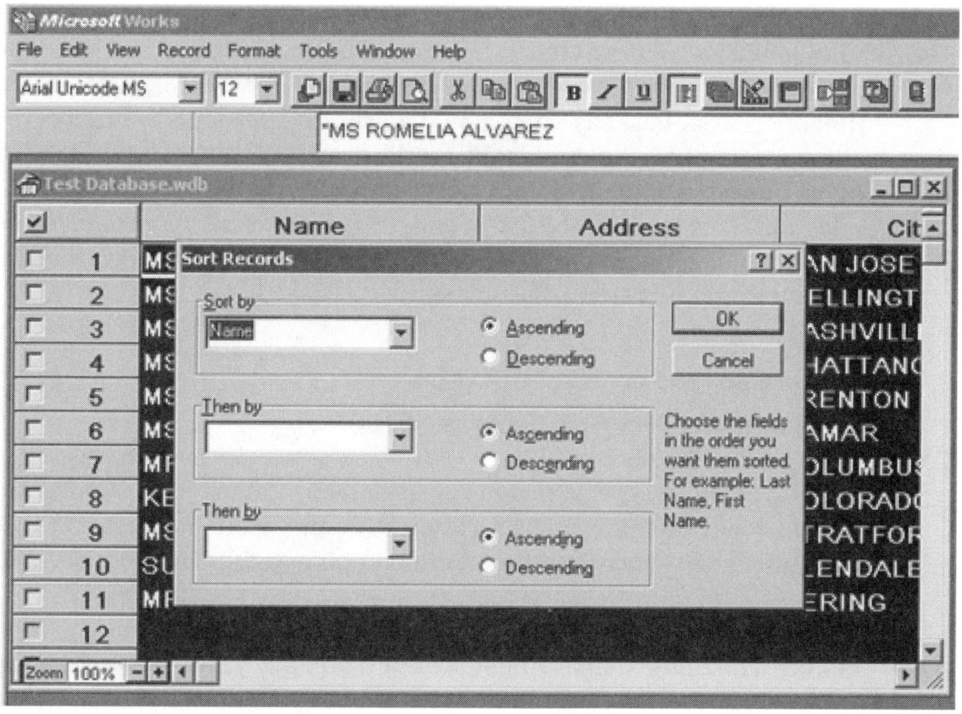

FIGURE 12-4. Sorting a database with Microsoft Works.

Screen shot reprinted by permission from Microsoft Corporation.

all persons who reside in the state of Texas. You can also use complex criteria. For example, in an accounts database, you may want a list of all persons within the 214 area code who have unpaid account balances as of September 1.

One advanced feature found on some database programs is the ability to perform mathematical functions. By creating a field that contains numerical information, a report can calculate totals for that field. This feature comes in handy when you are using a database program for keeping track of financial records.

Database management software handles all these tasks easily. You tell the database what type of information you need; the database extracts and displays only those records that meet your requirements. This process of extracting information is also called **querying the database**. You ask the database questions, and it gives you the answers.

Conducting a Search

The fastest way to find specific information in a database is to conduct a **search.** Most database management programs have a search feature that can be accessed via a keyboard command or a pull-down menu. When the command Search is selected, you are asked to type in comparison information. The program then searches the database for any records containing the comparison information and displays any that do.

To find more complex associations between your data, record selection rules, often called **arguments,** are used. These special commands combine the power of sorting with searching to find records that match a certain combination of criteria. Let's say you wanted a list of people who live in a certain state and have purchased a product or service from you but spent under $100 on it. Many database management programs use Boolean logic to narrow down the selection. This involves the use of *and, or, not, less than, more than, equal to, not equal to, blank, not blank,* and so forth. For example, our record selection argument might be listed as following:

State Field Contains: Texas

Purchase Field Contains: Not Blank

Purchase Amount Field Contains: <$100

To create a record selection, most database management programs use a menu system that allows a user to type in comparison information (arguments) and to select from various choices to combine arguments (Figure 12-5).

Printing the Information

Finally, a database management program organizes and prints the information you've selected in the form that you need it. Printed output from a database is referred to as a **report.** A report may be a list of names, a customer invoice, or a monthly statement. In any case, most database management programs allow

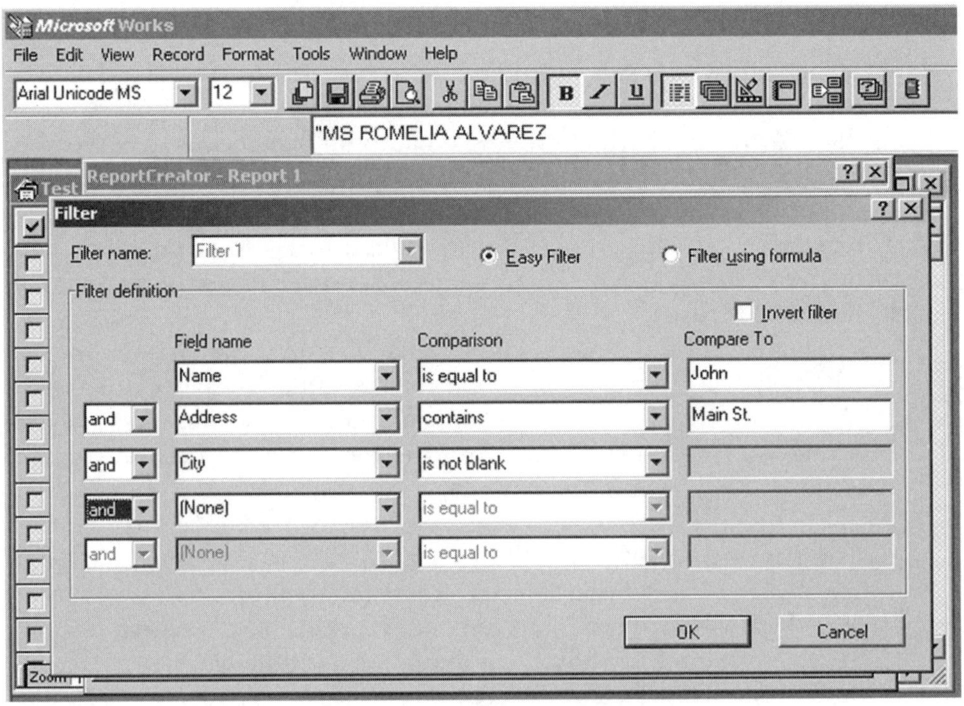

FIGURE 12-5. Creating a search report in Microsoft Works.

Screen shot reprinted by permission from Microsoft Corporation.

you to design your reports to include as much or as little information as you want in a layout that suits your needs. Some programs are designed to display and print data on specific forms such as insurance forms, tax forms, and other business forms. Many office forms suppliers have a list of forms and compatible database software.

Types of Databases

As an administrative assistant, you'll probably most often see two basic types of databases: The **file manager** and the **relational database.** The file manager is the simpler type of database, acting much like a regular filing cabinet. You use it when you need to organize a single group of information, such as a name and address file or a telephone record. Some database management applications are mainly designed for use with file manager software.

Other programs allow you to create a more complex type of database—a relational database. This type of system relates information in one database file to information in another by tying together key fields using a link such as a customer ID number. Suppose you had two databases: a customer address database and a customer order database. These two databases are linked by one common field: a customer ID number. When you type the customer ID number into an order, the order database retrieves the name and address of a customer from the address database. Thus, you would not have to type in the customer's name and address each time you completed a new order, saving you time and energy and reducing the opportunity for mistakes.

Applications

In general, software applications that allow you to develop only file-manager type databases are less expensive and easier to learn and to use than relational databases. Here is a list of some common file managers and relational database programs:

- Corel Paradox
- dBASE from dBASE.com
- FileMaker from FileMaker.com
- IBM's DB2
- IBM Lotus Approach
- IBM's Lotus Notes
- Microsoft Access
- Microsoft Works
- Oracle from Oracle
- Personal RecordKeeper from Nolo

Computer Networking

Connecting with Other Computers

Using a personal computer on the job can lead to substantial improvements in your productivity and organization. Being able to connect with other computers to share information or perhaps to share a printer can produce even more surprising results. There are two ways to connect computers together: telecommunications and networking.

Telecommunications involves connecting computers via telephone lines. This is accomplished with a hardware device called a **modem.** The computer that receives calls from other computers and stores information that can be retrieved is often called the **host computer.** Other computers that access the host computer are called **remote computers.** These terms are used as a way to distinguish the two computers when they are connected.

Networking involves linking computers together using special coaxial cable within an office or office building complex. Each computer connected to the network can communicate with any other computer on the network (Figure 13-1). This allows for sharing of files and printers and intra-office electronic mail. Usually, one computer is set up to provide storage for important data files and programs. This computer is called the **server,** because it provides access to needed resources whenever a computer user on the network needs them.

Modems

There are two general types of modems: **internal** and **external** (Figures 13-2 and 13-3). External modems connect to your computer through one cable and to a telephone line through another cable. An internal modem is inserted inside the computer into an expansion slot. It does not require a cable to connect it to the computer, but you still must connect it to the telephone line.

The purpose of a modem is to convert data to a form that can be sent over telephone lines. At the other end, another modem receives the transmission and converts it back into data that a computer can understand.

FIGURE 13-1. A diagram of a computer network.

Graphic by Jerome Brown.

FIGURE 13-2. External modem.

Courtesy of Zoom. All rights reserved.

FIGURE 13-3. Internal modem for a laptop computer.

Courtesy of Zoom. All rights reserved.

Modem performance is measured in the number of bits of data that can be transmitted per second, called the **baud rate.** The most common baud rate available for modems is 56K.

Communications Software

In order to use a modem with your computer, you must have a telecommunications program. There are many available, such as the dial-up networking feature available within Microsoft Windows. These programs are often called **dialers.**

A dialer will let your computer communicate with the modem to perform such functions as dialing or answering the telephone, establishing links with another computer, and automatically checking for errors in data transmissions.

Most communications programs allow the user to select a **communications protocol,** a set of rules and procedures used for transmitting data between two computers (see Figure 13-4). In most cases, the protocol you use will be determined by the host computer. Whatever protocol and settings the host computer is using, you must also use.

One of the main reasons to connect two computers is to transfer files. You might want to send someone a word processing document or a spreadsheet so he or she can review it, or you might want to get a similar document from this

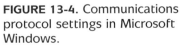

FIGURE 13-4. Communications protocol settings in Microsoft Windows.

Screen shot reprinted by permission from Microsoft Corporation.

person's computer. Most communications software has various commands that allow you to send or receive a file. When you send a file to another computer, it is called **uploading.** When you receive a file, it is called **downloading.**

Networking

Yet another useful purpose for computer communications is the linking of computers together within a single office or office building; this is known as **networking.** Networking requires two main components: special network hardware and network software. Together, the parts of this system are known as a **Local Area Network** (LAN).

Networks are useful for sharing data, storing large amounts of information, and sharing expensive equipment such as laser printers. With a network, you can run multi-user programs such as database and order-entry and accounting systems. Each worker in the office using a computer connected to the network can add or retrieve information or share common peripherals such as the printer or hard drive.

The Physical Setup

The physical setup of a network is called its **topology.** The best-known topologies are named roughly for their descriptions: **ring, star,** and **bus.** A ring topology contains computers and devices set in a closed loop. In a star topology, computers and devices are connected to a central computer like spokes on a wheel. A bus topology connects the devices in a line with additions put at the end. Also, you can connect various smaller networks together.

In a small business, a network may just be two computers linked together to share a printer. In small networks like this, each computer has equal status so that each person can access the disk drives of the other computer or the printer. This is called a **peer-to-peer** network. In larger businesses, there may be a central dedicated computer with a large-capacity disk drive to which all the other computers are connected. The central computer is known as a **file server,** and the other remote computers are called **nodes.**

The benefits of networking are twofold: lower costs and greater efficiency. By having its employees share hardware, such as a storage server, a business doesn't have to purchase expensive devices for each user. Sharing software allows everyone who uses it to perform tasks in exactly the same way. Sharing software also allows multiple users to work on projects together. When working collaboratively, groups of users can complete large projects in less time. Improved communications using e-mail software allows users to coordinate schedules and encourages other efficiencies throughout an organization.

Networks can be configured using different hardware, protocols, and transmission media depending on the type of network being created. A protocol is a data transmission convention encompassing timing, control, formatting, and data representation. Most of the differences between network types are based on what protocol is used. The following is a list of network protocols and their speeds. Speeds are usually calculated in megabits per seconds: 100 megabits per second (100 Mbps) is equal to 1 megabyte (1 MB) per second. 1000 megabits per second is equal to one gigabit per second (1 Gbps) (see Table 13-1).

Hardware and Software

Network hardware usually consists of a network interface card along with special cables to link the computers together. Some computers, such as Macintosh computers with their Appletalk networking capability, have built-in network interfaces. All that is needed in these cases is cabling to link the computers.

Peer-to-peer LANs are usually smaller localized networks for a single workgroup, for example a single office. A peer-to-peer network is usually the first type of network utilized by a workgroup, because it causes the least amount of disruption and is the least expensive. Users can continue working on their computers as they've done before the network was installed; however, they can now share resources and data.

A peer-to-peer LAN requires the following:

■ A network interface card installed in each computer

■ Cabling that links all of the network interface cards

■ An operating system, such as Windows or Macintosh OS

■ Optionally, a network hub may be used as a central connection point for all the computers on the network

To manage the network, special LAN software is required. This software keeps up with the sending and delivering of information and manages use of the printer and other common peripherals.

Every user on a network has a password. You can connect to the network by typing in your name and your password. Once you are on, you have access to the extra disk drives and printers. You can run programs stored on other computers and access data files. In some cases, you can prevent other users

TABLE 13-1 Network Protocols and Their Speeds

Network Protocol	Speed
Token Ring Type 3	4 Mbps
10Base-T Ethernet	10 Mbps
Token Ring Type 1	16 Mbps
100Base-T Fast Ethernet	100 Mbps
Fiber Distributed Data Interface (FDDI)	100 Mbps
Asynchronous Transfer Mode (ATM)	155 to 622 Mbps
Gigabit Ethernet	1.25 Gbps
Fibre Channel	1.3 Gbps to 4 Gbps
SONET (Optical)	10 Gbps to 20 Gbps
Dense Wavelength Division Multiplexing (DWDM)	Up to 240 Gbps

from having access to certain confidential files stored on a particular computer. For instance, accounting records or personal data can be locked so that a special password is required for access.

Internet and Intranets

The Internet has existed for decades as a tool for scientists and the military. However, in 1989 a hypertext language with links was created that gave birth to the World Wide Web. The Internet is now a vast network of networks that link the world. It is accessed by hundreds of millions of users using dial-up modems, Digital Subscriber Line (DSL), cable, and satellites. Web information is distributed to personal computers, palmtops, personal digital assistants, smart phones, set-top boxes, and televisions.

The speed of computer connections on the Internet is increasing. Table 13-2 shows the three primary means of connecting to the Internet along with an approximate number of users in the United States.

Intranets are networks connecting computer resources within an organization or company. Unlike the Internet, intranets are private and restrict access. Usually intranets are extended LANs using Ethernet or another dedicated network protocol.

TABLE 13-2 Approximate Number of Users in the United States Connected to the Internet

Medium	Data Rate	Users in year 2000	Users (projected) in year 2006
Cable	1.5 Mbps to 10 Mbps	1.3 million	40 million
DSL	1.5 Mbps to 6 Mbps	300,000	25 million
Modem	56 Kbps	48 million	135 million

E-Mail

E-mail is short for **electronic mail.** It involves the exchange of written messages sent over computer networks such as the Internet. In many offices, e-mail has replaced written memos, drop-by office visits, and even phone calls. E-mail provides a written record of office communications. You can send messages to groups of people simultaneously, attach files, and include hyperlinks to Web sites. E-mail is one of the most popular and effective tools for communicating with others over the Internet. With e-mail, you can send a message to anyone in the world who has e-mail access—and, barring technical difficulties, the message will be received in a matter of minutes.

E-Mail Accounts

An e-mail account allows you to connect to a network and the Internet. This is done through an Internet Service Provider or **ISP.** The ISP helps you get connected to the network using a dial-up telephone connection, DSL, cable modem, or satellite modem. When you establish an account with an ISP, the ISP will provide you with the following:

- E-mail Address—In most cases, this will be your name or nickname, followed by the @ sign and an ISP identifier that will most commonly end with the extension .com or .net.

- POP Server—This is the name of your incoming mail server. POP stands for Post Office Protocol. This is the ISP's computer that receives incoming e-mail messages addressed to you.

- SMTP Server—This is the name of the outgoing mail server. SMTP stands for Simple Mail Transfer Protocol. This is the ISP's computer that processes the e-mail messages you send.

- User Name—This is usually the part of your name that appears in your e-mail address before the @ sign. Some ISP's use your entire e-mail address. The user name is used to access the ISP's system along with your password.

- Password—This is the secret code you'll use to keep your e-mail private.

In many offices, an administrative assistant will obtain an e-mail account from the company's system administrator. This person will assist you in setting up your computer to send and receive e-mail and will provide you with your user ID, password, and e-mail address.

Passwords

Passwords can sometimes be case sensitive. If your e-mail password is all uppercase letters, you will need to press the SHIFT key while entering your password.

You should never store your password around your computer. You password should be something that is easy to remember. If you are assigned a hard-to-remember password, change it yourself. Most e-mail systems encourage you to change your password often. The best passwords combine letters and numbers and are at least six characters in length. Never use your name, your user name, your telephone number, birth date, social security number, or family names as passwords. Also, never use any real word that can be found in the dictionary without combining it with numbers.

E-Mail Programs

E-mail can be accessed from a Web site. This is often called Web mail. You can also use e-mail software provided by your ISP. However, in most businesses the most commonly used e-mail programs include:

- Microsoft Outlook Express

- Microsoft Outlook

- IBM Lotus Notes

All e-mail programs have similar features such as file folders for organizing mail, toolbars, menu bar, message list, and a message view window. The most commonly used toolbar or menu bar commands include:

- New Message—to create a new message

- Print—to print a paper copy of a message

- Read—to view a message in a separate window

- Reply—to reply to a particular message

- Reply to All—to reply to everyone copied on a previous message

- Send and Receive—to send out mail you've written and receive new messages

- Forward—to send an e-mail you've received to someone else

- Attachment—to send a computer file along with your e-mail message

Microsoft Outlook Express

Microsoft Outlook Express is provided with Microsoft Internet Explorer version 5.0 or later. It is designed for home users, small businesses, and Microsoft Office for Macintosh users who access their e-mail using a dial-up ISP connection. Microsoft Outlook Express users can send plain text or HTML-formatted e-mail. HTML-formatted e-mail allows a user to format an e-mail using fonts, bullet lists, and so forth. Microsoft Outlook Express includes a customizable toolbar, an address book, inbox filters, and support for multiple e-mail accounts.

Figure 14-1 shows a screen image of Microsoft Outlook Express with the various components identified.

Microsoft Outlook

Microsoft Outlook is a more advanced e-mail management program that is included with the Microsoft Office suite of programs. Microsoft Outlook is one of the most common e-mail programs used by businesses today. In addition to sending and receiving e-mail, users can also manage their personal calendar, schedule meetings with other co-workers, and manage contacts. Microsoft

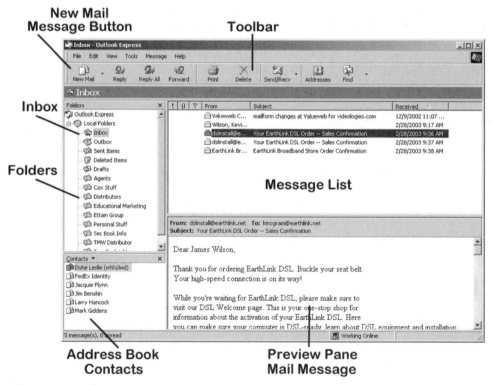

FIGURE 14-1. Outlook Express.

Screen shot reprinted by permission from Microsoft Corporation.

Outlook can also be integrated with voice mail systems so that voice messages can be retrieved and played on your computer.

Figure 14-2 shows a screen image of Microsoft Outlook with the various components identified.

IBM Lotus Notes

IBM's Lotus Notes is an e-mail messaging and collaboration program that includes e-mail, schedule, to-do list, calendar, address book, personal journal, Web pages, and databases. Lotus Notes can be integrated with voice mail, pagers, fax, and wireless devices such as cellular telephones and handheld Personal Digital Assistants (PDAs).

Figure 14-3 shows a screen image of IBM Lotus Notes with the various components identified.

Managing E-Mail

When you receive mail, the e-mail program stores it in your Inbox. When you click the inbox, you will see a list of messages you have received. When you select a message from the list, the body of the message is displayed in a window. You may read other messages by clicking on the listings in the Inbox window.

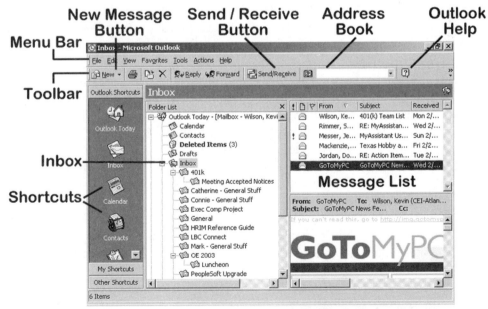

FIGURE 14-2. Microsoft Outlook.

Screen shot reprinted by permission from Microsoft Corporation.

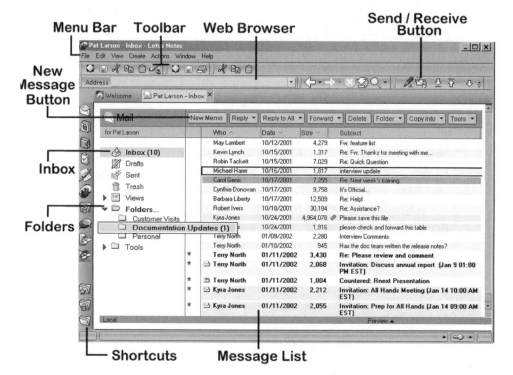

FIGURE 14-3. IBM Lotus Notes.

Screen captures (© 2003) IBM Corporation. Used with permission of IBM. IBM Lotus SmartSuite and IBM Lotus Notes are registered trademarks of IBM.

The icon to the left of the message indicates whether or not a message has been read. In Microsoft Outlook, unread mail has a sealed envelope to the left of the message. When you read a message, its icon automatically changes to an open envelope.

After you have read a message, it will remain in your Inbox. You can reduce the clutter in your Inbox by moving the messages to other folders. You can also use menu items to move a message to the Deleted Items folder or, once the message is highlighted, simply press the DELETE key.

You can print a message by opening it and clicking the **Print** icon on the toolbar. To compose a new message, you click the **New Mail** icon on the toolbar. A New Message window then appears. Figure 14-4 shows the New Mail window in Microsoft Outlook.

To send a message, click the **Send** button on the toolbar. The message will be stored in the Outbox folder until you click **Send and Receive.** In Lotus Notes, you have to click **Replicate** to send and receive mail.

Sending Attachments

Whenever you e-mail a message to someone, you have the ability to send additional files along with your message as an attachment. In Microsoft Outlook,

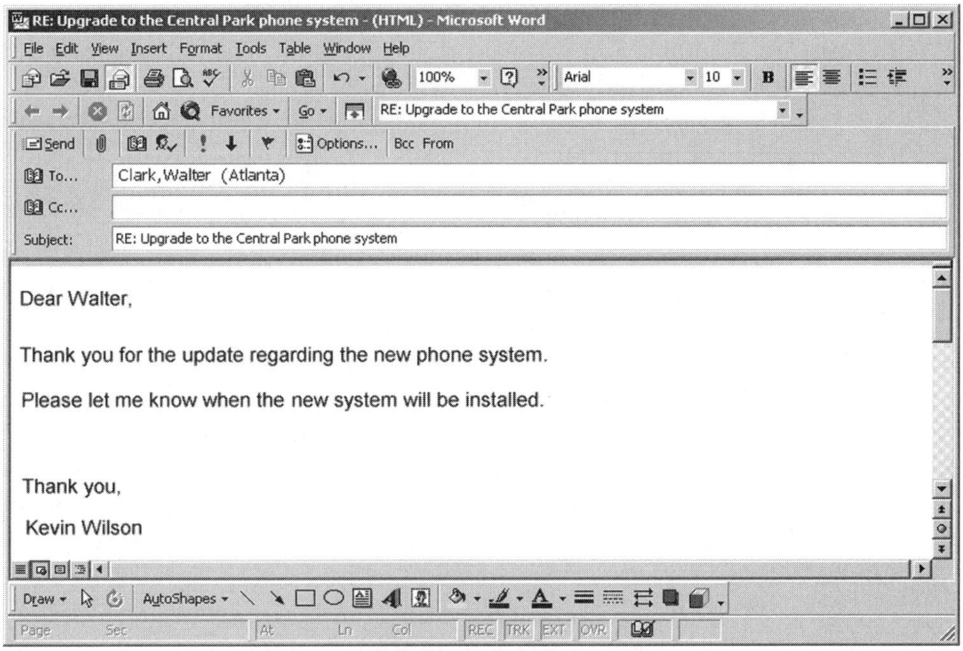

FIGURE 14-4. New Mail window in Microsoft Outlook.

Screen shot reprinted by permission from Microsoft Corporation.

you click the **Attach** icon on the toolbar. The Insert Attachment dialog box will appear. You can navigate to the appropriate file and attach it to the e-mail message. You'll then see the attachment listed or shown as an icon, along with your message.

When you receive an attachment, the e-mail program lets you know by showing you a small icon next to the message in your inbox. In programs like Microsoft Outlook, an attachment shows up as a paperclip icon. When you open the message, you will see a listing for the attachment or an icon embedded within the document. Double-clicking the icon will open the attachment file.

Problems with Attachments

E-mail attachments can be big and take a long time to download, depending on if the recipient has a slow dial-up connection. There can also be translation problems when the recipient doesn't have the right program or the correct program version for opening and using the attachment. In addition, many viruses spread across the Internet through infected attachments.

E-Mail Protocol for Attachments

Unless you send attachments to someone on a regular basis, you should always check with the recipient before sending. Make sure the person has the right software and can handle downloading the file.

When you send an attachment, use the e-mail message as a cover letter. Explain what the attachment is and why you are sending it. You can use compression software such as WinZip if you are sure the recipient also has the same software. Compression software reduces the file size and download times for users with slower dial-up Internet connections.

Always keep in mind that the formatting of a document may change on the recipient's computer. Many files, such as Microsoft Word documents, are printer dependent. That means, their layout on the screen and on paper is dependent on what model printer is installed.

If you want to make sure a document will look the same on the screen and when printed on a recipient's computer, use Adobe Acrobat. Adobe Acrobat uses a file format called Portable Document Format (PDF). Adobe Acrobat Reader can be downloaded for no charge from Adobe.com. To create an Acrobat document, you need to purchase Adobe Acrobat creation software. After Adobe Acrobat is installed on your computer, you will be able to create Acrobat documents by printing your document to the Acrobat Distiller. Adobe Distiller acts as a software-only printer connected to your system. Instead of printing your document on paper, your document is printed as a PDF file and stored on your hard drive.

Reasons for Sending Attachments

Here is a partial list of reasons for sending someone an attachment:

■ The recipient will use the file to add, edit, or make revisions.

■ You need a document to arrive ready to print and distribute.

■ The recipient needs the document immediately.

■ You need to send a single document to many different recipients.

■ The recipient is going to distribute the document to others.

Alternatives for Sending Attachments

You should avoid sending attachments when they are unnecessary. You can avoid sending attachments by:

■ Cutting and pasting word processing data into your e-mail message

■ Placing the files on a Web site or File Transfer Protocol (FTP) site for downloading

■ Sending the files on a diskette or CD-ROM

■ Faxing the document

■ Printing the document and sending it via mail or overnight express

Attachment Protocol for Recipients

Don't get upset when you can't open an attachment. When this happens, send a reply and explain the problem. If necessary, ask for word processing documents to be saved as text or have the document printed and mailed.

You should know what kind of attachments you can open. Each program has a file extension of a dot and three characters added to the file name. The file extension is used by a program to identify its own data files. When you examine an attached file extension, it will tell you what program is needed. The following is a list of common file extensions and the program needed to open them:

- doc—Microsoft Word
- txt—Microsoft Word, WordPad or Notepad
- rtf—Microsoft Word
- pdf—Adobe Acrobat Reader
- xls—Microsoft Excel
- ppt—Microsoft PowerPoint
- pps—Microsoft PowerPoint

- jpg—Windows Paint
- bmp—Windows Paint
- gif—Windows Paint
- mp3—Windows Media Player
- mov—Quicktime Player
- avi—Windows Media Player
- zip—WinZip

Be careful with executable file attachments. File extensions like *exe, vbs, com, drv, dll, bin,* and *sys* can easily be viruses. You should always use anti-virus software and keep it up-to-date. Don't open file attachments from people you don't know. Some viruses come embedded within legitimate files, such as Microsoft Word macro viruses. Because of this, you should always download file attachments to your hard drive and scan them with your anti-virus software before opening them.

Hyperlinks in E-Mail Messages

In most e-mail programs, when a World Wide Web address appears in the body of a message, it shows up as a hyperlink that the recipient can click to view.

Organizing Your E-Mail

When you receive messages in your e-mail program, they automatically go to the Inbox. In time, the number of messages you receive may crowd the Inbox and make it difficult to keep track of information. You can create new folders to organize your messages. You can then drag and drop messages from the Inbox to the various folders to store and save them.

It is important for an administrative assistant to keep a good filing system for e-mail messages. You may want to create separate file folders for projects, personnel, clients, or subjects. You can create folders within folders to further organize your messages.

E-Mail Address Book

All e-mail programs have an address book to help you manage your e-mail contacts. There are two ways to generate listings for the Address Book. You can enter the information manually, or you can add to a list through a menu command. Once you've added names to your Address Book, you'll want to start using it to address messages.

Newsgroups

Usenet is a series of newsgroups, maintained on host computers, which act as electronic bulletin boards open to the public. There are thousands of newsgroups. Some are designated for specific regions or cities. Some are geared to specific pastimes and hobbies, and others are directed to specific fields of scientific inquiry.

To join a newsgroup and read the messages, you must first subscribe. After you subscribe, the newsgroup will be added to the list of subscribed newsgroups, and the messages will download into your e-mail program. You can then view and read the messages just like e-mail.

You can determine what a specific newsgroup is devoted to by its name. The naming structure is hierarchical, moving from general concepts to specific issues. The first part of a newsgroup name is used to designate the most general level of interest. For example:

- rec.—used to indicate recreational groups

- soc.—contains newsgroups devoted to social issues

- chi.—is the prefix for groups centered around Chicago

The remaining elements of a newsgroup's name indicate more specific areas of interest:

- sci.physics—is a general science newsgroup about physics

- sci.physic.quarks—narrows the focus to the subatomic particles called quarks

Subscribing to newsgroups tells your e-mail program to keep track of those newsgroups you are particularly interested in following. While it's not required that you subscribe to a particular group to read and view messages, there are some distinct advantages to subscribing. Every time you open the newsgroup reader, your e-mail program loads all of the available newsgroups your provider carries. By subscribing to a specific newsgroup, you will not have to scan through all of the newsgroups to find the one you're looking for. Besides being a time saving issue, subscribing to a newsgroup may also prove to be a money saver if your Internet on-line time is monitored.

The messages list window displays all of the postings and replies from other users of the newsgroup. The first column lists the subject of the message, containing a short description of the contents of that posting. The second column lists the name of the sender. The third column includes the date and time that the message was posted. The last column shows the size of the message.

Mailing Lists

Like newsgroups, another message-board-like resource is a mailing list. People who are interested in a particular topic use a mailing list to carry on a group conversation. You can subscribe by sending an e-mail message to the list's subscription address, where you will be added to the list.

The first question that pops into most people's minds when they hear about sending an e-mail to a subscription address is, "Where do I find these addresses?" Mailing lists, unfortunately, are not as easily determinable through guesswork as Web addresses are. You'll soon find, however, that mailing lists are surprisingly accessible—you just have to know where to begin.

A simple way to find a mailing list is to conduct a search using a search engine such as Google.com or Yahoo.com.

Signature Files

A signature file is a small text file that can be added automatically at the end of your e-mail messages. Signature files are created in ASCII text format, which is a format that can be read by any program on any computer.

The content of this file can be anything you want used as a sort of personal "tag line"—your name, e-mail address, a quote, or a saying you use frequently. Sometimes people include a favorite quote. If you do have a quote, make sure it is up-to-date. Don't use pictures. You can include a link to a Web site.

Returned Mail

Sometimes a message you send cannot be delivered. When this happens, you will receive a message notifying you that your mail has been returned. There are a number of reasons why this could happen. Often, the cause may be temporary problems with your ISP. Or, the host server of the intended recipient may not have been on line when your message arrived. Also, you may have made an error in the intended recipient's address. Should a message be returned to you, read the routing information that appears at the top of the message. Verify that you sent the message to the proper address. If the problem persists, notify your ISP or the person you're trying to send mail to.

NetMeeting

Another method of collaborating on the Internet is NetMeeting. This software allows you to transmit video, voice, and data nearly anywhere in the world in real time while you pay local telephone rates.

As a conferencing tool, NetMeeting can be used to share information with two or more meeting participants in real time. You can share information from one or more applications on your computer, exchange graphics or draw diagrams with the whiteboard, send messages or take meeting notes and action items with the chat program, as well as send files to other participants using the file transfer capability.

Lotus Notes has a similar software tool available called Sametime. Figure 14-5 shows an example of Lotus Notes Sametime.

E-Mail Protocol for Administrative Assistants

Since e-mail is a written form of communication, you should follow proper e-mail protocols in order to look professional. You can do this by using proper language and accepted rules.

Addressing Your E-Mail

To send a message to someone, enter his or her e-mail address in the To field. Always verify the correct e-mail address of a recipient. Sending just one e-mail to the wrong person could be a disaster. If a person is already in your address book, many programs fill in the address automatically when you click on the name.

The CC field is for carbon copies. You should add recipients to this field when you want them to have a copy of a message, but do not need a response.

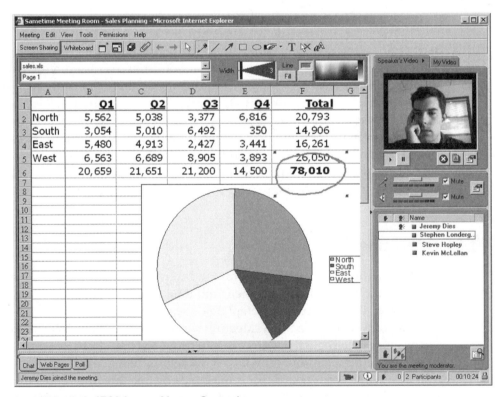

FIGURE 14-5. IBM Lotus Notes Sametime.

Screen captures (© 2003) IBM Corporation. Used with permission of IBM. IBM Lotus SmartSuite and IBM Lotus Notes are registered trademarks of IBM.

You should use this field sparingly, unless you are certain the recipient knows why they are receiving a copy of the message. Using this field can be confusing, since many people consider CC messages as FYI (for your information).

The BCC field is for blind carbon copies. When you add a recipient to this field, any recipients in the To or CC field will not know the person in the BCC field was copied. In most cases, you should not use the BCC field to send secret messages behind someone's back. This can be an e-mail etiquette disaster. Instead, use the BCC field to send out a message to a list of people in order to keep the e-mail addresses private.

Subject Line

Most e-mail recipients decide when and whether to read a message based on the subject line. Always add a subject to the subject line. Some computer novices and ultra-busy executives forget to add a subject line. Even if you have to reply to a message without a subject line, always add one yourself.

Keep your subject short. Many e-mail programs limit the subject line message to 40 characters or less. Avoid starting your subject out with "RE." Many programs automatically insert "RE:" in the subject line when you reply to a message. You may want to capitalize the subject like a book title; capitalize the first letter of each word except for articles.

Always be very specific with your subject lines. A subject like "ISS Meeting on Tuesday" is better than "Meeting." Make the subject meaningful. If the message generates a back and forth conversation, you'll know what the message is about after you received it for the third time.

Message Greetings

E-mail should always have a personal greeting and include customized information. With e-mail, there's no need for the inside address, date, and all the normal things that go into a business letter. However, standard business letter protocol still applies with e-mail.

If this is the first time you have sent an e-mail to a recipient, introduce yourself, and explain why you are writing. Be respectful of people you don't know.

Body of the Message

Be respectful of the recipient's time. Keep your messages short. If one sentence will do the job, use one sentence. If you have to switch subjects, it's best to send a separate e-mail so it can be filed separately.

Use the active rather than passive voice in your message. The passive voice incorporates various forms of the word to be followed by another verb. For example, "Documents were drafted by the committee," is passive. An active voice alternative is, "The committee drafted documents."

Keep your language gender neutral. Avoid using sexist language such as, "The salesman should configure his e-mail program." Instead, you could say, "The sales person should configure the e-mail program."

If you make a request in an e-mail message, don't forget to add "please" to your request. If someone does something for you, a polite "thank you" is always nice.

Always spell check your messages. Most e-mail programs have a built-in spell check feature. Always proofread your messages before you send them. Many people don't bother to read their messages, and it shows. Most spelling and grammar errors can be eliminated if you read your messages before clicking **Send.**

You can use common abbreviations and acronyms used in your business if you are certain the recipient understands them.

Avoid using all capital letters in the body of your message. In Internet tradition, this means yelling. However, if you need to emphasize a word like DANGER or WARNING, that's okay.

HTML Format Versus Plain Text

You can choose whether to send your messages in HTML format or plain text. In Microsoft Outlook, this feature can be set by accessing the Tools Menu, clicking **Options,** and then clicking the **Mail Format** tab. The HTML format allows you to format your message just like word processing; however, the recipient must be using an e-mail program that recognizes HTML format. Within an office where everyone is using the same e-mail program such as Microsoft Outlook or Lotus Notes, it's okay to send formatted messages using HTML format. With plain text messages, all formatting information is disregarded.

For external e-mails you should assume that the recipient is using a plain text e-mail system. Therefore, when you send external e-mails you should not use:

- Italics
- Bold
- Underlining
- Multiple colored or sized fonts
- Bullets
- Any special symbols or fonts
- Tabs
- Spacing to indent paragraphs

Even for internal e-mails, you should refrain from formatting your e-mail to look like a desktop publishing job. Your message format should be basic and easy to read. Use paragraphs, and double-space between them. Don't double-space after periods. Most people now use a publishing style that requires only one space after a period.

Emoticons

Emoticons are little sideways faces created using punctuation marks. For example, :-) means smile. Emoticons are often used in online chat rooms and to signal to your reader you are being sarcastic or making a statement with a tongue-in-cheek attitude. They can also be used to soften a message.

Use emoticons sparingly. Use them only when necessary, directly after the comments that require them. Don't use them in every message you write, and do not include them in your signature file.

Sign-Offs

For business e-mail, you should always end your message with a formal sign-off. *Sincerely, regards,* or *best wishes,* followed by your name, are the best salutations for formal messages. For informal communications, you can sign off with just your name. For external e-mails, always include your contact information: Name, title, company name, address, e-mail address, phone, and fax, numbers. Or, include your contact information in your signature file.

When to Respond to E-mails

In deciding how often to read and respond to e-mail, you must balance your workload between productive work and spending all day doing e-mail. Of course, your manager or a customer should get a quicker response than someone else if you are busy.

With most e-mails personally addressed to you, you should respond by the end of the business day. Even if the e-mail requires that you perform a task or do some research, you should let the sender know you got the message and when they can expect you to complete the task.

You can use templates for frequently asked questions, such as directions to your office. You can create a template message in your word processor and cut and paste it into your e-mail message. You can also use software like ReplyMate for Outlook.

When you send e-mail to external recipients, you should not expect a reply as quickly as you would with an internal e-mail. Unless a message is urgent, you should wait a few days, even up to a week, before resending the message. Remember, if a message is urgent, you can always call them on the phone.

Messages Sent to the Wrong Address

If you ever receive an e-mail message by mistake, send a reply to the sender along with a copy of the message, and let them know they used the wrong e-mail address. Of course, this does not apply to any junk e-mails you may receive.

Quoting From a Previous E-Mail

When you reply to a previous e-mail, send a copy of the previous message or a few lines as a quote. This will help the recipient know to which message you are replying. Most e-mail programs automatically copy the previous message if you click **Reply** on the toolbar. You have the option of including the entire message or deleting everything except the section you want to reference. You should quote when you are answering a question, commenting on a point made in a previous e-mail, or when you think it will be helpful. If you use selective quoting, you can mark the previous message by using two << (less than) and (>>) greater than symbols on each side of the quote.

When you include a copy of a previous message or a quote, always type your message below the quote or copy. This will prevent the recipient from having to scroll down to find your message.

Handling E-Mail Overload

When you find your inbox swamped with messages, answer the most recent messages first. This will help you avoid answering questions or dealing with issues that may have already been resolved. In addition, by answering the most recent messages first, you maximize your appearance of promptness.

Don't spend all day reading and replying to e-mail. You should read and respond to all nonurgent messages at one time—perhaps after lunch or at the end of the business day. File or delete messages you have already read and responded to. This will reduce the clutter in your inbox.

Filtering Messages

There are filters built-in to e-mail programs like Microsoft Outlook and Lotus Notes. Filters allow you to sort messages directly to specific file folders, bypassing your Inbox. Filters do take some time to set up, but they are well worth the time. Some ideas for filters include separating:

- Mail from particular people
- Internal e-mail from external e-mail
- Messages that do not include your company's domain name
- Messages where your e-mail address is in the CC or BCC field
- Messages from mailing lists or newsgroups
- Personal e-mail from family and friends

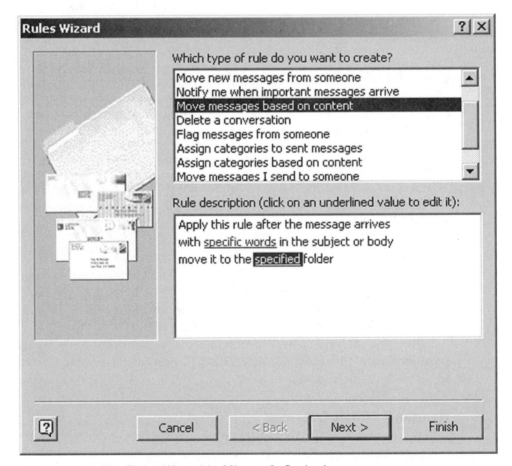

FIGURE 14-6. The Rules Wizard in Microsoft Outlook.

Screen shot reprinted by permission from Microsoft Corporation.

Urgent Messages

You should mark a message as "urgent" or "high priority" only when it really is. Never cry wolf with your e-mail by getting in the habit of marking all your messages "urgent." In fact, when you have an urgent message to send, you should consider whether e-mail is the best medium for the message. Perhaps a telephone call would be more effective.

Return Receipt

On an internal e-mail system, you can choose whether to be notified via e-mail when a recipient receives your message. When the message is read, you get a read receipt.

Return receipts are usually not supported for external e-mails sent over the Internet. In many cases, the receipt only tells you that the message made it to the recipient's e-mail server. There are delivery receipt options in Microsoft Outlook that give the recipient the option of acknowledging the delivery of the message.

Some e-mail programs allow you to read a message in a preview window without actually opening the message. If the recipient never actually opens and reads your message, you won't get a return receipt.

If you send a message with a return receipt and do not get a receipt, or if you request something and do not get a response, send out a reminder message. For internal messages, give the recipient until the end of the day to respond. For external messages, give the recipient several days to a week to respond.

Rules for Forwarding Messages

Forwarding a message can be both good and bad. It's good because it allows you to easily share information with others. It's bad because any message you forward may end up in public.

When is it okay to forward messages? Not as often as most people think. Unless a person gives you permission to forward a message, you should not forward it. There may be many reasons why someone would not want their message forwarded. The message may be for you only, the tone might not be appropriate for others, or the sender may not want to share his or her e-mail address.

If you don't want a message you send to someone to be forwarded, how should you let the recipient know? Make it clear that the message is just for them.

Before forwarding a message that contains a history of replies, check to make sure that everything in the message is appropriate before you forward. Remove any unnecessary or sensitive content.

Always keep in mind that e-mail is not private. Anything you write might be forwarded. Not everyone follows the correct protocols. One of the best rules to follow for e-mail communication is to not write anything in an e-mail you would not want someone else to read.

You should never forward jokes and chain letters to anyone at work. You never know when someone might find them offensive. However, if you receive a lot of forwarded messages, you can set up a filter that looks for messages with FW on the subject line.

Is it necessary to reply to forwarded messages? The answer is usually no, unless you find there is something in the message that specifically applies to you or one of your responsibilities.

Mass Mailings

Any time you need to send a single message to a group of people, you can always just add all of the addresses to the To and CC field. However, this means you are sharing everyone's e-mail address with everyone in the list. To avoid this, you can either create a group or use the BCC field. When you use the BCC field, none of the e-mail addresses are revealed. You do need to put at least one e-mail address in the To field, however, that can always be your own e-mail address.

You should never use the BCC field to send a message behind someone's back, as it is considered to be impolite.

Creating a Group

Many e-mail programs like Microsoft Outlook will allow you to create a group of e-mail addresses from your address book and save the list with a unique name. When you send a message to the group, everyone in the list receives the message.

Some company e-mail systems have pre-configured groups. Be careful when sending e-mails to these groups. Know who these individuals are before you include them in a mass mailing.

Reply to All

If you receive a mass mailing and click **Reply to All,** everyone on the list will get a copy of your reply. This can be dangerous if Reply to All is used by mistake. When replying to a message, always make sure you click **Reply** rather than Reply To All, unless you really do intend to send a reply to everyone on the list.

Some e-mail programs will allow you set a preference that will prompt you when you click Reply to All. This feature helps prevent clicking Reply to All by mistake.

What Messages Are Appropriate for Business E-Mail?

E-mail is not always the best medium for a message. Sometimes it is best to use the telephone or speak with a coworker in person rather than sending an e-mail message.

E-mail is appropriate in business communications for things like directions, requests, information to be saved, information to be copied, and company-wide announcements.

What Messages are Inappropriate for Business E-Mail?

The following are examples of situations where e-mail is an inappropriate medium for communication:

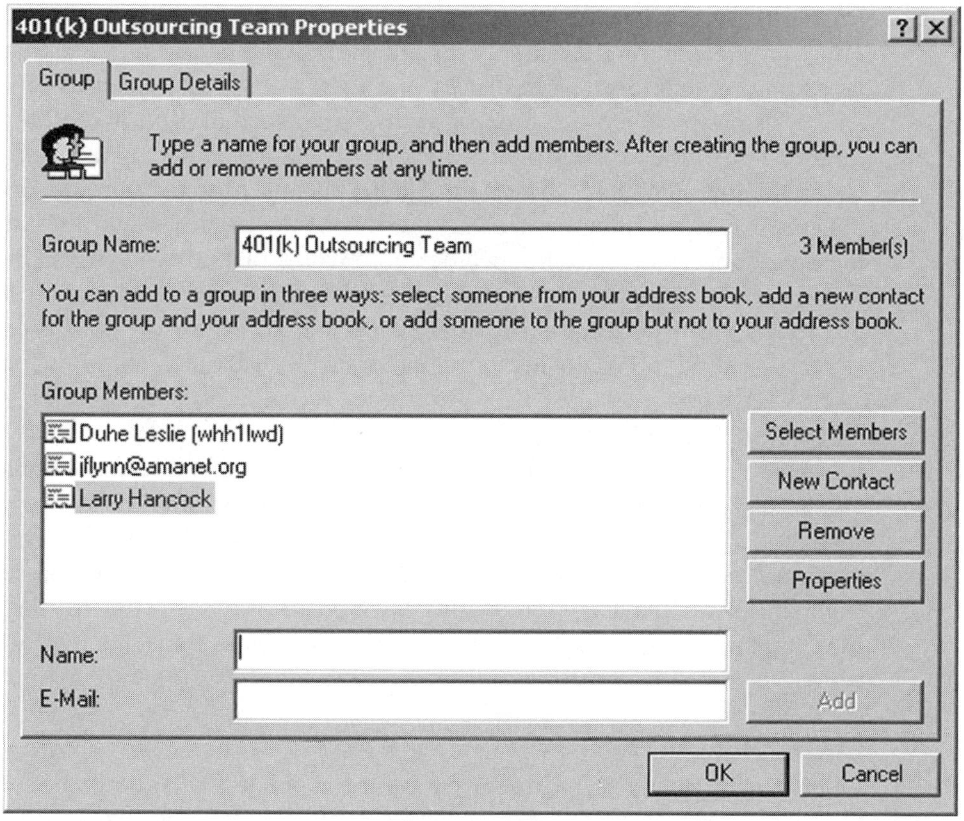

FIGURE 14-7. Creating a group in Microsoft Outlook.
Screen shot reprinted by permission from Microsoft Corporation.

- Thank you notes
- Long memos
- Yes or no answers
- Job praise
- Telling your boss you are sick
- Requests for raises, promotions, or resignations
- Jokes
- Flirting
- Gossip
- Anything illegal or unethical

The Tone of Your E-Mail at Work

When you e-mail your boss, do not use a casual tone, even if you are friends. Keep your e-mails business-like. You never know when your boss may need to forward one of your messages to a superior.

Never write an e-mail when you are angry. Take time to calm down before you fire off a message you'll later regret.

International E-Mail

There are special rules that apply for international business e-mails. Start by addressing the recipient as Mr. or Ms. and their surname. Do not use the recipient's first name. Keep the tone of your e-mail formal, and avoid humor that might be misunderstood. Convert all your measurements to metric, and be careful about calendar dates. The date 2/06/05 means June 6, 2005 in Europe, not February 6, 2005. To be clear, always write out the month, day, and year. If your message concerns money, be specific about what currency you are talking about. If you ask the international recipient to call you, provide them with the appropriate telephone country code. Also watch out for time-zone confusion. If you say you'll call the recipient at 5 p.m., make sure you are clear about whose 5 p.m.

Auto Respond Messages

When you are out of the office for longer than one business day and will not be able to respond to your e-mails, you should use an out-of-office notice that auto responds to your e-mails. An auto-respond message can be set up in your e-mail program. It will automatically send a message to anyone who sends you a message while you are away. Your auto-respond message can inform the senders that you are away and will respond to their e-mails at a specific time when you return.

E-Mail Hoaxes

From time to time you may receive forwarded hoaxes. You should be suspicious of any message that says, "Forward this to all your friends." Many times, these chain letters are simply ways to harvest e-mail addresses for junk e-mailers.

If you are suspicious that a message may be a hoax, you can check the following Web sites dedicated to exposing Web-related hoaxes:

- Urbanlegends.about.com
- Hoaxbusters.ciac.org
- Cdc.gov

You can also do a search of the particular message content in Yahoo.com or Google.com.

Spam

Spam is another word for junk e-mail. These are the unsolicited sales offers and scams that try to trick the unsuspecting e-mail user. Many Internet Service Providers have filters that attempt to eliminate spam; however many spam messages still slip through. You can reduce the amount of spam you receive by setting up filters that look for subject line phrases like *free, hot, money, hi, hello,* and *info*. You should also report any spam messages to your Internet Service Provider. You can also report spammers to the U.S. government's Federal Trade Commission at uce@ftc.gov or fill out a complaint form at www.ftc.gov.

Never reply to spam. This will cause you to receive even more, because now the junk e-mailer will know your e-mail address is real. Also, never click on any Web links in a spam message or call any telephone numbers listed.

E-Mail Viruses

There are many different types of computer viruses that spread via e-mail. These viruses can clog up your hard drive and slow down your computer, destroy files, compromise access to your computer, and automatically spread viruses to other computers.

One of the most common ways to get a computer virus is from an e-mail attachment. The attached file is either infected or is itself a virus. You should always use anti-virus software and keep it updated. Anytime you receive a file attachment, download it and scan it with your anti-virus software.

E-Mail Privacy

E-mail is not private. Not only may your messages be forwarded to others, but your company has the right to read anything you write or receive via e-mail. Because your employer pays for the computer, Internet connection, and your time, your business e-mail account belongs to the company. Even if you delete e-mail, it is still available for a company to view. The same rules apply for Web surfing and telephone usage.

Using the Internet

The Internet represents a vast global resource for collecting, disseminating, and distributing information. The Internet's underlying technologies enable instantaneous communication and collaboration across the entire globe. Individuals, businesses, educational institutions, communities, libraries, government bodies, and so on are able to share information like never before. The popular media have come to call this vast new digital world "cyberspace."

With the Internet, the possibilities are infinite. Business people can check in with the home office from anywhere, or they can e-mail proposals to sales prospects instantaneously. In short, the Internet has changed our perception of time and space.

Simply put, the Internet is composed of millions of computers linked into tens of thousands of computer networks. These networks, which span the globe, are then connected to one another.

World Wide Web

Today the World Wide Web (WWW) makes up a very large percentage of total Internet traffic. Just about every for-profit and nonprofit company, university, library, school, government, and millions of individuals now have a presence on the Web. The Web uses the same underlying protocols as the Internet, but has supplemented them with several additional technologies that have made the Internet far more accessible to computer users around the world. These include browser software, search engines, and HTML (HyperText Markup Language).

The Web was originally introduced to the Internet as a text-only system. With the release of the Mosaic browser—the first graphical browser—in 1993, the popularity of the Web grew. Soon after, Netscape appeared on the scene with its first Web browser—Netscape Navigator. Microsoft also developed its web browser—Internet Explorer. Both Netscape and Explorer were quickly accepted and surpassed Mosaic in use. Both browsers were faster, contained more features, and were easily acquired by downloading them from web sites.

Today, Web documents can include text, graphics, video, and sound. The World Wide Web gives you access to true multimedia documents from all over the globe.

Connecting to the Internet

In order to connect to the Internet, you will need the following.

Modem

A modem is a device that translates and transmits signals sent over the phone lines. Many computers today have modems already built into them. For machines without a built-in modem, you can purchase a modem and attach it to your computer.

Software

Once you have a modem installed, you need to add **browser software** to read the documents available on the World Wide Web. Browser programs read, interpret, and present documents. Netscape Navigator and Microsoft's Internet Explorer are two of the most widely accepted Web browsers.

ISPs

ISPs, short for Internet Service Providers, are companies or organizations that provide access to the Internet. ISPs maintain several **servers,** which are computers dedicated to providing high-speed access to the Internet. Your computer's modem dials a server at your ISP, which then establishes your connection to the Internet. This type of connection is called a **dial-up connection.**

The speed at which data can travel to and from your computer is determined by a number of factors including: The processor in your computer, the speed of the ISP's servers, and the type of phone or data line connecting computers along the way. Data can be carried on a standard phone line. However, improving technology has resulted in the creation of the ISDN line, which can carry data about four times faster than a standard phone line, and the T1 line, which can carry data about 100 times faster than an ISDN line. Even faster is a T3 line. A T3 line represents 28 T1 lines and has the "backbone" speed of major Internet connections in the U.S.

Fast Internet connections are sometimes referred to as "broadband." Broadband connections can be 50 times faster than dial-up connections. Broadband connections include the following:

- DSL—digital subscriber line service that connects at high speed over a telephone line

- Cable modem—a high-speed connection provided by a cable television company

- Satellite modem—a high-speed connection provided by a satellite subscription service

Besides providing direct access to the Internet, some ISPs also contain several options to make your online activity user-friendly and more interesting. These options may include chat rooms, entertainment ideas, travel services, online catalogs for home shopping, and so forth.

Browsers and HTML

The software programs that allow you to view the Internet are called browsers. Netscape Navigator and Microsoft's Internet Explorer are two of the most common browsers in use today. Browsers are designed to read the content of Web pages and display the data on your screen.

The Web is based on the principle of **hypertext.** Hypertext is a method of navigating through documents using **links.** You've probably encountered hypertext even if you've never used the Web. For instance, CD-ROM encyclopedias often have highlighted terms in the text of the entries. Clicking on these terms connects you to a related entry or to a definition of a term. Similarly, the Help Menu that you can open in a software application usually presents you with a Hypertext Menu that links to various topics.

Hypertext is a "nonlinear" medium. That is, aside from a site's home page, there is no beginning, middle, or end to hypertext documents. You may link from a home page to a page that discusses the latest news and then link from that page to a different site altogether for related information.

Links are embedded into a Web page through a coding system called HyperText Markup Language (HTML). When you activate one of these links by clicking on it, the Web makes the connection to the host computer that houses the document you requested, and it retrieves the documents without involving the user in the underlying file-transfer process.

Web Pages and Web Sites

A **Web page** is a document almost like a word processing document that can be displayed by your Web browser. Web pages contain text, graphics, sounds, animation, downloadable files, and hyperlinks.

A **Web site** is an organized group of Web pages. For example, this book could be put on the Web and would be considered a Web site. Each of the chapters could be considered a Web page.

When you visit a Web site, the first page that appears is called the **home page.** The home page contains links to other pages on the Web site. If this book were a Web site, the home page would likely contain a table of contents, with each listing being a hyperlink that would take you to the chapter or page you select.

Internet Addresses (URLs)

How does the browser find a particular document? It employs an addressing method known as the Universal Resource Locator (URL). Each page on the

Web has its own URL. A look at how a URL is put together might make it easier to visualize how documents are found.

Here is an example of a URL: http://www.videologies.com/assistant.htm. The first section (http) is the **protocol.** This indicates the type of Internet service the URL uses, in this case hypertext transfer protocol—http. When typing a URL using a modern browser, you usually do not have to include the http:// prefix. It is automatically added when you access the site. The two slash marks (//) indicate that the next section of the URL will be a domain name. In our example, the **domain name** consists of videologies.com. This is enough information to direct the browser to the host computer. When it reaches the site, it will pull up the default home page, unless a particular file is specified.

Each type of organization has its own domain. A few of the more common domains are listed in Table 15-1 below.

The last section of the URL—after the slash (/)—specifies a file located within that domain. If you do not enter a specific file name, the URL will generally take you to the home page of the site you are requesting. In this case, we want to reach a particular file named assistant.htm.

Using a Web Browser

Many of the features and functions of the Microsoft Explorer browser are the same or very close to those of Netscape Navigator. The features you will use the most often include:

- Menu bar
- Help
- Toolbar
- Address box
- History list
- Status bar
- Favorites

The following illustrations (Figures 15-1 and 15-2) show the major features of Microsoft's Internet Explorer and Netscape Navigator.

The Menu Bar

Menu bars are common to most Windows and Macintosh applications. They include categories of functions you'll use the most often when working. The

TABLE 15-1	Common Domains
Domain	**Organization**
.com	Business/Commercial
.org	Organization
.gov	Government
.edu or .k12	Educational Institution
.net	Network Provider
.mil	Military Agency

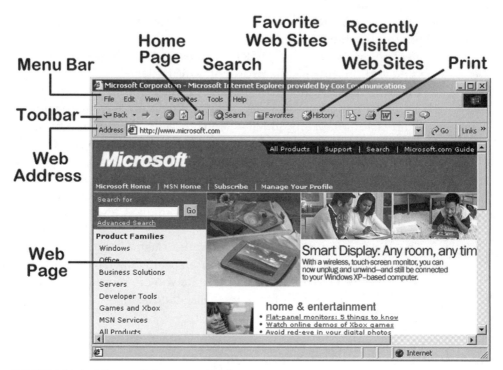

FIGURE 15-1. Microsoft Internet Explorer.

Screen shot reprinted by permission from Microsoft Corporation.

menu bars for Netscape Navigator and Microsoft Internet Explorer have different menu bar choices. Netscape Navigator includes choices for: File, Edit, View, Go, Bookmarks, Tools, Windows, and Help. Microsoft Internet Explorer includes menu bar choices for: File, Edit, View, Favorites, Tools, and Help.

The Toolbar

The toolbar includes buttons for the most common functions you'll use when browsing the Web. Like their differences in menu bar choices, the toolbars for Netscape Navigator and Microsoft Internet Explorer differ slightly in their look. Toolbars can be customizable with features you use the most often; however, the default versions of the programs include the following:

■ Back—to view the last Web page you viewed

■ Forward—to return to the original Web page after you have clicked the **Back** button to view a previous Web page

■ Stop—to stop loading a Web page

■ Refresh—to reload a Web page to check for an update

■ Home—to load the Starting Web page that opens whenever you start your browser

■ Search—to access the browsers Web search function

Menu Bar   Reload Web Page
Back   Forward   Search   Print   Toolbar

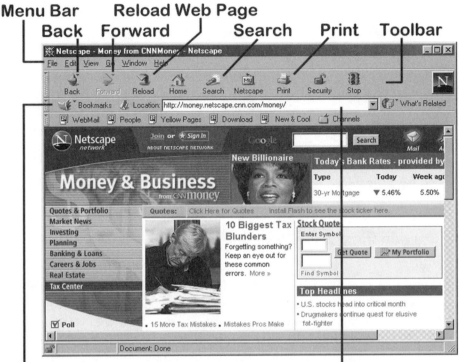

Bookmarks (Favorite Web Sites)   **Web Page Address**

FIGURE 15-2. Netscape Navigator.

Screen shot reprinted by permission from Netscape.

■ Favorites—to access a Web site you have added to your list of favorite Web sites

■ History—to access any of the Web pages you have viewed in the past

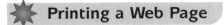

Bookmarks

Both Netscape Navigator and Microsoft's Internet Explorer feature a bookmark function that keeps an electronic record of favorite pages. (In Explorer the bookmark feature is called "Favorites.") No matter what it is called, the feature maintains a list of URLs that can be accessed whenever you want to return to your favorite Web sites.

Printing a Web Page

To print a Web page, you can either click the printer icon on the browser's toolbar, or you can click the **File Menu** and then click **Print.** Depending on the type of Web page, the Print window may ask which frame you wish to print. Frames are a way of dividing up the information on a Web page so that it almost looks

like a magazine page layout. You can choose to print one particular frame or all of the frames on the page.

Saving a Web Page

You can download and save a Web page to your computer's hard drive. By doing this, you can view the page again without having to be online.

To save a Web page, click the **File Menu,** then click **Save As.** The Save Web Page window will appear and allow you to browse to a location where you want to save the page.

Downloading and Uploading Files

When you are viewing Web pages with your Web browser, your browser is **downloading** files to your computer. These files are stored temporarily in your computer's memory as you view them. As just described, you can chose to save a Web page to your hard drive in order to access it when you are offline.

Downloading involves the transmission of a file from the Internet to your computer. Sometimes you will find links to files on Web pages that are available for downloading. These files may be data files, new programs, drivers for particular devices, graphics, music, and so forth.

Uploading is the opposite process. You transmit a file from your computer to another computer on the Internet. For example, if you apply for a job online, you might want to upload your resume. In most cases, this is done by clicking the appropriate link to upload a file, then browsing your computer's hard drive to locate the file you want to send.

If you are involved in publishing documents and other information to Web sites, you will need to use an **FTP** program. FTP stands for File Transfer Protocol. An FTP program works similar to Windows Explorer. After logging onto a Web site with a user name and password, you will see two windows on your screen. One window shows the files on your computer's hard drive. The other window shows the files on the Web site. You can then drag and drop files using your mouse from your computer to the Web site in order to start the FTP process.

Cookies

Whenever you visit a Web site, your browser stores information about your visit on your computer. This information is called a **cookie.** A cookie stores information such as your user ID and user preferences, so you don't have to retype them the next time you visit the site. Cookies are often used by Web marketers to learn your likes and dislikes so they can try to sell products. Unfortunately, this means your privacy is at risk.

You can set your browser to disable cookies if you wish. You can do this by viewing your browser's preferences or Options Menu.

Search Tools

There are millions of pages on the World Wide Web. How do you begin to find the information you're interested in? Various companies have developed programs that search the Web for the information you're looking for. **Search Engine** is the name commonly given to a number of different sites on the Internet which provide this service.

Search engines serve as a sort of automated reference librarian. Search engines will find pages on the Web based on keywords you provide. There are a variety of engines and tools to help you find what you're looking for. For example, AltaVista, Metacrawler, Lycos, Yahoo!, and many others, can help you find sites on the Web. Alta Vista searches the database that it maintains. Metacrawler, created at the University of Washington, is considered a **metasearch** engine. It queries eight different databases but does not maintain one of its own. The metasearch engines are typically a bit slower but will give search results based on multiple databases instead of only one.

Yahoo! is a Web guide which organizes listings into categories and subcategories. It is among the most popular search tools because it allows users to register their own Web sites. You'll be able to find the latest additions to the Web using Yahoo!

The list of categories in a Web guide is most useful when you have a broad subject in mind. The guide's hierarchical structure can help you narrow your topic as you go along. For instance, you could search an extremely broad topic, such as "weather," using the categories provided by a Web guide.

The following is a list of search sites:

- AltaVista—*www.altavista.com*
- Ask Jeeves—*www.ask.com*
- Direct Hit—*www.directhit.com*
- Excite—*www.excite.com*
- Go.com—*www.go.com*
- Google—*www.google.com*
- Hotbot—*www.hotbot.com*
- Lycos—*www.lycos.com*
- Northern Light—*www.northernlight.com*
- OpenText—*www.opentext.com*
- Search—*www.search.com*
- Snap—*www.snap.com*
- Webcrawler—*www.webcrawler.com*
- About.com—*www.about.com*

- Looksmart—*www.looksmart.com*
- Netcenter—*www.netcenter.com*
- Suite101—*www.suite101.com*
- Dog Pile—*www.dogpile.com*
- Mamma—*www.mamma.com*
- Profusion—*www.profusion.com*
- Savvysearch—*www.savvysearch.com*

Conducting a Search

Due to the sheer volume of information on the Web, broad searches generate a great number of results. Yahoo! provides the very useful service of breaking the results down for you.

Some search engines don't return results based on categories and concepts. Instead, they look for the occurrence of the keywords within all the documents in their registries. This approach has both advantages and disadvantages.

The main advantage is breadth. A search for the key word "hurricane" may turn up interesting documents that refer to hurricanes but are not entirely devoted to hurricanes. For instance, a general science magazine may have a good article on hurricanes. While you may not find it in a directory search, because it wouldn't be listed under the category "hurricanes," you would likely find it in a keyword search.

A disadvantage is that in addition to useful references, you'll also pull up every page with the word "hurricane," whether it's relevant or not.

The simplest way to get good results from a search engine is to determine in advance precisely what you are looking for and then enter as many words as you can think of to describe it.

For this particular search, you will use the engine AltaVista. AltaVista ranks the search findings by matching them to the search text. If your search text involves a number of words or phrases, AltaVista will rank Web pages that have all the search text requirements above those which only contain a single element of the search text. For example, Web pages containing all the words of the search text "hurricane, radar, image, Atlantic, ocean," will be ranked above those which contain only one or two of those words.

Effective Search Strategies

Two key terms used in comparing search engine performance are **recall** and **precision.** Having a high recall rating indicates that a search engine returns a great number of documents from a search. High precision refers to the percentage of returns that actually match your search criteria. The goal on which to focus is to increase the precision of your searches.

You can achieve more efficient search results through the use of **search syntax.** There are a few simple syntax elements that can greatly help to refine your search. Incorporating search syntax into your queries will make each search far more effective in finding the information you want. In other words, it will increase the precision of your search.

Advanced searching alerts the search engine to the relationship between your key terms. You can specify that *all* your terms must appear, *any* of your terms must appear, or that the terms must appear in a specific order. Moreover, you can specify that certain words do not appear. This feature would be helpful if you were searching for information on pythons and wanted to exclude documents dealing with the British comedy group Monty Python.

You can indicate the relationships between your key terms by placing **operators** between them. For example, adding a plus sign (+) between words in your search will produce results that include all of the words in your search. *Note: Be sure to refer to a search engine's Help page before doing an advanced syntax search. The Help page will indicate which operators are recognized.*

Boolean Searches

AltaVista and HotBot also let you perform Boolean searches. This is the search syntax that professional research librarians use.

While Boolean searches can get complicated, knowing a few of the operators will help you refine your searches. The following are some useful operators. (Note that they are typed in all capitals.)

AND Placed between two words to indicate that the document must contain both words

OR Placed between two words to indicate that the document can contain one or both words

NOT Placed before a word to indicate that this word must not appear in the document

NEAR Placed before a word to indicate that these words must occur within 10 words of each other

Searching Within a Site

You've seen that there are many ways to search. However, just because you have found a good site, it doesn't mean that the search is over. You'll find that even good sites contain a lot of filler. The goal is to cut through the filler and find the material that is useful and helpful to you. It is easy to get lost in a large Web site. Here are some standard rules for searching a very large Web site:

- Clearly identify the desired information—clarify the search.
- Think through the possible search terms that could be used.

- Remain focused in your search. Don't be pulled into surfing if you are trying to find something specific.

Error Messages

When using a browser, an error message can come up for a number of reasons. Different problems will generate different error messages.

The Web is a dynamic and ever-changing environment. While pages are constantly created, others are removed. If you encounter a page or a site that does not exist, you will receive an error message.

Unable to Locate Server—If the browser is unable to locate a particular host computer (also called a server), you will receive a message indicating the situation.

Page Does Not Exist—If you try connecting to a specific Web page that does not exist, you receive another type of error message. Rather than a dialog box, an actual Web page appears, advising you that the site you requested is not a valid URL.

Server Busy or Unavailable—When there is too much traffic on the Internet, or if you try to access an overwhelmingly popular site, you may receive an error message.

Plug-Ins

Your Web browser has various features that allow it to display graphics, play sounds, and run animations. There are some specialized tools required to access content on certain Web sites. For example, some sites provide streaming audio or video content. These sites usually require a special plug-in be installed in order to access the content.

Some of the most common plug-ins include RealNetworks' Realplayer, Apple Computer's Quicktime player, Macromedia's Shockwave and Flash, and Adobe's Acrobat Reader.

Web Sites of Interest to Administrative Assistants

The following is a list of Web sites that may be of special interest to administrative assistants:

- 1-800-Flowers—*www.1800flowers.com*—An online florist

- About Work—*www.aboutwork.com*—A Web site with information on job hunting and career advancement

- All-In-One Search—*www.allonesearch.com*—A search engine for finding reference sources, quotes, and other language usage resources

- Amazon.com—*www.amazon.com*—An online bookstore that is searchable by title, author, or topic

- Ask An Expert—*www.askanexpert.com*—Specialized answers to questions ranging from business and industry to science and health

- Barnes & Noble—*www.barnesandnoble.com*—An online bookstore that is searchable by title, author, or topic. There are also free online courses available from this Web site.

- Better Business Bureau—*www.bbb.org*—A list of Better Business Bureau services

- BusinessTown.com—*www.businesstown.com*—A Web site dedicated to business resources that includes sample letters and forms, travel information, accounting and finance, and office procedures

- Career City—*www.careercity.com*—A listing of job postings

- Career Mosaic—*www.careermosiac.com*—A listing of thousands of job postings, resume listings, and employer information

- City Search—*www.citysearch.com*—A listing of entertainment, restaurants, hotels, and shopping for various U.S. cities

- CNN—*www.cnn.com*—An online news resource

- Cool Jobs—*www.cooljobs.com*—A listing of job postings

- Cybershop.com—*www.cybershop.com*—An online shopping resource for corporate gifts

- Dictionary—*www.dictionary.com*—An online dictionary and thesaurus

- EDGAR Online—*www.edgar-online.com*—A repository of corporate filings by public companies to the Securities and Exchange Commission

- Encarta—*www.encarta.msn.com*—An online encyclopedia

- E-Trade—*www.etrade.com*—An online stock trading resource

- Federal Express—*www.fedex.com*—An express shipping service for overnight letters, packages, and freight

- Fodor's Restaurant Index—*www.fodors.com/ri.cgi*—A listing of restaurant reviews for various cities around the world

- Foreign Language Translation—*www.travlang.com/languages*—A list of common phrases in various foreign languages

- Hoaxes—*www.kumite.com/myths*—Information on Internet hoaxes

- Idea Café—*www.ideacafe.com*—A collection of resources available for small businesses

- Insurance—*www.insuremarket.com*—A Web site with information on various types of insurance products

- Internal Revenue Service—*www.irs.ustreas.gov*—The IRS' Web site with downloadable tax forms and tax information

- Learn2.com—*www.learn2.com*—An extensive resource of online courses on many different subjects

- Legal Issues—*www.findlaw.com*—A directory of legal resources, law firm listings, and legal news

- Maps—*www.mapquest.com*—An online map that can provide driving directions between any two streets in the United States

- Monster—*www.monster.com*—A listing of job postings

- National Fraud Information Center—*www.fraud.org*—Information on common scams

- New York Times—*www.nytimes.com*—An online newspaper

- Office Depot—*www.officedepot.com*—An online office supply store

- Office Max—*www.officemax.com*—An online office supply store

- Organizer—*www.eorganizer.com*—A service that helps you remember important dates, such as anniversaries, birthdays, and meetings

- People Search—*www.infospace.com*—A search engine that finds telephone numbers, addresses, and e-mail address of people nationwide

- Priceline.com—*www.priceline.com*—A resource for purchasing air travel, hotels, and car rentals at reduced prices

- Real Estate—*www.bankrate.com*—A listing of mortgage rates across the country

- Small Business Administration—*www.sbaonline.sba.gov*—A listing of resources available for starting, financing, and running a small business

- Small Office—*www.smalloffice.com*—A collection of resources available for small businesses

- Staples—*www.staples.com*—An online office supply store

- The American Management Association—*www.amanet.org*—Resources and training information for administrative assistants and their managers

- Travel—*www.expedia.com*—An online travel agency for booking airline flights, hotels, and car rentals

- Travelocity—*www.travelocity.com*—An extensive travel guide for booking air travel, hotels, and car rentals anywhere in the world

- U.S. Census Bureau—*www.census.gov*—A Web site with statistical listings for individuals and businesses

- U.S. Federal Government—*www.fedworld.gov*—A resource listing U.S. Federal Government publications, agencies, tax information, and jobs

- United Parcel Service—*www.ups.com*—A shipping service for packages

- USA Today—*www.usatoday.com*—An online newspaper

- Wall Street Journal—*www.wsj.com*—An online newspaper

- Weather.com—*www.weather.com*—An online weather report for anywhere in the world

- Web MD—*www.webmd.com*—A Web site with an extensive library of health-related information

- Women's Issues—*www.femina.com*—A listing of information for women

- Yahoo! Metros—*www.yahoo.com/promotions/metros*—A city guide with links to resources for various U.S. cities

- Zip Codes—*www.usps.gov/ncsc*—Locate zip codes by typing in an address and a city

Spreadsheet Software

What Is a Spreadsheet?

Many administrative assistants use computerized spreadsheet software to handle accounting chores, assist with budgets, and for similar tasks. Spreadsheet software takes the place of the columnar pad that was so popular in the past. A columnar pad is divided into columns across the top and rows that run down the side. The rows and columns intersect at a small box. Altogether, there are hundreds of these little boxes on each page. An electronic spreadsheet is a large grid of columns and rows. A box where a column and row intersect is called a **cell.** Each cell has a unique **address.** Most spreadsheets label columns using letters, and rows using numbers. Therefore, the cell at the intersection of column C and row 5 is cell C5.

The largest spreadsheet can contain millions of cells depending on the memory size of the computer running the software. However, most of the applications you'll be working with use only 500 to 1,000 cells.

There are two spreadsheet programs used most commonly in business today: Microsoft Excel and IBM Lotus 1-2-3. The following figures (16-1 and 16-2) show screen images of Microsoft Excel and Lotus 1-2-3 with their key components labeled.

Navigating Around a Spreadsheet

When you are using a spreadsheet, one cell is always active—that is, ready for you to input data. This cell is designated by a cell pointer, highlighted area, or flashing cursor. To make another cell active, you use the arrow keys, numeric keypad, or mouse to move to another location. Due to the limits on screen size, only a small group of cells can be displayed at any one time. If you wish to view additional cells, use a mouse or the arrow keys to move even farther on the spreadsheet.

Navigating around on a spreadsheet is much like looking through a window. Moving the window around to view additional cells is called **scrolling.** There

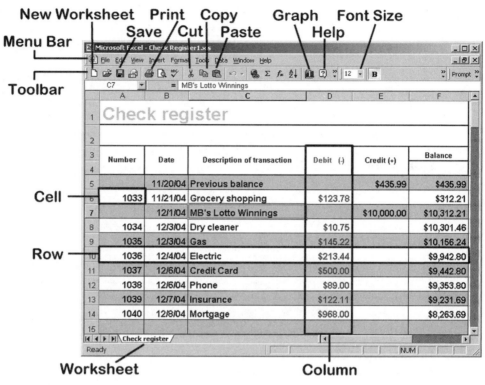

FIGURE 16-1. Microsoft Excel.

Screen shot reprinted by permission from Microsoft Corporation.

are also special commands that will take you to predefined locations on a spreadsheet, such as the bottom or top.

To make using a spreadsheet as simple as possible, most spreadsheet software programs have some type of control panel. Some have the control panel at the bottom of the screen, and others have it at the top. The control panel displays information about the active cell and a space where a user can type information into the active cell. In addition, it displays menus for activities such as saving, printing, and loading, as well as a list of special built-in functions in some cases. To select a choice, you move the cursor around using the arrow keys, numeric keypad, or mouse to highlight your choice and then press EN-TER/RETURN or click the mouse.

Spreadsheet Data

Any entry into a cell can be one of three possible items: A label, number, or formula. A **label** is a word used to describe information in your spreadsheet. For example, you might want to calculate a budget for office expenses. Therefore, you would create a list of those expenses: Paper, pens, computer supplies, stamps, and so forth. These words describe the numbers in another column or row, which is why they're called labels.

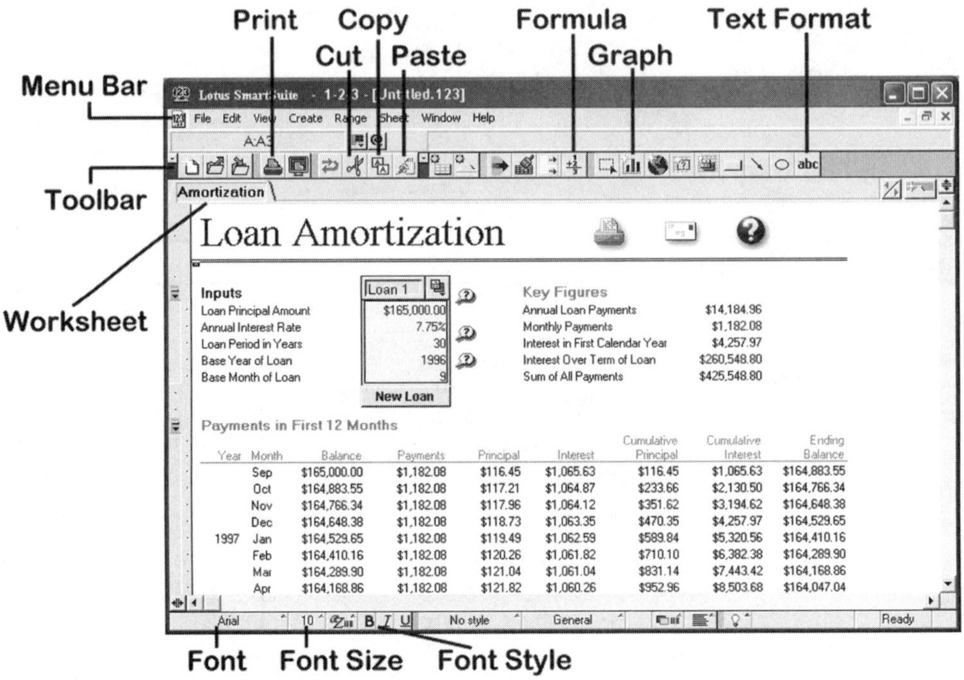

FIGURE 16-2. IBM Lotus 1-2-3.

Screen captures (© 2003) IBM Corporation. Used with permission of IBM.
IBM Lotus SmartSuite and IBM Lotus Notes are registered trademarks of IBM.

The actual expenses for the office supplies are the **numbers.** In order to add up a total of all the expenses at the bottom of the list, you need to enter a **formula,** a combination of cell addresses connected by mathematical symbols, for instance A1 + A2 + A3.

To enter a label, number, or formula into a cell, place the cursor on the cell you want to make active, then begin typing. As you type, the information you enter will be displayed in the control panel. When you are ready to put that information in the active cell, you either click the mouse or press ENTER/RETURN on the keyboard.

Formulas

A formula will work correctly only with numbers. Therefore, in order for a spreadsheet to distinguish labels, numbers, and formulas, most spreadsheet software programs use special predefined characters so that a user can specify the difference. For example, if the first character you type in a cell is a number, the spreadsheet will assume that entry is a number. If the first character you type is a letter, the spreadsheet will assume the entry is a label. And if you type in a special software-defined character such as "=", the spreadsheet will assume your entry is a formula.

Spreadsheet formulas can get complicated. Formulas can link information from one area to another so that totals from one group or section can be added to an overall summary. For example, an accounting system could be set up that allows you to enter expenses into various accounts. One formula would calculate the total expenses for each account; another would be used to link the total of a particular account to an overall profit-and-loss statement.

The simplest formula is one that moves the data from one cell to another. If you entered the following formula in cell A1: "=Sum(A2)"—whatever amount appeared in cell A2 would automatically also appear in A1.

The use of parentheses is an important aspect of formulas. For example, a formula such as "=Sum(A1:A10)" would provide a total of all the numbers in cells A1 through A10. When combined with other mathematical symbols for division, multiplication, and subtraction, a formula containing multiple sets of nested parentheses could be created, for example, "=Sum(((A1:A10) * A20) – A30)."

In order to create a formula correctly, you must know the order in which the mathematical operations will be performed by the computer. The natural order is to perform any calculation involving exponents first, followed by multiplication and division, and then addition and subtraction. For example, to solve the formula =Sum($(2^2 \times 10)$ + ((144/12) – (5+6))) you do the following:

- 2^2—first square the 2 to get 4 =Sum((4×10) + ((144/12) – (5+6)))

- 4×10—multiply 4 by 10 to get 40 =Sum(40 + ((144/12) – (5+6)))

- 144/12—Next you divide 144 by 12 to get 12 =Sum(40 + (12 – (5+6)))

- Then do the addition and subtraction, starting inside the parentheses: 5 plus 6 equals 11 =Sum(40 + (12 – 11))

- 12 minus 11 equals 1 =Sum(40 + 1)

- To finish, 40 plus 1 equals 41 =Sum(41)

Whenever a continuous group of cells is involved in a formula such as a row or column or block of numbers, rather than type in each individual cell address, a **range** is specified instead. For example, A1:A10 specifies a range of cells from cell A1 to cell A10 including all cells in between. A range can be as small as two cells or as large as the entire spreadsheet. It can be a row, a column, part of a row or column, or a block of several rows and columns. Most often a range is specified by identifying the beginning cell, followed by a colon or an ellipsis, followed by the ending cell.

Automatic Recalculations

One of the nice features of a spreadsheet is the ability to recalculate formulas automatically if you change any of the numbers in the cells included in the formula. If you have formulas that link various columns, rows, or sections, changing one number in a cell can cause numbers to change throughout the entire spreadsheet as each formula automatically recalculates. This recalculation feature is extremely useful for performing a "what-if " analysis.

If you want to see the effect of a change on one particular area on a spreadsheet, enter the new number, and see what it does to the overall total. This feature allows you to build what are sometimes called **spreadsheet templates.** For example, if you create a spreadsheet to keep track of petty cash or a project budget, once you create the spreadsheet and the formulas, you can go back and change the labels and the numbers and have a whole new spreadsheet with a lot less work. By saving the new spreadsheet with a new name, both the old version and the new version will be stored for future use.

Functions

Spreadsheets have a variety of built-in functions that can replace complicated formulas. One of the simplest is the **sum function.** It allows you to calculate the total of a range of cells. Functions are identified by first typing either "=" or "@" depending on the particular software and then the function name. This lets the software know that the entry is a function, and not a label. Some spreadsheet programs allow users to select functions from a pull-down menu. Functions are available for many different mathematical, statistical, and financial formulas.

Editing Spreadsheets

Another feature that can save you much time is the spreadsheet's ability to copy labels, numbers, and formulas from one location to another. For example, you might want to list your petty cash expenses by months, with each month in a separate column. Rather than recreating the labels and formulas for each month, you could copy the entire first month's information and paste it into the next column or the next group of columns. The spreadsheet software automatically compensates for the differences in cell labels from column to column and row to row and adjusts the new column so that the formula calculates the numbers in the new column, not in the original month column. The commands for selecting, copying, and pasting can all be found in the control panel of the spreadsheet.

Arranging Layout

Arranging your layout to look the way you want is another useful feature of an electronic spreadsheet. You can change the contents of any cell; add or delete rows or columns; and copy, cut, and paste data from one cell, row, column, or block to another similar area.

Editing Commands

Most spreadsheets have editing commands listed in their control panels. The simplest editing feature is to access the contents of a single cell and to alter the data there. When you make a cell active by selecting it with the cursor or mouse, its contents appear in the control panel. There you can insert text, type in completely new text, change a number—or do anything else.

You create new cells by inserting a new row or column. The Insert command or Create New Column or Row command allows you to do this easily. You select a column to the left of where you want to insert a new column and then select the **Insert** command from the control panel. For inserting rows, you select the row where you want the new row to appear. Pointing to the very top of a column or the extreme left of a row with a mouse will allow you to select it. If you do not have a mouse, position your cursor at the top of a column or on the cell on the far left of a row and choose **Select** from your Control Panel Menu. Then move your cursor to highlight the row or column.

To delete a row or column, select the entire row or column, and choose **Delete** from the Control Panel Menu.

Whenever you insert or delete a row, it's important to note that some cells and formulas will move in the spreadsheet to a new cell address. Most spreadsheets automatically adjust to compensate for these moves so that you don't have to go back and make changes. Therefore, if you have a formula that adds up the total of a column of 10 cells, and you insert five new rows in the middle, the formula will automatically be changed to add up a total of 15 cells instead.

Formatting features help you align the numbers and text to make your spreadsheet look good when printed out on paper. Formatting commands, found in the control panel, allow you to justify the text in a document, center text or numbers, or make them flush left or flush right. You can format individual cells or rows to specify how many decimal points will be displayed or to create dates, dollar signs, commas, percentages, and scientific notations. You can change the width of a cell or column in order to display more information, such as a long label or a very large number. Some of the newest spreadsheets allow you to change the spacing of rows, the typeface style, and even the type size of your text and numbers.

Other Spreadsheet Functions

Saving and Printing

When you get your spreadsheet looking the way you want, you may print it or save it. Printing and saving are commands you can select from the control panel. If you select **Save,** you'll be asked where you want to save your spreadsheet and to give it a name. You choose the disk drive where you want to save the file—a diskette or a hard drive—and then type in the name. Whenever you work with a spreadsheet that has been saved previously and you wish to save it again, it will automatically be saved under the same name on the same disk. If you want to save two or more different versions of a spreadsheet, you will need to change the name slightly. This can be accomplished by selecting **Save As** from the control panel or by selecting **No** when asked if you want to save the file with the same name.

When you wish to print a spreadsheet, you'll be given an opportunity to determine how much of your spreadsheet you want printed, whether you want a header or footer, if you want borders or a grid, column and row numbers, and so forth. Some spreadsheets display a menu asking if you want to print the spreadsheet to a printer or to a file.

Printing to a file is a way of saving a spreadsheet on a diskette or hard drive so that it can later be incorporated into another program such as a word processor.

Online Help

Many spreadsheets are equipped with online help features, which provide detailed explanations of spreadsheet commands, functions, and procedures. These online help files can be accessed while you are in the middle of working on a spreadsheet by choosing Help from the spreadsheet's control panel and selecting the topic you need help on.

Templates

To help get you started, many spreadsheets have built-in **templates,** which are pre-built spreadsheet models for common applications in business such as budgets and financial analysis. By loading a template, you can edit the spreadsheet to customize it to your particular business. This can be a great time saver.

Spreadsheet Macros

Spreadsheet macros are another great time saver. As you may already know from your word processing work, a **macro** is a way to minimize repetitive keystrokes. You can create a macro by selecting Macro from your spreadsheet's control panel. You will then be asked to type in the keystrokes you want to record. Once these are recorded, you'll be asked to assign a simple keyboard command to trigger the macro. Many spreadsheets come with built-in macros that you can customize and access with special keyboard commands.

Data Security

 Information = Profit

Information about your company is valuable—not only to your company but also to unscrupulous people outside your company. Such information includes confidential records such as bank transactions or corporate credit card numbers. It also includes paper or computer files about customers, new products, sales strategies, and so on. Consider how damaging it would be to your company if such records were lost or destroyed or if they were stolen by a competitor. That's why data security is critical to protect computer information from theft, misuse, and disaster.

The misuse of computer information ranges from unauthorized use of computer time to criminal acts like sabotage. It all falls under one general category many people call "computer crime." Surveys show that over half of the government departments and industrial organizations in the United States have experienced some form of computer crime. Because of this growing epidemic, it's important that you understand the different types of computer crime in order to protect yourself and your company's information.

Determining What Is a Crime

There are different degrees of computer crime, from breaking into other people's computers in order to steal or sabotage data to making illegal copies of software to give to a friend. All of it is wrong.

Probably the most often committed offense is theft of computer time. It ranges from the innocent borrowing of someone's computer without permission to the theft of computer time from a business for personal use and gain. Theft of computer time—especially involving large computers, such as one running an office network—can easily translate into a theft of money. Besides the theft of time, unauthorized use of a computer also involves unnecessary wear and tear on the equipment and software.

The best way to judge whether a personal activity might be considered a criminal act is to compare it with the use of a company vehicle. Would it be wrong to borrow a company car or truck without asking? Would it be wrong to use the company car on the weekend for personal use? Would it be wrong to fill up one's personal car with gas and charge it to the corporate account? We know your answer is, "Yes, it would be wrong," so keep this comparison in mind when using business computer equipment and software yourself and when overseeing others' use of it.

Threats from Outside

Today's companies are using computer communications in ever-increasing ways, and these same applications are in the hands of criminals. Working from the privacy of their own homes, would-be criminals often gain access to an organization's computer for the purpose of stealing or altering information. This electronic trespassing or vandalism has several variations, which are referred to by their own slang terms:

- *Hacking*—Breaking into computer systems to gain access to restricted or private information
- *Freaking*—The defrauding of a telephone company using stolen long distance access codes or credit cards
- *Crashing*—Breaking into a computer system in order to shut it down or turn it off
- *Trashing*—The altering or erasing of a computer's data files
- *Viruses*—A malicious computer program that destroys data or opens unauthorized access to a computer

Threats from Inside

One of the most serious threats to the security of business data comes from insiders: Those working within a company who decide to misuse computer or data files as a form of vengeance or for financial gain. This type of computer crime is extremely harmful, since it may involve information worth thousands and thousands of dollars. If a computer crime happens in your company, any insider could be a suspect. However, there are certain individuals who are likely to be investigated first:

- Disgruntled employees may often take their vengeance out on the computer system in the form of sabotage.
- A competitor or an employee who has recently quit or been terminated may be responsible for theft of computer data or software.
- Outside users of a computer system via a communications system may attempt unauthorized sale of information, such as customer lists.

- Computer programmers may attempt to take their programs with them or to create hidden embezzlement schemes.

- Computer operators may alter or erase data on purpose.

- Computer system engineers may attempt to alter security information or passwords.

Software Piracy

Software piracy is another major computer crime problem. Individuals are sometimes allowed to make copies of their programs for protection purposes, but the sale and/or the distribution of those copies to friends and other computer users is a violation of federal copyright laws.

With the growing concern over the copying problem, many software publishers have been forced to devise elaborate copy protection schemes. Piracy may not affect your own company directly, but the cost of combating piracy is eventually passed along to you as the consumer.

Apprehending Criminals

Computer criminals have often been hard to apprehend due to a lack of understanding on the part of law enforcement agencies and the judicial system. However, things are beginning to change. Many states are leading the way with special legislation aimed at stopping software piracy. Other new laws make it a crime to trespass electronically on a computer system even if there is no damage or theft. And many cities are establishing special police units to combat computer crime.

Protecting Your Company's Data

Audit Logs

In order to protect your company's data from these human threats, there are steps you can take. Audit logs are a record of who has been using a computer system. As a user logs onto a computer, it records the time, the name of the user, the files that person accesses, and when the person logs off. The computer then keeps the data in a special security file.

In some cases an audit log can tell whether files have been altered. The use of audit logs is usually provided as part of security password software that can be installed on individual computers. If a computer crime occurs, the log can furnish the authorities with evidence they might need to prosecute.

Codes

Special data encryption techniques code your data files and your communications automatically. Someone who is attempting to intercept and manipulate the information would receive a file that looks like random symbols, thus preventing use of the data.

Computer Viruses

One type of computer crime that is a big concern to even the smallest business is the computer virus. A virus is a program developed by a computer vandal who finds pleasure in creating havoc. This program "infects" other programs, causing them to malfunction or to fail completely. Viruses are passed from computer to computer via communications services and by copying diskettes and files from one computer to another. Some viruses will display only messages, others can damage your hard drive and the files stored there. Some virus programs even try to extort money from victims in order to receive a software antidote.

To combat the rapidly growing virus problem, there are a variety of virus protection software programs available on the market (see Table 17-1). The key to selecting one of these programs is to purchase the most current edition and then update it from time to time.

Most virus protection programs are designed to look for and destroy viruses that are known at the time the program was written. As new viruses appear, an older virus protection program may fail to detect them.

Symptoms of Viruses

When a virus attacks your computer, there may be the following effects:

■ The virus continuously makes a copy of itself and uses up all the free space on your hard drive.

■ A copy of the virus may be sent to all the addresses in your e-mail address list.

■ The virus may reformat your hard drive and wipe out all your files.

■ The virus may install hidden programs that allow people to access your computer without your knowledge or permission.

■ You experience a sudden degradation in system performance.

■ Your anti-virus software stops working for no reason.

■ Strange messages appear on your screen.

■ Strange music or sounds play from your speakers.

■ A program installed on your computer suddenly disappears.

■ Your computer will not start.

■ There is a lot of communications activity.

■ The computer takes a long time to start.

■ You get "out of memory" error messages.

■ You cannot install new programs.

■ A disk utility such as Scandisk reports serious errors.

TABLE 17-1	Anti-Virus Software	
Company	**Internet Address**	**Anti-Virus Software**
Aladdin Knowledge Systems	*www.aks.com*	*eSafe*
Alwil Software	*www.asw.cz*	*Avast*
Anyware Software	*www.helpvirus.com*	*Anyware Anti-Virus*
AVG AntiVirus	*www.grisoft.com*	*AVG Anti-Virus*
Cat Computer Services	*www.quickheal.com*	*Quick Heal*
Central Command Software	*www.centralcommand.com*	*Vexira Antivirus*
Command Software, Inc.	*www.commandsoftware.com*	*Command AntiVirus*
Computer Associates	*www.ca.com/virusinfo*	*eTrust*
Cybersoft	www.cyber.com	wave Antivirus
DialogueScience	*www.dials.ru*	*SpIDer Guard*
Frisk Software	*www.f-prot.com*	*F-Prot Antivirus*
F-Secure	*www.fsecure.com*	*F-Secure Anti-virus*
Kaspersky Labs	*www.kaspersky.com*	*Kaspersk Anti-Virus*
Messagelabs	*www.messagelabs.com/viruseye*	*global e-mail scanning (service not product)*
Network Associates	mcafee.com OR nai.com	*McAfee Anti-Virus*
NetZ Computing	*www.invircible.com*	*InVircible AV*
Panda Software	*www.pandasoftware.com*	*Panda AntiVirus*
Per Systems	*www.persystems.com/antivir.htm*	*Per AntiVirus*
Proland Software	*www.pspl.com*	*Protector Plus*
Safetynet	*www.safe.net*	*VirusNet PC and VirusNet LAN*
Softwin	*www.bitdefender.com*	*BitDefender*
Sophos	*www.sophos.com*	*Sophos Anti-Virus*
Sybari Software	*www.sybari.com*	*Antigen for Microsoft Exchange*
Symantec	*www.symantec.com*	*Norton Antivirus*
TREND Micro	*www.trendmicro.com*	*Trend Virus Control System*

■ A disk storage partition suddenly disappears.

■ Anti-virus software indicates a virus has been found.

Maintaining Your Computer's Security

To prevent virus infections, hacker attacks, and other types of computer crime, do the following:

■ Always use anti-virus software, and keep it updated with the latest virus signature files.

■ Install operating system security updates and software updates.

■ Install and use firewall software.

Acts of Nature

Mother Nature can be an enormous threat, even causing a computer system to fail and lose data permanently. Floods, lightning, tornadoes, hurricanes, and fires could completely destroy your office computer and all your data files, resulting in the failure of the business and loss of everyone's job, since business records, client lists, accounting records, and much more would all be lost.

Electrical surges or voltage spikes can damage the computer's important electronic components. These surges can also disrupt and scramble data storage media like the hard drive. A complete power outage can shut down a computer system, causing loss of all data in the memory.

Mechanical Problems

Mechanical problems can cause storage mediums such as the hard drive to fail, resulting in the loss of all data stored there. Sudden changes in temperature or humidity, or bumping or dropping a computer system when the hard drive is operating can result in what's called a head crash—or hard drive failure. Diskettes can be damaged by a variety of accidents, ranging from spilled drinks to exposure to magnets located in telephones and speakers.

A Security Checklist

Following is a variety of ways to protect your company's data and make it more secure from both human and natural threats. Some of these methods you may wish to use for your own computer. If you have office management responsibilities, you may also want to make changes for your entire department or company.

■ Investigate theft prevention devices that can lock a computer to a desktop.

■ Install small cooling fans inside the computer system to help control high temperatures. They will add to the life of your system.

■ Prevent electrical noise and power surges from damaging your computer system through the use of surge suppressors. A surge suppressor plugs into the wall, and the computer system plugs into it for power.

■ Get even more security with a device known as an **unintcrruptible power supply.** It will power your computer system for a limited period of time in the event of a power outage. Then if an outage does occur, you'd have ample warning to save your data.

■ Make a backup copy of all data stored. The methods to back up your data range from printing out your files on paper; to using a tape backup system, CD-RW, or DVD-RW; to making an extra copy of your data files on a backup diskette.

Coping with Disaster

It is a good idea to insure your company's computer system and software. If you work in a small company, you may want to check with your boss to see if he or she has this insurance. But in the case of a disaster, getting reimbursed for the cost of the equipment can't ever replace the valuable data that the business relies on.

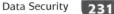

Most large organizations have disaster plans that shift data processing jobs from one location to another and protect data by storing them in two or more different locations. A small business should also have a disaster plan just in case. As secretary, you can get the ball rolling.

A good disaster plan should consider the following points:

- Is backup computer equipment available?

- Are backup software and data files available?

- What should employees do in the event of a disaster?

- What projects and tasks have priority?

- Are essential business supplies available?

Taking the time to create a disaster plan and to inform all employees in the company is essential. If the company is very small, even having an extra computer system, software, and supplies at someone's house may be a good start. It's like an extra insurance policy, and it may help all of you keep your jobs should disaster strike.

chapter 18

Keyboarding Skills

Keyboards

Whether you use a computer, a dedicated word processor, or a typewriter, you are using a keyboard. There are many differences in keyboards depending on the particular system you use. There are also differences in typing on each. For instance, computers and word processors require greater sensitivity than the heavy stroking of a regular manual typewriter.

No matter what keyboard you use, basic typing skills are a must. If your typing skills are not up to the level you feel are necessary for your job, computer programs such as *Mavis Beacon Teaches Typing* can help. If you don't use a computer, there are various touch-typing books that can provide assistance.

Since computer keyboards are growing fastest in importance, the focus of this chapter will be on these. In many cases, electronic typewriter keyboards now have many of the same functions, and we will compare these at the conclusion of the chapter.

Common Keyboards

The most common keyboard layout is the QWERTY keyboard. It gets its name from the first five alphabetical keys on the top left-hand corner of the keyboard. This is the same style used on typewriters in the United States. An alternative keyboard layout is the Dvorak keyboard. It places the keys in different locations on the keyboard and is said to be faster and easier to use once you learn to touch type with this layout. However, most people learn touch-typing with a QWERTY style keyboard.

Keyboard Features

If you examine a typewriter and a computer keyboard side by side, you'll find many similarities. For instance, you'll see on each the normal alphanumeric keys, along with a space bar, an Enter or Return key, Tab keys, Shift keys, Caps Lock, and Backspace. The alphanumeric keys can be used to type letters or numbers. Typing a Shift along with a letter or number key produces an uppercase letter or, in the case of numbers, a special symbol. If you want to type all uppercase letters, you select the Caps Lock key once rather than holding down the Shift key. Touch the Caps Lock key again, and it toggles back off.

On both a typewriter and a computer keyboard, the Tab key moves your next keyboard entry to the next tab stop. However, with a computerized word processor or a modern electronic typewriter, tabs are no longer set mechanically. Instead, you use special software commands, menu or ruler choices, or a special key on the keyboard to set tabs and release them.

The space bar adds spaces between words or characters, and it can insert spaces between words and characters typed previously. The Enter or Return key on a computer keyboard may look similar to the carriage return found on a typewriter, but it is used much differently. On some typewriters, you type a Return at the end of a line in order to begin a new line of type. However, with a word processing computer or modern electronic memory typewriter, a special feature called **word wrapping** is standard. This automatically moves your text to the next line when it will not fit at the end of the previous line. The Enter or Return key is used only to skip lines, such as when starting a new paragraph.

Figure 18-1 shows a QWERTY-style keyboard.

Function Keys

Because of the increased functionality of a computer over a standard typewriter, a variety of extra keys have been added to computer keyboards to use with word processing software, electronic spreadsheets, and database applications. Early computer systems had just a few extra keys, but most modern keyboards have many special-purpose keys.

Numeric Keypad

The numeric keypad is a set of number keys just like those you might find on a calculator. In fact, it is often used for computerized accounting and electronic spreadsheet applications. Many computer systems have built-in calculator soft-

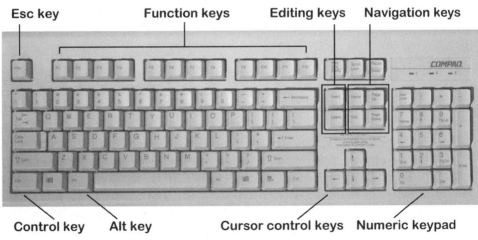

FIGURE 18-1. QWERTY style keyboard.

Photo by Jennifer Wauson. Digital photography courtesy of Kyocera Optics.

ware that can be called up on the monitor screen, allowing the user to make quick calculations and then return to another application to insert the result. The numeric keypad is also sometimes used for navigational purposes in some software applications. For example, if you want to move a pointer up on the screen, you hit the number 8 key. If you want to move down, you hit the number 2 key. To go left, hit 4. And, to go right, hit 6.

The numeric keypad includes several mathematical function keys as well. The "+" key is used for addition, the "−" for subtraction, the "*" for multiplication, the "." for decimals, "/" for division, and " = " for equals or totals. There's also usually an extra Enter key, which is used similarly to the Total key on a calculator. In addition, you may find a Num Lock key. The Num Lock key, which stands for "number lock," toggles the numeric keypad so that it can be used to navigate or to type numbers. When the Num Lock is on, the numbers are entered when typed.

Navigation Keys

Along with the numeric keypad's navigational features, there are special-purpose navigation keys on many keyboards. Most have some form of arrow keys, allowing you to move a pointer on the screen up, down, left, or right. Other navigational keys include the Home, Page Up, Page Down, Insert, and Delete keys. These may also have special functionality in certain applications. For example, in some word processing programs, pressing the HOME key will take you to the beginning of your document. In a spreadsheet program, pressing HOME will take you to the top left-most cell, Al, sometimes called the **home cell.** The Page Up and Page Down keys in a word processing application will cause your document to scroll up or down one page at a time. The Insert key is useful in some word processors for editing and inserting text in the middle of an existing sentence. The Delete key works similarly to a Backspace key. It can also be used to eliminate entire blocks of text that have been previously selected.

Special Function Keys

The special function keys found on many computer keyboards are usually labeled Fl through F10 or F12, although some keyboards have fewer. Located across the top of the keyboard or along the left side, special function keys are used in many applications to allow easy menu selection or to perform common tasks like saving documents, loading documents, printing, and editing. In addition to assigning one command to a particular function key, additional commands are available by pressing the SHIFT or the ALT keys along with a function key. Without the guidance of the software, these keys have little purpose. However, when specially programmed by a particular software application, they can have a multitude of uses.

There is no real standardized method for assigning commands to particular keys, although Fl is often the Help key. To find out the assignments, check the manual for the software you're using. Some software publishers and other third-party vendors make keyboard templates available that connect to the top of your keyboard. These quick reference templates list the commands for each function key, as well as other special key combinations.

Special Command Keys

The special command keys found on most computer keyboards include keys like ALT, CONTROL, and ESCAPE. The ESCAPE key is often used to back out of a series of menu choices or to leave a program. The ALT and CONTROL keys are often used on computers without special function keys. By pressing the ALT or CONTROL key and another designated key, a variety of commands, such as printing or saving, can be given from the keyboard. For keyboards with special function keys, using the ALT or CONTROL keys in combination with the special function keys provides access to additional commands.

IBM-Compatibles Versus Macintosh

Perhaps the greatest differences between computer keyboards are those between IBM-compatible and Macintosh computers. Most of the keys we have been describing are common to IBM-compatibles. Macintosh computers have different special function keys such as the Open-Apple Command key and the Option key. These are used in combination with another keystroke. For example, pressing the OPEN-APPLE COMMAND key along with the S key will save a document. A list of these keyboard commands is available in the software manual, as well as in the pull-down menus. Many of the Macintosh command key combinations have been standardized and are the same from one program to the next.

Keyboard Macros

In addition to using special function and command keys to access specific commands from the keyboard, users can define their own keyboard commands with the help of special keyboard shortcut software. There are a variety of these accessory programs available for both IBM-compatibles and Macintosh computers. These programs allow a user to assign a particular series of commands or keystrokes to a single multi-key combination. For example, use Option-C as a user-assigned command to bring up the calculator. Use Option-D to type today's date automatically.

Another similar keyboard shortcut tool, available in many software applications on both IBM and Macintosh, is the **macro.** A macro can be used to record a long series of keystrokes and menu choices. The recording of these keystrokes and commands can be saved and given a name. In addition, a user-definable key combination can be assigned to call up and play the recorded macro automatically.

The Mouse

Both IBM-compatibles and Macintosh computers use a mouse as an addition to the computer keyboard. A mouse is a hand controller that contains a small, round ball connected to a series of sensors. When you move the mouse around on your desk, the ball inside rolls, and the sensors translate this into movement of a pointer on the monitor screen. Thus, if you pick up the mouse and move it in the air, it does not affect the monitor screen at all.

Today it's impossible to discuss keyboarding skills without also discussing the use of a mouse. Most people use a mouse in conjunction with a mouse pad, a piece of foam rubber that gives the mouse extra traction. The amount of movement on the screen that a mouse can produce can be controlled by the computer's operating system. On IBM-compatible Windows-based systems, the mouse control is found in the Control Panel folder. With Macintosh computers, the mouse control is found in the control panel under the Apple pull-down menu option.

The IBM-compatible mouse has two or three buttons. The left mouse button is used for making selections. The right mouse button is used for accessing special function menus. If the mouse is equipped with a third button, it can be programmed to perform special functions. A left-handed user can switch the functionality of the mouse buttons.

The Macintosh mouse usually only has one button that is used for making selections.

A wheel mouse differs from a standard mouse in that it includes a little wheel between the two buttons. When you roll the wheel, you can scroll up or down on the screen without having to click the scroll bars. This comes in handy when viewing long documents.

As an alternative to a mouse, track balls are available. They are almost like a mouse turned upside down. By rolling the ball with your fingers, you can move a pointer on the screen. Track balls are common with some laptop computers where operating conditions make it difficult to access a mouse.

Another alternative to a mouse and track ball is the track pad found on many laptop computers. The pressure-sensitive pad allows you to move the cursor around on the screen by moving your finger over the pad. The track pad usually includes two buttons that act like mouse buttons. Some laptop computers also include a pointing stick positioned in the middle of the keyboard keys. By pushing or pulling the pointing stick with your finger, the cursor is moved on the display screen.

Using Typewriters

Modern electronic typewriter keyboards provide many of the same features found on IBM-compatibles and Macintosh computers. In addition to the common keys such as Tab, Space, Shift, Backspace, and Return, there are special navigation, special function, and command keys. Depending on whether a typewriter has memory capability, the number of special keys will vary. They also vary greatly by manufacturer. However, even the most modest electronic typewriters now have some small amount of memory available and thus several additional keys for editing.

Common keyboard layouts include correction keys for correcting a character, word, or line, along with navigational keys for moving around within a document. Typewriters with built-in spelling checkers usually have a key for turning this feature on or off. Special formatting keys can justify text in several different ways. A special command or code key is often used to access additional formatting commands as well as special symbols.

Word Processing

The use of word processing can greatly improve your overall productivity. Even if you don't use a computer, most typewriters now have some form of word processing built in. And although there are great differences between word processing typewriters and word processing software for computers, almost all allow you to create documents—edit and format these documents—and print them. Other features include spelling checkers, style and grammar checkers, mail-merge features, and the ability to store documents electronically.

The most common word processors found in businesses are microcomputers equipped with word processing software. When the word processing program is run by the computer, the computer becomes an intelligent typewriter with the ability to create, edit, format, and store documents.

Creating Documents

In order to get started using a word processor, you must first create a fresh blank document. This is like loading a sheet of paper into a typewriter. Some word processors require the user to create a new document and to name it. However, most allow you to wait until you save the document for the first time before assigning it a name.

Typing

When a new document has been created, you can begin typing and entering data. Some types of word processors, such as those for the Macintosh or Windows environment, allow you to begin typing immediately. As you type on the keyboard, the letters and words appear on the display screen. The text or data you type are stored in the computer's memory temporarily, until the document is saved or discarded or the power is turned off.

Positioning

On the screen a pointer called a **cursor** shows where text will appear when typed. Cursors can take many forms: A vertical line, an underscore, or a rectangle. They may also flash on and off. It all depends on the particular word processing software used. You can move the cursor from one character to another, up or down, or left and right in order to make corrections, edit, or format the text. To move the cursor, some word processors employ the arrow keys on the computer keyboard. On keyboards that don't have arrow keys, special combinations involving the number keys on the numeric keypad or two or more keys pressed simultaneously will also move the cursor. Some word processing software programs allow the use of special function keys on the keyboard or special key combinations to jump to the top or bottom of the page.

You can also use a mouse to move around your document. By moving the mouse, a pointer moves on the screen. When you click the mouse, the cursor jumps to that location. If you want to change a word a few lines up from where you're currently typing, move the mouse up to that line; click; delete the incorrect word by using the BACKSPACE or DELETE key; and retype a new word in its place.

As you continue typing, you'll notice one of the main differences between word processors and typewriters when you reach the end of a line of text. On a typewriter, you type a carriage return and start a new line. Other more advanced typewriters with built-in computer memory automatically move a word that will not fit down to start the next line. This is a feature common to all word processors called **word wrap.** Thus, when typing on a word processor, you never have to type a carriage return unless you want to begin a new paragraph.

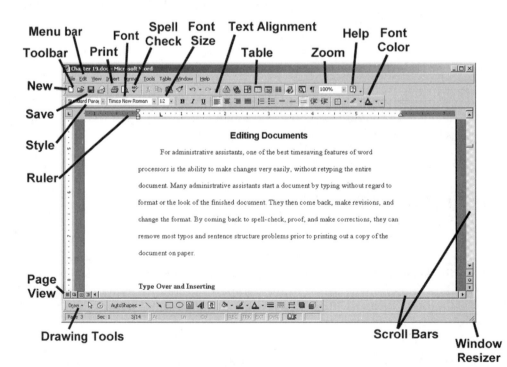

FIGURE 19-1. Microsoft Word.

Screen shot reprinted by permission from Microsoft Corporation.

✴ Editing Documents

For administrative assistants, one of the best timesaving features of word processors is the ability to make changes very easily, without retyping the entire document. Many administrative assistants start a document by typing without regard to format or the look of the finished document. They then come back, make revisions, and change the format. By coming back to spell-check, proof, and make corrections, they can remove most typos and sentence structure problems prior to printing out a copy of the document on paper.

Type-Over and Inserting

For some word processors, a user must first select the proper editing mode in order to make revisions. This is done by typing a special function key, such as the INSERT key, or a key combination. One editing function is the type-over mode that allows a user to type over mistakes. New characters appear on the screen in place of existing characters. If new characters or words must be inserted instead, an insert mode is available. When the insert mode is activated by pressing the INSERT key, new characters appear when typed, and all characters and words to the right of the cursor move to the right to make room.

Word processors written for Windows and Macintosh are always in insert mode by default. The user does not have to type any special function keys or key combinations to turn on insert mode.

Deleting Text

To delete text from a document, several choices are available. The simplest method is similar to the BACKSPACE key on a typewriter. Some keyboards have BACKSPACE keys, and others have a key marked DELETE.

When you type the BACKSPACE key, the cursor moves to the left one space and erases the character that was displayed there. When you type the DELETE key, the character that occupies the same space as the cursor is erased. Some word processors require you to move the cursor to highlight the specific character to be deleted and then to type the DELETE key.

Undo

In case you inadvertently delete something you did not mean to, most word processors have an Undo function. This can be accessed via a special function key or key combination or, in the case of Windows and Macintosh, a pull-down menu choice. When you delete text, it's stored in a temporary buffer memory. The buffer stores the last thing you deleted, such as a word, sentence, paragraph, or even whole pages. Select the Undo function, and your text is restored.

Cutting and Pasting

Moving text from one location to another is one more useful feature of word processors. For Windows and Macintosh environments, just click and drag the mouse to highlight a block of text such as a sentence, paragraph, or group of paragraphs. Once the text is highlighted, select Cut or Copy from a pull-down menu to put the text (or a copy of it) into the temporary memory buffer. Next, use the mouse to navigate through the document to the location where the text should be inserted. By clicking the mouse on this location and selecting Paste from the pull-down menu, you remove the text from the memory buffer and insert it into the new location. Thus, moving text from one location to another is called **cutting and pasting.**

Searching

Most word processors provide the ability to search for and find a particular string of characters or words anywhere in a document. This feature comes in handy for finding names in a mailing list or other specific information from a document. Some word processors call this a **Search** function, others a **Find** function.

In order to search an entire document, position the cursor at the beginning of the document. On Windows- and Macintosh-based word processors, a Search or Find function is available on a pull-down menu. Once Search has been selected, you'll be asked to type in the characters or words you want to find.

Searching and Replacing

A related function is Search and Replace. Many users save time by using Search and Replace like a macro. If these users frequently have to type a long, complicated word or phrase in a document, they will type substitute characters instead, such as "xxx." Since "xxx" would normally not appear in a document, the user can later access the Search and Replace function. This function then finds "xxx" and allows the user to type in a replacement string—the long, complicated word or phrase.

Formatting Documents

Many users of word processors start by typing in text and later go back to make adjustments to the way the document will look when printed on paper. This is a process known as **formatting.** There are many different ways to format a document, for example, by changing the margins, the line spacing, or the type style and size of the characters.

Margins

All word processors allow you to set the left and right margins. Most often a ruler is used to show where on a piece of paper the text will be positioned when printed. For Windows and Macintosh, margins are set by moving a margin guide on the ruler, and tabs are positioned by moving a tab guide—both with the mouse.

Line Spacing

For the Windows and Macintosh environments, the spacing is changed by selecting a choice from the ruler or menu bar. There are icon choices for single spaced, double spaced, and triple spaced. They can be selected at any time when entering text; the text entered after the selection will be spaced according to your choice. You can also alter the spacing of already existing text by first highlighting the text with a mouse or pointer, and then selecting your line spacing choice from the ruler.

Tabs

Word processing programs let you set tabs and can be programmed to indent a specified number of spaces at the beginning of a new paragraph automatically. Windows- and Macintosh-based word processors use pointers, which can be placed on the ruler at various points to determine tab stops and indentions.

Justification

The remaining line-formatting option is justification. Any block of text can be aligned flush with the left margin or the right margin. Another choice is full justification, which aligns the text flush with both the left and the right margin—like typesetting in a book. This is done by adding spaces between the words of each line. A fourth option is centered justification, used to center titles and other text in the middle of a line.

For Windows- and Macintosh-based word processors, select your justification option from the ruler or pull-down menu with the mouse or pointer. A previously written block of text may be justified by first highlighting the block with the mouse, and then selecting the justification choice from the ruler or pull-down menu.

Character Formatting

Another major document-formatting tool is the character format. Text can be printed in a variety of different styles, such as underlined, bold, and italics. In addition, the characters themselves can be printed in many different sizes and typefaces called **fonts.**

Often, word processing programs come with a limited number of fonts and font sizes already installed. Additional fonts can be purchased as software to increase your number of choices. Some fonts are used to display text on the screen, and others are used by the printer. Some printers will print only fonts that are installed in the printer hardware.

Windows and Macintosh word processors use pull-down menus to select font style choices, which appear on the monitor screen almost the way they'll appear printed on paper. The font and size of existing text can be changed by highlighting the text with the mouse or pointer and then selecting the font choice from the pull-down menu.

Page Formatting

Additional formatting options are available for entire documents and sections of a document. For example, the page format determines the top, bottom, left, and right margins for all text on a page. In addition, headers and footers can be inserted on each page for page numbers, the date, or the name of a document.

Styles

If you create a specialized format for a document, rather than manually format each section, you can create what are called **styles.** Styles allow you to define individual formatting characteristics such as margins, justification, font size, and font style and give them a name that can be accessed from a menu on the ruler.

Printing Documents

When a document has been created and formatted, getting that document printed on paper is the ultimate goal for most word processor users. The Print function allows you to specify additional information about the way the document should appear on paper: for example, which pages of the document are to be printed, whether the printing itself should be draft mode or letter quality, how many copies should be made, page orientation (portrait versus landscape), paper size, and whether the printing will be one-sided or two-sided.

Most word processors have a print-preview feature, which displays on the monitor the overall layout of the printed document on paper. In this way, you can see the formatting options before time and paper are wasted printing an incorrect document. Before printing any document, it's important that you first save the document on a diskette or the computer's hard drive. Since printing involves a hardware connection between two different devices, occasionally there are problems that cause a computer to "hang up" on the printer. If you have not saved your document, you could lose it if this happens.

Some of the biggest problems for many word processing users are printer related. The printer might print something you didn't intend, or perhaps it might not print at all. In order for the computer to communicate with a printer, print driver software is required. This software is usually supplied with the printer but can also be found included with some word processing software. It's important that you specify the type of printer you are using and how it's connected to the computer. For Macintosh and Windows word processors, this can be done from the pull-down menus.

Saving and Loading Documents

One of the main benefits of using a word processor is the ability to save your documents electronically and to retrieve them to use again. In this way, common business documents such as letters, invoices, and contracts can be created once, saved, and then customized as needed. This feature eliminates having to re-create a letter or document every time it is needed.

Saving a document is an electronic way of recording the data on a diskette or on the computer's hard drive. Before you can save a document, you'll be asked to name the document and to designate where you want to save it. Some word processors limit the number of characters that can be used in a name, so many people resort to using codes that can be easily remembered, such as

M92604 for "memo written on 9-26-2004." Other word processors will allow longer names.

If your computer is equipped with multiple disk drives and hard disk drives, you must specify on which drive you want to save the document. One good rule of thumb is to save your data on diskettes rather than on your hard drive since the storage space on the hard drive is limited. Another good practice is to save your documents twice, on two different diskettes. In this way, if something happens to one of the diskettes, you'll have a backup copy for protection.

Loading or opening a document that has been previously saved involves specifying the name of the document you want to open and telling the computer which drive it is saved on. When a document is loaded from a diskette or hard drive into the computer's memory, only a copy of the document is loaded. The original saved version is still stored on the disk. If you make changes to the document and save it again using the same name, only the most recent version will be saved on the diskette. The original version is wiped out, and the new version is saved in its place. To save both versions of a document, you need to alter the name of the new version. Even if you change just one letter or character in the name, the new version will be saved in a different space, and the original version will still be intact on the disk.

Fortunately, most word processors have built-in protection that warns you when an original version of a document is about to be **overwritten.** The word processor tells you that a previous version of the same document already exists and asks you to confirm that you really want to wipe out the old version. Other word processors use Update, Replace, or Revise commands to wipe out or protect your original version of a document.

Advanced Word Processing Features

Many word processors have advanced features that may be of use to you in your job. For example, if you create long manuscripts or reports, features such as indexing, sorting, footnote tracking, automatic hyphenation, and tables may be of help. Check the manual for your word processing software if you wish to employ these powerful tools.

Spelling and Grammar Checkers

Spelling checkers automatically look for spelling errors. Grammar and style checkers analyze the mechanics of your writing. Thesaurus programs can provide synonyms for words used in your document.

Just because you use a spelling, grammar, or style checker to analyze a document doesn't mean that you shouldn't proofread the material, too. Many times a word or phrase that appears correct to the computer is not correct in a given context.

Mail Merging

One of the most useful business-related features, **mail merging** allows you to create a single form letter and to merge it with a list of names and information to create individualized letters. For example, you might want to send a personal letter to customers telling each one about your company's new product or service. First you create a document containing the names and addresses of your customers. Then you create a form letter with special symbols or commands inserted where the customer's name and address and the greeting would normally go. These special symbols or commands are determined by your particular word processing software. These commands link the form letter with your address list so that, when you print out the form letter, it automatically picks up elements of the list, such as name and address, and positions them in the proper place. The result is individualized letters by the dozens or even hundreds, while you typed only one. The exact procedures for creating a mail merge vary; the software manual outlines the steps for your particular program.

Macros

Many word processors utilize macros to help customize and shorten repetitive processes. A macro is a way of recording a series of keystrokes or commands and recalling them by using a single keystroke or key combination. For example, you might have to type a long medical term repeatedly throughout a document. Rather than type it over and over, you might create a macro that with just a two-key combination automatically types the longer word.

Macros can also be created for a series of command choices from a menu, such as those required to select special formatting. Word processors such as Microsoft Word call these special formatting macros **style sheets.** Style sheets can be very helpful when the format changes often within a document. By highlighting a particular block of text, you can assign a name to this style, and it will be assigned a place on the ruler or pull-down menu, where it can be easily selected in the future.

Popular Word Processing Software

Here is a partial list of popular word processing software available:

- Microsoft Word
- Corel WordPerfect
- Lotus Word Pro

Desktop Publishing

What Is Desktop Publishing?

Desktop publishing allows you to create brochures, fliers, newsletters, advertisements, and manuals without having to visit a print shop. Many administrative assistants use desktop publishing software to create high quality publications that can be printed one at a time in the office or taken to a local print shop for mass duplication. Many desktop publishing programs have predefined templates that allow you to add your own text and graphics to quickly customize a publication. You can create your own letterhead, business cards, and business forms with the help of desktop publishing.

While it is similar to word processing in theory, desktop publishing focuses on the layout of text and graphics on a page. Some sophisticated word processing programs, such as Microsoft Word, can be used for desktop publishing. However, there are other more specialized tools available for creating graphics, adding special effects, and for layout of multi-page brochures in desktop publishing software.

In addition to desktop publishing software, you will need an office computer system complete with a keyboard, monitor, and mouse. Optional desktop publishing hardware includes: A graphics tablet, color printer, scanner, and digital camera.

Desktop Publishing Software

There are five general types of software used for desktop publishing. These programs make up your desktop publishing toolbox.

Word Processing

Word processing programs such as Microsoft Word and Corel WordPerfect are used to type and edit text, check spelling and grammar, and format text. These programs are best suited for working with words, not for page layout. Word processing programs can be used in conjunction with page layout software to create text and then export it to the page layout program. Figure 20-1 shows a simple desktop publishing layout created in Microsoft Word.

Page Layout

Page layout programs such as Adobe PageMaker, QuarkXPress, and Microsoft Publisher are the software most closely associated with desktop publishing. Page layout software allows for the integration of text and images on the page, manipulation of the page elements, and for creation of artistic designs. High-end or professional level tools available within these programs include separations, imposition, and typographic controls. Figure 20-2 shows a page layout in Adobe PageMaker. Figure 20-3 shows a page layout in Microsoft Publisher.

Illustration

Illustration programs are vector-based drawing tools for creating artwork, logos, and other drawings made by hand. Art can be created by drawing with a mouse or by using a graphics tablet. The most popular illustration programs include Adobe Illustrator and CorelDRAW. Figure 20-4 shows a screen from Adobe Illustrator.

Photo and Image Editing

Bitmap graphics, such as photographs, are manipulated using photo editing software. These photo-realistic images can be obtained by scanning photos, using a digital camera, or by purchasing stock digital images. These programs al-

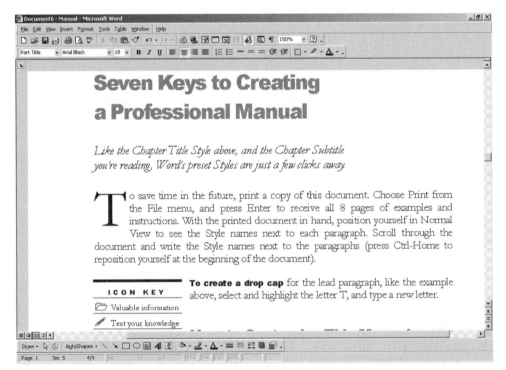

FIGURE 20-1. A page layout in Microsoft Word.

Screen shot reprinted by permission from Microsoft Corporation.

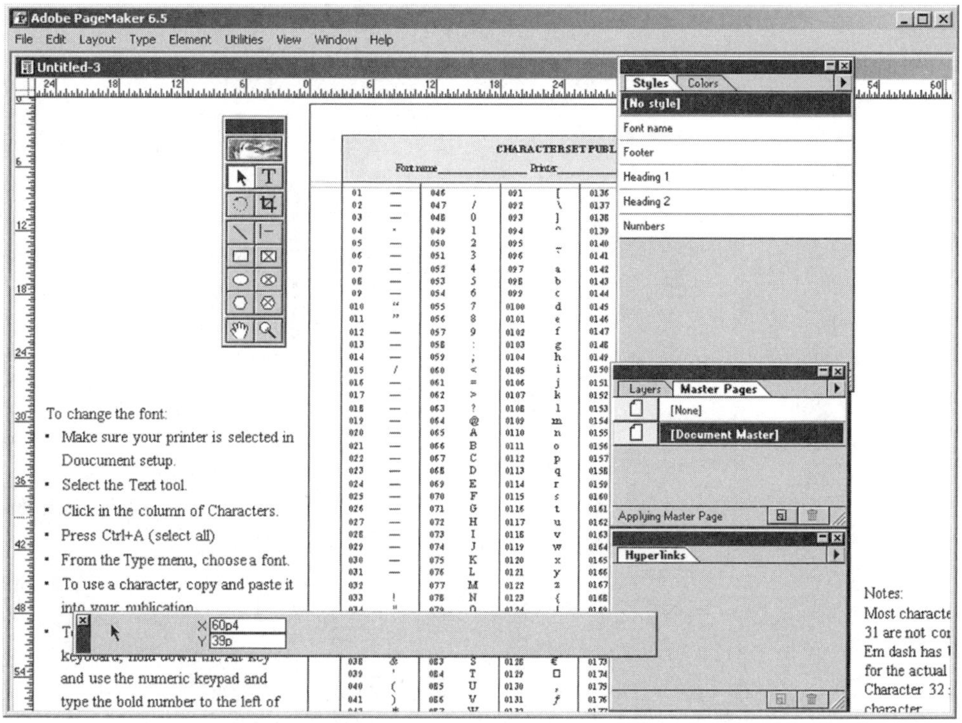

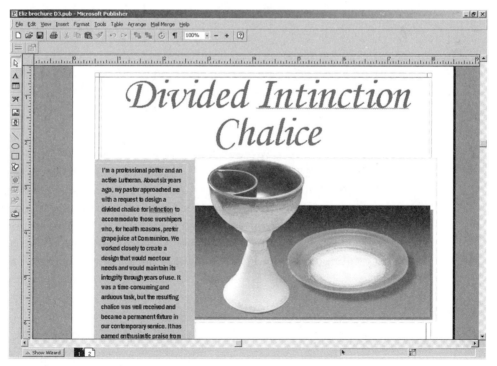

FIGURE 20-2. Adobe PageMaker.

Screen shot reprinted by permission from Adobe Systems, Inc.

FIGURE 20-3. Microsoft Publisher.

Screen shot reprinted by permission from Microsoft Corporation.

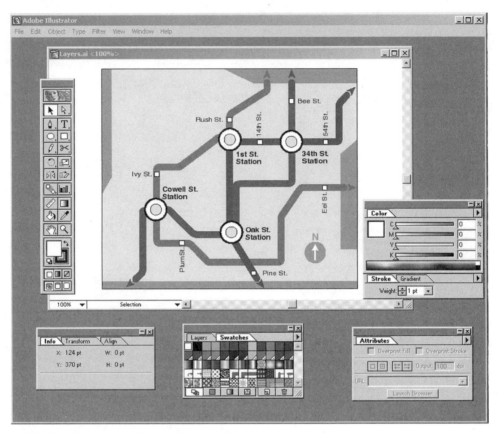

FIGURE 20-4. Adobe Illustrator.

Screen shot reprinted by permission from Adobe Systems, Inc.

low you to color-correct images, crop them, manipulate them by copying and pasting elements, add text, combine and layer images, and add special effects. The most popular photo editing programs include Adobe Photoshop and Corel PhotoPaint. Figure 20-5 shows a screen from Adobe Photoshop.

Font and Image Management Utilities

The various text styles available for desktop publishing projects are called **fonts.** There are thousands of font choices available, and special tools are needed to manage them. Adobe Type Manager and Bitstream Font Navigator are used to organize and group fonts into families so they can be more easily selected. Image management programs such as ThumbPlus and HiJaak make it easier to locate pictures and do batch conversions or cataloging.

Types of Desktop Publishing Documents

The first step in desktop publishing is deciding what type of document is going to be produced. Will you create a brochure, a newsletter, or a business card? Depending on the document, the general format may already be predetermined. For example, if you need to create a business card, the document size

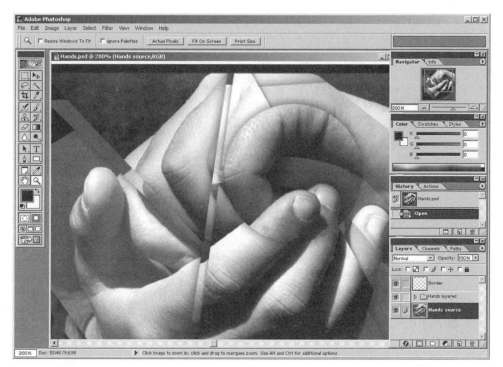

FIGURE 20-5. Adobe Photoshop.

Screen shot reprinted by permission from Adobe Systems, Inc.

and general characteristics will already be known. You might use a business card template available in a program such as Microsoft Publisher and customize it with your company's logo and text information.

There are a variety of desktop publishing documents you may be asked to produce as an administrative assistant including: Advertisements, direct mail, holiday messages, identity package, and sales information.

Advertising Information
Advertisements come in many different sizes, so the first step is determining the type of ad. Is it a Yellow Pages display ad, a small newspaper ad, an online ad for a Web site, or a flyer? Figure 20-6 shows a template available in Microsoft Publisher for creating an advertisement.

Direct Mail
Direct mail marketing can take various forms ranging from postcards to flyers to letters to brochures. You must decide which format is best based on the amount of information you will include, the purpose of the mailing, and the budget for postage.

Holiday Message
Customized corporate greeting cards are popular, but so are holiday newsletters, customized calendars, and postcards. Explore the templates available in your desktop publishing program, or create something new.

FIGURE 20-6. Advertisement Template in Microsoft Publisher.
Screen shot reprinted by permission from Microsoft Corporation.

Identity Package

Business cards, letterhead, and envelopes are the first steps in creating a corporate identity, and all three can be created using desktop publishing software. In addition, you can also create note cards, notepads, rolodex cards, fax forms, and custom invoices.

Sales Information

If your company is involved in sales, you may be asked to help create a sales brochure. The type of product, the size of your marketing budget, and the amount of information you need to include will determine the size of the brochure. Other sales-related documents include fliers, price lists, catalogs, and online catalogs.

The Desktop Document

While there are a variety of processes and procedures involved in desktop publishing, the basic desktop publishing techniques involve six different areas: Design, setup, text, images, file preparation, and printing.

Design

Design is an on-going process that begins prior to creation of the document. During this phase you may:

- Determine document format and type
- Conceptualize and brainstorm
- Create rough drafts
- Select colors
- Select fonts
- Select images

Document Setup

This is the phase where desktop publishing begins. During this phase you may:

- Select a template
- Set page size and margins
- Set up columns and grids
- Set up master pages
- Customize the color palette
- Create paragraph styles

Text and Fonts

The text used in your desktop publishing document can take many forms. Text may be created by typing directly into the page layout software or by using a word processor and then exporting the text. During this phase you may:

- Create text
- Import and place text
- Compose the text layout
- Select fonts
- Apply paragraph style settings

Images

Depending on the type of document and the elements you are using, image creation and selection can occur at any point in the process. While working with images you may:

- Take digital photographs
- Scan images using a scanner
- Browse and select images from clip art and stock photo collections
- Create and edit photo-realistic bitmap graphics using an image editor
- Create vector-based artwork graphics using an illustration program
- Convert images to the proper graphics file format
- Import and place graphics into the page layout
- Create boxes, add callouts, captions, and titles to images

File Preparation

After you get your desktop publishing document looking the way you want it, you must prepare the file to make sure it will print as planned. This is known as the **prepress phase.** During this phase you may:

- Do soft- and hardcopy proofs
- Embed fonts
- Specify color trapping

- Verify color specifications
- Package fonts and graphics with the file
- Impose the file
- Create a PostScript or Adobe Acrobat PDF file

Printing

With the creation process complete and the file prepared for printing, the last step is to print. During this phase you may:

- Print to a desktop laser or inkjet printer
- Deliver the digital files to a commercial printer
- Finish the document by trimming or folding

Desktop Publishing Software Tools

Most desktop publishing software share certain common tools. They allow you to arrange and format text and graphics. Of course, each program has its own procedures, but there are four basic tools that almost all desktop publishing programs have available: Selection, text, graphics, and magnification. You will find these tools in your program's toolbox.

Selection

The selection tool, also known as the **pointer,** is the most basic tool in any desktop publishing application. It is usually represented by an arrow and is used to select one or more page elements and move them around on the page. The selection tool can also be used to resize page elements.

Text

The text tool is usually represented by a T or A in the program's toolbox. It is used for adding text to your layout. By selecting the text tool, you can position your cursor on the page and then click your mouse. You will then be able to use it to draw a text box and enter text. You can also use this tool to select a text box to change the formatting to a different size, color, font, or style.

Graphics

Most desktop publishing programs have graphics tools for drawing boxes, lines, and for importing graphics. The toolbox may have tools for drawing freehand, making circles, rectangles, lines, and curved lines. Some graphics tools allow you to format the shapes by changing their size, color, texture, transparency, and shape.

Magnification

In order to see your page layout up close for fine tuning, most desktop publishing programs have a magnification tool for zooming. Usually the tool is a magnifying glass.

Typography

The style, size, and type of text used in desktop publishing is known in the printing world as **typography.** In the computerized desktop publishing world we call them **fonts.**

Fonts are measured in picas and points. **Picas** measure the length of a line of text. **Points** are 1/12 of a pica. Font sizes are measured in points. The larger the number, the bigger the type.

Leading is the space above and below the characters in a font for ascenders and descenders so they do not touch the next line. **Kerning** refers to the space between letters in a word. Both leading and kerning are adjustable in most desktop publishing programs and word processing programs such as Microsoft Word.

There are two main classifications of typefaces: Serif and sans-serif. **Serif** fonts have tiny trailing lines that finish the stroke of each character. These fonts are generally used for normal text because they are easier to read. Popular serif fonts include Times Roman.

Sans-serif means no serif. This type is clean and normally used for headings within documents. Helvetica is the most popular sans-serif font.

Page Layout

A master page layout is a common design that will be used throughout a publication. For example, the master page layout determines:

- The number of columns
- The use of horizontal and vertical bars
- The placement of illustrations and logos
- The settings for page size
- The settings for portrait versus landscape page orientation
- The page margins
- The use of facing or single-sided pages
- The use of footers and headers
- The page numbering

Graphics Formats

Graphics come in a variety of file formats, and not all are suitable for every purpose. Some are best for the Web; others are more suitable for printing. Table 20-1 lists graphic formats and their applications.

What Is PostScript?

One of the things you may have noticed in Table 20-1 is the term **PostScript.** PostScript was developed by Adobe, one of the leading producers of desktop publishing software.

TABLE 20-1	Graphic Formats and Their Applications
File Format	**Application**
BMP	Screen display in Windows.
EPS	Printing to PostScript printers and image setters. Best choice for high resolution printing of illustrations.
GIF	Screen display, especially for the Web. Best choice for publishing illustrations and screen shots online.
JPEG	Screen display on the Web. Good choice for online publishing.
PICT	Screen display on the Macintosh and for printing to non-PostScript printers.
TIFF	Printing to PostScript printers. Good choice for high resolution printing of images.
WMF	Screen display under Windows or printing to non-PostScript printers. Good choice for vector graphics.

PostScript is a programming language used to communicate between a computer and a printer. The language describes what a page should look like to the printer. Printers print tiny dots on the paper. How these dots are arranged determines what your finished document looks like. A PostScript printer uses the language to translate the digital document created by your desktop publishing software into a raster image of dots a printer can print.

Some sophisticated documents with an intricate combination of graphics and fonts are best output when using PostScript. PostScript is generally device-independent; that is, it will print just about the same on any PostScript compatible device.

If your desktop publishing work consists of letterhead, business cards, and simple brochures, you probably don't have to worry much about PostScript. You can use a non-PostScript printer and achieve pleasing results. If you need to send your desktop publishing files to a commercial printer for output, you may need to use a PostScript printer to proof your documents in advance.

One way to confirm your document will print the same anywhere it is printed is to use Adobe Acrobat. Acrobat generates special files called PDF files. PDF stands for Portable Document Format. PDF files include all the PostScript information necessary to make sure your desktop publishing documents are truly portable.

Adobe Acrobat allows you to print to the Acrobat Distiller. This is a software-only printer that converts your print output into the PDF file. Figure 20-7 shows a screen from Adobe Acrobat.

Scanners

Scanners have become an important part of the modern office. Not only can they be used to scan photographs into digital images for use in desktop publishing applications, but they can also be used to digitize images of paper documents for storing them electronically. In addition, optical character recognition soft-

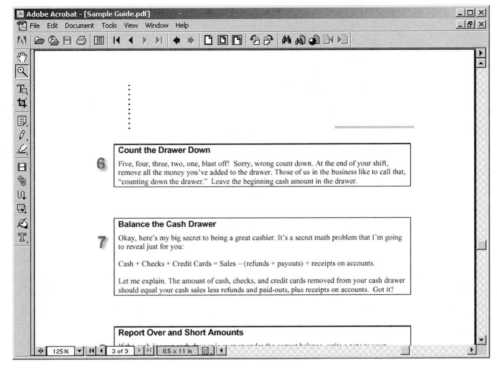

FIGURE 20-7. Adobe Acrobat for creating PDF files.

Screen shot reprinted by permission from Adobe Systems, Inc.

ware can examine a scanned image of text and convert that text into digital text for editing and use in a word processor or desktop publishing application. Some office machines combine the features of a scanner, printer, and copier into one unit. Figure 20-8 shows a combination scanner, printer, and copier.

The most common types of scanners used in business are flatbed or desktop scanners and handheld scanners. For most business applications, a flatbed scanner capable of scanning legal size documents is the best choice.

Scanners use a photographic process similar to digital cameras. They use Charge-Coupled Device (CCD) arrays. These are light-sensitive diodes that convert light into an electric charge. When a document is placed on the glass plate of a scanner, and the cover is closed, a lamp shines a bright light on the document. The CCDs are located on the scanning head, which is moved slowly across the document. By using a series of filters and mirrors, color information is captured.

Scanners vary in resolution and sharpness. Resolution is measured in dots per inch (dpi). The scanner's dpi is determined by the number of sensors in the CCD. Most scanners have a dpi of at least 300×300. For most business applications a resolution of 600×600 dpi is best. This will allow you to scan and reproduce full color photographs, as well as use Optical Character Recognition (OCR) software to convert hardcopy text to digital text.

Scanners can increase the perceived resolution using a technique called **interpolation.** This is accomplished by creating extra pixels or dots between

FIGURE 20-8. Combination scanner, printer, and copier.

Photo courtesy of Xerox Corporation. All rights reserved.

the ones scanned by the CCD. When evaluating a scanner for your business, you should focus on true DPI resolution and not interpolated resolution.

Another term associated with scanning is **bit depth.** This is also called **color depth.** This refers to the number of colors the scanner is capable of reproducing. Each pixel requires 24 bits to create true color, and almost all scanners support this. Some scanners offer 30 or 36 bit depth; however for most business applications a scanner with a bit depth of 24 is sufficient.

Images are transferred from the scanner to your computer using one of four connections:

- Parallel—Connects through your printer parallel port and is the slowest transfer method available

- Small Computer System Interface (SCSI)—Requires a special SCSI connection card or interface in your computer. Most SCSI scanners come with an interface card.

- Universal Serial Bus (USB)—Connects to your computer's USB port and is fast and affordable

- FireWire—Requires a FireWire port or interface card on your computer, but is the fastest transfer method available

One additional component in a scanning system is the scanning software. You will need a driver and scanning application installed on your computer. Most scanning software is used in association with another application such as a drawing program or a word processing program. Scanners speak a language called **TWAIN.** The TWAIN driver acts as an interpreter between any application that supports the TWAIN standard and the scanner. For example, Microsoft Word and Adobe Photoshop both support the TWAIN standard.

Digital Photography

Digital photography is rapidly replacing the film camera and has many applications in business. You can use a digital camera to take pictures and then import your pictures into your computer for use in desktop publishing applications. You can create images for high-quality newsletters, photo ID cards, and Web sites for your company with a digital camera.

The key difference between a digital camera and a film-based camera is that the digital camera has no film. Instead it has a sensor (a CCD similar to a scanner or a CMOS chip) that converts light into a digital form. Images can be saved in a graphic file format, typically JPEG.

Many of the illustrations in this book were photographed using a digital camera provided by Kyocera Optics, Inc. Figure 20-9 shows the three-megapixel camera that was used.

The key features you need to consider when choosing a digital camera include:

- Resolution
- Sensor technology
- Storage
- Compression formats
- LCD
- Optical viewfinder
- Lens
- Interface to the computer

- Exposure control
- Image stabilization
- Focus
- Macro
- Movie mode
- Batteries
- Flash
- Image processing software

Resolution

The resolution of a digital camera is measured in megapixels. Pixels are the image elements in a CCD or CMOS chip. The more pixels, the better the image quality. For most business and home applications you need at least three megapixels. This will allow you to take a picture that is 2048 × 1536 pixels in size and will allow you to reproduce a large 8 × 10 inch image.

Even though a camera is capable of three megapixels, you can take pictures at different resolutions. For example, if your images are only going to be published on the Web, you can use a resolution of 640 × 480 pixels. This will allow you to store more pictures in your computer's memory without having to off-load them to your computer.

FIGURE 20-9. A digital camera.

Photo courtesy of Kyocera Optics, Inc.,
All rights reserved.

Sensor Technology

The choice in sensor technology is between CCD and CMOS sensors. CCDs have more pixels and take better pictures in low light. However, they tend to be more expensive and use more power.

CMOS sensors are lower resolution and don't work as well in low light. However, if you need a low-end camera suitable for photography published on the Web, a CMOS equipped, low-cost camera may be a good option.

Storage

Images are stored in the camera's memory. Most digital cameras use some form of storage device. Some common choices include a writeable CD or DVD, hard disk, diskette, CompactFlash, SmartMedia, and Memory Sticks. Removable memory cards are sold with a specified amount of memory.

Compression Format

Images are typically compressed by the camera as they are saved on the memory card. In uncompressed mode a 3 megapixel image is approximately 3 megabytes in size. Most cameras store images in JPEG graphics file format. Some high-end cameras also support the TIFF format. JEPGs are compressed images, TIFFs are not.

LCD

Most digital cameras have a Liquid Crystal Display (LCD) screen that allows you to view a picture right away. If you don't like the image, you can delete it and take another picture.

Viewfinder

Some cameras do not have an LCD display and use a simple optical viewfinder. Other digital cameras have both an LCD and a viewfinder. By turning off the LCD you can save power and make your batteries last longer. In addition, sometimes in bright sunlight it is difficult to see the LCD. In that case, you can use the optical viewfinder.

Lens

The more expensive the digital camera, the better the lens, number of pixels, and other features. An optical zoom is better than a digital zoom. An optical zoom has an adjustable focal length lens. A digital zoom expands the image by enlarging it electronically. Some cameras combine both an optical and digital zoom.

Overall, you will find four different kinds of lenses on digital cameras:

- Fixed-focus, fixed-zoom
- Optical-zoom with automatic focus
- Digital-zoom
- Replaceable lens systems

Interface

The interface with your computer allows you to transfer images from your camera to your computer for image processing and desktop publishing applications. There are four different interfaces available:

- USB—A cable connects from your camera to the USB port on your computer.

- Serial—A cable connects from your computer to the serial port on your computer. This is a slow way to transfer images.

- Disk—The camera uses a diskette or a writeable CD or DVD to store images. You can put the disk or CD/DVD into your computer's diskette or CD/DVD drive to read the graphic files.

- Flash Memory Slots—A flash memory reader is attached to the computer that will allow you to remove a memory card from the camera and insert it into the reader in order to transfer the images to your computer.

Exposure Control

Most digital cameras have automatic exposure. Some cameras offer manual exposure control and special settings for specific situations such as sports, landscapes, and portraits.

Image Stabilization

Some cameras offer a special feature to steady the camera to help you take clearer pictures. This feature is popular on video camcorders.

Focus

Most digital cameras have fixed focus—where you can't adjust focus at all—or automatic focus. Some digital cameras have a manual focus option.

Macro

If you plan to take extreme close up pictures, you'll want a camera that has macro focusing capability. This feature allows you to move a camera very close to a subject and still be able to focus.

Movies

Many digital cameras offer an MPEG movie feature that allows you to take short movies with the camera.

Batteries

Digital cameras, especially those with CCD sensors and LCD displays, use a lot of power. Rechargeable batteries can help lower the cost, but the batteries themselves are expensive. When evaluating a digital camera, check to determine whether it uses standard-size rechargeable batteries.

Flash

Most digital cameras have a built-in flash. The normal modes of operation are: Automatic, forced flash, fill flash, and no flash.

Software

A digital camera usually comes with some type of software for use in downloading images from the camera into a computer. Microsoft Windows comes with software for transferring images from digital cameras, so no additional software is necessary.

Multimedia and Presentation Software

✴ What Is Multimedia?

Multimedia in a computer context is defined as the integration of more than one medium, such as animation, audio, graphics, text, and video. Multimedia is a step beyond traditional presentation graphics used by many people in business. Rather than use a software program such as Microsoft PowerPoint to create overhead transparencies, the computer is used as the presentation tool. When the computer is connected to a video projector, the presentation can be presented as a slideshow and projected on a screen for everyone in a meeting to see. When you add graphics, animation effects, audio, and video files to the presentation—you've created multimedia.

The term multimedia was used long before computers appeared in the office. Originally, multimedia was a term to define presentations or lectures that included any elements other than just the spoken or written word. Slide projectors, audiotapes, movies, and pictures were often combined with a lecture or demonstration to provide a more dynamic presentation.

Why Is It Called Multimedia?

Today, the term **multimedia** has come to mean something different to different types of users. To the computer industry, multimedia often refers to a computer system that includes a CD-ROM and a set of speakers. To a computer game enthusiast, it may mean being able to "walk" through a virtual world and interact with characters. To an Internet user, multimedia could mean having the ability to click on a link on a Web page that provides a picture or audio file. To someone in business, it might mean using PowerPoint to provide a visual presentation for a lecture.

While these specific uses of multimedia vary slightly in emphasis, the basic elements remain much the same. They all include the combination of text, sound, graphics and/or video delivered through or controlled by a computer.

A related term, often heard these days, is **hypermedia.** Hypermedia is multimedia whose sequence is determined by the learner or user. For example, most World Wide Web pages provide **hot links** to other documents or Web sites that provide additional information. It is up to the user whether to jump out of the linear presentation of information and explore in other directions.

While all hypermedia is also multimedia, not all multimedia is hypermedia. A PowerPoint presentation, which consists of a series of slides, typically is a very linear (non-hypermedia) type of multimedia.

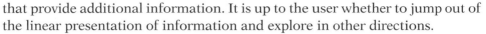

Multimedia System Requirements

The requirements of a multimedia computer depend upon whether the user is a viewer or a producer. All commercial multimedia programs require ever-increasing amounts of memory (RAM). The production of a multimedia presentation requires an even more complex system. To distinguish between the two types of requirements, the terms **user system** versus **production system** will be used. Remember that technology is changing very rapidly, and these guidelines may be quickly outdated. System requirements need to be re-examined often.

The following lists represent suggested system requirements if you are purchasing a new system. If you already have a system that is less than four years old, and it has a CD-ROM drive, the system can probably be used to run multimedia software. However, when you are ready to create your own multimedia, you will probably need a computer with more capacity. Check the system requirements for any software before buying it to make sure you will be able to run the program on your computer.

Low-End Multimedia System
First, examine a basic user system for a Microsoft Windows machine.

- Pentium processor running at 200 MHz
- 32 MB RAM
- 10 GB hard drive
- Windows 95 or higher
- 4X CD-ROM drive
- Video card with 8MB RAM
- 16-bit sound card and speakers
- 56 Kbps modem

Low-End Software
If your current system meets or exceeds these specifications, it can be used to run many of the commercial multimedia applications, such as Microsoft PowerPoint or Lotus Freelance Graphics, to create low-end multimedia projects.

High-End Multimedia System
For serious multimedia production, a high-end system is necessary. The list below is considered a minimum high-end system, because it is easy to add capacity either when you initially purchase it or later when you might need to add to it.

- Intel Pentium IV
- 256 MB RAM
- 80 GB hard disk drive

- Windows XP or higher
- CD-RW drive (8X or higher)
- 64-bit video card with 2 MB RAM and 24-bit color monitor
- 32-bit sound card with Wavetable and good quality speakers
- Microphone
- 56 Kbps (or greater) modem

High-End Software

High-end systems can do everything a low-end system can do, plus high-end systems have the capability of running more sophisticated multimedia production programs, such as Macromedia FreeHand, Adobe Photoshop, Macromedia Director, Multimedia Studio, and Adobe Premiere. When coupled with peripherals (scanner, digital camera, camcorder, etc.), you will be able to create full-blown multimedia productions that rival those that only commercial video production houses were capable of producing in the past.

Presentation and Authoring Programs

Multimedia presentation and authoring software are tools that allow the user to bring all the multimedia components into a coherent presentation or product. While there is some overlap between presentation and authoring tools, a comparison of the two is valuable.

Presentation programs like Microsoft PowerPoint are typically called slide show programs. They are simple to use and basically present information in a linear fashion, one slide after another. On any slide, you can attach a media file with an image, animation, or sound. Some of them will allow very simple branching out of a linear sequence.

Authoring programs have the distinct advantage of allowing more sophisticated branching. They also allow numerous media elements with overlays and logic attached. The disadvantage is that they are typically harder to learn to use. On the other hand, third grade students have successfully created wonderful interactive multimedia presentations.

This chapter will focus on the use of Microsoft PowerPoint because it is well established as a business presentation tool and is relatively easy to learn.

Using Microsoft PowerPoint

Microsoft PowerPoint (Figure 21-1) is included as part of the Microsoft Office Suite of software that is very popular in business today. If PowerPoint is installed on your computer, you can create a multimedia presentation or an overhead slide presentation by following the AutoContent wizard that is built-in to the program.

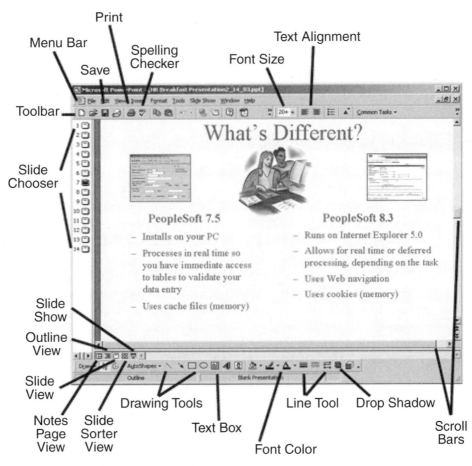

FIGURE 21-1. Microsoft PowerPoint.

Screen shot reprinted by permission from Microsoft Corporation.

Using Views

PowerPoint allows you to view your presentation in several different ways. The view selection buttons are along the bottom left edge of the presentation window.

Slide View is used for designing the look of the slides. Here you can work with the various fonts, colors, backgrounds, drop shadows, and so on.

Outline View is best for working with text only. You can see your presentation in context, since you see the text of a number of slides at once. Also, Outline View gives you a sense of the relative importance of the various points you're making. Finally, you can easily add, rearrange, or delete slides in this view.

In Slide Sorter View you see all the slides in reduced size. This view is used for arranging slides in the sequence you want as well as setting transitions, builds, hidden slides, and other features.

In the Notes View you can compose notes about each slide. The notes can be used to print a script for yourself or handouts for your audience.

In the Slide Show View, the screen will change radically to show only the slide. This is the view you use to present your presentation if you are going to do so on a computer screen or computer projector. In this view, since there are no toolbars or menus available, you primarily use keys to operate the show. For example, use the SPACEBAR to move to the next slide. After reaching the final slide in a presentation, the program exits from Slide Show, and the screen returns to the view you had before running the slide show.

Getting Help in PowerPoint

The primary help feature of PowerPoint is the Office Assistant, which is designed to suggest Help topics based on your current activity as well as provide answers to your specific questions. The Office Assistant displays possible help topics based on your search criteria. Sometimes the Office Assistant will appear with a light bulb on it. This is to let you know that the Office Assistant has a tip relating to your current action. To see the tip, just click on the light bulb.

Another way to access help is through PowerPoint's Help Menu, which conforms with the standards for most Microsoft Windows software. There are several navigational and control functions that can help you better use the help program.

If you need help on a certain screen feature, such as a button, the status bar, or the ruler, you can click on the **What's This?** button. It will activate the Help pointer. Then, point to the item in question, and click on it.

Moving Through Slides in Slide View

When you are in Slide View (where you'll likely be most of the time), you can move through the slides by using the scroll bar on the right. You can click on the small buttons with double-arrowheads at the bottom of the scroll bar to move among slides. The up-pointing button moves to the previous slide, and the down-pointing button moves to the next slide. Depending on your Zoom setting, you can also click in the gray area above and below the slider to move between slides.

Using Zoom

While working with slides in Slide View, you can change the size of the image to make it more convenient to work with. Near the right-hand end of the toolbar, you'll find a drop-down list of percentages, called the Zoom Control. By clicking one of the percentages in the list, you can enlarge or shrink the size of the slide.

Working with Multiple Presentations

Like many Windows programs, PowerPoint permits you to work with more than one file at a time. You can open several presentation files at once in PowerPoint, and each can occupy its own window within the PowerPoint application window. Each window is called a document window.

The AutoContent Wizard

A Wizard is a feature that allows you to automate certain actions in PowerPoint (and other Microsoft products). PowerPoint's opening menu offers you the opportunity of choosing from several Wizards. Among these templates is the AutoContent Wizard (Figure 21-2) that will guide you by presenting suggested topics and discussion items, then automatically choose the "look" of your presentation by selecting a template.

The AutoContent wizard creates a presentation by taking the information you type and applying it to a pre-existing format. The presentation is displayed on your screen in Outline View.

Working with Outline View

In Outline View (Figure 21-3), each slide is represented by the slide icon that appears just to the left of the slide title. From Outline View you can add new slides, delete slides, edit the text of slides, and rearrange the sequence of slides. The floating window labeled Color displays a miniature version of the slide you're working on. It allows you to see the effects of your changes without having to switch back to Slide View.

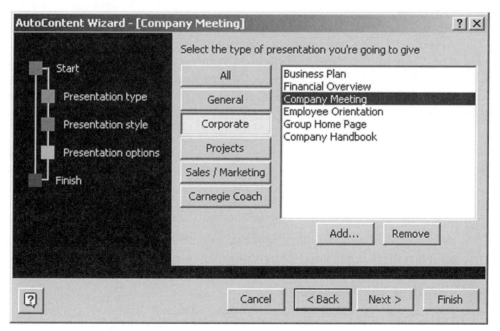

FIGURE 21-2. AutoContent Wizard in Microsoft PowerPoint.
Screen shot reprinted by permission from Microsoft Corporation.

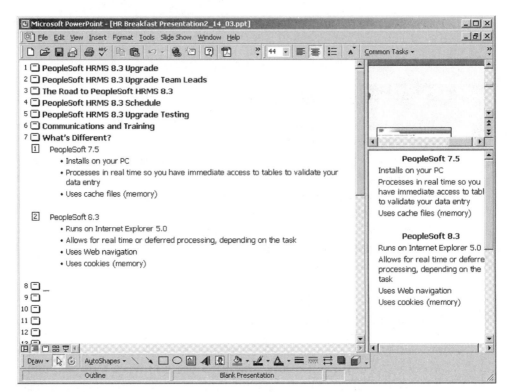

FIGURE 21-3. Outline View in Microsoft PowerPoint.

Screen shot reprinted by permission from Microsoft Corporation.

Adding a New Slide

You can add a new slide by selecting where you want the new slide to be and clicking on the **New Slide** button. Another way to create a new slide is to begin a new line in the outline at the top level. You begin a new line by pressing ENTER at the end of the previous line. The first text you type will be the title of the slide. When you press ENTER, you will start a new line of text.

Moving Text

If you need to move text from one slide to another you can easily do it by selecting the text and dragging to another slide in the Outline View. When you release the mouse button, the text will be pasted into the second slide.

Adding Text to a Slide

If you need to add some additional text to an existing slide, the easiest way to do that is to press CTRL and ENTER at the end of the title line. This will automatically make a bullet appear and allow you to enter the next line.

Demoting and Promoting Lines

One of the most common features of a PowerPoint presentation is bulleted text or numbered lists. You can also have lines of text that are indented below another line. Indenting text is called **demoting.** Moving indented text out even with the rest of the lines or bulleted list is called **promoting.** For example, if you need to demote a new line to become an item under the title, you can do that by clicking on the **Demote** button.

As you might guess, you can promote items using similar methods (except you use the Promote button, of course). If you promote an item all the way to the top level, it creates a new slide and becomes the title of the slide.

Rearranging Slides

To change the sequence of a slide, you should switch to Slide Sorter View. You can do this by clicking the **Slide Sorter View** icon (Figure 21-4). This gives you a thumbnail view of the various slides in your presentation. To rearrange the order of your slides you simply drag a slide icon to the new position. For example, if you wanted to move slide number 3 to the second position, you would click on the icon for slide number 3 and drag it until a horizontal line appears beneath slide 1.

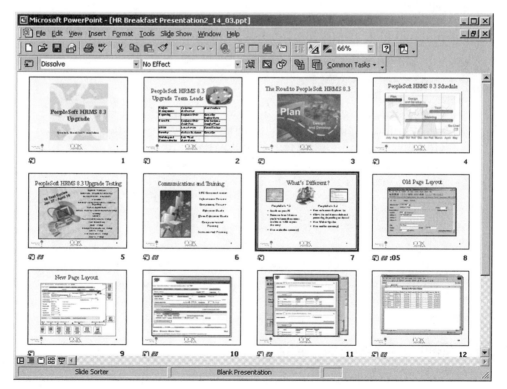

FIGURE 21-4. Slide Sorter View in Microsoft PowerPoint.

Screen shot reprinted by permission from Microsoft Corporation.

21 ■ MULTIMEDIA SOFTWARE

Deleting Slides

To delete a slide in Slide Sorter View, you select it and press the DELETE key. As with most Windows applications, you can undo a deletion (or any action) by using the Undo command. You can access the Undo command by clicking the **Edit Menu** and then clicking **Undo.** The deleted slide is then returned to the screen.

Using Transitions

Slide Sorter View also permits you to create transitions between the slides in your presentation. These transitions can take the form of fades, dissolves, and wipes, and are applied to the "incoming" (next) slide in a sequence. The Slide Sorter View has a button that is used for this purpose, called the Slide Transition button.

The Text Preset Animation button can create new slides for individual items on a bulleted list. You'll see more about that in a few moments. Remember that transitions are applied to the incoming, or following, slide.

The Slide Transition dialog box is where you specify the type of transition, the speed at which it occurs, and whether to advance automatically or under your manual control. There are several types of transitions available. All are previewed in the upper left corner of the dialog.

The Slide Transition dialog box not only specifies which effect to be used, it also allows you to see what the effect of the transition will be before you use it. Each time you click on the transition icon, the slide previews what the transition will look like in your final presentation.

Using Build Effects

In PowerPoint terminology, a **build** is a sequence of slides that displays each point, one at a time, in a bulleted list. While you could create each slide individually, using the build feature allows you to concentrate on other aspects of your presentation. To use a build effect, you first select the slide, then select an animation effect from a list.

When you return to the Slide Sorter View screen, you'll see an icon beneath the slide. This is a visual indication that you have an animation effect active for that slide.

The animation effect icon does not respond to a click the way the transition icon does, but that's only because PowerPoint doesn't support previewing build effects while in Slide Sorter View mode. You can see the effects when you run the slide show.

Saving a Presentation

Once you've created a presentation, you'll want to save it to the disk. If you've used any Windows applications before, you already know how. You click the **File Menu** and then click **Save** or **Save As.**

You may have seen this Save As dialog box in other Windows applications. It's called a **common dialog box,** because it's used throughout the Windows environment and in other Windows applications.

The Summary Info dialog permits you to add comments and other descriptive text to your presentation file which you can search later. You might add some comments about how you created the presentation or the names of departments that can use the file. Other data you can track include the author's name, keywords, and the title of the presentation.

Switching to Slide View

In Outline View you can concentrate on the content of the presentation—the text and arrangement. To work with the appearance of the presentation, you'll use Slide View. To switch to Slide View, click on the **Slide View** button.

This view shows you the appearance of the slide, permitting your visual inspection. From here, you can see if the colors are what you want and if the general look and feel of the slide is proper.

Notes Page View

In Notes Page View (Figure 21-5), you can create notes about each slide in your presentation. These notes can be printed to serve as a script or as handouts for the audience. To switch into Notes Page View, click the **Notes Page View** button.

The slide appears on a representation of a sheet of paper, with an area below it for notes. To type a note, you can click inside the notes box to make a cursor appear. However, at this size it will be difficult to read your note as you type it. To solve that problem, you can use the Zoom feature. The Zoom Control appears on the right side of the standard toolbar.

Running the Slide Show

One nice feature about PowerPoint is that you can run your slide show at any time while you're in the process of creating it. It's so simple to preview the show at any time that you may find yourself running the slide show often just to be certain that the effects come out right and the look is just what you want.

Table 21-1 lists keyboard commands you can use while in the Slide Show. This table is taken from the online help screen, which you can display by searching for *keyboard shortcuts,* then choosing *slide show shortcuts.*

Your screen will go blank for a few moments while PowerPoint prepares to run the slide show. To move from slide to slide, you'll use the space bar. Because different computer systems work at different speeds, you may experience a slight delay in getting to the first slide. Please be patient.

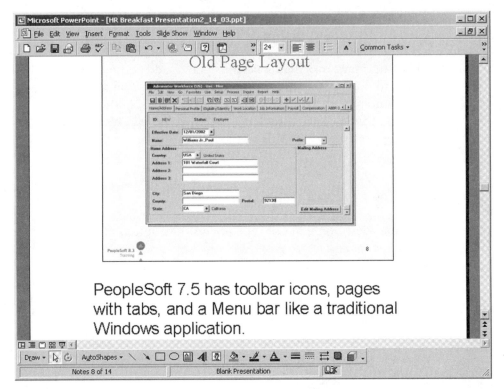

FIGURE 21-5. Notes Page View in Microsoft PowerPoint.

Screen shot reprinted by permission from Microsoft Corporation.

TABLE 21-1	Slide Show Keyboard Commands
To do this. . .	**Press. . .**
Go to slide <number>	<Number>+ENTER
Black/unblack screen	B, . (period)
White/unwhite screen	W, , (comma)
Show/hide pointer	A, =
Stop/restart automatic show	S, +
End show	ESC, CTRL+BREAK, − (minus)
Erase screen annotations	E
Use new time	T
Use original time	O
Advance on mouse click	M
Advance to hidden slide	H
Go to slide 1	Hold both mouse buttons for 2 seconds
Advance to next slide	Mouse click or spacebar
Return to previous slide	Press BACKSPACE

Using Fonts in Your Presentations

Fonts are usually thought of as the specific typeface design for letters, numbers and other characters that make up the text of a slide. Windows supports an almost unlimited array of fonts, so using the correct one for the job is a fairly important issue. Picture the front page of a typical newspaper in your mind for a moment. There are headlines that are presented in larger, bolder fonts than the rest of the page, designed to catch your eye as you read. Smaller sub-headlines may punctuate sections of an article and allow the reader to browse through the content more quickly. The text of the stories is in a smaller, less dramatic font so that reading them won't become tiring on the eyes. The point here is that fonts are to be used as a design element to make your work more easily absorbed by the audience. When you make presentations with a tool like PowerPoint, you want your material to be easily understood with enough pizzazz to keep everyone's attention long enough for you to make your point. Fonts can go a long way toward getting your point across to an audience.

Changing Fonts

When you choose a template, an appropriate font is selected for you. You can easily change the font for the entire presentation by making the change on the Slide Master, which we'll discuss later in this chapter.

As a general design rule, you should stay with one font for all of the presentation. A single font will give your work a cleaner, more consistent look. If you mix fonts, you may end up with very tacky looking slides.

Although there are many different styles of fonts available, many of them fall into two basic categories called **serif** and **sans serif.** A serif is a short line or stem at the end strokes of individual letters. This lends a particular flair or style to the typeface design. Sans serif means without the serif. A sans serif font has letters with no end strokes. Studies show that serifs help guide the eyes and make text easier to follow. For this reason, publications with dense text, such as books, magazines, and newspapers, almost always use serif fonts. Typical examples of serif fonts include Times Roman, Times New Roman, New Century Schoolbook, Bookman, Palatino, and Courier (typewriter font).

For screen design, where text is kept to a minimum, a sans serif font may provide a cleaner look to your presentation. This is why television commercials and magazine ads frequently use sans serif fonts. Examples of sans serif fonts include Helvetica, Swiss, Arial, Avant Garde, and Modern. At least a few, if not all, of these fonts should be available on your particular computer system.

For presentations, you may use either a serif or a sans serif font, but you should avoid mixing them.

Changing the Font Size and Color

You can set each font type to a number of different sizes measured in units called **points.** The title of the slide is in a larger point size than the body text. To see the point measurement for the font size, simply look at the Toolbar.

To increase or decrease the size of the currently selected text, simply click on one of the font size buttons until you get the font size you want. Each time you click this button, the text will become a bit smaller, shrinking to the next smaller point size available on your system. The other button will do just the opposite—that is, it will make the selected text get just a bit larger.

Color is an important aspect of character formatting. Here you have to be careful. The chosen template uses appropriately coordinated colors. To help protect you from choosing an inappropriate color, the template uses a color scheme. A small drop-down box appears with several colors shown. There's a reason why so few colors are shown—these are colors matched to the color scheme you're using for the current slide and will blend in easily. Other colors are available, in case you need them, from the More Font Colors . . . option.

There is another button on the Toolbar that gives you the ability to set shadows behind your text.

Changing Alignments

With PowerPoint, you can use various paragraph alignments to reposition text. You can change the alignment for any text area, or for any individual paragraph, to centered, left, right, or justified.

While text is an undeniably important aspect of your presentation, the way your text is presented is also very important. PowerPoint allows you to modify the background using a wide variety of colors and gradients, or fill patterns, to make your presentation as visually appealing as possible.

Shading the Background

Shading means displaying a color which ranges from a lighter shade to a darker shade. Sometimes, shading is performed by adding what is called a **gradient,** which means a gradually changing range of colors. Gradients can display a range from light to dark, or one color to another, and in general add to the visual depth of your presentation. An example of shading is shown in the Slide Color Scheme dialog box. You can make adjustments to the shading in several different ways:

- The Color Scheme dialog box lets you adjust the color scheme for shadows, background, fills, etc. You can also select different colors from this dialog box.

- The Slide Color Scheme option allows you to specify colors for each component of the slide.

- The Variants section offers four versions for shading: From top to bottom, from left to right, from right to left, and from the center to each corner.

Changing the Color Scheme

Changing the color scheme can dramatically influence the look of your presentation. Unlike a template, a color scheme can be applied to individual slides as well as to the entire presentation.

The Color Scheme dialog box gives you several choices for changing colors. When you view this dialog box, notice that the upper right corner of the dialog box displays buttons for applying any changes to the current slide only (Apply) or to every slide in the presentation (Apply to All).

There may be instances where you want to use different schemes for different slides as a sort of color coding method. In the absence of careful planning, however, varying schemes may cause problems with visual consistency, which may in turn annoy or distract your audience.

Using the Slide Master

The Slide Master controls the format for each slide in your presentation. For instance, when you want to change the size of the title on each slide, you simply have to change the title area one time on the Slide Master.

PowerPoint lets you look at different masters that correspond with different ways of viewing your work. There's a Slide Master, a Notes Master, and a Handout Master. The master shows you sample text to indicate the area size and placement of the title and body text. This helps you eye the layout of the template and gives you a way to reformat text on the master level.

Notes Master

The Notes Master gives you the ability to format your speaker notes. You can see your slide and type notes into the area shown to help remind you of important items to be covered in that slide, and any other related issues that may not be shown on the slide.

Handout Master

The Handout Master is used to add text and artwork to your audience handouts. You can see the master slides by holding down the SHIFT key while clicking on one of the buttons in the lower left-hand corner of the PowerPoint window.

PowerPoint Templates

A template is a presentation whose color schemes and layout formats can be applied to another presentation (see Figure 21-6). PowerPoint comes with

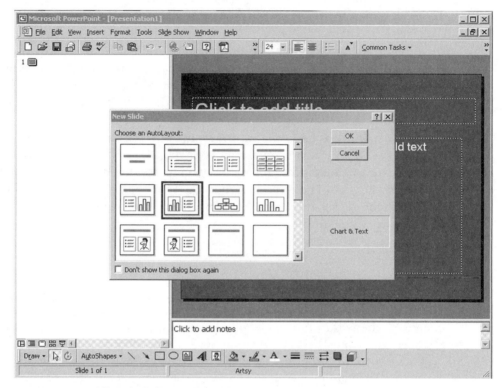

FIGURE 21-6. Microsoft PowerPoint Templates.

Screen shot reprinted by permission from Microsoft Corporation.

dozens of professionally designed, pre-built templates you can use when creating your own slide shows. In fact, new presentations can be patterned after a default template called Blank Presentation.pot, or you can select from a variety of templates.

After creating your presentation, you can even save its look and feel and use it again in another presentation by applying the template to the new file.

Changing a Template

Changing templates is a very powerful way to instantly reformat your entire presentation. When you change templates, all formatting revisions you've made to the Slide Master, including font types and sizes, colors, and text position, are reset. However, changes that you made on individual slides will remain intact. Again, any formatting changes you made to individual slides will remain even though you changed templates.

Inserting Visuals

The word "visuals" implies images, and educators know that a picture is frequently worth at least a thousand words. Visual media, which include graphics, photographs, movies, and animations, can be added to multimedia productions in a wide variety of ways. These can come from commercial sources, such as the wide variety of computer clip art or CD-ROMs full of images, or from photographic or computer supply companies. Clip art is one of the most commonly used sources of images for multimedia developers.

When PowerPoint is first installed, the clip art files are placed in a subdirectory on your hard drive. To open any of these files, use the Clip Art command on the Insert Menu.

PowerPoint may take a few moments to compile available images the first time you use the Insert Clip Art command. Be patient if you see several dialogs with a meter showing the progress of the operation.

Each clip art category contains a number of different images related by subject, as suggested by the titles. The Microsoft Clip Gallery is actually a miniature application within PowerPoint. You'll be able to add your own images and create your own categories, to better organize your clip art collection.

You can use the Clip Gallery program to preview clip art you wish to use in a presentation. Each image is represented by a **thumbnail** or tiny version of the real thing. You might not be able to see all the detail in each picture, but you can get an overall idea about content, layout, and colors used from the thumbnail.

Once you've found the clip art that really complements your presentation, you may find that a small amount of tweaking is needed to get it just right. PowerPoint allows you, like many other Windows-based drawing programs, to resize and move your graphics in almost any way you need.

You can also insert clip art images using the AutoClipArt tool. This feature searches your presentation for concepts and then suggests images in the Clip Gallery you might use to express your ideas.

Moving and Sizing Clip Art

Once an image is pasted on your slide, you can manipulate it by moving it or resizing it to fit your needs. Also, as a general rule, you should avoid using more than one clip art image per slide. Too many images can clutter a slide and detract from your message.

Inserting Charts

Since your presentations cannot be dependent on clip art alone, it's nice to know that you can insert other types of graphic images into your slides. Charts can communicate mathematical relationships in a visual way. PowerPoint actually has a graphing module built into the program, and whenever you need it, all you have to do is click on a button in the toolbar.

When the datasheet is on the screen, you're actually using Microsoft Chart, a program included with PowerPoint. You could think of it as a (much) scaled-down version of Excel, or some other Windows-based spreadsheet application.

Organization Charts

One other type of chart you can use in PowerPoint is the organization chart, often simply called an **org chart.** These are frequently used to show the relationships between departments or other groups within an organization. Inserting an org chart is just as easy as inserting a chart, and it's done almost the same way—by clicking a button in the toolbar. From here, you can build a chart that reflects the structure of the organization.

Creating Artwork

In addition to using clip art, graphics can be created from scratch on the computer by using simple paint programs, such as Microsoft Paint, or more complicated drawing programs such as Adobe Photoshop. They can also be created outside the realm of the computer by pen, pencil, paint, crayons, photography, or any other media, and then brought into the computer for editing and incorporation. You can digitize images with a scanner, shoot digital photos with a digital still camera, or have your camera film processed and the images digitized on a PhotoCD.

Drawing with AutoShapes

Another special tool, called AutoShapes, gives you the ability to create less conventional shapes such as stars and arrows. You'll find it on the Drawing toolbar.

The AutoShapes tool can help when you need something other than a simple rectangle or oval, and PowerPoint treats an AutoShape just like any other object. You can move and resize AutoShapes, type text onto them, or copy them for use elsewhere in your presentation. Using the SHIFT key will **constrain** your drawings—rectangles will become squares, ovals will become circles, and so on. Use the SHIFT key whenever you want symmetrical images.

Using Videos

You can incorporate videos in your presentations as simply as you can place graphics on the screen. Videos can be shot with a digital camcorder and transferred to the computer using a special cable or a video capture card. You can then edit the video using a program such as Adobe Premiere and export it for use in the PowerPoint presentation.

Using Sound Media

In addition to still images and video, sound is another powerful medium. Audio in a multimedia presentation, just as graphics, can originate from a wide variety of sources—from commercial pre-recorded music or historical speeches, stand-alone sounds or part of a video, to narration recorded with a microphone connected to your computer.

Playback of audio usually involves a sound card, now built into most multimedia Windows systems. The quality of the sound will vary drastically depending upon whether the sound card supports 8-bit or 16-bit sampling resolutions. Most multimedia computers include 16-bit sound cards as a standard feature. Without getting too technical, a comparison between the two is similar to the difference between AM radio and compact disc audio.

Planning a Presentation

Consider the following guidelines as you plan your presentation.

Determine Your Goal and Objectives

Begin by defining your goal. What do you hope to accomplish? Is your goal to persuade or merely to inform? Persuasion may require getting your audience emotionally involved in your argument, getting them to care. On the other hand, if you are simply making a report, you may want your audience to remain objective, clear-headed, and somewhat emotionally detached.

Define your objectives. What topics will support your thesis?

Keep It Simple

Regardless of the purpose of your presentation, always try to keep it simple and focused. A simple, clear message can be delivered with greater impact to your audience and is more likely to achieve results. A complicated or muddled message will leave your audience confused and frustrated, which may severely hinder your chances for success. Keep the number of topics to a minimum. When expounding on each topic, make sure the information on each slide is clear and easy to understand.

Design for Flow

Outline your content in a topical format with a beginning, middle, and end. Try to keep your ideas focused and organized toward a logical conclusion. While sound reasoning and logic are not the only ways to effectively communicate or persuade, they are tried and true methods.

Design for Drama

Timing is everything. Design your presentation with a dramatic curve in mind. Peak your audience's interest toward the end, and deliver the central conclusion of your message when you have the full attention of everyone.

Plan Your Media Selection

Be sure to plan your media selection so that it's appropriate to the environment and audience. Do you need to prepare slides, overheads, or handouts?

Think and Plan Ahead

If you plan to use handouts along with a screen or slide show, consider whether you want to give them out before or after the presentation. If you give the audience handouts before the show, they can follow along, write notes directly on the handouts, and have an immediate reference should they have trouble seeing the screen. Yet, in some cases, saving the handouts till the end may help avoid giving away any surprises you may have planned.

Consider Subject Matter

Consider your subject matter. Are you presenting a training seminar, a presentation to managers or employees, or a sales presentation? This may determine the scope of your presentation and the tone you want to set.

Consider Your Audience

Consider your audience. Employees, customers, business people, professionals, or mixed? Conservative or progressive? Formal or informal? Are they people you know personally, or total strangers? Consider the audience's familiarity with the subject matter. If they are unfamiliar, or if the subject is somewhat technical, present one concept at a time and move in progression.

Both subject matter and audience should help you determine the tone of your presentation. Do you want a lot of humor, or a more subdued approach?

Consider the Size of Your Audience

Larger audiences may dictate the need for more structure and formality. A smaller audience may be less formal, giving you more room for improvisation and one-on-one interaction.

Consider Environment

Office, small conference room, or hotel meeting room? How visible is the screen from each part of the room? If visibility is questionable, you may want to include handouts with printed versions of each slide. If you're not familiar with the equipment, try to arrange time for setting up and rehearsing your presentation before delivering the real thing.

Practice

Practice delivering the presentation to a co-worker or friend. Your friends can offer helpful critiques by letting you know if your presentation is clear and focused, if your style and manner are tasteful, and if your treatment is interesting enough. They can also help you smooth over some of the rough spots.

✴ Presenting Your Presentation

Once a multimedia presentation has been created, you'll need to prepare to present it to your audience and then follow up once the presentation is complete. Below is a set of steps you might follow for this process. These guidelines will help you become a better developer and presenter. It's really true—practice does make perfect in the world of multimedia development.

Step 1: Set Up

Now that a multimedia presentation has been created, you are ready to deliver the presentation. The first step is to set up the necessary equipment.

Step 2: Test Run

Make a test run through the presentation. This is especially necessary if the presentation was prepared on a different computer. If the presentation is a long distance from the original computer, be sure to move and test the presentation before traveling.

Step 3: Back-Up Plan

Develop a plan B. If the computer breaks or does not make it to the room in which the presentation will take place, what will you do? Having a back-up plan is always a good idea!

Step 4: Deliver

Deliver the presentation. This may seem obvious, but don't be afraid to just do it! If everything goes perfect, you will be lucky. If not, relax, smile, and work through the problems.

Step 5: Evaluate

Take time to reflect on the experience now that the presentation is over.

- What went well?
- What needs to be improved?
- What was frustrating?
- What was exciting?
- What did you learn from the process?

Office Ergonomics

Office Ergonomics

You can think of ergonomics as a way of designing tools and equipment to suit individual needs. For a number of years, there have been efforts to improve ergonomics, primarily in manufacturing and product design. But improvements can also be made for office workers.

Ergonomics addresses three aspects of your workplace: the physical, the environmental, and the personal. An example of a physical aspect is creating a good fit between you and your computer workstation. An example of an environmental aspect is eliminating glare on your monitor screen by improving the lighting in your work area. An example of a personal aspect is the need to take periodic breaks throughout the day to restore your energy and improve comfort.

Early recognition of physical symptoms will allow you to make adjustments, seek help, and eliminate further discomfort. So how can you recognize the early signs and symptoms? Well, only you can listen to what your body is telling you. If you feel any fatigue, tension, or discomfort in any part of your body, take immediate action to relieve it. It's important to pay attention to the early signs and symptoms to avoid conditions that may lead to further discomfort.

Other symptoms include limbs that feel heavy, or you might feel a dull ache. You might also have joint or muscle discomfort. Be aware of dry or itchy eyes, redness, aches, or blurred vision. You can also get headaches from eye strain.

How can you recognize the advanced signs and symptoms of work related problems? Consider the following:

- Do you notice tingling, numbness, or coldness in joints and extremities?
- Is there a loss of strength or dexterity in your hands?
- Do you have difficulty turning door knobs, grasping, or holding onto things?

What should you do if you experience these symptoms? Well, first of all, remember that these symptoms are likely temporary and might have nothing to do with your work. For example, these symptoms might result from recreational activities, such as sports, hobbies, and home projects, or from medical conditions, such as arthritis, diabetes, pregnancy, or obesity.

Whatever their source, it's important to address these symptoms early and seek appropriate medical attention. Early intervention is the key to avoiding prolonged discomfort.

Whether at work or play, examine the risk factors in your activities.

- Are you involved in prolonged, intensive activities without breaks?

- Is your desk arranged so that you must extend yourself to reach the phone or reference materials?

- Do you often sit in one position without moving about? No rest breaks? No stretching? You should take a break at least once each hour.

- Do you use too much force when gripping a pen or pencil?

- What about leaning or rubbing against hard surfaces such as the edge of a desk?

- Do you perform visually intensive tasks without breaks?

- Do you work in an area where there are wide temperature shifts, drafts, breezes, poor or irregular lighting, or excessive noise?

Your Desk and Chair

There are three preferred ways to sit at your desk. Sitting upright is perhaps the most familiar posture when working at a computer. When seated, the angle between your upper and lower body should be approximately 90 degrees. Your back should be supported and erect. Your feet should be supported by the floor or a footrest. This is a good all-around posture for working at the computer.

A second popular sitting position is called reclining. In this position, you lean back in your chair. Make sure your back is fully supported and your buttocks are not shifted forward. This causes your lower back to not be supported. Your feet should be supported by the floor or a footrest. This is a good posture for viewing information on your monitor or for reading documents.

The third way to sit is called declining. In this posture, your upper body is upright while your thighs are declining slightly and your feet are firmly on the floor or a footrest.

The seat back is adjusted almost vertically to provide back support. This is also a good posture for keyboarding work.

To enhance your comfort, you can make four main adjustments to a chair. These include adjusting the seat pan height, the backrest height, the backrest tilt, and the armrests. Let's look at each of these adjustments in more detail. (See also Figure 22-1).

You should adjust the seat pan height so that your elbows are approximately at keyboard height when your elbows are next to your body. Your thighs should be approximately parallel to the floor with your feet resting firmly on the floor.

FIGURE 22-1. Ergonomic desk chair.

If your feet are not resting firmly on the floor, you will need a footrest. This seat pan height adjustment prevents your thighs from being compressed so blood flow is not restricted. This reduces fatigue in your legs. This adjustment also encourages you to sit more erect and to use the backrest of your chair, which reduces stress on the lower back.

The backrest height adjustment makes sure that your lower back is supported. For most people, their lower back is at the same height as their elbows when the elbows are next to their body. When adjusted correctly, the lumbar support of the backrest should fit the curvature of your lower spine. This adjustment helps your lower back to maintain its natural curvature and thereby provides even compression on spinal disks and less fatigue of your back muscles.

The backrest tilt adjustment involves the angle between the backrest and the seat pan. It should be no less than 90 degrees. You should avoid adjusting the backrest too far back to where your arms are stretched out to reach the keyboard. You should also avoid adjusting the backrest too far forward where you are too close to the keyboard and cause too much bend in your elbow.

The armrest adjustment involves adjusting the height of the armrests so that the elbows rest naturally on the armrests without slouching or shrugging your shoulders. If possible, you should adjust the width between armrests so that the armrests are directly underneath your elbows. The correct adjustment of the armrests reduces the loading of the arm on the shoulder.

What if you must use a nonadjustable chair? Well, just because the chair is "nonadjustable" doesn't mean you can't still make adjustments. You can make an existing chair more ergonomically sound by physically adjusting the height and adding lumbar support. You can adjust the height by adding a cushion on top of the seat pan. Finally, you can add a back support cushion, pillow, or even a rolled up towel to give yourself lumbar support.

You can lower the height of your work surface by obtaining a lower-height work surface, or, as a last resort, have Facilities or a similar group cut down the height of the legs. You might also consider adding an adjustable-height or lower fixed-height keyboard tray to your work surface.

You can raise the height of a work surface by obtaining a higher height work surface or by adding blocks under the workstation's legs.

Positioning Your Computer Keyboard and Mouse

The keyboard and mouse are typically the main interface between a user and computer system. Therefore, if you work with a computer system, you probably use your keyboard and mouse extensively.

So how can you set up your keyboard and pointing device to maximize comfort? There are several things you can do. You can place them properly, and, if necessary, you can acquire keyboard and mouse accessories.

To set up your keyboard properly, start by placing it directly in front of the monitor with the home position keys, G and H, centered to the screen. Sit so that your elbow angle is approximately 90 degrees. Maintain a straight line across the hand and forearm. This might require you to lower the keyboard off the rear legs. Placing your keyboard properly helps you maintain a neutral posture, thereby improving comfort (see Figure 22-2).

FIGURE 22-2. Positioning your keyboard.

Pointing devices such as a mouse, trackball, or glidepoint should be positioned to maximize comfort. You should place the device at the same height as the keyboard and as close to the keyboard as possible. For right-handed people who don't use the 10-key pad, you might want to consider using a keyboard without a 10-key pad. Positioning your pointing device correctly helps you maintain a neutral posture, thereby improving comfort.

Several keyboard and mouse accessories are available that can assist you with your comfort. Adjustable keyboard trays and platforms are designed to position the keyboard at various heights to help keep your wrists and arms in a neutral, relaxed position. Adjustable keyboard trays can slide in and out from underneath a work surface. Some models have a separate height and tilt adjustment.

Palm rests (Figure 22-3) can be helpful in the use of both keyboards and mice. These soft foam or gel strips are designed to raise your palms and keep your wrists straight. If you use a palm rest, it should not be used while keying but only to rest your palms between periods of keying.

Positioning Your Computer Display

The location and orientation of your display depends on the lighting characteristics in your work area, the viewing distance and angle, and glare control.

Glare control is key to avoiding eye strain and the accompanying discomfort it can cause. You should keep in mind that the best way to correct screen reflections is to remove their source. The need for antiglare screens (Figure 22-4) suggests that the workplace is not arranged or lit properly.

Many sources that can cause glare reflections on a properly positioned display will likely cause distracting glare in a person's normal field of vision. Screen glare can result from too much light falling on the screen, for example, light from windows or lamps, or bright areas of the environment that reflect onto the screen such as a white shirt or blouse.

If possible, choose a workplace setup location where the screen is perpendicular to any windows and away from any bright light sources such as lamps. You should consider using an antiglare screen if it is impossible to control the source of the glare.

FIGURE 22-3. Keyboard and mouse palm rests.

FIGURE 22-4. Antiglare screen.

You should also adjust the monitor's contrast, brightness, and color controls to suit your individual comfort level. This may require changing these controls during the day as room light varies.

Special screen cleaners are available to clean dust, dirt, and fingerprints from the display or anti-glare screen. You can also try a damp cloth.

After you've located your display properly in your work area to avoid glare, you need to fine-tune the position in relationship to your body. Your display should be centered behind your keyboard. The height of your display depends on your eye height while seated. The top of the display, not the top of the screen, should be even with or a little lower than your horizontal line of sight.

For people of shorter stature, you should avoid placing the display on top of your desktop computer system. This makes it nearly impossible to position the keyboard and display properly. Either the monitor will be too high, or the keyboard too low. If, in your work, you look primarily at source documents, place the source documents directly in front of you and the display slightly off to the side.

If you need to raise the display, stands are available that can provide a comfortable viewing height in order to reduce eye and neck discomfort.

If you wear glasses with bifocals, trifocals, or progressive lenses, and you find yourself looking through the bottom or top of your glasses to view the screen, you should adjust the display until you don't have to tilt your head up or down to see the screen. What if you have a laptop instead of a monitor? In a fixed office setting, you might consider getting a "Y" connector and using an external keyboard and mouse. You can then set the laptop on a raised platform behind the keyboard to raise the screen to the proper height. Another option is to obtain a separate display for office use.

The distance between your eye and the display should be whatever is comfortable for you. You should be able to easily read the characters on the screen. You should not have to lean forward or back to read the screen. One good rule of thumb is to sit at an arm's length from the display with your hand in a fist position.

You can tilt the display up or down as necessary. Try to maintain a 90-degree angle with your line of site. Also be careful not to pick up glare from overhead lighting. By following these simple placement guidelines for displays, you can avoid possible eyestrain, awkward neck positions, and neck and back discomfort.

Arranging Your Workstation

The way you organize the elements of your workplace to fit your individual needs is an important consideration in working comfortably. Make sure you have sufficient desk area to allow you to position your keyboard, pointing device, display, and other items in a way that works best for you.

Organize your desk to reflect the way you use work materials and equipment. Place the equipment you use most often, such as your telephone, within the easiest reach. Avoid placing objects where they reduce your freedom of movement. For example, don't place a computer tower or boxes under your desk too close to your legs. The key here is to maintain an orderly desktop to reduce unnecessary movements or awkward postures. This will help to improve your comfort.

Proper lighting is really a relative term. Lighting that is good for one task may be inappropriate for another. The general attitude in most offices is that more is better, but this is not necessarily true for working at your computer. If you are reading paper documents, you need bright light, but if you are viewing a display, you need less light. The best solution for most offices is to reduce the overhead lighting so that the screen is more easily read. Task lamps can be used to provide lighting for reading documentation or to illuminate specific work areas. You should be careful when placing task-specific lighting to avoid glare on the screen and to avoid getting direct light in your eyes. Having the proper lighting will help you reduce eye strain and the accompanying discomforts.

If your job involves working with documents, you should place the source documents properly to avoid eyestrain and awkward neck positions. One useful accessory is a document holder. When positioned properly, a document holder reduces the amount of movement required when looking back and forth between the screen and the document. Some document holders sit on your desk and are adjustable. Other models attach to the side of the display.

You should position the source document at the same distance as your display and next to your display. The main thing is for the document to be on the same plane and angle as the display.

If you spend most of your time transcribing, you should position your source documents directly in front of you and place your display off to the side.

How many times a day do you pick up a telephone? It's probably a lot, right?

The main thing is to avoid cradling the handset between your ear and shoulder. This can lead to neck discomfort. If you use a telephone for the majority of your day, you should consider obtaining a telephone headset. A variety of sizes and types of telephone headsets are available. You should find one that fits you comfortably and that is compatible with your telephone. If you are unsure of compatibility, consult with the telephone manufacturer's literature.

Sustained Work

No matter how well your workstation is set up, you should take frequent breaks. These breaks in your work are important as they help you to avoid fatigue. Frequent ergo-breaks are important when you perform sustained, intensive, or highly repetitive work. Even if you just change positions, or stand up and stretch at your workstation, it will help.

When working at your computer, it is recommended that you take a short break at least once each hour. These breaks can be from 30 seconds to five minutes and can go a long way toward reducing fatigue. If you do take a short break from your workstation, don't just go somewhere else to sit. It is more beneficial to get up and move around. For example, stand while taking a phone call. Stand while having a face-to-face conversation with a colleague. Go make copies at the copy machine. Or just take a break from the keyboard and change your position in your chair and read mail or other documentation.

It is also a good idea to rest your eyes occasionally throughout the day. Your eyes can become fatigued; however, this is a temporary condition and is not harmful to your eyes. The muscles in your eyes that work to focus on near and far objects become fatigued when they focus for extended periods of time on near objects. Your eyes experience the least stress when they are focused on objects 20 feet away or farther.

Computer display users tend not to blink as frequently as people performing other reading tasks. Eye dryness from this staring effect is increased by low humidity in the office.

If you have difficulty reading your screen, you might consider increasing the default font size or improving the screen resolution.

If you wear glasses, you should keep the lenses clean and keep your prescription current. In fact, even if you don't wear glasses, you should have periodic eye exams. Most people's vision changes over time.

Keyboarding

The ergonomic principles behind proper keyboarding technique start with your body position relative to the keyboard. Maintain a relaxed and neutral hand and arm posture to improve comfort. Your shoulders should not be hunched up. Your arms should be comfortably at your side with your elbows bent at approximately 90 degrees. The keyboard should be approximately at elbow height, which allows the forearm and hand to be in a straight line and parallel to the floor.

The proper keyboarding technique involves a few guidelines you should keep in mind while you are working. If you notice that you are doing something incorrectly, you should stop and make adjustments.

Keep a soft touch on the keyboard. Use as little pressure as possible. Your hands should glide over the keys. If your hands remain in a fixed position, your fingers tend to overreach for the keys. Keep your fingers in a relaxed posture similar to when you rest your hand gently and naturally on a table. Try not to extend your pinky fingers and thumbs while typing. Avoid resting your hands on the palm rest while typing. Use the palm rest only when you are not typing. To reach the keys that are farthest away, such as the function keys, move your entire hand instead of reaching with your fingers.

Glossary of Computer Terms

A

Accelerator key ✳ A keyboard equivalent of a mouse click, signified by an underlined character in a menu or dialog box. You can press the key (often in combination with the alt key) instead of clicking with the mouse.

Access ✳ To get to, to bring up and display, as "to access a file" or "to access a menu." In computer terminology, *access* is a verb.

Active window ✳ The application or document window to which the next keystroke or mouse click will apply. Sometimes called the *foreground* window or *current* window. See **Window.**

Address book ✳ A feature of a browser that holds personal information (for example, name, e-mail address, phone number) for reference.

Alphanumeric ✳ Refers to any combination of the letters of the alphabet and the ten numeric digits. Contraction of **alphabet** and **numeric.**

Append ✳ To add to the end of existing text or an existing file.

Apple, Inc. ✳ A major developer of microcomputers that chose to use a different type of microprocessor chip from those found in IBM machines and their compatibles. Software designed for Apple computers will not work on IBM machines, and vice versa.

Applet ✳ A small-scale application that is included with Windows. Examples include Write, Paintbrush, Notepad, Cardfile, Calendar, Clock, and Calculator.

Application ✳ A computer program. Examples include word processors, spreadsheets, and database management systems. Sometimes, applications are differentiated from programs that perform a task like computer operation and maintenance, which are called utilities or applets. See Also: *Utility software, Applet.*

Application window ✳ A window containing a running application, along with its work area and menu bar. An application window may contain multiple *document windows.*

Applications ✳ See *applications software.*

Applications software ✳ An organized collection of computer programs that provides powerful tools for performing a variety of tasks in a specific area—for example, word processors, spreadsheets, and database management systems.

Archie ✳ A search engine designed specifically to find files and information on FTP sites.

Argument ✳ Additional information added to a command to define the scope of an operation. In a spreadsheet, an argument tells a function values to use in a calculation. Compare *parameter.*

ARPAnet (Advanced Research Project Agency) ✳ A wide area network developed in the 1960s by the Advanced Research Project agency of the U.S. Department of Defense.

ASCII ✳ The American Standard Code for Information Interchange is a 7-bit character set almost universally available on all personal computer systems. It is a common denominator for exchanging data between computers. Files that consist only of ASCII characters are called *text files.*

ASCII file ✳ A text file made up of only letters, numbers, or symbols.

Associate ✳ To identify a document or data file with a particular application through the file's extension. When you open a file in Windows Explorer with an extension that has been associated with a particular application, that application will start automatically.

Attachment ✳ A graphics, text, or HTML file sent with an e-mail message.

Attributes ✳ Hidden codes which assign certain properties to files. For instance, there are attributes to make a file read-only, or hidden, or to indicate if modified since the last backup. You can display and modify a file's attributes by selecting the file in Explorer, then pressing ALT + ENTER.

B

Back up ✳ To copy the information stored on the hard disk onto another medium, such as a set of floppy diskettes; usually done as a safeguard against malfunction of the hard disk. Used as both a noun and a verb.

Background ✳ In a multiprocessing environment, the program that runs unattended while another is running in the "foreground." Typically, with Windows you might print a document in the background while working with another application.

Backslash ✳ The "\" character; represents the root directory in DOS paths and serves as a separator between elements of a path name.

Batch files ✳ See *batch processing files.*

Batch processing files ✳ A file containing DOS instructions to be performed automatically or with little input from the user.

Baud rate ✳ A measure of speed referring to movement of serial data, usually applied to modems and serial printers.

BCC ✳ Blind Carbon Copy. When you BCC an e-mail message recipient, other recipients cannot see that you have sent a copy of the message to this person.

Binary ✳ A system of counting using only two digits, 1 and 0.

Binary file ✳ A file which is in machine readable form, like an executable program.

Bit ✳ Short for "binary digit;" the smallest unit of information.

Bitmap ✳ An image or graphic produced by paint programs such as Paint.

Block ✳ In word processing, text that is highlighted and treated as a unit.

Bookmark ✳ A way that a Web browser can keep a permanent record of Internet addresses.

Boolean operators ✳ These operators are designed to put conditions on a search. The most common Boolean operators are AND, OR, and NOT.

Boot ✳ Starting (or restarting) a computer. Since a computer must start itself by loading its own startup software, it is said to "lift itself by its own bootstraps." When you boot the computer, its operating software, e.g., Windows, starts.

Border ✳ Any of the four sides of a window which serve as the boundary lines for that window. The border can be used to reshape and resize a window.

Browse ✳ To look through drives and folders for a file. Some dialog boxes have a Browse button that will list available drives and folders from which you can select the appropriate folder and file.

Browser ✳ A software program that requests, interprets, and presents World Wide Web documents. Frequently used browsers include Netscape Navigator, Internet Explorer, Lynx, and Mosaic.

Buffer ✳ Temporary storage in memory for data or other information. A disk cache and a print buffer are two examples.

Bus ✳ See *data bus.*

Bus topology ✳ A network arrangement connecting computers together along a common set of electrical conductors so that each can communicate with the others. Compare *Ring topology; star topology.*

Button ✳ A graphically defined clickable area of the screen.

Button bar ✳ See *toolbar.*

Byte ✳ A unit of computer data, usually equivalent to one alphanumeric character.

C

Cache ✳ The storage area on a person's computer that has copies of original data stored so that the computer doesn't have to go to a remote server to get information every time it is requested.

CAD ✳ See *computer-aided design.*

Cascade ✳ A way of arranging open windows on the desktop so that they overlap but still show each window's title bar.

Categorical directory ✳ A search tool that contains a directory in which the contents are organized by category, for example, Yahoo!

CC ✳ The Carbon Copy message header. This field contains the e-mail addresses of additional message recipients.

CD ROM ✳ Compact disk read-only memory. An advanced storage medium capable of holding up to 550 megabytes of data.

Cell ✳ In spreadsheets, the intersection of a row and column. A cell may contain a value, a label, or a formula.

Cell address ✳ The identification of a spreadsheet cell by its row and column coordinates.

Central processing unit (CPU) ✳ A term often used interchangeably with the microprocessor of a personal computer.

Character ✳ A single letter, number, or symbol (including a "space"). Sometimes used interchangeably with byte.

Character set ✳ The letters, numbers, and symbols available for use by personal computers and printers. The first 128 of these symbols are standardized and referred to as the *ASCII character set*. They include letters A-Z and numbers 0-9, among others.

Character string ✳ A group of alphanumeric characters treated as one unit. A text string can be a single character, several characters, or many words.

Check box ✳ A small square box appearing in dialog boxes denoting an option that can be set. An "X" or checkmark in a check box means that option is turned on.

Chip ✳ A small electronic component that contains microscopic electronic circuits.

Choose ✳ To begin an action using either the mouse or the keyboard.

Circuit board ✳ A nonconductive surface on which electronic paths or circuits are imprinted.

Click ✳ To quickly press and release a mouse button without moving the mouse, usually to select an on-screen item. Compare *double-click.*

Client ✳ A computer or software program that can access particular services on a network.

Clipboard ✳ The temporary storage area used by Windows to transfer text and images between applications and/or documents. It is a holding area within the computer's memory.

Clone ✳ Informal term for an IBM-compatible computer.

Close ✳ To remove an application or document window from the desktop.

Close button ✳ A small button at the right end of the title bar, which closes a window.

Column ✳ In spreadsheets, the vertical divisions of the worksheet. On a computer monitor, one character space; most monitors display 80 columns. Compare *row.*

Command ✳ An instruction that controls the activity of a computer system, normally entered by the user through the keyboard.

Command button ✴ A rectangular button found in a dialog box and labeled with the action it will carry out.

Compatible ✴ A computer that is functionally identical to a competitor in appearance, operation, or both; a clone.

Compound document ✴ A document which contains data created in more than one program, usually employing links to other files through OLE or DDE.

Computer aided design (CAD) ✴ Software application commonly used by engineers, designers, and architects to simplify their work.

Conference ✴ An application developed to provide real-time conferencing over the Internet. It includes live audio transmission, Internet chat, a white board, file transfer, and collaborative browsing.

CONFIG.SYS ✴ A configuration file that is read each time the computer starts. This is where 16-bit device drivers are loaded and other system resources are customized. The CONFIG.SYS file is not necessary unless you need to load 16-bit drivers.

Control menu ✴ In application windows, this list of options allows Restore, Move, Size, Minimize/Maximize, Close, and Switch To other applications. The menu appears when you click the tiny icon at the left end of a window's title bar.

Control panel ✴ A utility program that permits system-wide adjustments to Windows.

Copy ✴ A frequently used operation to duplicate text, data, or a file without disturbing the original. Compare ***move.***

CPU ✴ See ***central processing unit.***

Cross posting ✴ A method by which you can post a single article to multiple newsgroups.

Cursor ✴ A blinking bar indicating where characters will appear when typed; usually called the *Insertion Point* in Windows.

Cursor control keys ✴ The Arrow Keys, PAGE UP, PAGE DOWN, HOME, and END keys.

Customer support ✴ Telephone assistance provided by software manufacturers to address problems arising from specific user situations.

Cut ✴ To place a copy of text or other data in the Clipboard and remove the original selected text from the screen. Compare ***copy, paste.***

Cylinder ✴ Circumferential tracks on disk storage surfaces. For example, track 3 on side 0 of a disk when combined with tracks 3 of sides 1, 2, 3, etc., are collectively called "cylinder 3."

D

Data ✴ In general, any information being processed by the computer system.

Database ✴ An organized collection of related information (data) stored on the computer's hard disk.

Database management system ✻ Applications software that contains tools for defining, organizing, storing, and retrieving data.

Database manager ✻ See *database management system.*

Database structure ✻ The basic, initial design of the database according to the wishes and needs of the user; what different items of information are included in a database.

Data bus ✻ A common path of printed circuits through which data pass from one part of a computer to another.

Data file ✻ One of the two primary types of files DOS works with. Data files are generally created by the user or by computer programs themselves. Compare *program file.*

Daughter board ✻ See *expansion board.*

DDE ✻ *Dynamic Data Exchange* allows application programs to pass commands and data to other applications. With DDE, one program can remotely control another.

Default ✻ A value assigned or an action taken automatically by a software program unless another is specified. Can be thought of as a "factory setting."

Default button ✻ In some dialog boxes this is the button Windows will select automatically if ENTER is pressed. Shown with a bold border.

Delete ✻ To erase or remove data from a computer's memory or disk storage.

Desktop ✻ The main screen. The desktop is any part of the screen not appearing within a window.

Desktop computer ✻ Another term for microcomputer.

Desktop publishing ✻ A powerful type of applications software for manipulating text and graphics, allowing a computer user to prepare near print shop quality documents.

Device ✻ A component of the computer's hardware system, like a mouse, a printer, a disk drive, or a modem, among others.

Device driver ✻ A software program that controls communications between the computer and a device attached to it.

Dialog box ✻ A rectangular box that opens temporarily and requests additional information or provides command options.

Digital ✻ The representation of information using only arrangements of binary numbers (1 and 0) to represent all characters and values.

Directories ✻ Structures on a disk or Web site that contain files or other subdirectories.

Directory ✻ A convenient logical division for storing related files. See *folder.*

Directory path ✻ The route from one area on a disk to another through the levels of directories and subdirectories.

Directory tree ✻ A graphic (or imagined) representation of levels of hierarchical directories. Similar in shape to a family tree.

Disk ✻ See *diskette.*

Disk cache ✸ Memory buffer set aside for temporarily storing data being read from, or to be written to, a disk. Its purpose is to make the computer operate faster.

Disk controller ✸ The circuitry (often an expansion board) that directs the operation of the disk drives and their respective read/write heads.

Diskette ✸ A single disk of recording material that is a portable but relatively limited form of data storage.

Disk operating system (DOS) ✸ See *operating system.*

Display ✸ A video display device, often called the "monitor" or the "screen."

Display adapter ✸ The circuitry (often an expansion board) that converts the computer's commands to "show this" to a visible picture on the display.

DNS (Domain Name System) ✸ The addressing protocol that lets computers connected to the Internet find each other.

Document ✸ A general term for most types of work created with applications. In many contexts, *document* is synonymous with *file.*

Documentation ✸ The collection of books and other materials that explains the use and operation of a software program.

Document icon ✸ Graphic representation of a document window that has been minimized.

Document window ✸ Window within an application window containing a document created or modified by that application. In many applications, there can be more than one document window within the application window.

Domain name ✸ The name given to any computer registered on the World Wide Web as an official provider of information and files. Domain names are usually two or more terms separated by periods. Examples include Microsoft.com or www.mus.edu.

DOS ✸ Disk operating system.

DOS prompt ✸ *See* **prompt.**

Double-click ✸ To quickly press a mouse button twice in succession without moving the mouse. Used to choose an item or start a process. Compare *click.*

Download ✸ To copy data or files from another computer. Compare *upload.*

Drag ✸ To move an object onscreen by pointing at it, then pressing a mouse button and moving the mouse while keeping the button pressed.

Drag and Drop ✸ A process in which you use your computer's mouse to click and hold objects on the monitor, move them around while continuing to hold the mouse button, and release the mouse button when you have moved the object to the desired location.

Drop-down list box ✸ A single line text box (sometimes with a default value already highlighted) that opens to display a list of additional choices.

Drop-down menu ✳ A list of command options that drops down from a menu bar.

DVD ✳ A storage medium capable of storing 4 to 9 gigabytes of data.

E

E-mail ✳ Electronic mail sent from one computer to another over a network or by telecommunications.

E-mail address ✳ A unique address assigned to a person allowing him or her to receive e-mail messages. It consists of a user ID, followed by an @ sign and a domain name. For example: athomas@nasa.gov.

Embed ✳ To insert data created from one document into another and allow the embedded object to be edited (through OLE) just by double-clicking on it.

Emoticons ✳ Short for emotional icons. These character combinations are one way of trying to get across emotion in what you say. For example, :) is a smile.

Enhance ✳ In word processing, to make specific text stand out from the rest (by underlining or using boldface type, for example).

Enter key ✳ The key pressed to begin the execution of a command. Also called the RETURN key.

Erase ✳ See *delete.*

Executable file ✳ File that starts programs. You can start an executable file in Explorer by double-clicking its name. The following extensions are reserved for executable files: .EXE, .COM, .BAT.

Expansion board ✳ Additional circuit boards to enhance the performance or capabilities of the computing system.

Expansion card ✳ See *expansion board.*

Expansion slot ✳ An opening along the data bus for the addition of expansion boards.

Extension ✳ See *filename extension.*

F

FAQ ✳ Stands for Frequently Asked Questions. Many times, newcomers to a newsgroup will ask questions that the old-timers have heard over and over again. FAQs are written and posted periodically to reduce the number of redundant questions.

Field ✳ In a database, an item of information; similar to a blank on a form.

File ✳ A named collection of information stored on a disk or other storage device. Files include text, programs, graphics, databases, etc.

File manager ✳ In older versions of Windows, an application that organizes, copies, deletes, and renames files and directories, and runs programs. Windows uses an updated version called Explorer.

Filename ✳ A number or letter designation assigned to a file.

Filename extension ❋ An optional one-to-three letter addition to a filename separated from that filename by a period. Application programs use the filename extension to identify compatible files.

File server ❋ A central computer that supervises the operation of a network. Compare *node.*

Fixed disk ❋ IBM's term for a non-removable hard disk.

Flame ❋ An Internet message that often uses profanity or otherwise berates and belittles the recipient.

Flat file ❋ A simple database management system used to organize a single group of information. Compare *relational database.*

Floppy disk ❋ An informal term for a diskette. The actual media inside the diskette shell is flexible, hence the nickname "floppy."

Folder ❋ A container object that holds files and other folders. Also called a *directory.*

Font ❋ A set of letters, numbers, and symbols that are a particular size and design. Usually available in a range of sizes and a variety of styles.

Footer ❋ Repeated text that appears at the bottom, or "foot," of each printed page.

Foreground ❋ Area of the screen occupied by the active window. This is always the application with which you are currently interacting.

Format ❋ The basic layout or appearance of a document or spreadsheet, including such things as margins, line spacing, and column width.

Formatting ❋ The process of preparing a disk or diskette to receive data; a new disk must be formatted before it can be used. When a disk is formatted, all previous data will be erased and replaced by new sectors and tracks.

Frames ❋ A feature available on the World Wide Web that presents text, links, graphics, and other media in separate portions of the browser display. Some sections remain unchanging, while others serve as an exhibit of linked documents.

Freeware ❋ Free software that is available on the Internet and can be downloaded, used, and redistributed at no cost to the user.

FTP ❋ An abbreviation for File Transfer Protocol. FTP is a set of rules for transferring files on the Internet.

FTP site ❋ A location on the Internet where one can either download or upload files using FTP.

Function keys ❋ Programmable keys whose purposes depend on the software program being used.

G

Gigabyte (G or GB) ❋ Roughly, a billion bytes.

Global ❋ An operation that affects an entire document or spreadsheet.

Gopher ✳ Developed at the University of Minnesota, a system whereby many types of information can be displayed and accessed in a simple, menu-based structure.

Gopherspace ✳ The term used to describe the portion of the Internet that contains Gopher sites.

Graph ✳ A visual representation of data, such as a bar graph or pie chart. (Not to be confused with *graphics*).

Graphic interface ✳ The use of pictures, symbols, and icons to provide a menu of operations and applications available to the user. Usually a mouse is used to point to a particular icon to run that program.

Graphics ✳ The production of lines, angles, and curves by a computer on a monitor display or printer.

Graphics mode ✳ A way of presenting visual data in which the screen is treated as an array of tiny dots. Anything shown on the screen (pictures or alphanumeric characters) is built up from these dots. Compare *text mode*.

H

Hard disk ✳ An internal, usually non-removable data storage device.

Hardware ✳ A general term referring to all of the physical and electronic components of the computer system.

Header ✳ (1) Text within a Web page, e-mail message, or newsgroup message that indicates the main point of a document or a section within it. (2) Repeated text that appears at the top, or "head," of each printed page.

Help ✳ In applications software, a set of instructions or operating reminders that can easily be displayed on-screen.

Hierarchical directories ✳ The formal term for the arrangement of directories and subdirectories in a directory tree.

High density ✳ Diskettes that have increased storage capacity.

Hits ✳ (1) When you are conducting an Internet search on the Web, each result of a particular search is called a hit. (2) The number of visits to a Web site. Each time a Web site is accessed by a viewer, there is one additional hit to that Web site.

Home page ✳ Frequently, this term refers to the cover of a particular Web site. The home page is the main, or first, page displayed for an organization's, or person's, World Wide Web site. Sometimes also called a *start page.*

Hover ✳ To place the mouse over an area of the screen (but not clicking).

HTML ✳ An abbreviation for HyperText Markup Language, HTML is the coding language for the World Wide Web that informs browsers how to display a document's text, links, graphics, and other media. This language forms the foundation for all Web pages.

HTTP ✳ HyperText Transfer Protocol. The way information gets exchanged between HTTP servers and their clients.

Hyperlink ✳ Sometimes called a link, a pointer within a document that, when clicked, transports you somewhere else.

Hypertext ✳ Text that is organized by means of links from one piece of information to another.

I

I/O (Input/Output) ✳ A general term to describe any input/output device or the data that flows to or from it.

IBM ✳ International Business Machines, Inc.

Icon ✳ A graphic symbol or picture used to represent various objects or options, such as applications, documents and devices.

Inactive window ✳ An open window that is not currently selected or being worked within.

Inbox ✳ The place a person goes to get his or her incoming messages within his or her e-mail program.

Ink jet printer ✳ A type of letter-quality printer that "paints" its characters by squirting tiny drops of ink onto the paper.

Input ✳ Any data or information that goes into the computer.

Insert ✳ In insert mode, characters typed at the cursor will push existing text to the right as the new characters are typed. Compare ***overwrite.***

Insertion point ✳ The place text will appear when you type. Usually shown as a flashing, vertical bar or line. Sometimes referred to as a *cursor.*

Integrated circuit ✳ A large number of electrical components and connections densely and microscopically placed on the surface of a semiconductor; often called a *chip.*

Integrated software ✳ A comprehensive applications software package, usually including word processor, spreadsheet, database manager, and communications programs.

Interactive ✳ Requiring input or responses from the user.

Interface ✳ The point where two data processing components meet, for example, where a printer cable plugs into a parallel port. The user interface refers to how information is conveyed to the human user, such as the design of the screens and the functions of the keys.

Internet ✳ The global network of computers that enables people all over the world to electronically communicate with each other.

Internet phone ✳ An application that transmits a user's speech across a network (in this case, the Internet) to another user's machine.

Internet Service Provider (ISP) ✳ An organization or company that provides users access to the Internet.

Intranet ✳ A network of computers that is set up like the Internet, except that only certain people, like those who work for a company, are given access.

J

Joystick ✳ An input device often seen with computer and video games.

Justification ✳ In word processing, arranging and spacing words and letters so that margins are aligned. Left justification (that is, along the left margin) is common, right justification less so.

K

Keyboard ✳ Most frequently used input device; resembles a typewriter keyboard.

Keyboard shortcut ✳ Special key sequence used to choose a command directly without first highlighting and displaying a menu.

Keypad ✳ Supplemental set of keys resembling a calculator keypad. Convenient for entering a large amount of numerical data. *Cursor control keys* are superimposed on the numerical keypad and may be *toggled* back and forth with the NUM LOCK key.

Kilobyte (K or KB) ✳ 1,024 bytes.

L

Label ✳ In spreadsheets, the contents of a cell beginning with either a letter or one of several text characters. Although they may contain numerals, labels are not affected by arithmetic operations. Compare ***value.***

LAN ✳ See ***local area network.***

Laser printer ✳ A sophisticated letter-quality printer that combines laser and photocopying technology.

LCD ✳ Liquid crystal display. A popular technology for flat-screen monitors and laptop computers.

Letter-quality printer ✳ Any of several printers that produce printed documents comparable in quality to those produced by good typewriters.

Light pen ✳ An input device that optically scans and "reads" data, often in the form of a bar code.

Link ✳ Short for hypertext link. A link provides a path that connects a user from one part of a World Wide Web document to another part of the same document, a different document, or another resource.

Link ✳ In spreadsheets or databases, two or more separate files may be linked through a common field.

Linked object ✳ The visual representation of a drawing, a sound file, or other media element that can be embedded, updated, and accessed from within a document through OLE.

ListBox ✳ Column of available choices arranged in alphabetical sequence. Usually only one, but sometimes more, can be selected.

Listserv ✳ An e-mail address that is configured to forward every message it receives to the e-mail addresses of those who have subscribed to it. You can think of it as an electronic, interactive newspaper.

Load ✳ To place or copy a program into memory in preparation for running it.

Local Area Network (LAN) ✳ A group of computers connected together to allow users to share resources and files.

Login ✳ The name or identity used when you access a remote computer system.

M

Macro ✳ Macro instruction. A work-saving procedure in which a series of frequently used keystrokes and commands are recorded by a software program to be later "played back" by just pressing one or two keys.

Mail merge ✳ A word processing feature allowing information from two files (such as text in a form letter and addresses from a mailing list) to be combined quickly and simply so that each form letter looks individually typed.

Mailbox ✳ A place where your e-mail program stores mail.

Mailing List ✳ See *listserv.*

Mainframe computer ✳ A very large computer, usually requiring specialized staff and support.

Math co-processor ✳ An optional, supplemental microprocessor that speeds up complex mathematical calculations.

Maximize ✳ Enlarge an application window to occupy the entire desktop, or enlarge a document window to fill the entire application window in which it resides.

Maximize button ✳ Small button located near the right end of the Title Bar. It enlarges the window to its maximum size.

Megabyte ✳ 1,048,576 bytes, or roughly one million bytes. Abbreviated "M" or "MB;" often referred to as a "Meg."

Memory ✳ The high-speed working area of the computer where both the program currently being run and the data being processed are temporarily stored.

Menu ✳ In applications software, a list of several options or commands available to the user.

Menu bar ✳ The row beneath the Title bar that lists the names of command menus which are available.

Merge ✳ See *mail merge.*

Message box ✳ An information-only type of dialog box that requires a single user response, usually the selection of an OK or CANCEL button.

Message headers ✳ The part of an e-mail message (or newsgroup posting) that contains basic information such as sender, receiver, and subject.

Microcomputer ✳ A small, relatively inexpensive, free-standing computer designed for individual use. Also known as a personal computer.

Microdiskette ✳ A 3½-inch diskette contained in a hard plastic shell.

Microprocessor ✳ The small computer chip in a personal computer that interprets programs and performs instructions.

Minicomputer ✳ A medium-sized computer, usually able to run several programs simultaneously.

Minimize ✳ To reduce an application or document window to an icon. Some windows cannot be minimized.

Minimize button ✳ Small button near the right end of the Title Bar. It shrinks the window down to an icon and places it on the desktop.

Modem ✳ Modulator-demodulator. A device that allows computer data to be fed back and forth over telephone lines.

Moderated listserv ✳ Just as a debate has a moderator to make sure both sides stick to the rules, so, too, do some listservs have a human moderator who makes sure the rules of the Listserv are being followed. These listservs are called moderated listservs.

Moderated newsgroup ✳ A newsgroup which features a human moderator to review messages before they are posted.

Moderator ✳ Anyone who moderates, or filters, the content on a Listserv or newsgroup.

Monitor ✳ The computer's video display.

Monochrome ✳ A monitor capable of displaying only one color (usually green or amber) against the background.

Mother board ✳ The primary board of the computer; contains the main circuitry, including the microprocessor.

Mouse ✳ An input device that controls pointer movement by sliding on a flat surface. It has one or more buttons used to initiate actions.

Move ✳ The transfer of text, data, or files from one location to another. The original material is then erased. Compare *copy.*

MS-DOS ✳ A proprietary *operating system* distributed by the Microsoft Corporation. Usually simply called *DOS*. PC-DOS is a licensed version distributed by IBM that is functionally equivalent. The functions of DOS are built into Windows, so a separate version of DOS is not required.

Multimedia ✳ The combination of a variety of media, including sound, animation, video, text, and graphics.

Multitasking ✳ The capability of some computers to perform more than one task or run more than one computer program at a time.

Multiuser ✳ The capability of some computers and computer systems to support several interactive terminals at the same time, with the appearance that each terminal is enjoying exclusive use of the system.

N

Netiquette ✳ The acceptably polite method of talking via electronic communication.

Network ✳ A group of computers connected through cables or telephone lines for the purpose of transferring information from place to place. See *local area network.*

Newsgroups ✳ Topical areas of Usenet that operate much like bulletin boards for the discussion of topics regarding recreation, society, culture, business, and computers. Currently, there are more than 12,000 newsgroups available.

Newsreader ✳ Software designed to download, display, and transmit newsgroup postings.

Node ✳ Peripheral computers connected to a network. Compare *file server.*

Number crunching ✳ Informal term for a spreadsheet's ability to take a large table of related numbers and formulas and perform multiple calculations in a short time.

O

Object ✳ Items such as files, folders, and icons that are visually represented on the screen. Objects have properties and can usually be manipulated, as in copying, deleting, or modifying.

OLE ✳ Object Linking and Embedding, the inclusion (embedding) of data from one program, such as a table, chart, or drawn object, to another data file. OLE permits changes to embedded items by simply double-clicking on them in the current document.

Online ✳ To be currently connected to a remote network or computer.

Online services ✳ Services provided to connect your computer to the Internet.

Open ✳ To make a document available for revision or printing, or to enlarge an icon to a window. Also, to start an application.

Operating system ✳ A program which supervises and controls the operation of a computer, the operation of other software programs, and the user's communication (interface) with the computer. Windows is an operating system.

Operators ✳ Anything that modifies a term or equation. In the equation 2 + 2 = 4, the plus sign is an operator. When searching on the Web, you can often use special symbols or words to build a search "equation" that is often more effective than searching for a single word or phrase.

Option board ✳ See *expansion board.*

Option button ✳ Round button in a dialog box used to select an option. Within any group of option buttons, only one button can be selected. Sometimes called *radio buttons.*

Outbox ✳ The place within an e-mail program where messages are queued, ready to be sent.

Output ✳ Any information or results from the computer for the user.

Overwrite ✳ In overwrite mode, any characters typed at the cursor will erase pre-existing text as the new characters appear. Compare *insert.*

P

Parallel port ✳ A connection or outlet on the system unit that can transmit 8 bits at a time. Usually connected to printers. Compare **serial port.**

Parameter ✳ An addition to a command that governs software, selects options, or establishes limits. Compare **argument.**

Parent directory ✳ The directory one level higher than another.

Password ✳ In applications software, a specific word required to gain access to protected information.

Paste ✳ To insert *cut* or *copied* text from the Clipboard into a document.

Path ✳ See **directory path.**

PC ✳ Abbreviation for personal computer. See **microcomputer.**

PC-DOS ✳ A proprietary operating system distributed by IBM. Functionally equivalent to MS-DOS, both of which are usually simply called *DOS.*

Peer to peer ✳ A network arrangement whereby each computer has equal status and access to all resources.

Peripheral device ✳ Any external piece of equipment attached to the system unit; same as an I/O device.

Peripherals ✳ See **peripheral device.**

Personal computer (PC) ✳ See **microcomputer.**

PIF ✳ Program Information Files tell Windows how to control and run DOS (non-Windows) applications.

Pixels ✳ The smallest graphic unit that can be displayed onscreen. Also called *picture elements* (PELS).

Platform ✳ A particular computer environment with specific operating protocols. Windows, Macintosh, and UNIX are platforms.

Plotter ✳ A specialized printer used to draw pictures, graphs, schematics, and other pictorial representations.

Plug in ✳ A small program that enhances the capabilities of a Web browser. Plug-ins enable browsers to display file types beyond images and text.

Point ✳ To move the mouse until the tip of the pointer rests on the item to be selected or chosen.

Pointer ✳ Usually an arrow-shaped cursor that indicates the current mouse position, and the screen location where your next click will take effect. Can also be a double-headed arrow, I-beam, hourglass, crosshair, small hand, or other shape, depending on what you are currently doing.

Pointing device ✳ Any control that allows the user to position the cursor, select items, or perform commands. Examples include: mouse, trackball, and joystick.

Port ✳ Connections used for transferring information between peripheral devices and the system unit. See **parallel port; serial port.**

POST ✳ Power On Self Test, a self-checking program automatically run every time the computer is switched on.

Post ✳ What a message to a newsgroup is called. When you submit messages (also called articles) to newsgroups, you are said to be posting a message.

Printer ✳ A peripheral device for producing permanent printed copies of computer output.

Program ✳ A complete set of coded instructions that tells a computer how to do something.

Program file ✳ A complete set of coded instructions that tells the computer how to do something. In Windows, a program usually has a file extension of **.COM, .EXE, .BAT,** or **.PIF.**

Program icon ✳ A graphical representation of a program.

Programming ✳ The process of writing coded instructions for a program.

Prompt ✳ A message or symbol (such as the DOS prompt) displayed by interactive software, requesting information or instructions from the user.

Properties ✳ Attributes of an object. For instance, a text object might have a particular font, a certain color, and a certain size.

Protocol ✳ A set of rules. On the Internet, this translates into the set of rules computers use to communicate across networks.

R

RAM ✳ See *random access memory.*

Random Access Memory ✳ RAM. Temporary computer memory which can be read or written to. It is the workspace of the computer, and it's contents are lost when the computer is shut down.

Read ✳ The ability or process of acquiring data from memory storage, or a peripheral device. Compare *write.*

Read-Only Memory ✳ ROM. Permanent memory which can be read but not written to except by special means. It contains instructions for starting the computer, as well as special routines which perform many functions of the operating system.

Read/write slot ✳ The exposed area on a diskette where the disk drive head can read and write data.

Reboot ✳ To restart the computer and reload the operating system. See *boot.*

Record ✳ One complete entry in a database file.

Relational database ✳ A database management system that allows two or more files to be linked together, forming relations on common data or "tables." Compare *flat file.*

Resolution ✳ The degree of clarity of characters on a video display or printer.

Restore ✳ To return a window to its size and position prior to being minimized or maximized.

Restore button ✳ Small box at the right end of the Title Bar that makes the window resume its prior size and location on the screen.

Return key ✳ See *enter key.*

Ring topology ✳ A type of network whereby each node receives and passes along all messages in a closed loop until the messages reach their destinations. Compare *bus topology; star topology.*

ROM ✳ See *Read-Only Memory.*

Root ✳ See *root directory.*

Root directory ✳ The highest level folder in the system of hierarchical folders; the one that is automatically created when a disk is formatted.

Row ✳ In a spreadsheet, the horizontal division of a worksheet. On a computer monitor, the vertical space for one line of text; most monitors can display 25 rows.

Run ✳ To start or execute an application program or other process.

S

Save (to disk) ✳ To write data to a disk or other storage device.

Scroll ✳ The action of moving through text and graphics in order to see parts of the file or list which cannot fit on a single screen.

Scroll bars ✳ Bars in the right-hand and bottom borders of a window representing a document's current position on the screen. Boxes within the scroll bars (called *scroll boxes* or *sliders*) may be dragged with a mouse to move the cursor more rapidly.

Search ✳ To look for a specific character string of information.

Search and replace ✳ To look for specific information and replace it with different data.

Search engine ✳ A computer program that indexes a database and then allows people to search it for relevant information available on the Internet.

Search syntax ✳ The phrasing and symbols used in directing a search tool.

Sector ✳ A subdivision of a track on a disk constituting a unit of disk storage space.

Select ✳ To mark an item by highlighting it or clicking on it. In Windows, objects are selected prior to an action, which will be applied to the selected object. For instance, if you select text then press the DELETE key, the selected text is deleted. In Explorer, if you select an icon (single-click), then open the File menu, the options on the menu will apply only to the selected icon.

Serial port ✳ A connection or outlet on the system unit that can transmit only 1 bit at a time. Used for a variety of peripheral devices, including modems, printers, and mice. Compare *parallel port.*

Server ✳ Any computer that delivers or transmits information and data.

Shortcut key ✳ A key combination that carries out a command or action without first accessing a pulldown menu.

Signature ✳ A small text file that contains information your e-mail or newsgroup client automatically attaches to the bottom of every message you send.

Software ✳ The set of instructions that make computer hardware perform tasks. Software includes both the *operating system* as well as *application programs.*

Sort ✳ To arrange records or data in a particular order.

Split bar ✳ Used to divide a document window into panes when dragged with the mouse. Usually located at the top of a vertical scroll bar, or to the left of a horizontal scroll bar. The Explorer uses split bars to separate the directory window from the file contents window.

Spool ✳ To store a print job on disk so that it can be printed at the same time you are working with another application or document. Abbreviation for *simultaneous peripheral operation online.*

Spreadsheet ✳ Applications software that is an electronic version of the traditional financial analysis tools: the columnar pad, the calculator, and the pencil. The spreadsheet is represented on the screen as a grid of columns and rows.

Star topology ✳ A network arrangement in which all lines converge on a central "host" computer. Compare **bus topology; ring topology.**

Start page ✳ Frequently, this term refers to the cover of a particular Web site. The start page is the main, or first, page displayed for an organization's, or person's, World Wide Web site. Sometimes called a *home page.*

Status bar ✳ The horizontal bar near the bottom of the typing screen showing the cursor's current position and which special function keys (if any) are active. Not found in all Windows applications.

String ✳ See **character string.**

Subdirectory ✳ Lower-level directories subordinate to a parent directory.

Sub domain ✳ A distinct section contained within a domain.

Subscribe ✳ Adding a discussion group to your subscription list.

Surfing the Internet ✳ Slang expression for using the Internet. Also, "surfing the Web."

System board ✳ See **mother board.**

System reset ✳ See **reboot.**

System unit ✳ Hardware unit that houses the majority of the computer's electronic components, including the microprocessor and the disk drives.

T

Task ✳ A running program; an open application or active process.

Task List ✳ A window that is used to show all open applications and switch between them. Can also arrange windows and icons and terminate any running programs or processes. Sometimes called *task manager.*

Task switching ✳ The act of suspending one program's operation while running another. Only one program is actually running or active at a time, as opposed to multitasking, where two or more programs are running simultaneously.

TCP/IP ✳ A set of protocols that applications use for communicating across networks, including the Internet.

Telecommunications ✳ Data communications via telephone circuits.

Teletext ✳ Commercial services that provide information and other services to computers via telecommunications.

Template ✳ In some applications software, a template is a pre-designed form automatically set up to receive certain information or to perform specific procedures. Also, a plastic or paper cutout to be placed on or near the keyboard to remind users of key operations and procedures.

Text attribute ✳ An enhancement of text, such as underlining or boldface, for adding emphasis.

Text box ✳ An area within a dialog box where data needed for a chosen command is typed. May contain default text or be blank. The standard Windows editing keys can be used while typing here.

Text editor ✳ A program that is used to create, edit, and view text files (ASCII). *Notepad* is an example of a Windows-based text editor. See *ASCII*.

Text mode ✳ A way of presenting the entire character set quickly by having all characters built in to the computer's memory. Compare **graphics mode.**

Thread ✳ A series of newsgroup articles all dealing with the same topic. Someone replies to an article, and then someone else replies to the reply, and so on.

Thumbnail image ✳ An image that is a smaller version of a larger one.

Tile ✳ A way of arranging open windows on the desktop so that none overlap and all are visible. Each window occupies a portion of the screen.

Time slice ✳ Amount of processing time allocated to an application by the computer while multitasking, usually expressed in milliseconds.

Title bar ✳ The horizontal bar located along the top of a window that contains its title.

Toggle ✳ An action typical of certain keys allowing a function to be alternately turned on and off by pressing the same key (much like a light switch).

Token ring ✳ Local area network software methodology that works with networks arranged in a ring topology.

Tool bar ✳ A row of graphical rectangles that suggest push buttons. Each push button represents a command that can be executed directly by clicking the appropriate button. Also called *button bar, icon bar, tool palette,* and other names.

Topology ✳ The design and physical arrangement of a network.

Touchscreen ✳ A combination input device/monitor that allows information to be conveyed to the computer by touching specific areas on the monitor screen.

Track ✳ A logical concentric circle on a disk for storing information. Compare *cylinder.*

Trash ✳ A folder containing unwanted messages that can be emptied when the person desires.

True Type fonts ✳ Scaleable fonts that can be sized to any height and will print exactly as they appear onscreen.

Tutorial ✳ Practice sessions that are frequently provided by software manufacturers as an aid to learning their software. Tutorials may be printed in a book or displayed onscreen.

U

UNIX ✳ A multi-user, multi-tasking operating system developed by AT&T and originally designed for use of minicomputers. Versions of UNIX are now available for the more powerful versions of microcomputers.

Upload ✳ To copy data or files to another computer. Compare *download.*

URL ✳ An abbreviation for Uniform Resource Locator. A URL serves as identification for all Internet documents.

Usenet ✳ A large network of computers that are home to the message forums called newsgroups.

User ✳ Commonly used term for the person currently operating the computer and its software.

User interface ✳ See *interface.*

Utility program ✳ A general-purpose computer program that performs an activity not specific to any one applications program. Often used for computer "housekeeping" operations, such as managing files.

V

Value ✳ In spreadsheets, the contents of a cell beginning with either a numeral or one of several symbols. Values can be manipulated by arithmetic operations. Compare *label.*

Veronica ✳ An acronym for the Very Easy Rodent-Oriented Net-Wide Index to Computerized Archives. This is a search engine designed to search Gopherspace.

VGA ✳ See *video graphics array.*

Videodisc ✳ A disk-based medium for storing and accessing video and audio information. Also called *laserdisc.*

Video graphics array (VGA) ✳ An advanced color display adapter that allows for 16 colors (from a palette of 256), high-resolution text, and graphics.

Virtual memory ✳ Hard disk space used to swap tasks and other information when actual system RAM runs low. Allows applications to work as if there were more RAM installed than actually present in the system.

Virus ✳ A program designed to interfere with the normal operations of computers.

W

Web guide ✸ A type of search tool for locating information on the Web. Yahoo! is an example of a Web guide.

Web page ✸ An HTML document that can be browsed and edited.

Web phone ✸ See *internet phone.*

Web Site ✸ A collection of World Wide Web documents, usually consisting of a home page and several related pages. You might think of a Web site as an interactive electronic book.

What if ✸ A powerful feature of spreadsheets using formulas and functions to compute the values at cell addresses rather than computing the values themselves. Once the spreadsheet has been constructed, new data can be introduced, and the entire spreadsheet recalculated to show the effect of the new data.

Window ✸ Rectangular area on the desktop containing an application or document file. Windows can be sized and moved, minimized and maximized, opened or closed.

Windowing ✸ The division of a single display screen into more than one viewing area.

Windows application ✸ Programs designed for the Windows environment that can only run with Windows.

Wizard ✸ A Wizard is a step-by-step procedure to help lead you through what might otherwise be a complex set of steps.

Word processor ✸ A powerful applications package for creating, revising, and printing text documents.

Word wrap ✸ A word processing feature that automatically breaks a line of text at an appropriate point, continuing to the next line.

Workspace ✸ The main work area in an application window that displays the program and any documents being used. Also called *drawing* or *layout area,* or *client area.*

World Wide Web ✸ The graphical interface portion of the Internet.

Write ✸ The ability or process of moving information from one place to another and saving it at the destination, such as in memory or on disk. Compare *read.*

Write protect feature ✸ A method of protecting storage media (diskettes) from being accidentally altered or written over.

X

XENIX ✸ A version of UNIX.

BUSINESS
DOCUMENTS

SECTION THREE

An administrative
assistant faxes a
business document.
Photo by Kevin Wilson.

The Business Letter

Appearance

Despite constantly improving forms of communication such as e-mail, the business letter still exerts enormous influence and deserves your close attention. Business letters are more formal and personal than e-mail. They are also more private.

Very few customers ever see the home office or a branch office; this is often true even of small businesses. What customers do see is company correspondence. An untidy or ungrammatical letter gives the instant impression that the company's product or service is equally flawed. On the other hand, upon receiving a handsomely spaced, well-constructed, and well-organized letter, a customer unconsciously assumes it has come from an up-to-date, well-organized, and successful business.

Letter writing occupies at least one-third of all office work, and good writing is the most effective advertisement of your capability. Any skills you can acquire or improve in this area do double duty: They help you work more quickly and effectively while advancing your career.

Besides the skills you need for your own writing, you need to learn techniques of letter writing to handle your boss's correspondence. Most successful businesspeople have already mastered the mechanics of language, but many in authoritative positions lack such skills. They rely on their administrative assistants to see that their letters are satisfactory.

Any letter that comes from your keyboard—whether composed by you or your employer—must have a businesslike appearance that does not distract from the message it has to convey. The letter must be neat and symmetrical, and with no typographical, grammatical, or spelling errors. Its language should clearly and simply go to the heart of the matter discussed. Its language and appearance should also be within the conventions of the commercial world. That is the reason each company selects its own style for presentation to its public.

The way in which a company is known to its customers, its good name, its reputation, and the quality of its products or services all comprise the *corporate image.* Image is very important, and many companies spend fortunes to have the image instantly recognized by the consumer, so no matter what style the company uses, use it consistently. This helps make the company's correspondence characteristically its own. That consistency also translates into dependability in the customer's mind.

Paragraphing

If you are new to the company, it's not likely you'll be invited to decide on which style of letter to use. A certain style may have already been selected long ago after various experiments. In accordance with that style, you'll be instructed to indent paragraphs or to block them and to put a double-space between paragraphs that are single-spaced. Your boss will no doubt also tell you his or her way of closing a letter, perhaps with the company's name and his or her signature with title below. You should conform to your employer's preference without question.

At the same time, you'll be told of **open punctuation** (no marks at the end of each line outside the text of the letter) or **closed punctuation** (marks after the date line, after each line of the addressee's name and address, after the complimentary close, and after the signature). Closed punctuation is usually used with blocked paragraphs.

Parts of a Business Letter

The various parts of a business letter (Figure 24-1) include:

- Dateline—two to six lines below the last line of the printed letterhead. The date should be written out in this form: January 1, 2006.

- Reference line—a numerical file number, invoice number, policy number, or order should appear on a new line below the date.

- Special mailing notations—special notations such as "confidential" should appear two lines below the date.

- Inside address—should include addressee's title and full name, business title, business name, and full address.

- Attention line—if the letter is not addressed to any specific person, skip one space after the inside address and add, "Attention: _____ ." You can make the letter go to the attention of a department.

- Salutation—one line after the attention line or the inside address. Dear _____ , Ladies and Gentlemen, Dear Sir or Madam, Dear (company name).

- Subject line—gives an overview of what the letter is about. Can be used in place of a salutation.

- Message—the body of your letter with paragraph breaks, optional indentions for paragraphs, bullet lists, and number lists.

- Complimentary close—appears two lines below the last line of the message. Either left justified or five spaces to the right of center.

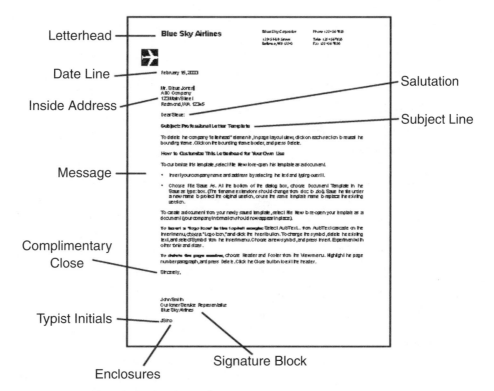

FIGURE 24-1. Parts of a business letter.

- Signature block—justified with the complimentary close with options of typed name and title, signature, or just signature.

- Identification initials—the initials of the typist appears left-justified two spaces below the signature block.

- Enclosure notation—located with the identification initials or in place of them with the notation enc, encl, enclosures (3), or 3 encs.

- Copy notation—left-justified two lines below identification initials with the notation cc: (person's full name or initials).

- Postscript—two spaces below the last text on the page with a P.S. and then a short sentence.

Beginning the Letter

The Date Line

Some offices show the **standard date line** near the body of the letter, ending at the right margin two spaces above the name of the addressee, which is written flush with the left margin. If the **centered date line** is chosen, it is placed two spaces below the letterhead as though it's part of the letterhead and centered exactly. This is an effective and well-balanced look if the company name and address in the letterhead fall in the center. If the letterhead is spread out across the whole top of the page ending at the right margin, then the standard date line seems more graceful and more balanced. When paper without a letterhead is used, the date line must be standard and must be a part of the three-line heading. This consists of the address of the writer and the date of the letter:

1501 Guadalupe St
Austin, Texas 78702
May 27, 2004

Never place the name of the writer in the typewritten heading of the letter, for that belongs only at the end of the letter.

In typing the date line, never abbreviate the name of the month or use figures for it. Also, use numerals only for the day of the month; never add *nd, d, rd, st,* or *th.* These sounds are heard but are never written.

WRONG:	RIGHT:
May 27th, 2005	May 27, 2005
June 22d, 2005	June 22, 2005

The Inside Address

The name and address of the addressee should be exactly as typed on the envelope.

If a street address is long enough to require two lines, place the less important of the two above:

Student Union Building
Northwestern State Teachers College
Alva, Oklahoma 76021

If an individual in a company is addressed, show the individual's name (and title) with the company's name below that, single-spaced. If there is a long address that must be carried over to a second line, indent the second line three spaces:

Mr. Rick Ritenour, President
San Francisco National Bank and Mortgage Association
1200 Market Street
San Francisco, California 99001

Never abbreviate part of the company name unless the company's registered name uses an abbreviation (Co., Inc., or &), and such abbreviation is shown on the company's official letterhead.

Figures are used for all house numbers except "one" (which is spelled out). If there is a numerical street number, separate the house number and street number by a dash:

3780-87 Street (note: no *th* after 87)

Names of cities are never abbreviated; the names of states are also never abbreviated. There is one exception: Use the official U.S. Postal Service postal state abbreviations on the envelope address. (See Chapter 4, Mailing and Shipping.)

Never use an abbreviation such as a percentage mark for "care of;" always spell the words out. Never use "care of " before a hotel name if the addressee is a guest there, and never use it before a company name if the addressee is employed there. However, if the addressee is temporarily receiving mail at the office of the company, "care of " may be used before the company name:

> Mr. Steve Eichman
> Care of The Rockwell Corporation
> 60 Wall Street
> New York, New York 10022

Titles

An individual's name is always preceded by a title—for example, Mr., Ms., Mrs., Miss, Dr., or Col. It's permissible to place honorary initials after the name of an addressee; in that case, always omit the beginning title:

WRONG:	RIGHT:
Dr. Gary K. Wilson, Ph.D.	Gary K. Wilson, Ph.D.

Reverend and Honorable are titles of respect and are preceded by the word *The. Mr.* is omitted:

WRONG:	RIGHT:
Rev. John Wilson	The Rev. John Wilson
Reverend Jim Seckman	The Reverend Jim Seckman

Women and Men

In addressing a woman, it's useful to refer to previous correspondence from the individual to see whether she included a courtesy title when she typed or signed her name. If you have no previous correspondence, use these general guidelines: *Miss* is used for an unmarried woman; *Mrs.* with her *husband's* full name (if known) is used for a married woman or a widow; if a divorcee retains her married name, use *Mrs.* plus her own name, not her husband's; *Ms.* is used in any of the above cases if the woman prefers it; it's also used if you do not know the woman's marital status or if you're addressing a divorcee who has resumed her maiden name.

Address a professional woman by her title, followed by her given and last name:

> Dr. Bernice Wilson

Previous custom was to use *Mr.* as the title when the gender of the addressee was in doubt. Current custom, to avoid giving offense, is more likely to use the addressee's full name without a title in both the address and the salutation:

> Dear Eric Wilson

However, if the letter has some importance, it's worth making a quick call to the other party to get the proper title. Simply say to whomever answers the telephone: "I'm addressing a letter to Pat Richardson. Is that Mr. Richardson or Ms.?" This can save you and your employer much embarrassment later on.

Business Titles

Business titles are never abbreviated:

WRONG:	RIGHT:
Mr. Mark Giddens, Sr. Ed.	Mr. Mark Giddens, Senior Editor
Ms. Julie Seckman, Asst. Mgr.	Ms. Julie Seckman, Assistant Manager

When you are writing to a person holding more than one office within a company, use the highest title unless you are replying to a specific letter signed by him or her under another title as applying to the subject covered. When you are writing to a department of a company, rather than to a person within the company, place the company name on the first line and the department on the second line:

MB's Department Store
Electronics Department
120 Irving Mall
Irving, Texas 76022

Attention Line

An **attention line** refers the letter to the person or department in charge of the situation covered. The word *Attention* is followed by the name of the individual or department. Do not abbreviate the word *Attention* or follow it with a colon.

The attention line is placed two spaces below the last line of the name and address of the addressee, either flush with the left margin of the letter or in the center of the page when paragraphs are blocked. When paragraphs are indented, the attention line is placed in the center of the page.

The attention line is never used in a letter to an individual but only in a letter having a plural addressee, in which case the letter is written to the entire company and not to the person named in the attention line. The salutation must always agree (singular or plural) with the name of the addressee, not with the name on the attention line. For example:

Johnson Smith & Company, Inc.
1500 Main Street
Greenville, Texas 75401

Attention Mr. Horace Wauson

Gentlemen:

Salutation

The salutation is typed two spaces below the addressee's address or the attention line, flush with the left margin. The first word of the salutation begins with a capital, as does the name of the addressee. In business letters the salutation is followed by a colon. In personal letters, the salutation is followed by a comma:

Dear Governor Thompson:
My Dear Mrs. Thomas:
Dear Jane,

Sometimes you'll be required to write a letter addressed to no particular person or firm (such as a letter of recommendation); then you will use capitals for the salutation:

TO WHOM IT MAY CONCERN:

Subject Line

The **subject line** of a letter is an informal way of categorizing or titling a letter. Many letters in business must begin with a subject line after the salutation, a valuable aid in the distribution of mail that also facilitates filing. The subject line can be centered, but when the paragraphs are blocked, it is flush with the left margin.

Do not show "Re" or "Subject" before the subject line. Underline the subject line, but if it occupies more than one line, underline only the bottom line, letting the line extend the length of the longest line in the subject.

Be sure to word the subject line so that it is helpful. If the letter is about an order of silk, a subject line reading simply "Silk" would contribute nothing. If, however, the subject line should read,

Silk Returned, Our Shipping Order 8939

the clerk opening the letter could promptly route it to the person within the organization best able to reply.

Contents

With the body of the letter, first consider its appearance. You must judge how long the letter will be and how much space it will occupy in order to place it on the page as within a picture frame—never too high, never too low, always with proper side margins. If you create the letter with word processing software, you can add spaces to the top of the letter or change the page margins after you have written the letter.

The body of the letter should be brief and straightforward. The letter should have the same ease as a personal conversation. Although you must write whatever your boss dictates, many times while typing you can ease the language a bit to improve its impression on the reader; it's possible to do this with just a word or two more or less that won't call attention to any change. It's your responsibility to see that the letter going forth is creditable in every way to your employer's interests.

The length of the letter should be in accordance with its importance. If too short, the letter may have a curt tone and may seem to slight the recipient. If the letter is too long, the recipient's attention may wander after the first page, and he or she may not read the letter in its entirety.

Closing the Letter

Complimentary Close

When the salutation has been "Dear Sir" or "My Dear Sir," the complimentary closing can be "Yours truly" or "Very truly yours;" no personal connection exists between the writer and the recipient.

"Sincerely" or "Sincerely yours" is appropriate when there is an established personal as well as a business relationship, but it is used only in letters to individuals, never to a company. "Respectfully yours" appears only on letters addressed to a person of acknowledged authority or in letters of great formality.

Avoid the use of such complimentary closes as "Yours for lower prices" or "I remain" and other hanging phrases. "Cordially yours" is not suitable in a business letter. It is often used but used incorrectly as it is too familiar for business. Avoid it.

The Signature

If in the body of the letter the writer has referred to *we, us,* or *ours,* the company, and not an individual in the company, is writing the letter. Consequently the signature would then consist of the typed name of the company under the complimentary close, the space for the writer's signature, and the typed name of the writer with his or her title. The whole signature is typed in block form beginning under the first letter of the complimentary close. In some blocked paragraph letters the complimentary close begins at the left margin; then the signature also begins at the left margin.

Very truly yours,
GRAM'S QUILT COMPANY

Evelyn Wauson, President

Never put a line for the writer's signature. This is a superfluous and old-fashioned practice.

When the writer has referred within the letter to *I, me, my,* or *mine,* this means that he or she, not the company, is writing the letter. Therefore the writer's name is typed with his or her title, omitting the company name entirely.

Very truly yours,

Evelyn Wauson, President

A woman should include a courtesy title in her typed signature so as to allow the recipient of the letter to reply appropriately. Parentheses may be used:

(Miss) Louise A. Scott
Ms. Tina Anderson-Tate
Mrs. Pat Brueck

The courtesy title is blocked with the complimentary close, not extended to the left of it. For a married woman, the signature may consist of either the woman's first name and her surname or her husband's name preceded by Mrs. (no parentheses).

Sincerely yours,

Mrs. Ruth Wilson

A widow may sign as though her husband were living. A divorced woman no longer uses the given name or initial of her former husband. She may use whatever courtesy title she wishes, whether or not she keeps her married surname.

Other Elements

REFERENCE INITIALS

It's no longer considered necessary to type reference initials—the initials of the letter writer and the typist. However, if the company requires identification of this kind for the files, show these on the file copy only not the original. The writer's initials are typed in capitals, the typist's in lowercase. To separate the two, use a colon or a slash. Many companies require only the typist's initials since the writer's initials are obvious from the signature of the letter.

When using a word processor, write the initials or name of the person dictating the letter on the office file copy.

ENCLOSURES

Mention of enclosures should be placed two lines below the reference initials. It may seem to serve no purpose to add "Enc. 2" if the body of the letter mentions the enclosure of two papers. However, the mailing department may find this notation helpful to sort outgoing mail. In addition, as the recipient of such mail, this helps you keep the contents of letters together as you prepare to distribute them without having to read every line.

POSTSCRIPT

Sometimes the letter writer will take advantage of the postscript—following the initials, "P.S.," two spaces below the signature or reference initials—to dramatize some bit of information. Never use the postscript to add something that was forgotten during the writing of the letter. Instead, rewrite the letter.

A Last Look

Before you consider the letter finished, decide if it looks like a picture on the page; that is, have you centered the whole thing? Ask yourself: If you received this letter, would you be favorably impressed? Now check your grammar, spelling, and punctuation again.

A business letter should be folded neatly and precisely. The side edges must match, the typing inside the folds must seem to be protected, and only the fewest folds for the perfect fit into the envelope must be used. Upon taking the letter from the envelope, the recipient should be able to begin reading the letter immediately and should find it attractive. Remember that this is the reader's first impression of your organization.

Letters Written by the Administrative Assistant

Letters written over your own signature usually include acknowledgments of correspondence received while your boss is away, letters requesting appointments, follow-up letters, and letters requesting information that another secretary can furnish. While these letters are an excellent opportunity to show your capability and initiative, always keep in mind that service to your boss and the company is the main factor in deciding which letters to write without dictation.

Many of the routine letters described in this chapter may be handled electronically through e-mail. However, because business letters are more formal and personal, and usually generate results better than e-mail, many executives prefer them over e-mail for certain types of correspondence. Regardless of whether the document is printed on paper or transmitted as an e-mail or fax, you should follow the same guidelines.

Planning the Letter

Good ideas can be clouded by verbosity, while clear forceful words make for quick understanding. Therefore, plan your letters before you write a word. You'll save yourself precious time and effort and add to the company's bottom line because the time element is the greatest cost connected with writing a letter.

To begin, ask yourself: Is this letter supposed to serve the writer, the reader, or both? Will the letter give information, or will it request information? Will it ask for action? What other data must it contain? Before you write, be sure that you have all necessary information on the subject so you can readily refer to previous correspondence or double check your information. If you're hazy about the subject of the letter, so will be the reader.

In the first sentence, mention your purpose in writing so that the reader immediately knows what the letter is about; then follow with whatever explanation is necessary, using a positive tone at all times—that is, words chosen to evoke a positive response. Speak directly to the reader from his or her own point of view, not from yours. The reader must see the advantages of replying favorably.

Use concise language, but be as natural as possible, as though you were speaking to the other person. Reserve the last sentence to request a response if there is to be further correspondence on the subject. Always make that last sentence complete, never hanging. A hanging statement is one that leads into the signature, such as "Hoping this meets with your approval, I am . . ." If that's the thought you wish to express, state it as, "I hope this meets with your approval."

In a business letter, there's no place for cute or clever remarks, or for slang. Your use of slang may be misinterpreted as your not knowing the correct English equivalent. Also avoid exaggeration, sarcasm, or any remarks derogatory to any person or to any product—even competitors.

For the Employer's Signature

Your boss may prefer that all letters be written over his or her name rather than having some letters written over yours. This may be true even if you compose the letters and have permission to sign the boss's name yourself.

When you're composing such a letter, use the boss's characteristic language and style. If your employer usually dictates in a short, concise manner, word the letter in the same way. If your boss usually goes into detail, do the same. And when you sign your employer's name, try to duplicate his or her handwriting as nearly as possible. In other words, make the reader think that your employer took the time to dictate the letter and sign it. To do less is an insult to the recipient.

Never write "Dictated but not read" or "Signed in Mr. Wilson's absence." It's insulting to the recipient, implying that your employer either didn't have or didn't take the time to read and sign the letter personally. It also hints that you could not be trusted to write what your employer asked you to write.

For the same reasons, don't sign the boss's name and then add your initials beside it. If you find it useful to show the true writer and true signer, make a notation on the file copy for future reference.

When you write a letter on your employer's behalf but in your own name, sign it, but do not type your name below the signature line. Instead, type:

Sincerely yours,

Secretary to Mr. Wilson

★ Routine Letters

Encourage your boss to trust you with routine correspondence by emphasizing the enormous time savings it will produce. Then when the boss discovers you can prepare such letters for signature without dictation, he or she may reward you with more challenging correspondence. Following are the types of routine letters you should be able to handle with ease.

Appointments and Acknowledgments

You may request an appointment for your boss or acknowledge letters requesting an appointment. In each letter, always refer to the reason for the appointment and the suggested time; always request a confirmation.

If a certain time has been requested, and your employer approves, confirm the appointment accordingly. If your boss will be occupied at the requested time, suggest another, and ask for confirmation. Be sure to keep a record of appointments suggested and not yet confirmed. If there is ever an argument that your employer broke an appointment, you will have proof otherwise in writing. For this reason, if the back-and-forth process of setting an appointment moves from the letter to the telephone, always send a letter to confirm it in writing.

Reservations

In writing for hotel reservations, state the type of accommodation desired, the name of the person desiring it, and the date and time of arrival, with the probable date of departure, then request confirmation.

Usual reservations for plane or train travel may be made through a travel agent who understands your employer's requirements and makes every effort to satisfy. Travel agents can be invaluable to a business, and their services are free, because their fees are paid by the airline or hotel. When using a travel agency, a telephone call will substitute for a letter to request arrangements; however, do request written confirmation once arrangements have been made.

Follow-Up

In some offices, secretaries use a follow-up file (or a tickler file) to check on delayed replies after a certain lapse of time. When you write a follow-up letter, refer to the previous correspondence, identifying the last letter by date as well as content, and perhaps enclosing a copy if it contains a great deal of detail that could be useful should the original not be available to the addressee.

If you have many follow-up letters to write, instead of composing separate reminders, prepare a form request that can be duplicated on the copier machine or in your word processor. When follow-ups are sent outside the company, often the enclosure of a stamped return envelope will speed a reply.

Sample Model Letters

When a letter is typical of ones you send out frequently, make an extra copy and place it in a special binder, or keep a copy in the memory of your computer so you can refer to it as a model when you have to write that sort of letter again. On a typed letter, note the space plan for margins and center measurements so you'll have the format already arranged. With a computer or word processor, these margins and center measurements are much easier to reset.

Personal Letters

You'll find that many of the letters in this "letter bank" will be from your boss to another businessperson, yet the subject will be personal in nature. These letters are among the most difficult to write, since they must display sincerity in a variety of situations: Sending congratulations, declining invitations, offering condolences, and the like.

Figures 24-2 through 24-4 are samples of personal letters to business associates that you may adapt for your own use. Such letters should use the salutation that your boss would normally use for the recipient and should sign the name your boss is called by that recipient.

Personal Service and Hospitality

When a person has done your employer a personal service or has entertained the boss without financial remuneration when he or she is out of town, that person should be thanked in a letter that can be written by you (Figure 24-5).

Dear John,

I have just read in *The Wall Street Journal* of your promotion to General Sales Manager. I don't think that Smith and Company could have chosen a better person for the job.

Sincerely yours,

[signed] Phil

Dear John,

I appreciate your generous letter about my promotion to Executive Vice President. Such good wishes and kind words will help me do a better job, I'm sure.

Thanks for your note and for your valued friendship.

Sincerely yours,

[signed] Phil

FIGURE 24-2. Sample letters of congratulations and acknowledgments.

Introductions
Letters of introduction written by you for the boss's signature may be mailed or prepared for delivery in person. Such letters should contain the name of the introduced person, the reason for the introduction, the personal or business qualifications of the person, and a courtesy statement (Figures 24-6 and 24-7).

Invitations
Letters of invitation should be gracious without undue formality. Always tell when, where, and why (Figures 24-8, 24-9, 24-10).

Acceptance of Invitations
Letters of acceptance should be brief, appreciative, and enthusiastic. If the letter of invitation failed to include complete details, the letter of acceptance should ask for specific information (Figures 24-11 and 24-12).

Declinations
Letters declining an invitation should express appreciation and enthusiasm, with an assurance of regret or an explanation (Figures 24-13, 24-14, 24-15).

Dear Mrs. Wilson:

It is with great regret that I just read of your son's passing.

I know no words of mine can console you in this sorrowful time, but I do want you to know of my deepest sympathy. You have many friends who are thinking of you.

Sincerely yours,

Philip Brown, President

Dear Mr. Crenshaw:

All of us at Thorne and Sons were saddened to learn of your wife's death. We know there is nothing we can say to help you in this time of grief, but we do want you to know that we extend to you our very deep sympathy.

Sincerely yours,

Philip Brown, President

Dear Mrs. Holmes:

We at Liberty Oil Company were sorry to read of the tornado that struck your Denison factory. We know the loss was very great, but we know also that you will rise and go ahead with rebuilding.

If we can be of service in helping you overcome your present problems, please call on us. We have enjoyed doing business with R. G. Holmes Corporation and look forward to resuming our enjoyable relationship in the near future.

Sincerely yours,

Philip Brown, President

FIGURE 24-3. Sample letters of condolence.

Dear Henry,

Your card and beautiful bouquet of roses helped a great deal to make last week bearable.

I am back at the office and feel I shall be good as ever very soon. The accident was a shock, but with good friends like you, I know the days ahead will be brighter.

You may be sure that I appreciate your friendship all the more at a time like this.

Sincerely yours,

[signature only]

FIGURE 24-4. Sample letter of thanks.

Dear Janet,

If it hadn't been for your keen mind and able assistance, our recent sales meeting might have been a complete flop. Because I had never before conducted such a meeting, I certainly was lucky to have your help.

Thank you for your good judgment and wise suggestions.

Sincerely yours,

[signature only]

FIGURE 24-5. Sample letter of personal service and hospitality.

Dear Mr Fielding:

This will introduce a good friend of mine, John August, who is associated with our state's Department of Commerce. He has heard of the fine work you are doing in Ohio and hopes he will have a chance to talk with you for a few minutes when he visits Cincinnati next Tuesday, March 22.

I have asked Mr. August to telephone you upon his arrival in Cincinnati to learn whether you can see him on that day. If you can, I shall appreciate it. I think you will enjoy meeting him.

It was great to see you at the Boston convention, and I look forward to the Buffalo convention in September.

Sincerely yours,

Philip Brown, President

FIGURE 24-6. Sample letter of introduction to a business associate.

To a personal friend

Dear Tom,

A very good friend of mine, John August, will be passing through Nashville on his way to Boston next Tuesday, and I have asked him to stop by your office. John is a fellow you will enjoy meeting.

I shall appreciate any courtesy you may extend to him while he is Nashville—his first visit to your great city, by the way.

Sincerely yours,

[signature only]

FIGURE 24-7. Sample letter of introduction to a personal friend.

Dear Mr. Brueck:

The American Consolidated Life Insurance Company is holding a dinner next Thursday evening honoring its million-dollar-a-year salespeople. Will you join us as our honored guest?

Since you would be seated at the head table, we are asking you to join us in Room 200 of the Waldorf Hotel at seven-thirty, so that we may arrive at the banquet room in a group.

Sincerely yours,

Nora Drake, President

FIGURE 24-8. Sample invitation to attend a luncheon or dinner.

Dear Roger,

Arthur Whitfield is coming to town next Friday, and Mary Smith and I are entertaining him at a luncheon at the Ritz. We hope you can set aside a couple of hours so as to join us. I am sure Arthur will be happy to see you, as I shall also.

The luncheon will be held in the Persian Room at twelve-fifteen.

Sincerely yours,

[signature only]

FIGURE 24-9. Sample invitation to attend a luncheon or dinner.

Dear Mr. Lee:

As President of the Chicago Rotary Club, I have been asked to arrange the program for our next Thursday noon meeting. I know that all of our Chicago Rotarians would like to hear the address you gave in Detroit last week (I was privileged to be in attendance there) on the subject of "The International Situation."

Next Thursday's meeting will be held in the Benetian Room of the Drake Hotel. I hope you will be with us to give our members the same treat you afforded the Detroit Rotarians.

Sincerely yours,

Philip Brown, President

FIGURE 24-10. Sample invitation to give an address.

Dear Ms. Drake:

It is a pleasure to accept your invitation to attend the dinner next Thursday evening honoring your million-dollar-a-year salespeople.

I shall be in Room 200 of the Waldorf Hotel promptly at seven-thirty, as you request.

Thank you very much for your invitation.

Sincerely yours,

Bob Brueck

FIGURE 24-11. Sample acceptance of an invitation.

Dear Mr. Brown:

I shall be delighted to speak to the Chicago Rotary Club next Thursday. Thank you for inviting me.

Your suggestion that I repeat my Detroit address means that I won't have to prepare a new one.

I shall look forward to seeing you in the Venetian Room at noon.

Sincerely yours,

Barry Lee

FIGURE 24-12. Sample acceptance of an invitation.

Dear Ms. Drake:

Only yesterday, I accepted an invitation to speak in Boston on July 12, the date of your dinner meeting honoring your million-dollar-a-year salespeople. This will make it impossible for me to be your guest that evening.

It was kind of you to invite me, and I regret my inability to attend. I hope the occasion will be a very successful one.

Sincerely yours,

Steve Wauson

FIGURE 24-13. Letter of declination.

My Dear Mrs. Scott:

In reply to your letter of May 3 inviting me to participate in your association's fundraising campaign, I appreciate your thoughtfulness in writing to me.

I am familiar with your association's good work, and in the past it has been my pleasure to contribute to it. It is with regret, therefore, that I must tell you that all my available funds for purposes of this nature have been pledged. It is not possible for me to be a party to your worthy program at this time.

You have my best wishes for a highly successful campaign.

Sincerely yours,

Mrs. Susan Wilson

FIGURE 24-14. Letter of declination.

Dear Mr. Bryson:

I dislike writing a letter that will cause someone inconvenience, but this one falls within that category, to my regret.

This morning, I was advised that a close relative had passed away in Denver, and I shall be leaving this afternoon to attend the service tomorrow, the day of your meeting.

I am sorry that I shall not be able to speak to your group and especially that you will have to find a speaker to replace me at this late date. I hope you understand that I am helpless to avoid this trip.

I hope your meeting will be successful in every way.

Sincerely yours,

Elizabeth Wright, President

FIGURE 24-15. Letter of declination.

Because this cancellation comes so close to the date of the speech, this letter would immediately be delivered by messenger or would be faxed or e-mailed if the addressee is in another city. It is wise to follow-up with a phone call.

★ Interoffice Memorandums and E-Mails

If the company you work for is large, much of your correspondence will be with other departments or perhaps with branch offices scattered throughout the company. The office memorandum, commonly called a memo, is a popular and inexpensive method of communicating with these fellow employees.

In many offices, paper memos have been replaced by e-mails. However, there are many types of communication that are inappropriate for e-mail. For example, confidential information, or information that should not be forwarded should be printed on paper and not sent as an e-mail.

Memos should be directed only to persons within the organization and should be signed or initialed by the sender. If a memorandum is confidential in nature, enclose it in a sealed envelope. If copies are sent to individuals other than the person or persons addressed, a notation to that effect should be made at the lower left corner of the form.

If you wish to create memo forms from scratch, use plain white paper. If your office is equipped with a word processing computer, store the basic form in the computer's memory, and retrieve it when needed. Figure 24-16 contains an example.

TO: Mary Anne Scott, Shipping Department Manager

FROM: Bob Brueck, President

DATE: May 12, 2006

SUBJECT: Meeting to discuss various overseas carriers

A meeting has been scheduled for Tuesday, May 12, in my office to discuss with several carrier representatives suggested methods and costs to deliver our products to international markets. Your attendance is requested.

Distribution:

Tom Alberton

Martha Reeves

FIGURE 24-16. Sample interoffice memorandum.

Paper Selection

Paper selection is important for some written communications. Paper and envelopes come in various sizes, colors, and qualities. One way to rate a particular paper is by its basis weight. For example, 20 lb paper is often used in copy machines and laser printers. For report covers, 100 lb paper can be used.

Paper with rag content and cotton is more expensive than other varieties and is often a choice for letterhead. The standard size for letterhead is 8 1/2 × 11 inches.

Envelopes

Envelopes come in a variety of sizes. Security envelopes have extra thickness so that documents cannot be read through the envelope by holding it up to a light source. Windowed envelopes have a clear plastic window that allows an address to show through. Typical envelope sizes include:

- No 6 —3 5/8 inches × 6 1/2 inches
- No 9—3 7/8 inches × 8 7/8 inches
- No 10—4 1/8 inches × 9 1/2 inches

Addressing Envelopes

Envelopes can be addressed by using a typewriter, by printing on sheets of adhesive-backed labels, or by using the envelope feature of your word processing software. Regardless of which method you use, the address should contain the following:

- Name
- Title
- Company
- Street address, suite or apt number
- City, State Zip + 4

You should capitalize the first letter of every word in the address, except prepositions (*of* and *for*), conjunctions under four letters, and articles. You should leave one space between the state name and zip code. The state name can be spelled out, or you can use the two-letter abbreviation. The next to the last line in the address should be the street address, P.O. Box, rural route, or highway address.

Word Processing Envelope Feature

When using the envelope feature in your word processor, you should accept the defaults for the envelope size. This will ensure that the address will fall within the OCR read area for the U.S. Postal Service. If the software allows, include the USPS POSTNET bar code above or below the address block.

In Microsoft Word, you can access the envelope feature by clicking the **Tools Menu,** then clicking **Envelopes and Labels.** On the Envelopes and Labels dialog you can enter the delivery address and return address. If you click the **Options** button, you can click the checkbox to add Delivery Point Barcode to the envelope or label. Figure 24-17 shows the Envelopes and Labels dialog in Microsoft Word.

Creating Envelopes By Merging an Address List

With Microsoft Word, you can print envelopes for a mass mailing by merging addresses from an address list. The first step is to create a new blank document. On the **Tools Menu,** if you click **Mail Merge** you can view the Mail Merge dialog. It allows you to select a main document, a data source, and then to merge the two documents. The Mail Merge function can be used to print form letters, address labels, or envelopes. Figure 24-18 shows the Mail Merge dialog.

Windowed Envelopes

When using windowed envelopes, adjust the placement of the inside address so there will be a 1/8-inch clearance around the edges of the address inside the window.

Return Addresses

A return address should always be included; however, the writer's name is not necessary. The return address should include the company name, street address, city, state, and zip. It should be aligned at the left about 1/2 inch from top and 1/2 inch from the side of the envelope. Any special notations such as *confidential, personal,* or *hold for arrival* should be typed three spaces below the return address.

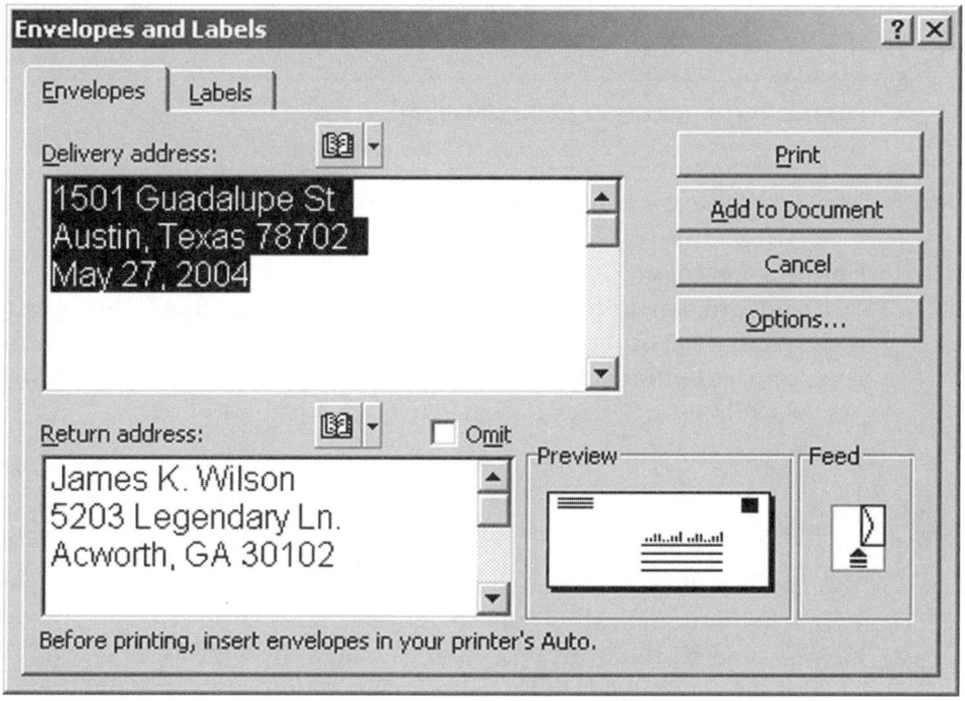

FIGURE 24-17. Microsoft Word Envelopes and Labels Dialog.

Screen shot reprinted by permission from Microsoft Corporation.

Mail Merge Helper `?` `X`

The main document and data source are now available. Choose the appropriate Edit button to work on either one.

1 Main document

[_Create_ ▾] [_Edit_ ▾]

Merge type: Form Letters
Main document: D:\Kevin's Work\...\Chapter 24.doc

2 Data source

[_Get Data_ ▾] [_Edit_ ▾]

Data: D:\...\Tape Labels.doc

3 Merge the data with the document

[_Merge..._] [_Query Options..._]

Options in effect:
  Suppress Blank Lines in Addresses
  Merge to new document

[Cancel]

FIGURE 24-18. Microsoft Word's Mail Merge Feature.

Screen shot reprinted by permission from Microsoft Corporation.

Folding Letters

The standard way to fold letters is to fold them into thirds. Start by bringing the bottom third of the letter up and then making a crease. Fold the top of the letter down to within 3/8 inch of the bottom crease. Then make a second crease. The second fold side goes into the envelope first.

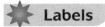 **Labels**

You can use the labels feature of a word processing program just like the envelope feature. You can purchase adhesive label sheets from companies such as Avery and set the word processor to match the label number.

You can type single addresses or a page of the same address (useful for creating return address labels). Figure 24-19 shows an example of the labels ready to print in Microsoft Word.

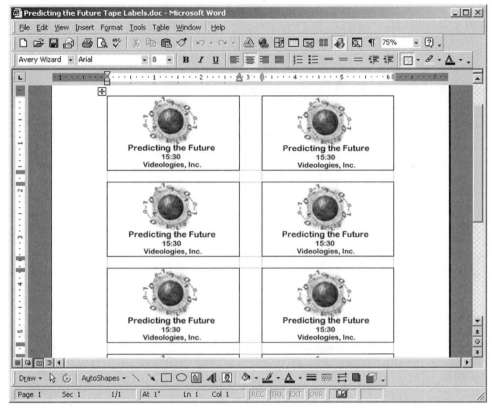

FIGURE 24-19. A page of labels in Microsoft Word.

Screen shot reprinted by permission from Microsoft Corporation.

Other Written Communications

⭐ Reports

As an administrative assistant, you may be asked to create a variety of different reports for your boss. Some of the reports will be routine and will be created from various sources already available. Other more formal reports will require input from your boss in the form of dictation, supplied documents, and a series of reviews and revisions. There are four general types of reports that will be created by administrative assistants. They include:

- Memorandum report
- Letter report
- Short report
- Formal report

Memorandum Report

The memorandum report is a routine and informal report that might be prepared on a weekly basis to report the status of projects to upper management. This report is objective and impersonal in tone. There may be some introductory comments; however, they will be very brief. Headings and subheadings will be used for quick reference and to highlight certain aspects of the report. Usually, the memorandum report is single-spaced and printed on plain paper; however, in some businesses this report may be sent as an e-mail or e-mail attachment.

Letter Report

The letter report is normally a one-page letter that is printed on company letterhead. Letterhead second sheets are used for continuation pages. The letter report is most often sent outside the company to consultants, clients, or to the board of directors. The report should have headings and subheadings to organize the content.

Short Report

The short report differs from the memorandum and letter reports because it will have a title page, a preliminary summary with conclusions and recommendations, authorization information, a statement of the problem, findings, conclusions, and recommendations. The short report may contain tables and graphs, and can be either single- or double-spaced. Headings and subheadings will be used to organize the content and to emphasize certain aspects.

The title page has the name, title, and address of the person or company to whom the report is being submitted. In addition, the title page includes the preparer's name, title, and address. Long report titles are divided and centered.

Formal Report

The formal report is more complex and has a greater length compared to the short report. Included in the formal report are the following:

- Report Cover
- Fly leaf
- Title fly
- Title Page
- Letter of authorization
- Letter of transmittal
- Foreword or Preface
- Acknowledgements
- Table of contents
- List of tables
- List of illustrations
- Synopsis
- Report body
- Footnotes or endnotes
- Appendix
- Glossary
- Bibliography
- Index

The margin settings for a formal report are: first page top margin, 2 inches; subsequent pages top margin, 1 inch. Bottom margins on all pages are 1 inch. The left and right margins on all pages are 1 inch. For bound reports the left margin should be 1 1/2 inches to allow extra room for the binding.

Spacing for the body of the report can be single- or double-spaced. Set-off quotations should be single-spaced, as are footnotes.

Paragraph indentions should be 5 spaces. Long quotations should be indented 5 spaces in from body. Numbered and bulleted lists should also be indented 5 spaces in from the body. Footnotes should match paragraph margins.

Primary headings should be left justified, bold, with additional space above and below. A 20 to 24 point sans serif font such as Helvetica should be used. Secondary headings should be left justified, bold, with a 16 to 18 point sans serif font. Third level headings should also be left justified, bold, with 12 to 14 point sans serif font.

There should be no page number on the title page, although a page number should be assigned for numbering purposes. The front matter should use small roman numerals for numbering. The body of the report should use Arabic numerals starting with 1. Page numbers should be either centered or in the right margin, 1/2 to 1 inch from the top, or 1/2 inch from the bottom.

Headings and Subheadings

You should use a numbering system for headings. You can use numbers or a combination of numbers and letters. Figure 25-1 shows two alternative heading numbering systems.

1. Main Heading
    1.1 Subheading
    1.2 Subheading
         1.2.1 Third level heading
         1.2.2 Third level heading

I. Main Heading
    a. Subheading
    b. Subheading
        1. Third level heading
        2. Third level leading

FIGURE 25-1. Heading numbering systems.

Headings and subheadings should be parallel in structure. The following are examples of non-parallel and parallel structure.

Non-parallel

1. Reading the Manual

2. The Instructions

3. How to Install the Software

Parallel

1. Reading the Manual

2. Following the Instructions

3. Installing the Software

Report Cover

The cover should have the title and author's name. The title should be in all capital letters. The cover may optionally be printed on card stock paper.

Flyleaf

The flyleaf is a blank page that is inserted after the cover. A flyleaf is also sometimes added to the end of the report just before the back cover.

Title Fly

The title fly is a single page with just the report title in all caps, centered on the upper third of the page.

Title Page

The title page should include the title of the report in all caps and subtitle if there is one. It should also contain the recipient's name, corporate title, department, company name, and address. It should also include the preparer's name, corporate title, department, company name, and address. The date the report is submitted should be included on the title page.

Letter of Authorization

The letter of authorization should be printed on letterhead and should explain who authorized the report and any specific details regarding the authorization.

Letter of Transmittal

The letter of transmittal is a cover letter for the report. It explains the purpose of the report, the scope, limitations, research used, special comments, and acknowledgements. The letter of transmittal may take the place of a foreword or preface.

Acknowledgements

The acknowledgements page should list individuals, companies, or institutions that assisted in creating the report.

Table of Contents

The table of contents should include headings, subheadings, and third level headings with page numbers. You can use an outline style with a heading numbering system. If you are using a word processor, you can automatically generate a table of contents based on the heading styles.

List of Tables

If tables are used in the report, you should include a list of tables in the front matter. The list should include table numbers, page numbers, and the descriptions that are used as table titles in the body of the report.

List of Illustrations

If illustrations are used in the report, you should include a list of figures in the front matter. The list should include figure numbers, page numbers, and the captions that are used with the figures in the body of the report.

Report Body

The body of the report should include an introduction to the report, introductions to major sections—headings, subheadings, and third level headings—and a summary at the end of the major sections. The body should include normal paragraph breaks, bulleted lists, numbered lists, illustrations, and tables.

Appendix

If there are supplementary reference materials or sources of research, you can include them at the end of the report in a separate section titled "Appendix."

Glossary

The glossary should include technical terms with definitions along with any abbreviations. Abbreviations should be spelled out the first time they are used in the body of the report.

Bibliography

The bibliography should list all sources of information that were used to compile the report.

Index

An index may be optional for many reports. If you are using a word processing program such as Microsoft Word, an index can be generated automatically similar to the way a table of contents is created. However, you will need to mark index entries throughout your document before you ask the program to create the index.

An index is an alphabetical listing. The first word of each entry has an initial capital letter. The rest of the words are lower case. Subentries in the index are like subheadings and are indented one or two spaces. Cross-references direct the reader to another location in the index. Punctuation is kept to a minimum.

✴ Documenting Sources

You should always acknowledge the work of other writers to allow readers to judge the quality of the information based on the quality of the source, and to enable the reader to verify information. Some writers use parenthetical references to documentation sources; others include footnotes or endnotes.

Footnotes and Endnotes

Footnotes are short notes set at the bottom of the page. Endnotes are placed at the end of the report. Usually, both footnotes and endnotes are numbered, with a small number inserted at the end of the text with the corresponding footnote at the bottom of the page. Endnotes are listed at the end of the report.

Footnotes and endnotes should include the author or author's names, the title of the source, publisher, date, and page reference.

For example:

James Stroman, Kevin Wilson, and Jennifer Wauson, *The Administrative Assistant's and Secretary's Handbook* (New York, AMACOM Books, 2003), page 201.

Parenthetical references are inserted within a document within parentheses. Sometimes a footnote is used for the first usage of a reference source. In subsequent references just the author names and the page number are listed. For example: (Stroman, Wilson, and Wauson, 2003).

Bibliographies

Bibliographies list all works cited in the report footnotes or parenthetical references. You may also include research that was not cited as a footnote but was used to create the report. The bibliography listings are ordered alphabetically by author's last name. If there is no main author, then the book title is used. The author's surname comes first. Additional authors are listed first name, last name. For example:

> Stroman, James, Kevin Wilson, and Jennifer Wauson, *The Administrative Assistant's and Secretary's Handbook* (New York, AMACOM Books, 2003), page 201.

Report Templates

If you are using a word processing program such as Microsoft Word, you can create a report by using one of the report templates that are available. By clicking **File, New,** and then clicking the **Reports** tab, you will see three default reports:

- Contemporary Report
- Elegant Report
- Professional Report

Press Releases

When writing a press release you should start with the main idea first, followed by major details related to the idea, followed by minor details, and then finally supplemental information. The major elements to include are the five Ws: who, what, when, where, and why. Also, don't forget to explain how.

A press release should be factual, interesting, and informative. All the details should be carefully verified and proofread.

Press releases should be printed on normal size office paper and double-spaced. All margins should be 1 inch.

The top of the press release should include contact information with name, address, phone number, and e-mail. The words *Press Release* and *For Immediate Release* or *For Release* (and then the date) should also be included.

If a press release is longer than one page, *MORE* is typed at the bottom in all capital letters, centered or on the right side. Subsequent pages are numbered and include a short title caption left justified.

At the conclusion of the press release, five number signs #####, *-end-* or *(END)* are used.

Tables

Tables are a good way to organize information into a compact easy-to-read form.

Word processing software, such as Microsoft Word, has features for creating and formatting tables.

The default table has horizontal and vertical grid lines. You can determine the number of rows and columns as you create the table. You can also add additional rows or columns as needed. The table grid will be the same width as regular paragraphs (see Table 25-1).

You can click within a table cell and move the column spacers in the ruler to make columns wider or smaller.

Column headings are usually added at the top of each column. The first row of each column can be merged to form a single row. This is where the title should be listed. The table title should be bold in all capital letters (see Table 25-2).

Other table cells can be merged to create cross headings that span several columns or several rows. To do this, select the cells, then click the **Table Menu,** then click **Merge Cells.**

Data in a default table will be left justified. You can select a row and then click on a different justification using the icons on the toolbar. Some types of data—such as money—should be right justified.

Heading text, as well as other text, can be made bold, italics, or both. You can change the color of the text and add shading to rows or columns.

You can change the height above and below the text within the table by selecting the table, then clicking **Format, Paragraph,** and then adjusting the settings for Spacing Before and After.

Using the borders and shading feature in the Format Menu, you can select the entire table or parts of the table and change the size or style of the grid lines. You can also remove the grid lines completely if you want (see Table 25-3 as an example).

You should capitalize the first word of each item in a table, plus any proper nouns or proper adjectives. Table text can include numbered lists and bullets, just like regular document text.

When placing tables within a report, the table should appear as soon as possible after it is mentioned in the text. Tables should always be introduced in the text. Avoid breaking a table at the end of a page and continuing it on the next page. Start the table at the beginning of a new page if necessary.

TABLE 25-1 A Table Grid

TABLE 25-2	Simple Table with Data

SALES BY REGION

North	South	East	West
$123,000	$145,221	$132,010	$90,321
$133,210	$111,301	$112,101	$99,781
$141,210	$98,989	$156,287	$101,341

TABLE 25-3	Table with Formatting Features

SALES BY REGION

North	South	East	West
$123,000	$145,221	$132,010	$90,321
$133,210	$111,301	$112,101	$99,781
$141,210	$98,989	$156,287	$101,341

Add two spaces after the last normal paragraph text before inserting the table. Leave two spaces after the table before resuming with the next paragraph.

Editing and Proofreading

Editing a document requires checking for the following:

- Grammar
- Spelling
- Punctuation
- Accuracy
- Style

The traditional lines between copyediting and proofreading have blurred with the use of computers in business. Many administrative assistants must proofread and edit their own documents before they are distributed. In some large offices, a technical writer or documentation specialist may edit reports that will be distributed to wide audiences within the company or communications destined for outside the company.

Sometimes a boss will proofread and copyedit documents and send them back with corrections. Depending on who is performing these tasks, an administrative assistant may need to make corrections to documents that contain proofreading symbols and abbreviations. (See Tables 25-4 and 25-5).

25 ■ OTHER WRITTEN COMMUNICATIONS

TABLE 25-4	Common Proofreading Symbols
Symbol	**Meaning**
⌃	insert a comma
⌄	Insert an apostrophe or single quotation mark
∧	insert something
⌄ ⌄	use double quotation marks
⊙	use a period here
℮	delete
∿	transpose elements
⌒	close up this space
#	a space needed here
¶	begin new paragraph
No¶	no paragraph

Copyediting
Use the following checklist when copyediting a document or manuscript:

- Are the headings and subheadings consistently used?
- Is the spelling correct?
- Are all proper names accurate?
- Are all lists parallel in structure?
- Do all nouns and verbs agree?
- Are numbered lists correctly numbered?
- Are all dates correct?
- Are all alphabetical lists in alphabetical order?
- Is all punctuation correct and consistent?
- Is all capitalization correct and consistent?
- Are all bibliographical references accurate and consistent?

Proofreading
Use the following checklist when proofreading a document or manuscript:

- Are all headings and other text elements consistent in style and layout?

TABLE 25-5	Common Proofreading Abbreviations
Abbreviation	**Meaning**
Ab	a faulty abbreviation
Agr	agreement problem:
P/A and S/V	subject/verb *or* pronoun/antecedent
Awk	awkward expression or construction
Cap	faulty capitalization
CS	comma splice
DICT	faulty diction
Dgl	dangling construction
- ed	problem with final -*ed*
Frag	fragment
| |	problem in parallel form
P/A	pronoun/antecedent agreement
Pron	problem with pronoun
Rep	unnecessary repetition
R-O	run-on sentence
Sp	spelling error
- s	problem with final -*s*
STET	Let it stand
S/V	subject/verb agreement
T	verb tense problem
Wdy	wordy
WW	wrong word

- (For letters) Is the dateline, reference line, initials, enclosure, and carbon-copy notation accurate?
- Are all cross-references accurate?
- Are all margins consistent and proper?
- Are all tables aligned correctly and consistently?
- Have any footnotes been omitted?
- Are all end-of-line word divisions accurate?
- Are there any accidentally repeated words in the document?
- Are the page numbers correct?
- Are call headings and captions separate?

Electronic Revisions

Rather than make edits on paper, you can make edits electronically on a word processing document. By using the Track Changes feature (Figure 25-2) in a word processing program like Microsoft Word, you can allow multiple people to add revisions and comments. Revisions show up in a different color font. After you have reviewed the revisions, you can accept them one at a time or reject them.

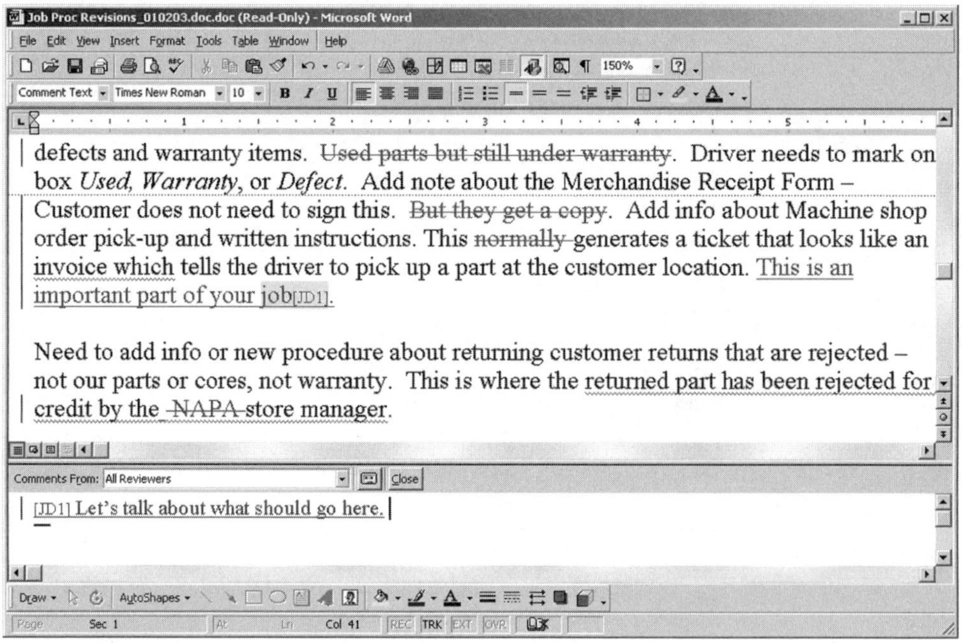

FIGURE 25-2. Revisions in a Microsoft Word document.

Screen shot reprinted by permission from Microsoft Corporation.

Forms of Address

The correct form of address helps to create a favorable impression, no matter whether you are communicating in a letter, by telephone, or in person.

Following is a chart of the correct forms in alphabetical order by the title of the person being addressed.

Chart Code:

EA	Envelope address
S	Salutation of a letter
C	Complimentary closing of a letter
SP	Speaking to
WR	Writing about

Abbot

EA	The Right Reverend Jackson Thomasson, O.S.B., Abbot of
S	Dear Father Abbot
C	Respectfully yours
SP	Abbot Thomasson OR Father Abbot
WR	Father Thomasson

Alderman or Selectman

EA	The Honorable Horace Wauson
S	Dear Mr./Mrs./Miss/Ms. Wauson
C	Very truly yours OR Sincerely yours
SP	Mr./Mrs./Miss/Ms. Wauson
WR	Mr./Mrs./Miss/Ms. Wauson

Ambassador (United States)

EA	The Honorable Regina A. Strauss, American Ambassador (but in Central or South America: The Ambassador of the United States of America)
S	Sir/Madam OR Dear Mr./Madam Ambassador
C	Sincerely yours OR Very truly yours
SP	Mr. /Madam Ambassador
WR	the American Ambassador OR the Ambassador of the United States

Ambassador (foreign)

EA His Excellency Tom Jowers, Her Excellency Rosemary Scalessa
S Excellency OR Dear Mr. /Madam Ambassador
C Respectfully yours OR Sincerely yours
SP Mr. /Madam Ambassador
WR the Ambassador of Spain OR the Ambassador

Archbishop (Roman Catholic)

EA The Most Reverend Archbishop of New York OR The Most Reverend
John C. Terrell, Archbishop of New York
S Your Excellency OR Dear Archbishop Terrell
C Respectfully yours OR Sincerely yours
SP Your Excellency
WR the Archbishop of New York OR Archbishop Terrell

Archdeacon

EA The Venerable Paul A. Morgan
S Venerable Sir OR My dear Archdeacon
C Respectfully yours OR Sincerely yours
SP Archdeacon Morgan
WR the Archdeacon of Los Angeles

Assembly Representative (see Representative, State)

Attorney General (of the United States)

EA The Honorable Carlton Patterson, Attorney General,
Washington, DC 20503
S Dear Mr./Madam Attorney General
C Sincerely yours OR Very truly yours
SP Mr./Madam Attorney General OR Attorney General Patterson
WR the Attorney General OR Mr./Mrs./Miss/Ms. Patterson

Attorney General (of a state)

EA The Honorable Marsha Smith OR Attorney General of the State
of Kansas
S Sir/Madam OR Dear Mr./Madam Attorney General
C Sincerely yours OR Very truly yours
SP Attorney General Smith
WR the Attorney General OR the State Attorney General, OR
Mr./Mrs./Miss/Ms. Smith

Bishop (Catholic)

EA The Most Reverend Phillip Johnson, Bishop of
S Your Excellency OR Dear Bishop Johnson
C Respectfully yours OR Sincerely yours
SP Bishop Johnson
WR Bishop Johnson

Bishop (Episcopal)
EA	The Right Reverend Mark Lessing, Bishop of
S	Right Reverend Sir OR Dear Bishop Lessing
C	Respectfully yours
SP	Bishop Lessing
WR	the Episcopal Bishop of

Bishop (Episcopal, presiding)
EA	The Most Reverend Peter Brown, Presiding Bishop
S	Most Reverend Sir OR Dear Bishop Brown
C	Respectfully yours OR Sincerely yours
SP	Bishop Brown
WR	Bishop Brown

Bishop (Methodist)
EA	The Reverend Andrew Carter
S	Reverend Sir OR Dear Bishop Carter
C	Respectfully yours OR Sincerely yours
SP	Bishop Carter
WR	Bishop Carter

Brother (of a religious order)
EA	Brother Robert, S.J.
S	Dear Brother Robert
C	Respectfully yours OR Sincerely yours
SP	Brother Robert
WR	Brother Robert, S.J.

Brother (superior of a religious order)
EA	Brother Thomas, S.J., Superior
S	Dear Brother Thomas
C	Respectfully yours OR Sincerely yours
SP	Brother Thomas
WR	Brother Thomas

Cabinet Officer of the United States (addressed as "Secretary")
EA	The Honorable Timothy Dutton, Secretary of State, Washington, DC 20044
S	Sir/Madam OR Dear Mr./Madam Secretary
C	Very truly yours OR Sincerely yours
SP	Mr. /Madam Secretary
WR	the Secretary of State, Timothy Dutton

Cabinet Officer (former)
EA The Honorable James Barker
S Dear Mr./Mrs./Miss/Ms. Barker
C Very truly yours OR Sincerely yours
SP Mr./Mrs./Miss/Ms. Barker
WR Mr./Mrs./Miss/Ms. Barker

Canon
EA The Reverend Thomas R. Milford
S Dear Canon Milford
C Respectfully yours OR Sincerely yours
SP Canon Milford
WR Canon Milford

Cardinal (Roman Catholic)
EA His Eminence John Cardinal Simonton, Archbishop of Chicago, Chicago, Illinois
S Your Eminence OR My dear Cardinal Simonton OR Dear Cardinal Simonton
C Respectfully yours OR Sincerely yours
SP Your Eminence OR Cardinal Simonton
WR His Eminence Cardinal Simonton OR Cardinal Simonton

Chairperson of a Subcommittee, U.S. Congress
EA The Honorable John Brown, Chairman, Committee on United States Senate/House
S Dear Mr. Chairman/Madam Chairwoman
C Sincerely yours OR Very truly yours
SP Senator Brown OR Mr. Chairman/Madam Chairwoman
WR Senator Brown OR Congressman Brown OR the Chairman/Chairwoman of the Senate/House Committee on

Chancellor of a university (see University Chancellor)

Chaplain (of a college or university)
EA The Reverend Dean A. Augustine, Chaplain
S Dear Chaplain Augustine
C Respectfully yours OR Sincerely yours
SP Chaplain Augustine
WR Chaplain Augustine

Charge d'Affaires ad interim, United States
EA Gary K. Wilson, Esq., American Charge d'Affaires ad Interim; OR, if in Central or South America, United States Charge d'Affaires ad Interim
S Dear Mr./Mrs./Miss/Ms. Wilson
C Sincerely yours

SP   Mr./Mrs./Miss/Ms. Wilson

WR   the American Charge d'Affaires in France OR if in Central or South America, the United States Charge d'Affaires in France

Clergy, Lutheran

EA   The Reverend Arthur Anderson (address of church)

S   Dear Pastor Anderson

C   Respectfully yours

SP   Pastor Anderson

WR   Pastor Anderson

Clergy, Protestant (no degree; excluding Episcopal)

EA   The Reverend Donald Reese (address of church)

S   Dear Mr./Mrs./Miss/Ms. Reese

C   Respectfully yours

SP   Mr./Mrs./Miss/Ms. Reese

WR   The Reverend Mr. Reese

Clergy, Protestant (with degree)

EA   The Reverend Dr. William Johnson

S   Dear Dr. Johnson

C   Respectfully yours

SP   Dr. Johnson

WR   The Reverend Dr. Johnson

Clerk of a Court

EA   Elizabeth Pym, Esq., OR Clerk of the Court of

S   Dear Mr./Mrs./Miss/Ms. Pym

C   Sincerely yours OR Very truly yours

SP   Mr./Mrs./Miss/Ms. Pym

WR   Mr./Mrs./Miss/Ms. Pym

Congressperson (see Representative)

Consul (United States or other)

EA   John Robert Henderson, Esquire, American (or other) Consul

S   Dear Sir/Madam

C   Very truly yours

SP   Mr./Mrs./Miss/Ms. Henderson

WR   the American Consul in Brazil

Dean (of a cathedral)

EA   The Very Reverend John C. Majors OR Dean John C. Majors

S   Dear Dean Majors

C   Sincerely yours OR Respectfully yours

SP   Dean Majors

WR   Dean Majors

Doctor of Dentistry/Divinity/Medicine/Philosophy

EA   Deana Fate, D.D.S. OR Deana Fate, Ph.D.
S   Dear Dr. Fate
C   Sincerely yours OR Very truly yours
SP   Dr. Fate
WR   Dr. Fate

Governor (of a state)

EA   The Honorable Penny Corson, Governor of New York
S   Dear Governor Corson
C   Respectfully yours
SP   Governor OR Governor Corson
WR   Governor Corson

Governor-elect (of a state)

EA   The Honorable Diane Jennings, Governor-elect of Ohio
S   Dear Mr./Mrs./Miss/Ms. Jennings
C   Respectfully yours
SP   Mr./Mrs./Miss/Ms. Jennings
WR   Mr./Mrs./Miss/Ms. Jennings

Governor (former)

EA   The Honorable Elizabeth Rietz
S   Dear Mr./Mrs./Miss/Ms. Rietz
C   Sincerely yours
SP   Mr./Mrs./Miss/Ms. Rietz
WR   Mrs. Elizabeth Rietz, Former Governor of Ohio

Judge

EA   The Honorable George Smithers, Justice (name of court)
S   Sir/Madam
C   Sincerely yours OR Very truly yours
SP   Judge Smithers
WR   Judge Smithers

King

EA   His Most Gracious Majesty, King Philip
S   May it please Your Majesty
C   Respectfully
SP   Your Majesty (initially; thereafter, Sir)
WR   His Majesty OR King Philip

Lawyer

EA   James Robert Judd, Esq., OR Mr./Mrs./Miss/Ms. Judd
S   Dear Mr./Mrs./Miss/Ms. Judd
C   Very truly yours OR Sincerely yours
SP   Mr./Mrs./Miss/Ms. Judd
WR   Mr./Mrs./Miss/Ms. Judd

Lieutenant Governor

EA   The Honorable Mary Brown, Lieutenant Governor of Maine
S   Madam/Sir OR Dear Mr./Mrs./Miss/Ms. Brown
C   Respectfully yours OR Sincerely yours
SP   Mr./Mrs./Miss/Ms. Brown
WR   Lieutenant Governor Brown

Mayor

EA   His/Her Honor the Mayor, City Hall (city, state)
S   Sir/Madam
C   Very truly yours OR Sincerely yours
SP   Mayor Starnes
WR   Mayor Starnes OR Mayor of Raleigh

Military Enlisted Personnel (United States)

EA   rank, full name, address
S   Sir/Madam OR Dear Sir/Madam
C   Very truly yours
SP   Sergeant Smith, Airman Jones, Private Jackson
WR   Sergeant Smith, Airman Jones, Private Jackson

Military Officer (United States)

EA   rank, full name, address
S   Sir/Madam OR Lieutenant Banks, Admiral Banks
C   Very truly yours
SP   Lieutenant Banks, Admiral Banks
WR   Lieutenant Banks, Admiral Banks

Minister (Protestant, no degree)

EA   The Reverend Richard W. Fate
S   Dear Mr./Mrs./Miss/Ms. Fate, or Reverend Fate
C   Respectfully yours OR Very truly yours
SP   Mr./Mrs./Miss/Ms. Fate OR Reverend Fate
WR   Mr./Mrs./Miss/Ms. Fate OR Reverend Fate

Minister (Protestant, with degree)

EA   The Reverend Robert R. Foley, D.D.
S   Dear Dr. Foley
C   Respectfully yours OR Very truly yours
SP   Dr. Foley
WR   Dr. Foley

Monsignor, Roman Catholic

EA   The Right Reverend Monsignor Johnson
S   Right Reverend Monsignor Johnson
C   Respectfully yours
SP   Monsignor Johnson
WR   Monsignor Johnson

Pope

EA His Holiness the Pope, Vatican City, Italy
S Your Holiness OR Most Holy Father
C Respectfully yours
SP Your Holiness
WR His Holiness OR the Pope

Premier

EA His/Her Excellency (full name), Premier of
S Dear Mr./Madam Premier
C Sincerely yours
SP Your Excellency
WR The Premier of OR The Premier

President of the United States

EA The President, The White House, Washington, DC 20500
S Mr. /Madam President OR Dear President Jackson
C Respectfully yours
SP Mr./Madam President OR Sir/Madam
WR The President OR President Jackson

President of the United States (former)

EA The Honorable Stephen Murray
S Sir/Madam OR Dear Mr./Mrs./Miss/Ms. Murray
C Respectfully yours
SP Mr./Mrs./Miss/Ms. Murray
WR Former President Murray OR Mr./Mrs./Miss/Ms. Murray

Priest (Episcopal)

EA The Reverend Ann Thomason OR if degreed, The Reverend Dr. Ann Thomason
S Dear Mr./Mrs./Miss/Ms. Thomason OR Dr. Thomason OR Reverend Thomason
C Respectfully yours
SP Mr./Mrs./Miss/Ms. Thomason OR Dr. Thomason OR Father/Mother Thomason
WR Father/Mother Thomason OR Dr. Thomason

Priest (Roman Catholic)

EA The Reverend Leland Smith (plus initials of his order)
S Reverend Father (formal) OR Dear Father (less formal)
C Respectfully yours
SP Father Smith
WR Father Smith

Prime Minister

EA His/Her Excellency, Prime Minister of
S Excellency OR Dear Mr./Madam Prime Minister

C   Respectfully yours
SP   Mr./Madam Prime Minister
WR   The Prime Minister of

Prince
EA   His Royal Highness
S   Sir OR Your Royal Highness
C   Respectfully
SP   Your Royal Highness
WR   His Royal Highness OR Prince George

Princess
EA   Her Royal Highness
S   Madam OR Your Royal Highness
C   Respectfully
SP   Your Royal Highness
WR   Her Royal Highness OR Princess Mary

Professor
EA   Professor (OR Dr., if Ph.D.) Brian A. Wilson, Department of Chemistry, Vanderbilt University, Nashville, Tennessee
S   Dear Professor Wilson
C   Very truly yours OR Sincerely yours
SP   Professor OR Dr. Wilson
WR   Professor OR Dr. Wilson

Queen
EA   Her Most Gracious Majesty Queen Anne
S   May it please Your Majesty
C   Respectfully
SP   Your Majesty (initially), Ma'am (thereafter)
WR   Her Majesty, Queen Anne

Rabbi
EA   Rabbi David L. Fader OR, if degreed, Rabbi David L. Fader, D.D.
S   Dear Rabbi Fader OR Dear Dr. Fader
C   Respectfully yours OR Sincerely yours
SP   Rabbi Fader
WR   Rabbi Fader

Representative, State (including Assemblyperson, Delegate)
EA   The Honorable Nancy Northcutt, The State Assembly OR House of Representatives OR The House of Delegates
S   Dear Mr./Mrs./Miss/Ms. Northcutt
C   Sincerely yours OR Very truly yours
SP   Mr./Mrs./Miss/Ms. Northcutt
WR   Mr./Mrs./Miss/Ms. Northcutt, the State Representative OR Assemblyperson OR Delegate

Representative, Congress
EA The Honorable Douglas Scrimshaw, United States House of
Representatives, Washington, DC 20515

S Dear Sir/Madam OR Dear Representative Scrimshaw

C Very truly yours OR Sincerely yours

SP Mr./Mrs./Miss/Ms. Scrimshaw

WR Douglas Scrimshaw, U.S. Representative from OR Congressman
Douglas Scrimshaw

Representative, Congress (former)
EA The Honorable Greg Linton (local address)

S Dear Mr./Mrs./Miss/Ms. Linton

C Very truly yours OR Sincerely yours

SP Mr./Mrs./Miss/Ms. Linton

WR Mr./Mrs./Miss/Ms. Linton

Secretary of State (of a state)
EA The Honorable James Cobb OR The Secretary of State of

S Dear Mr./Madam Secretary

C Sincerely yours OR Very truly yours

SP Mr./Mrs./Miss/Ms. Cobb

WR Mr./Mrs./Miss/Ms. Cobb

Senator, U.S.
EA The Honorable Larry Zezula, United States Senate, Washington,
DC 20510

S Dear Senator Zezula

C Sincerely yours OR Very truly yours

SP Senator Zezula OR Senator

WR Senator Zezula OR The Senator from OR The Senator

Senator (state legislature)
EA The Honorable Martin Allen, The Senator of (state)

S Dear Senator Allen

C Sincerely yours OR Very truly yours

SP Senator Allen

WR Senator Allen

Senator-elect
EA The Honorable Mary Branson, Senator-elect (local address)

S Dear Mr./Mrs./Miss/Ms. Branson

C Sincerely yours OR Very truly yours

SP Mr./Mrs./Miss/Ms. Branson

WR Senator-elect Branson

Sister (member of a religious order)
EA Sister Mary Martha, S.C.

S Dear Sister OR Dear Sister Mary Martha

C   Respectfully yours OR Sincerely yours
SP   Sister Mary Martha
WR   Sister Mary Martha

Sister (Superior of a religious order)
EA   The Reverend Mother Superior, S.C.
S   Reverend Mother OR Dear Reverend Mother
C   Respectfully yours
SP   Reverend Mother
WR   The Reverend Mother Superior OR The Reverend Mother

Speaker, U.S. House of Representatives
EA   The Speaker of the House of Representatives OR The Honorable
      Allan Carl, Speaker of the House of Representatives
S   Dear Mr./Madam Speaker
C   Sincerely yours OR Very truly yours
SP   Mr./Madam Speaker OR Mr./Mrs./Miss/Ms. Carl
WR   The Speaker OR Mr./Mrs./Miss/Ms. Carl

Supreme Court (United States; Associate Justice)
EA   Mr. Anthony Barrett, The Supreme Court, Washington, DC 20543
S   Dear Mr./Madam Justice OR Dear Justice Barrett
C   Sincerely yours OR Very truly yours
SP   Mr./Madam Justice Barrett
WR   Mr./Madam Justice Barrett

Supreme Court (United States; Chief Justice)
EA   The Chief Justice of the United States (NEVER The Chief Justice
      of the Supreme Court)
S   Dear Mr./Madam Chief Justice
C   Respectfully OR Respectfully yours
SP   Mr./Madam Chief Justice
WR   The Chief Justice of the United States OR The Chief Justice

Supreme Court (state; Associate Justice)
EA   The Honorable Lewis Ritenour, Associate Justice of the
      Supreme Court of
S   Dear Justice Ritenour
C   Sincerely yours OR Very truly yours
SP   Mr. /Madam Justice
WR   Mr. /Madam Justice Ritenour OR Judge Ritenour

Supreme Court (state; Chief Justice)
EA   The Honorable Margaret W. Smoot, Chief Justice of the Supreme Court of
S   Dear Mr./Madam Chief Justice
C   Sincerely yours OR Very truly yours
SP   Mr. /Madam Chief Justice OR Chief Justice Smoot
WR   Mr./ Madam Chief Justice

United Nations Delegate (United States)

EA   The Honorable Edwin L. Rutherford, United States Permanent Representative to the United Nations, United Nations, New York, NY 10017

S   Dear Mr./Madam Ambassador

C   Respectfully OR Sincerely yours

SP   Mr./Madam Ambassador

WR   The United States Representative to the United Nations

United Nations Delegate (foreign)

EA   His Excellency Charles Turner /Her Excellency Allison Turner

S   My dear Mr. /Madam Ambassador

C   Respectfully OR Sincerely yours

SP   Mr. /Madam Ambassador

WR   The Representative of Canada to the United Nations

United Nations Secretary-General

EA   His Excellency Juan Perez/Her Excellency Juanita Perez, Secretary General of the United Nations, United Nations, New York, NY 10017

S   Dear Mr. /Madam Secretary-General OR Your Excellency

C   Respectfully

SP   Sir/Madam OR Mr./Mrs./Miss/Ms. Perez

WR   The Secretary-General of the United Nations

University Chancellor

EA   Dr. Barbara R. Rodgers, Chancellor (name and address of university)

S   Dear Dr. Rodgers

C   Sincerely yours OR Very truly yours

SP   Dr. Rodgers

WR   Dr. Barbara R. Rodgers, Chancellor of (university name)

University or College Dean

EA   Dean Hamilton Smythe OR Dr. Hamilton Smythe, Dean (name and address of university)

S   Dear Dr. Smythe OR Dear Dean Smythe

C   Very truly yours OR Sincerely yours

SP   Dean Smythe OR Dr. Smythe

WR   Dr. Smythe, Dean of (university name)

University or College President

EA   Dr. Thomas A. Harmon, President OR President Thomas A. Harmon (name and address of university)

S   Dear President Harmon OR Dear Dr. Harmon

C   Sincerely yours OR Very truly yours

SP   Dr. Harmon

WR   Dr. Harmon

Vice President of the United States
EA	The Vice President, United States Senate, Washington, DC 20510
S	Dear Mr./Madam Vice President
C	Respectfully
SP	Mr./Madam Vice President
WR	The Vice President

Warrant Officer
EA	Warrant Officer John C. Calhoun, Jr., OR Chief Warrant Officer John Smith
S	Dear Mr./Mrs./Miss/Ms. Calhoun
C	Very truly yours
SP	Mr./Mrs./Miss/Ms. Calhoun
WR	Warrant Officer Calhoun OR Mr./Mrs./Miss/Ms. Calhoun

✴ Some Additional Guidelines

The Honorable and The Reverend

"The Honorable" is a title of distinction reserved for appointed or elected government officials such as congressional representatives, judges, justices, and cabinet officers. "The Honorable" is never used before a surname alone—for example, The Honorable Thomas Jones, NOT The Honorable Jones. Also, do not combine "The Honorable" with a common courtesy title, such as "Mr." or "Ms."—for example, NOT The Honorable Mr. Thomas Jones. Never abbreviate "The Honorable" in either forms of address or formal writing.

"The Reverend" should be used in official or formal writing. "The Reverend" is often abbreviated to "The Rev." or just "Rev." in informal and unofficial writing. However, when used in conjunction with a full name, "The Reverend" must be used—for example, The Reverend John Reeves or The Reverend Dr. Louise A. McGinnis. Notice that both titles are used with the full name on the envelope address but not in the salutation of the letter. Also note that "The" always precedes these titles.

Esquire

When the title "Esquire" is used, it is always abbreviated after the full name, and no other title is used before the name—for example, James Rogers, Esq. Although the abbreviation "Esq." is most commonly seen after the surnames of attorneys, it may also be used after the surnames of other professionals—engineers, consuls, architects, court clerks, and justices of the peace. "Esquire" is written in signature lines and addresses but is never used in salutations. It is commonly used regardless of sex, but there are some who object to using "Esquire" as a title for a woman professional.

Women Clergy

The issue of addressing women clergy reflects the problem of our ever-changing vocabulary. In many instances "Reverend" or "Doctor" will suffice for both men and women, but some denominations address their ordained male members as " Father." The natural tendency then is to address the female counterpart as "Mother," but there may be strong resistance to this title from both the individual and the group. Whenever possible in such a situation, try to discover the preference of the individual.

Retired Military

When military officers retire from active duty, they retain their highest rank, and this rank is always used when they are addressed.

Legal Documents and Terms

✸ Grammalogues

Business secretaries will probably not be called upon to take legal dictation, but it's helpful to have a brief knowledge of legal **grammalogues.** A grammalogue is a shorthand shortcut for full expressions used. When taking dictation, it's useful to be able to write in one stroke the representation for "time is of the essence," "writ of habeas corpus," "denied certiorari," and other phrases. You can have your notes complete before the person dictating has finished a sentence because you know what the dictator means to say and how to record it quickly.

✸ Document Formats

When you are asked to type or print a legal document, use plain white legal paper, 8 1/2 inch as by 13 or 14 inches, or legal cap paper of the same size having a wide ruled margin at the left and a narrow ruled margin at the right. The text must be kept within these ruled margins.

Wills are written on heavy non-correctable paper of legal size without ruled margins.

Always double-space papers and reports, with triple spaces between paragraphs. Retain a 2-inch margin at the top and a 1-inch margin at the bottom of the page. If plain paper is used rather than ruled, leave a 1 1/2-inch margin on the left and a 3/4-inch margin on the right.

Indent paragraphs ten spaces; for land descriptions or quotations that are single spaced, indent an additional five spaces.

If copies are to be signed (called duplicate originals), they are printed on the same kind of paper as the original.

Number the pages in the center of the bottom of the page (3/4 inch from the bottom edge), except for briefs that are numbered in the upper right corner, the first page number not marked.

Legal documents are bound with a sheet of heavy backing paper (9 inches by 15 inches). The backing sheet should be folded to provide four sections of the sheet 9 inches long. On one of these sections, type an endorsement, and label to briefly describe what the document represents. Following is an example of an endorsed mortgage backing:

No. A-31075
RELEASE OF OIL AND GAS LEASE
FROM
WILLIAM P ALLEN
TO
FIRST CITY BANK OF NEW YORK

Printed legal forms of many kinds, referred to as "law blanks," are obtainable at stationery and office supply stores and at legal stationers. They are easily filled in on the typewriter and are quickly read. They may sometimes serve as a guide in drafting a document.

When writing numbers in legal documents, write them in words, and repeat them immediately in numerals inside parentheses: ten thousand five hundred and seventy-five (10,575) or ten thousand five hundred and seventy-five dollars ($10,575). Dates may be spelled out, or you may express the day and the year in numerals, with the month always spelled out.

The following words and phrases often used in legal documents are customarily written in full capitals, usually followed by a comma, a colon, or no punctuation:

THIS AGREEMENT, made this second day of. . . .
KNOW ALL MEN BY THESE PRESENT, that . . .
IN WITNESS WHEREOF, I have this day . . .
MEMORANDUM OF AGREEMENT made this twenty-fifth day of . . .

Case Titles

Case titles are always underscored, followed by a comma, the volume and page numbers, and date:

Johnson v. Smith, 201 Okla. 433, 32 Am. Rep. 168 (1901).

Notary Public Forms

In a small office and even in many larger offices, the administrative assistant will probably also be a notary public. Figure 27-1 shows commonly used forms of notary public acknowledgments on legal documents.

For an individual

State of _____ SS

County of _____

On the _____ day of _____ , 200_____ ,

before me came _____ known to me to be the individual described

in and who executed the foregoing instrument and acknowledged that he

(or she) executed the same.

(S) _____

Notary Public

[Stamp and Seal]

For a corporation

State of _____ SS

County of _____

On the _____ day of _____ , 200_____ ,

before me personally appeared _____ to me known, who,

being by me duly sworn, did depose and say that he (or she) resides at

_____ ; that he (or she) is _____ (title)

of _____ (Company), the corporation described in and which

executed the foregoing instrument; that he knows the seal of said corporation;

that the seal affixed to said instrument is such corporate seal; that it was so

affixed by order of the (title) of said corporation; and that he (or she) signed his

(or her) name thereto by like order.

(S) _____

Notary Public

[Seal]

FIGURE 27-1. Commonly used forms of notary public acknowledgments.

For a partnership

State of _____ SS

County of _____

On the _____ day of _____ , 200 _____ ,

before me personally appeared _____ to me known, and known

to me to be a member of _____ (name of partnership), and the

person described in and who executed the foregoing instrument in the firm

name of _____ , and he (or she) duly acknowledged to me that

he (or she) executed the same as and for the act and deed of said firm of

_____ (repeat name of partnership).

(S) _____

Notary Public

[Seal]

FIGURE 27-1. Continued.

Codicils to a Will

Additions to and changes in a will are made by an instrument known as a **codicil,** sometimes written on the last page of the will. It must be dated, formally executed, signed, witnessed, and probated with the will (Figure 27-2).

Agreements and Contracts

Agreements or contracts should state the obligations of each party (Figure 27-3).

Proxy

A proxy is a form of power of attorney given by one person to another, authorizing the second person to vote in lieu of the first person at a meeting of a corporation (Figure 27-4).

I, JOHN PHILIP MOORE, a resident of the City of Chicago, County of Cook, State of Illinois, do hereby make, publish, and declare the following as and for a codicil to the Will and Testament heretofore by me executed, bearing date of the _____ th day of , 200_____ .

FIRST: [state provisions]

SECOND: [state provisions]

In all other respects and except as hereinbefore set forth, I hereby republish, ratify, and confirm my said Will, dated the _____ th day of _____, 200 _____.

WITNESS MY HAND AND SEAL this _____ day of _____, 200 _____.

(S) _____

[Seal]

Sample of attestation

The foregoing Codicil, consisting of one-half page, containing no interlineations or erasures, was on the date thereof signed by the above-named Testator and at the same time published and declared by him (or her) to be a Codicil to his (or her) Last Will and Testament. The said Testator signed this instrument in the presence of the undersigned, who acted as attesting witness at his (or her) request. Each of the undersigned signed as a witness in the presence of the Testator and in the presence of each other. At the time of the execution of this Codicil the said Testator was of sound mind and memory and under no undue influence or restraint.

NAME *_____ ADDRESS* _____

(S) _____

(S) _____

*The secretary usually types the name and address of each witness beneath these lines.

FIGURE 27-2. Sample of a codicil to a last will and testament.

THIS AGREEMENT, made this _____ day of _____ , 200 _____ ,

between _____ of _____ , First Party (hereinafter called the Seller), and

_____ a corporation under the laws of the State of _____ , with principal

place of business in _____ , _____ (city and state), Second Party

(hereinafter called the Purchaser),

WITNESSETH:

WHEREAS the Seller has this day agreed to _____ ; and WHEREAS the

Purchaser is willing to _____ ; and WHEREAS _____ ; NOW,

THEREFORE, it is agreed that _____ , WITNESS the signatures of the

parties hereto on the date aforesaid.

(S) _____

Seller

(S) _____

Purchaser

By _____

President

[Corporate Seal]

FIGURE 27-3. Sample contract.

[Corporate Seal]

I, JOHN WILLIAM SMITH, do hereby constitute and appoint HAROLD JACKSON attorney and agent for me, to vote as my proxy at a meeting of the stockholders of THE JOHN SMITH CORPORATION, according to the number of votes I should be entitled to cast if personally present.

Date: _____   (S) _____

FIGURE 27-4. Sample proxy.

✵ Legal Glossary, Including Real Estate Terms

Here is a partial list of common legal terms that you may have occasion to use:

A

Abstract of title ✵ A brief history of the title to a piece of real estate, including data regarding transfer of the property from the time of the first recorded owner to the present owner.

Acceleration clause ✵ A clause in a note or deed of trust causing the entire balance to become due and payable should a default in one of the provisions therein be triggered.

Accessory after the fact ✵ A person who aids one whom he or she knows to be a felon.

Accessory before the fact ✵ A person who instigates or contributes to the commission of a crime but does not actually take part in it.

Accrual method ✵ An accounting system that records income when earned and expenses as incurred.

Acknowledgment ✵ A certification appearing at the end of a legal paper showing that the paper was duly acknowledged and executed.

Administrator (male), Administratrix (female) ✵ A person appointed by a court to administer an estate.

Ad valorem tax ✵ Tax according to the market value of subject property.

Advocate ✵ A person who pleads the cause of another before a tribunal or judicial court.

Affidavit ✵ A certification attesting the authenticity of statements made in a legal paper.

Alienation clause ✵ A specific clause in a note and/or deed of trust stating that, should the property be sold or transferred in any manner, the entire balance of the note shall be immediately due and payable. To "alienate" is to transfer.

Answer ✵ A statement made by the defendant through an attorney stating his or her version of the situation (often called a plea).

Appeal ✵ The act of taking a legal case to a higher court.

Appurtenances ✵ Improvements that pertain to the land. See also **tenements.**

Arraignment ✵ The calling of an accused person into court, reading the indictment to that person, and asking that person whether he or she is guilty or not guilty.

Assessment ✵ A levy made on property for improvements.

Attachment ✵ A court order authorizing a seizure or a taking into custody of property or monies to satisfy a claim.

Attestation ✵ A certification as to the genuineness of a copy.

Attorney ✵ One who is legally appointed by another to transact business for him or her.

Attorney-in-fact ✵ One who is appointed by another, by means of a letter or a power of attorney, to transact business for him or her out of court.

B

Beneficiary ✳ The person who is benefited by a gift, proceeds of an insurance policy, income from a trust estate, etc.

Bequeath ✳ To make a bequest or to give personal property by will.

Brief ✳ The written argument of an attorney supporting his or her contention as to the correct interpretation of the law and the proper inference from the evidence in a particular case.

Burden of proof ✳ A term meaning that the party making a claim must prove it. Burden of proof rests on the plaintiff.

C

Capital punishment ✳ The death penalty.

Certified copy ✳ A copy of an instrument made from the records in a recorder's office and certified to by the recorder as being an exact copy of the paper on file or of record.

Certiorari ✳ A writ from a superior court to call up for review the records of an inferior court.

Change of venue ✳ A change in the place of trial.

Civil action ✳ An action to enforce a civil right or to remedy a private wrong.

Complaint ✳ A formal allegation against a party.

Conditional binder ✳ A sales agreement that contains certain conditions that must be met before it becomes unconditionally binding on all parties.

Conditional sale ✳ A contract covering goods sold and delivered to a buyer on condition that he or she make periodic payments thereon (or meet other stipulated conditions).

Contingency clause ✳ The clause in an agreement that makes the entire agreement conditional on the happening of a certain event.

Corporal punishment ✳ Punishment applied to the body of the offender.

Corporation ✳ An entity of joint ownership in which all parties have a share (equal and unequal) but that acts in the same capacity as an individual owner. Usually governed by a board of directors elected by the shareholders.

Criminal action ✳ An action in which it is sought to determine the guilt of a person who is accused of a crime specifically prohibited by law.

Cross-complaint ✳ A complaint seeking affirmative relief against a codefendant.

D

Defalcation ✳ A misappropriation of funds by one who has them in trust.

Demographics ✳ The study of population trends and/or buying habits of the public in a certain geographic area.

Demurrer ✳ A plea by the defendant asking the court to dismiss the action because of insufficient cause for complaint.

Deposition ✳ A testimony under oath in writing; often taken orally and signed after it has been recorded.

Due-on-sate clause ✳ The clause in the loan papers that gives the lender the right to call the loan due and payable upon the happening of a certain occurrence, such as sale of the property.

E

Easement ✲ An acquiring privilege or right of use or enjoyment that one person may have in the land of another.

Eminent domain ✲ That superior dominion of the sovereign power over property that authorizes the state to appropriate all or any part of it to a necessary public use, reasonable compensation being awarded.

Encumbrance ✲ A claim or lien upon an estate.

Environmental impact report ✲ Report required in some states that shows the effects a proposed development will have on the environment of the area. Such reports study the effects on the wildlife, traffic, schools, terrain, and so forth.

Escrow ✲ The procedure of placing all papers and money concerning a transaction in the hands of a disinterested third party with instructions on how such items are to be treated in the event all conditions are or are not met.

Exclusionary zoning ✲ Zoning sometimes used to exclude multiple-family dwellings from predominantly single-family neighborhoods.

Exclusive agency listing (real estate) ✲ A listing that contains a termination date in which an owner and broker enter into a written contract for the broker to sell a property. The broker, as agent for the seller, will receive a commission if the property is sold during the term of the listing by that broker or by any other, but not if the owner sells the property independent of the broker's efforts.

Exclusive right-to-sell listing (real estate) ✲ Similar to an exclusive agency listing, except that even if the owner sells the property before the termination date independent of the broker's efforts, the owner must still pay a commission to the broker.

Executed agreement ✲ An agreement that has been signed by all parties to it.

F

Factor times gross income ✲ An investment analysis formula for judging the worth of a piece of income property by multiplying the annual gross income by a factor derived from the ratio of gross income to the selling price of similar properties.

Farm Home Administration (FMHA) ✲ A branch of the U.S. Department of Agriculture concerned with making home loans in rural areas that lack the usual financing sources.

Federal Housing Administration Loans ✲ Loans made by conventional lenders but with a portion insured by the Federal Housing Administration.

Felony ✲ Any of various crimes graver in their penal consequences than those called misdemeanors.

Fiduciary ✲ The person named in a trust or agency agreement to act for another on his or her behalf and in the same manner as if acting for himself or herself.

First deed of trust ✲ A mortgage security instrument that has first priority over any other voluntary financing liens on a property.

Foreclosure ✲ The process in which property used as security for a mortgage is sold to satisfy the debt when a borrower defaults in payment of the mortgage note or on other terms in the mortgage document.

Foreclosure suit ✳ A suit brought to foreclose a mortgage.

Foreclosure under court action ✳ Foreclosure procedure that is handled in a court of law and allows the lender to obtain a deficiency judgment against the borrower. It also allows the borrower a year's right to redeem the property by paying all back monies and costs incurred to and from the date of foreclosure.

Foreclosure under right of sale (deed of trust) ✳ An automatic procedure that allows the lender to foreclose on the property through the power-of-sale provision in the contract. It usually takes about four months. The original borrower is released from responsibility for the debt in exchange for the sale of the property. However, in some cases, the borrower may be held liable for any difference between the loan amount and the sale amount.

Franchise ✳ Right to operate a business under the name and operating procedures of a large, often nationwide parent company.

G

Garnishment ✳ Legal notice to one to appear in court, usually regarding the attachment of property to secure a debt.

General agent ✳ One who performs continuing services for the principal.

General partnership ✳ An entity of ownership in which all partners in it hold voting rights as to decisions being made and in which all partners share in the profits and liabilities as their interests appear.

Grand jury ✳ An appointed group of citizens to examine accusations against persons charged with a crime and to issue bills of indictment if the evidence warrants.

H

Habeas corpus ✳ A common law writ to bring a party before a court or judge, usually when the party is confined to jail.

Hereditaments ✳ Rights and property inherited or inheritable. See also *appurtenances; tenements.*

Holographic will ✳ A will entirely written, dated, and signed in the handwriting of the maker.

I

Impeachment ✳ Arraignment of a public officer for misconduct while in office.

Indictment ✳ The formal written statement charging one or more persons with an offense, as framed by the prosecuting authority of the state and issued by the grand jury.

Inflation ✳ Abnormal increase in the volume of money and credit that results in a substantial, continuing rise in the general price level.

Injunction ✳ A court writ requiring a party to perform or to forbear certain acts.

Interlocutory ✳ Intermediate; not final or definite.

Intestate ✳ A person who dies without having a will.

J

Judgment ✳ The decree or sentence of a court.

Jurisdiction ✳ The legal power, right, or authority to hear and determine a cause or causes.

L

Larceny ✳ The unlawful taking of objects with intent to deprive the rightful owner.

Law of agency ✳ The section of statutes pertaining to the relationship that is created when one entity is authorized to act on legal matters for the benefit of another.

Legatee ✳ One to whom a legacy is bequeathed.

Letters of administration ✳ The instrument by which an administrator or administratrix is authorized to administer the estate of a deceased person.

Letters patent ✳ An instrument covering rights and title to an invention or public lands.

Letters testamentary ✳ An instrument authorizing an executor of a will to act.

Leverage ✳ The process whereby an investment can be burdened with a loan or loans and still provide a higher yield than if an investor had paid all cash for it.

Libel ✳ Written public defamation.

Limited partnership ✳ Syndication in which many parties can participate, except that the limited partners have no voice in the operation of the venture and do not suffer any recourse from potential liabilities beyond their initial investment.

Line of credit ✳ A prearranged commitment from a lending institution to advance up to a specific amount of money to a customer of that bank.

Liquidity ✳ The facility with which an asset can be converted to cash.

M

Malfeasance ✳ The performing of an act that a person ought not to perform.

Mandamus ✳ A writ issued by a superior court directing some inferior court or person in authority to perform some specific duty.

Misdemeanor ✳ A crime less than a felony.

Misfeasance ✳ A trespass or injurious act.

Money supply ✳ A figure issued weekly by the Federal Reserve Bank indicating the amount of money in circulation in the United States during the past week.

Mortgage ✳ A written conveyance of property intended to be a security for the payment of money. There are two parties to a mortgage: the mortgagor (the borrower) and the mortgagee (the lender).

Motion ✳ An application made to a court to obtain an order, ruling, or direction.

N

Net operating income (NOI) ✳ A figure arrived at in completing an investment analysis form that indicates the amount of income to be derived from the property after the vacancy factor and all other operating expenses have been deducted from the gross income but before any loan payments are applied.

NOI ✳ See *net operating income.*

Notary public ✳ A public officer who attests to or certifies deeds, affidavits, and depositions.

Notice of default ✳ A notice recorded by the trustee under a deed of trust that indicates that the trustor (borrower) is in default on the note and is in danger of foreclosure.

O

One-time capital gain credit ✳ A provision in the Internal Revenue Code that allows a taxpayer who is over fifty-five years of age to sell his or her home once without having to pay income tax on a certain amount of the profits.

P

PACs ✳ See *political action committees.*

Perjury ✳ False swearing; voluntary violation of an oath.

Petit jury ✳ A body of twelve persons selected impartially to hear cases and render decisions under the direction of a judge.

Plea ✳ An allegation of fact, as distinguished from a demurrer; in common law practice, a defendant's answer to the plaintiffs declaration or, in criminal practice, the accused person's answer to the charge against him or her.

Political action committees (PACs) ✳ Committees allowed by the federal government to collect contributions that are used for the political advancement of candidates or causes favorable to the aims of the organization forming the committee.

Prepaid interest ✳ Interest charged by a lender before it is actually due or earned.

Prepayment privilege ✳ The privilege spelled out in a loan agreement that allows the borrower to pay off a loan ahead of maturity.

Probate ✳ Official proof, especially of an instrument offered as the last will and testament of a person deceased.

Promissory note ✳ The note evidencing a debt and outlining the terms under which the debt is to be repaid.

Proxy ✳ Written power to act for another in a specific instance.

Q

Quasi-franchise ✳ An organization to which a company can belong that does not pose the requirements of a regular franchise.

Quiet Title suit ✳ Proceedings brought to perfect the title to property.

R

Rent control ✳ A practice that rigidly controls the amount of rents that a landlord can charge on his or her units.

Restraining order ✳ A court order temporarily restraining a party from committing a certain act until the court can decide whether an injunction should be issued.

Right of redemption ✳ The right to redeem a property foreclosed on through court action, usually because of default on a mortgage but sometimes on a deed of trust.

S

S corporation ✳ A special kind of corporation allowed by law that provides all of the protective benefits of a regular corporation but also allows income and deductions to pass through to the shareholders, much the same as in a partnership.

Second deed of trust ✳ A deed of trust second in priority to the first deed of trust.

Security device ✳ A device such as a mortgage or deed of trust that is used to secure real property for the repayment of the terms on a note.

Slander ✳ A false report maliciously uttered and tending to injure the reputation of another.

Square footage ✳ The area of a given property (either the land plot or the building alone). Land sales are often computed on a price per square foot, and commercial and industrial buildings are leased by this method.

Statute of limitations ✳ A statute assigning a certain time after which rights cannot be enforced by legal action.

Stay of execution ✳ Court order to withhold execution of a judgment.

Subpoena ✳ A writ commanding the addressee to attend court.

Subpoena duces tecum ✳ A subpoena that orders a witness to bring certain documents into court.

Summons ✳ A warning or citation to appear in court.

T

Tax-deferred exchange ✳ An arrangement under Section 1031 of the Internal Revenue Code that allows an owner to accept another property of like kind in exchange for his or her present holding, thereby eliminating payment of tax on the profit from the one he or she is disposing of.

Tax shelter ✳ An accounting term describing an investment that throws off tax deductions from interest and depreciation allowances.

Tenements ✳ Rights and interests that pertain to the land. See also *appurtenances; hereditaments.*

Testator (male), Testatrix (female) ✳ A person who leaves a will in force at death.

Title company ✳ A company that specializes in searching the abstract of titles to a property and then insuring that title for a new buyer for a fee. Some title companies in some areas of the country can also handle escrow for real estate transactions.

Transfer tax ✳ The tax charged by many cities, counties, and states for the privilege of transferring title to property.

Trust ✳ An equitable right or interest in property distinct from the legal ownership.

Trustee under deed of trust ✳ The entity under a deed of trust that holds a form of title to the property to ensure the repayment of a debt (usually a corporation formed by the lender).

Truth-in-Lending laws ✳ A group of laws enforced by the Federal Trade Commission to ensure that consumers are made fully aware of the cost of credit and are protected against false credit claims in advertising.

Two-party exchange ✳ An Internal Revenue Code Section 1031 tax-deferred exchange in which only two parties are involved as distinct from a three-party or multiparty exchange.

U

Usury ✳ Interest in excess of the legal rate charged to a borrower for the use of money.

V

Verdict ✳ The decision of a jury on the matter submitted in trial.

Vested rights ✳ Rights that are permanent and undisputed.

W

Waiver ✳ Act of intentionally abandoning some known right, claim, or privilege; also the instrument evidencing such an act.

Without prejudice ✳ Without effect on any rights that existed previously.

Writ ✳ An order issued by a court commanding the performance or nonperformance of some act.

Z

Zoning ✳ Laws in most cities, counties, and states that stipulate the uses to which any property may be put.

LANGUAGE USAGE

SECTION FOUR

Fellow assistants
review a report.
Photo by Kevin Wilson.

Grammar

The Parts of Speech

Within the English language there are eight parts of speech:

- Nouns
- Pronouns
- Verbs
- Prepositions
- Adjectives
- Conjunctions
- Adverbs
- Interjections or Determiners

Nouns

A **noun** is the name of a person, place, thing, or idea. A **proper noun,** which names a specific person, place, or thing (Kevin, Atlanta, God, English, Jennifer), is usually capitalized. A proper noun used as someone's name is called a **noun of address.** The remaining nouns for everything else are called **common nouns** and are not usually capitalized.

A group of related words can act like a noun within a sentence. This is called a **noun clause,** and it contains a subject and a verb. An example of a noun clause is:

- What he did for the country was unbelievable.

In this example, "What he did for the country" is the noun clause.

A **noun phrase** consists of a noun with several modifiers that act as a single noun. The following are examples of noun phrases:

- Professional football team
- Abnormally long fingers
- Money market account
- Real estate investment trust
- Grossly exaggerated totals

There are also groups of words that can form **compound nouns.** Some examples include:

- Son-in-law
- Stick-in-the-mud

Other Noun Categories

There are additional categories of nouns:

- Count Nouns—used for anything that can be counted, such as five dollars, a dozen, and seven continents.

- Mass Nouns—used for naming things that can't be counted like water, air, energy, and data.

- Collective Nouns—used for naming groups of individuals or things, such as team, class, or jury.

- Abstract Nouns—used for naming intangible things such as love, peace, justice, hope, hatred, and friendship.

Some words can be a count noun or a non-count noun, depending on how they are used. Whether a noun is a count or non-count noun, determines whether it can be used with articles and determiners. For example:

- The team got into trouble. (non-count)
- The team had many troubles. (count)

Noun Case

Nouns can be in the subjective, possessive, and objective case. The case tells you the role of a noun in a sentence. Here are some examples:

- The football player (subject) runs very fast.
- He selected a car (object).
- The football player's (possessive) jersey was torn.

Nouns in the subjective and objective case are identical. Nouns in the possessive usually require an apostrophe followed by the letter *s*.

Verbs

Verbs are used to describe an action or the idea of being in a sentence. Consider the following:

- I *am* an administrative assistant. (idea of being)
- The assistant *worked* late. (action)

There are many different ways to classify verbs. **Transitive** verbs require an object. For example, "Will you *lay* the book on the desk?" In this example, *the book* is the object. **Intransitive** verbs do not require an object. For example, "The dog *lies* down every day after lunch." Some verbs can be both transitive and intransitive depending on how they are used in a sentence. Others can only be used strictly one way.

Verb forms are also classified as either **finite** or **non-finite.** A finite verb form can stand alone as the main verb of a sentence. A non-finite verb form cannot. For example:

- The car *destroyed* the mailbox. (finite)
- The *broken* mailbox . . . (non-finite)

Verb Forms

There are four basic forms of verb inflections (endings). These include:

- Base form
- Present participle
- Past form
- Past participle

These are used to help determine the tense of the verb. Tense tells you whether an action is happening now, is going to happen, or has already happened. Unlike languages like French or Spanish, English verbs do not form their tense just with the endings. Instead, they use auxiliary words. For example:

- I write. (Base form)
- I am writing. (Present participle)
- I wrote. (Past form)
- I have written. (Past participle)

Linking Verbs

A **linking verb** is used to connect a subject and its complement (a noun or adjective that describes the subject). These are often forms of the verb *to be*, but sometimes include verbs related to the five senses (look, sound, smell, feel, taste) and verbs that relate to a state of being (appear, seem, become, grow, turn, prove, remain). Here are some examples of linking verbs:

- These children *are* all students.
- Those clouds *look* dark.
- Rain *seems* likely.

Mood

Mood in verbs refers to the attitude of the speaker or writer. There are three attitudes that can accompany a verb. **Indicative mood** is used to make a statement or ask a question. This is the most common verb mood. **Imperative mood** is used to give directions, give orders, or make a strong suggestion. Verbs used in the imperative mood do not need a subject, since it is understood to be "you." For example:

- Get out of here.
- Go to the store before you come home.

Subjunctive mood is used with dependent clauses to express a wish; used with "if" and a condition; used with "as if" and "as though" along with a speculation; or with "that" to express a demand. For example:

- He wishes she were here.
- We would have won the game if we played harder.
- They acted as if they were hungry.
- The letter demanded that membership dues be paid on time.

One of the most important things about a verb's mood is the ability to discern between factual statements and hypothetical statements. Hypothetical statements often use *could, would,* or *might.*

Phrasal Verbs

Phrasal verbs consist of a verb along with another word or phrase. Usually phrasal verbs are accompanied by a preposition. Usually phrasal verbs are casual conversational phrases that are accepted into mainstream language usage. Here are some examples:

■ The old people were *sitting around* doing nothing.

■ He *looked up* his old teacher in the phone book.

In each case the word that is joined with the verb is called a **particle.** The problem with phrasal verbs is that their meaning is unclear. They can be used in conversation, but it is best to avoid them in formal business writing.

Causative Verbs

Causative verbs are used to describe an action that is necessary to cause another action. For example, "The devil *made* me *do* it." In this example, "made" causes the "do" to happen. Other causative verbs include: let, make, help, allow, have, require, motivate, get, convince, hire, assist, encourage, permit, employ, and force. Most causative verbs are followed by an object (noun or pronoun) and an infinitive (*to* plus a verb). For example:

■ He *allows his dog to sleep* all day.

There are three causative verbs that do not follow this pattern: have, make, and let. These verbs are usually followed by an object and the base form of the verb. For example:

■ She *made her associates read* the entire report.

Factitive Verbs

Verbs like *make, choose, judge, elect, select,* and *name* are called **factitive verbs.** These verbs can take two objects. Here are some examples.

■ The people elected Mike Jackson President of the homeowners association. ("Mike Jackson" is the object and "President of the homeowners association" is the second complement.)

Verb Tenses

A **tense** shows the time of an action or state of being. There are three tenses that change the endings of verbs. The **present tense** means that something is happening now. "He is an executive. He wears nice suits." The **simple past tense** indicates that something happened in the past. "He was an executive. He wore nice suits." The **past participle** is combined with an auxiliary verb to indicate that something happened in the past prior to another action. "He has been an executive. He had worn nice suits."

Unlike other languages, English does not have special verb endings for future tense. Instead, future verb forms are created with the use of auxiliaries. "He will be an executive. He will wear nice suits."

Progressive Verbs

Progressive verbs, which indicate something being or happening, are formed by the present participle form (ending in -*ing*) along with an auxiliary. For example, "She is crying. She was crying. She will be crying. She has been crying. She had been crying. She will have been crying."

The progressive form occurs only with dynamic verbs (verbs that show the ability to change). **Stative verbs** on the other hand are those that describe a quality that is incapable of change. For example, you wouldn't say, "She is being tall."

There are a variety of **dynamic verbs:** activity verbs, process verbs, verbs of bodily sensation, transitional events verbs, and momentary verbs. The following provides some examples:

- Activity Verbs—ask, play, work, write, say, listen, call, eat
- Process Verbs—change, grow, mature, widen
- Verbs of Bodily Sensation—hurt, itch, ache, feel
- Transitional Events Verbs—arrive, die, land, leave, lose
- Momentary Verbs—hit, jump, throw, kick

There are two classifications of stative verbs: verbs of inert perception and cognition, and relational verbs. The following provides some examples:

- Verbs of Inert Perception and Cognition—guess, hate, hear, please, satisfy
- Relational Verbs—equal, possess, own, include, cost, concern, contain

Irregular Verbs

Most verbs form the simple past and past participle by adding *ed* to the base verb. For example, "He walked. He has walked."

There are some irregular verbs that do not follow this pattern. For example, common verbs such as "to be" and "to have" have irregular forms.

Sequence of Tenses

There is a relationship between verbs in a main clause and verbs in a dependent clause. The verb tenses do not have to be the same, as long as they are accurate about time and order. For example, "My father *will have returned,* before I *leave.*"

Verbals

Verbals are words that seem to mean an action or a state of being but do not function as a real verb. They are sometimes called **nonfinite verbs.** Verbals are frequently used with other words in what is called a **verbal phrase.**

Participle

A **participle** is a verb form that acts like an adjective. For example, "The *running* dog chased the *speeding* car." A present participle describes a present condition; a past participle describes something that has already happened. For example: "The *burned* tree fell down in the storm."

Infinitive

An **infinitive** is formed with the root of a verb and the word *to.* For example, "To be, or not to be." A **present infinitive** describes a present condition. For example, "I like to dream." The **perfect infinitive** describes a time earlier than that described by the verb. For example, "I would like to have slept until nine."

Gerund

A **gerund** is a verb form ending in—*ing,* which acts as a noun. For example, "Walking in the street after dark can be dangerous." Gerunds are usually accompanied by other words that make up a gerund phrase. For example, "walking in the street after dark" is a gerund phrase.

Because gerunds and gerund phrases are nouns, they can be used just like nouns. For example:

■ As a subject—"*Being President* is a difficult job."

■ As object of a verb—"He didn't really like *being poor.*"

■ As object of a preposition—"He read a book about *being careful.*"

Problems with Split Infinitives

One of the most common writing mistakes is the **split infinitive.** An infinitive is said to be "split" when a word (usually an adverb) is placed between the *to* of the infinitive and the root of the verb. For example, "To boldly go where no man has gone before."

The argument against split infinitives is based on the idea that an infinitive is a single unit and should not be divided. Because it is so easy to spot, many writers try to avoid this condition. However, many dictionaries now say the rule against splitting infinitives can be ignored. To avoid the argument, it is a good rule to avoid split infinitives in business writing.

Infinitives, Gerunds, and Sequence

Although infinitives and gerunds are not really verbs, they describe action. When combined with auxiliary verb forms, infinitives and gerunds can also express concepts of time (see Table 28-1).

Passive and Active Voices

Verbs can either be **active** (The assistant *used* the computer) or **passive** (The computer *was used* by the assistant) in voice. In the active voice, the subject and verb relationship is easy to understand. The subject is the "do-er" or "be-er," and the verb describes an action. In the passive voice, the subject is not a do-er or be-er. Instead, the subject is being acted upon by something else.

TABLE 28-1	Infinitives, Gerunds, and Sequence
Simple Forms	■ We had planned *to watch* the Super Bowl. ■ *Seeing* the Cowboys win is always a great thrill.
Perfect Forms	■ The Cowboys hoped *to have won* the Super Bowl. ■ I was thrilled about their *having been* in the big game.
Passive Forms	■ *To be chosen* as an NFL player must be the biggest thrill in any football player's life. ■ *Being chosen*, however, doesn't mean you get to play.
Perfective Passive Forms	■ The men did not seem satisfied simply *to have been selected* as players. ■ *Having been honored* this way, they went out and earned it by winning the Super Bowl.
Perfective Progressive Infinitive	■ *To have been competing* at this level was quite an accomplishment.

Computerized grammar checkers, such as the one built into Microsoft Word, can detect passive voice construction and suggest a revision. There is nothing incorrect about using passive voice verbs; however, if you can say the same thing using the active voice, you should do so. Your writing will be easier to understand.

The passive voice does have its uses. When it is more important to draw attention to the person or thing that was acted on, the passive voice can be used. For example, "George *was killed* while riding a bicycle." Another situation where the passive voice is more appropriate is when the subject is not important. For example, "The meteor shower *can be observed* just after dark."

The passive voice is sometimes required for technical writing, where the do-er or be-er can be anyone, and the process being described is more important. Instead of writing, "I developed a computer program that can print checks," you would write, "A computer program was developed that can print checks."

The passive voice is created by combining a form of the *to be* verb with the past participle of the main verb. Other helping verbs are sometimes used.

Only transitive verbs (those that can have objects) can be transformed into passive voice. However, some transitive verbs cannot be transformed into passive voice. "To have" is an example. You can say or write, "She has a new computer," but you can't say, "A new computer is had by her." Some other examples of verbs that cannot be used with the passive voice include: resemble, look like, equal, agree with, mean, contain, hold, comprise, lack, suit, fit, and become.

Verbals can also be used in the passive voice. An infinitive phrase in the passive voice can perform a variety of functions in a sentence. The same is true for passive gerunds and passive participles.

✵ Adjectives

Adjectives are words that describe or modify a person, place, or thing. Articles such as *a, an,* and *the* are adjectives. So are words like *tall, solid,* and *cold.*

A group of words containing a subject and verb may act as an adjective. These are called an **adjective clause.** For example, "My brother, *who is much older than I am,* is a psychologist." If the subject and verb are removed from an adjective clause, an **adjective phrase** results. For example, "He is the man ~~who is~~ *keeping my family fed.*"

One thing to keep in mind about adjectives is, don't ask too much of them. Use nouns and verbs to describe something. Sometimes adjectives don't add much to a sentence in the first place. For example, what do *interesting, beautiful, lovely,* and *exciting* really do for a sentence?

Adjective Position in a Sentence

Unlike adverbs, which can go almost anywhere in a sentence, adjectives almost always appear immediately before a noun or noun phrase that they modify. Sometimes adjectives appear in a string, and when they do, they must appear in a particular order according to category. When indefinite pronouns—such as *something, someone,* and *anybody*—are modified by an adjective, the adjective comes after the pronoun.

The order in which adjectives are arranged in a sentence is difficult for people learning English. They wonder why we wouldn't say "red big barn" instead of "big red barn." Adjectives are ordered as follows:

1. Determiners—articles and other limiters such as: a, an, five, her, our, those, that, several, and some
2. Observation—post-determiners and limiter adjectives and adjectives subject to subjective measure such as: beautiful, expensive, gorgeous, dilapidated, and delicious
3. Size and Shape—adjectives subject to objective measure such as: big, little, enormous, long, short, and square
4. Age—adjectives describing age such as: old, antique, new, and young
5. Color—adjectives denoting color such as: red, white, and black
6. Origin—adjectives denoting the source of the noun such as: American, French, and Canadian
7. Material—adjectives that describe what something is made of such as: silk, wooden, silver, and metallic
8. Qualifier—final limiter that is often part of the noun such as: rocking chair, hunting cabin, passenger car, or book cover

Sentences that run two or three adjectives together can be laborious to read. In addition, when adjectives belong to the same class, they are called **coordinated adjectives** and require a comma between them in a sentence. One good rule is to consider whether you could have inserted *and* or *but* between the adjectives. If so, then use a comma between them. For example, you could say "inexpensive but comfortable house." If the *but* is not in the sentence you would punctuate it as "inexpensive, comfortable house."

Degrees of Adjectives

Adjectives can express degrees of modification: positive, comparative, and superlative. We use the comparative for comparing two things and the superlative for comparing three or more things. Sometimes the word *than* accompanies the comparative adjective and the word *the* precedes the superlative adjective. The inflected suffixes *-er* and *-est* are used to form most comparative and superlatives. Sometimes *-ier* and *-iest* are added when a two-syllable adjective ends in *y*. The following in Table 28-2 are some examples:

TABLE 28-2 Degrees of Adjectives		
Positive	**Comparative**	**Superlative**
Rich	Richer	Richest
Lovely	Lovelier	Loveliest
Beautiful	More Beautiful	Most Beautiful

Some adjectives have irregular forms in the comparative and superlative degree, as in Table 28-3.

TABLE 28-3 Irregular Forms in the Commparative and Superlative Degree		
Positive	**Comparative**	**Superlative**
Good	Better	Best
Bad	Worse	Worst
Little	Less	Least
Much, Many, Some	More	Most
Far	Further	Furthest

You should be careful not to form comparative or superlative adjectives that already describe a unique condition or extreme of comparison. *Perfect* and *pregnant* are good examples.

Also be careful not to use the word *more* along with a comparative adjective formed with the—*er* suffix, or the word *most* along with a superlative adjective formed with the—*est* suffix. You'll end up with phrases such as *more larger* and *most largest*.

Less and Fewer

When making a comparison of quantities, we often have to make a choice between the adjectives *less* and *fewer*. When you are talking about countable things, you should use the word *fewer*. When you are talking about measurable quantities that cannot be counted, you should use the word *less*. For example, "He has fewer assets, but less worries."

Than I/Me

When making a comparison between yourself and something else, you'll often end with a subject form or object form: "taller than I/she." In the sentence, "He is taller than I am," or "He is taller than she is," normally we leave out the verb in the second clause, *am* or *is*.

Be careful with comparisons such as, "I like him better than she," or "I like him better than her." In the first case, you are saying you like him better than she likes him. In the second case you are saying you like the male person better than you like the female person. To avoid confusion with the word *than*, you should write, "I like him better than she does," or "I like him better than I like her."

Capitalizing Proper Adjectives

When an adjective's origin is a proper noun, it should be capitalized. For example: Christian music, Nixon era, Victorian poet, and Jeffersonian democracy.

Collective Adjectives

When the article *the* is combined with an adjective describing a class or group of people, the resulting phrase can act as a noun: the meek, the rich, the poor. The difference between a collective noun and a collective adjective is that the collective adjective is always plural and requires a plural verb. For example, "The *meek will* inherit the earth."

Adjectival Opposites

The opposite of an adjective can be formed in a number of different ways. One way is to find an adjective antonym. The opposite of cold is hot. A thesaurus can help you find an appropriate antonym. Another way to form a negative adjective is through use of a prefix. Consider the following pairs:

- Fortunate—unfortunate
- Honorable—dishonorable
- Prudent—imprudent
- Alcoholic—nonalcoholic
- Considerate—inconsiderate
- Filed—misfiled

A third way to form an adjectival opposite is to combine the adjective with *less* or *least*. In fact, this method allows for tact and a smoother tone in some cases. For example, "That is the least beautiful girl in the class," is somewhat more tactful than "That is the ugliest girl in the class."

Good Versus Well

Frequently we have to choose between using *well* and *good* in our sentences. *Good* is an adjective and *well* is an adverb. Therefore, when describing an action verb, the only choice is the adverb *well*. For example, "He speaks well."

When using a linking verb or a verb that has to do with the five human senses, you'll want to use the adjective *good* instead. For example, "You smell good today." Many writers use *well* after linking verbs related to health, since, in this case, *well* is an adjective, the opposite of *ill*. For example: "How are you doing? I am well, thank you."

Bad Versus Badly

The same rule that applies to *well* and *good* also applies to *bad* and *badly*. *Bad* is an adjective and *badly* is an adverb. Use the adjective *bad* when referring to human feeling. "I felt bad." If you said, "I felt badly," this would imply that there was something wrong with your sense of touch.

A-Adjectives

There are a group of adjectives that follow their own unique rules. These so-called a-adjectives are: ablaze, afloat, afraid, aghast, alert, alike, alive, alone, aloof, ashamed, asleep, averse, awake, and aware. These adjectives are used after a linking verb. For example: "The man was ashamed."

Sometimes you can use an a-adjective before the word they modify. For example, "the alert driver." A-adjectives are sometimes modified with "very much." For example, "The man was very much ashamed."

☆ Adverbs

Adverbs are words that modify verbs, adjectives, or another adverb. Adverbs often describe when, where, why, or under what circumstances something happened. Adverbs often end in *-ly*, however there are many words not ending in *-ly* that serve as adverbs. For example, the words *lovely, lonely, motherly,* and *friendly* are adjectives.

When a group of words containing a subject and a verb act as an adverb (modifying another verb in the sentence) it is called an **adverb clause.** For example, *"When this game is over,* we're going home for dinner."

When a group of words not containing a subject and a verb act as an adverb, it is called an adverbial phrase. Prepositional phrases frequently have the function of an adverb. For example, "She works *on weekends."*

An infinitive phrase can act as an adverb. For example, "The assistant ran *to catch the bus."*

Adverbs can modify adjectives, although adjectives can't modify adverbs. For example, "The executive showed a *wonderfully* casual attitude." Like adjectives, adverbs can have comparative and superlative forms. For example, "You should walk *faster* if you want to get some exercise. The candidate who types *fastest* gets the job." Sometimes words like *more* and *most, less* and *least* are used to show an amount. For example, "The house was the *most beautifully* decorated home on the tour."

Another construction used to create adverbs is *as . . . as.* For example, "He can't read *as* fast *as* his sister."

A small group of adverbs have two forms, one that ends in *-ly* and one that doesn't. In some cases, the two forms have different meanings. For example, "They departed *late."* *"Lately,* they can't seem to be on time." In most cases, the form without the *-ly* should be reserved for casual conversation and not business writing. For example, "He did her *wrong."*

Adverbs are often used as **intensifiers** in order to convey a greater or lesser meaning. Intensifiers have three different functions. They can emphasize, amplify, or tone down a verb. The following are some examples of each type:

- Emphasize—I *really* don't like him. He *simply* ignores me.

- Amplify—He *completely* wrecked his new car. I *absolutely* love fresh fruit.

- Tone down—I *kind of* like this restaurant's food. She *mildly* disapproved of his smoking.

Types of Adverbs
There are five main types of adverbs:

- Adverbs of manner—He spoke *slowly* and walked *quietly*.

- Adverbs of place—He lives *there* now.

- Adverbs of frequency—He drives to work *every morning*.

- Adverbs of time—He slept *late*.

- Adverbs of purpose—He drives his car slowly *to avoid getting a ticket*.

Adverbs in a Numbered List
Within normal text it is usually best not to number items beyond three or four. Anything more than that should be formatted in a vertical numbered list. When you create a numbered list, do not use adverbs with an *-ly* ending (secondly, thirdly, etc). Instead, use first, second, third, and so on.

Adverbs to Avoid
Adverbs like *very, extremely,* and *really* don't intensify anything. They are often too imprecise for business writing.

Positions of Adverbs
Adverbs have a unique ability to be placed in different places within a sentence. Adverbs of manner are unusually flexible in this regard. For example:

- Solemnly the President returned the salute.
- The President solemnly returned the salute.
- The President returned the salute solemnly.

Adverbs of frequency can appear at the following places within a sentence:

- Before the main verb—He *never* gets up before noon.

- Between the auxiliary verb and the main verb—I have *rarely* called my sister without a good reason.

- Before the verb *used to:* I *always* used to talk to him at the bus stop.

Indefinite adverbs of time can appear either before the verb or between the auxiliary and the main verb:

- He *finally* showed up for the date.
- He has *recently* traveled to France.

Order of Adverbs

There is a basic order in which adverbs can appear in a sentence when there is more than one (see Table 28-4).

As a general rule, shorter adverbial phrases precede longer ones, regardless of content. For example, "Mike takes a short swim *before breakfast every morning in the summer.*" Among similar adverbial phrases of kind (manner, place, frequency) the more specific adverbial phrase goes first. For example, "He promised to meet her *for coffee sometime next week.*" If you move an adverbial modifier to the beginning of a sentence, additional emphasis will be placed on that modifier. This is especially useful with adverbs of manner. For example, "*Slowly, ever so carefully,* the little boy crept into his parent's bedroom."

Inappropriate Adverb Order

Modifiers can sometimes attach themselves to the wrong word. For example, "They reported that Leslie Fiedler, a famous literary critic, had won the lottery *on the evening news.*" It would be better to move the modifier immediately after the verb it is modifying (reported) or to the beginning of the sentence. "They reported on the news that Leslie Fiedler, a famous literary critic, had won the lottery."

The adverbs *only* and *barely* are often misplaced modifiers. For example: "He *only grew* to be five feet tall." This would be better if, "He grew to be *only five feet tall.*"

Adjuncts, Disjuncts, and Conjuncts

Adverbs are usually neatly integrated into the flow of a sentence. When this is true, the adverb is called an **adjunct.** When an adverb does not fit into the sentence flow, it is called a **disjunct** or **conjunct** and is usually set off by a comma or a series of commas. A disjunct acts as if it is evaluating the rest of the sentence. Rather than modify the verb, it modifies the entire clause. For example, "*Honestly,* Bill, I don't really care." Conjuncts serve as a connector within the flow of the text, signaling a transition. For example, "If they start talking politics, *then* I'm leaving." One variation is the adverbial conjunction. These are words like *however* and *nevertheless.* For example, "I love this job; *however,* I don't think I can afford to stay."

TABLE 28-4	Order of Adverbs				
Verb	**Manner**	**Place**	**Frequency**	**Time**	**Purpose**
John jogs	enthusiastically	in the park	every morning	before sunrise	to keep in shape
Mary drives	hurriedly	into town	every afternoon	before dinner	to do her shopping

Special Adverbial Clauses

Some adverbs have special rules for their placement. For instance, the adverbs *enough* and *not enough* usually take a post-modifier position. For example, "Is your food *hot enough?* This food is *not hot enough.*" *Enough* can also be an adjective. When it is used as an adjective it comes before the noun. For example, "The teacher didn't give us *enough time.*" The adverb *enough* is often followed by an infinitive verb. For example, "They didn't play hard *enough to win.*"

The adverb *too* usually comes before adjectives and other adverbs. For example, "He ate *too fast.* He eats *too quickly.*" When *too* appears in a sentence after an adverb, it is a disjunct adverb and is set apart with a comma. For example, "John works hard. He works *quickly, too.*" The adverb *too* is sometimes followed by an infinitive verb. For example, "He talks *too slowly to keep* my attention." The adverb *too* can also be followed by the prepositional phrase *for +* the objective of the preposition + an infinitive. For example, "This food is *too spicy for grandma to eat.*"

Relative Adverbs

Adjectival clauses can be introduced by **relative adverbs:** *where, when,* and *why.* Although this is an adjectival clause and modifies a noun, the relative word itself serves in an adverbial function, modifying the verb within the clause. The relative adverb *where* begins a clause that modifies a noun of place. For example, "My family now lives in the *town where* my grandfather used to be sheriff." The relative pronoun *where* modifies the verb *used to be,* but the entire clause modifies the noun *town.*

A *when* clause modifies nouns of time. For example, "My favorite day of the week is *Friday, when* the weekend is about to begin."

A *why* clause modifies the noun *reason.* For example, "Do you know the *reason why* school is out today?" Sometimes the relative adverb is left out of these clauses, and the writer substitutes *that* instead. For example, "Do you know the *reason that* school it out today?"

Viewpoint Adverbs

A **viewpoint adverb** usually comes after a noun and is related to an adjective that precedes the noun. For example, "Investing all our money in technology stocks was probably not a *good idea financially.*"

Focus Adverbs

A **focus adverb** is used to limit a specific aspect of the sentence. For example, "He got a promotion *just* for being there."

Negative Adverbs

Negative adverbs can create a negative meaning in a sentence without the use of words like no, not, neither, nor, or never. For example, "He *seldom* smiles. He *hardly* eats anything since he got sick. After the team lost so many key players, *rarely* did anyone attend the games.

✳ Pronouns

Usually **pronouns** refer to a noun, an individual or group, or thing whose identity was been made clear previously. The word a pronoun substitutes for is called its **antecedent.** "Jeanne accepted Carmelo's proposal. She knew he was the right guy for her." Not all pronouns refer to an antecedent. For example, "Everyone on this floor charges over one-hundred dollars an hour." The pronoun *everyone* does not have an antecedent in this example.

There are a variety of different kinds of pronouns:

- Personal
- Reflexive
- Demonstrative
- Intensive
- Indefinite
- Interrogative
- Relative
- Reciprocal

Personal Pronouns

Personal pronouns change form according to their various uses within a sentence. The pronoun *I* is used as the subject of a sentence. For example, "I am tall." The pronoun *me* is used as an object in various ways. For example, "He gave me a car." The pronoun *my* is used for the possessive form. For example, "That's my house." The same is true for other personal pronouns: the singular *you* and *he/she/it* and the plurals *we, you,* and *they.* These forms are called **cases** (Table 28-5).

When a personal pronoun is connected by a conjunction to another noun or pronoun, it does not change case. For example, "I am taking a course in Latin. John and I are taking a course in Latin." You'll notice in the second sentence that "John" is listed before "I." The same is true when the object form is used. "The professor gave the Latin books to me. The professor gave the Latin books to John and me."

28 ■ GRAMMAR

| TABLE 28-5 | Various Cases for Pronouns |

	PRONOUNS		
	Subjective	Possessive	Objective
Singular first person	I	My, mine	Me
Singular second person	You	Your, yours	You
Singular third person	He, she, it	His, her, hers, its	Him, her, it
Plural first person	We	Our, ours	Us
Plural second person	You	Your, yours	You
Plural third person	They	Their, theirs	Them
Relative and interrogative pronouns	Who, whoever, which, that, what	Whose	Whom, whomever, which, that, what
Indefinite pronouns	Everybody	Everybody's	Everybody

When a pronoun and a noun are combined, you must choose the case of the pronoun that would be appropriate if the noun were not there. For example, "*We* teachers are demanding a raise." With the second person, there's not as much confusion because the pronoun *you* is the same for both subject and object form. "*You* teachers are demanding too much money."

Among the possessive pronoun forms, there are nominative possessives such as *mine, yours, ours,* and *theirs.* For example, "This new house is mine. Look at those houses. Theirs needs work. Ours is in good shape. Mine is newer than yours."

Demonstrative Pronouns

The **demonstrative pronouns,** *this, that, these, those,* and *such* can be used as either pronouns or as determiners. As pronouns, the demonstrative pronouns identify a noun. "*That* is marvelous! I will never forget *this. Such* is life."

As determiners, the demonstrative pronouns adjectivally modify a noun that follows. They are used to convey a sense of time and distance. For example, "*These* (strawberries that are in front of me) look delicious. *Those* (that are further away) look even better."

A sense of emotional distance can also be conveyed through the use of demonstrative pronouns. For example, "You're going to eat *that?*" Pronouns used in this way receive special emphasis in a spoken sentence.

When used as subjects, demonstrative pronouns can be used to refer to objects as well as persons. For example, "This is my mother. This is my book."

Relative Pronouns

The **relative pronouns** *who, whoever, which,* and *that* relate to groups of words, nouns, and other pronouns. The pronoun *who* connects the subject to the verb within a dependent clause. Choosing between *which* and *that* and between *who* and *whom* is difficult for many people. Generally we use *which* to introduce clauses that are parenthetical in nature. That means they can be removed from the sentence without changing the meaning of the sentence. For that reason, a *who* clause is often set apart with a comma or a pair of commas. We use *that* to introduce clauses that are indispensable for the meaning of the sentence. *That* clauses are not set apart with commas. The pronoun *which* refers to things, *who* refers to people, and *that* usually refers to things but also refers to people in a general way.

The expanded relative pronouns *whoever, whomever,* and *whatever* are known as indefinite relative pronouns. They do not define any thing or person in particular. For example, "The company will hire *whomever* it pleases. She seemed to say *whatever* came to mind. *Whoever* took the money will be punished." *What* can be an indefinite relative pronoun when used as in the following, "He will give you *what* you need for the trip."

Indefinite Pronouns

The **indefinite pronouns** *everybody, anybody, somebody, all, each, every, some, none,* and *one* do not substitute for specific nouns but act as nouns themselves.

One of the problems with the indefinite pronoun *everybody* is that it seems to be plural but takes a singular verb. For example, *"Everybody* is coming." The indefinite pronoun *none* can be either singular or plural. It is usually plural except when something else in the sentence forces it to be singular. *Some* can be singular or plural depending on whether it refers to something countable or not countable.

Some indefinite pronouns also double as determiners such as: *enough, few, fewer, less, little, many, much, several, more, most, all, both, every, each, any, either, neither, none,* and *some.*

Intensive Pronouns

The **intensive pronouns,** *myself, yourself, herself, ourselves,* and *themselves* consist of a personal pronoun plus the suffix "self" or "selves." They are used to emphasize a noun. For example, "I *myself* didn't play baseball."

Reflexive Pronouns

Reflexive pronouns indicate that the subject in a sentence also receives the action of the verb. "People who cheat on their taxes are only hurting *themselves.*" Whenever there is a reflexive pronoun in a sentence, there must be a person to whom the pronoun can reflect. For example, "Please give the food to *myself*" is incorrect because there is no "I" in the sentence.

There is a tendency to use reflexive and intensive pronouns (ending in *-self*) when they are not appropriate. For example, "These books will be read by *myself*" should be "These books will be read by *me.*"

The indefinite pronoun *one* has its own reflexive form. For example, "One must trust oneself." Other indefinite pronouns use either *himself* or *themselves* as reflexives.

Interrogative Pronouns

Interrogative pronouns are used to introduce questions. For example, *"What* is that? *Who* is coming? *Which* dog do you like best?" *Which* is used for specific reference rather than *what.* For example, in "Which dogs do you like best?", you are referring to specific dogs. "What dogs do you like best?" refers to general dog breeds you like best.

Interrogative pronouns can also act as determiners. For example, "It doesn't matter which road you take." In this role, the pronouns are called interrogative adjectives.

Interrogative pronouns are used to introduce noun clauses.

Reciprocal Pronouns

The **reciprocal pronouns,** *each other* and *one another,* are used for combining ideas. For example, "My brother and I give *each other* a hard time." If more than two people are involved, you would use *one another.*

Reciprocal pronouns can also take the possessive form. For example, "They borrowed *each other's* clothes."

Pronouns and Antecedent Agreement

A pronoun usually refers to its antecedent, and the two must agree in number. Therefore, if the antecedent is plural, the pronoun must be plural. The same is true if the antecedent is singular; the pronoun must be singular.

Certain pronouns like *anyone, anybody, everyone, everybody, someone, somebody, no one,* and *nobody* are always singular. This is perplexing for some people because they feel that *everyone* and *everybody* refer to more than one person. The same is true for *either* and *neither.* Even though they seem to be referring to two things, they are singular.

One of the most frequently asked grammar questions regards the pronoun *who (who, whose, whom, whoever,* and *whomever).* The choice of singular or plural is determined by what the pronoun refers to. It can refer to a single person or a group. For example, *"The person who* broke my window should confess. *The people who* have been without power should complain." One good way to understand the uses for *who* is to compare it with the pronouns *he* and *they,* as in Table 28-6.

So one good way to choose between the various forms of *who* is to think of the sentence in terms of the choice between *he* and *him.* If *him* feels right, choose *whom.* If *he* sounds better, pick *who.* For example:

- *Who* do you think is coming. (Do you think *he* is coming?)

- *Whom* shall we invite to the movie? (Shall we invite *him* to the movie?)

- Give the money to *whomever* you please. (Give the money to *him.*)

- Give the money to *whoever* wants it most. (*He* seems to want it most).

- *Whoever* guesses my age will win the prize. (*He* guesses my age.)

Another related problem is confusing *whose* with *who's. Who's* looks like it is possessive; however, it is really a contraction of who is.

Prepositions

Prepositions are used to describe relationships between other words in a sentence. Prepositions like *in, on,* or *between* are good examples because they describe the spatial nature of things.

TABLE 28-6	The Pronoun *Who* Compared to *He* and *They*		
	Subject Form	**Possessive Form**	**Object Form**
Singular	He	His	Him
	Who	Whose	Whom
Plural	They	Their	Them
	Who	Whose	Whom

Prepositions are almost always combined with other words to become prepositional phrases. Prepositional phrases consist of a preposition plus possibly a determiner and/or an adjective or two, followed by a pronoun or noun that is called the object of the preposition. The prepositional phrase takes on a modifying role of its own, acting as either an adjective or adverb to locate something in time and space, or explain when or where, or under what circumstances something occurred.

Prepositions can be divided into types: prepositions of time, prepositions of space, prepositions of location, and prepositions of movement.

Prepositions of Time: At, On, In, For, and Since

At, on, and *in* often serve as prepositions of time. We use *at* to designate specific times. For example, "Meet me *at* five o'clock." We use *on* to designate days and dates. For example, "I work all day *on* Saturdays." We use *in* for nonspecific times. For example, "He likes to read *in* the evenings."

The preposition *for* is used to measure time. For example, "He worked *for* 20 years." The preposition *since* is used with a specific date or time. For example, "I have known him *since* January, 2003."

Prepositions of Place: At, On, In

At, on, and *in* can also serve as prepositions of place. We use *at* for specific addresses. "I live *at* 5203 Legendary Lane." We use *on* to designate streets. "I live *on* Legendary Lane." We use *in* for the names of towns, states, and countries. "I live *in* Acworth."

Prepositions of Location: At, On, In

At, on, and *in* can be used as prepositions of location. Their usage is specific to certain places. For example, we say "in the bed," "in the bedroom," "in the car," "in the class," "in the library," "in the room," "in the school." We say "at class," "at home," "at the library," "at the office," "at school," "or at work." We can say "on the bed," "on the ceiling," "on the floor," "on the horse," "on the plane," or "on the train."

Prepositions of Movement: To, Toward

The preposition *to* is used to express movement to a place. For example, "I am driving to work."

Toward and *towards* are also used to express movement. They are both the same word with a spelling variation. You can use either one. For example, "We were working towards a common goal."

Preposition Combinations

Some prepositions are so commonly used with particular nouns, adjectives, and verbs that they have almost become one word. The following is a list of noun and preposition combinations:

- Approval of
- Belief in
- Awareness of
- Concern for

- Confusion about
- Desire for
- Fondness for
- Grasp of
- Hatred of
- Hope for
- Interest in

- Love of
- Need for
- Participation in
- Reason for
- Respect for
- Success in
- Understanding of

The following is a list of adjective and preposition combinations:

- Afraid of
- Angry at
- Aware of
- Capable of
- Careless about
- Familiar with
- Fond of
- Happy about
- Interested in

- Jealous of
- Made of
- Married to
- Proud of
- Similar to
- Sorry for
- Sure of
- Tired of
- Worried about

A combination of a verb and preposition is called a **phrasal verb.** The word that is joined with the verb is called a **particle.** The following is a list of verb and preposition combinations:

- Apologize for
- Ask about
- Ask for
- Belong to
- Bring up
- Care for
- Find out
- Give up
- Grow up
- Look for
- Look forward to

- Look up
- Make up
- Pay for
- Prepare for
- Study for
- Talk about
- Think about
- Trust in
- Work for
- Worry about

Conjunctions

Conjunctions are words that connect parts of a sentence. The simplest conjunctions are called **coordinating conjunctions.** They include: *and, but, or, yet, for, nor,* and *so.*

When a coordinating conjunction connects two independent clauses, it is often accompanied by a comma. For example, "John wants to play football for Texas, *but* he has had trouble with his grades." It is also correct to use a comma with *and* when used to attach a list item in a list. For example, "John needs to study harder in math, history, physics, *and* economics." When a coordinating conjunction is used to connect all the elements in a series, a comma is not used. For example, "Math *and* history *and* physics are the subjects that give John the most trouble." Commas are also used with *but* when a sentence expresses a contrast. For example, "John is a great player, *but* not very smart."

The most common coordinating conjunctions are *and*, *but*, and *or*. Each has it's own unique uses.

Coordinating Conjunction: And

The coordinating conjunction *and* can be used in the following ways:

- To suggest that one idea is sequential to another. For example, "Steve sent in his application *and* waited for the response in the mail."

- To suggest that an idea is the result of another. For example, "Linda heard the thunder *and* quickly took shelter inside the house."

- To suggest that one idea is in contrast to another. For example, "Lori is an artist, *and* her sister is a doctor." Frequently the conjunction *but* is used for this purpose.

- To suggest an element of surprise. For example, "Atlanta is a beautiful city and has symptoms of urban blight." Frequently the conjunction *yet* is used for this purpose.

- To suggest that one clause is dependent. For example, "Drink too much water before the trip, *and* you'll soon find yourself stopping at every rest area."

- To make a comment on the first clause. For example, "Horace became addicted to gambling—*and* that's why he moved to Las Vegas."

Coordinating Conjunction: But

The coordinating conjunction *but* can be used in the following ways:

- To suggest an unexpected contrast. For example, "Tom lost money in his investments, *but* he still maintained a comfortable lifestyle."

- To express positively what the first part of the sentence implies negatively. For example, "Tom never invested foolishly *but* listened carefully to the advice of investment newsletters."

- To connect two ideas with the meaning "with the exception of." For example, "Everyone *but* Tom is making money in the stock market."

Coordinating Conjunction: Or

The coordinating conjunction *or* can be used in the following ways:

- To suggest that only one possibility is realistic and excludes the other. For example, "You can sell your investment now *or* you can lose all your money."

- To suggest alternatives. For example, "We can go out to eat and to a movie, *or* we can just stay home and see what's on TV."

- To suggest a refinement of the first clause. For example, "The University of Texas is the best school in the state, *or* so it seems to every UT alumni."

- To suggest a correction to the first part of the sentence. For example, "There's no way you can lose money in this investment, *or* so Eric told himself."

- To suggest a negative condition. For example, "You have two choices: pay taxes *or* die."

Other Conjunctions

The conjunction *nor* is used occasionally by itself, however, it is most commonly used in a correlative pair with *neither*. For example, "He is *neither* rich *nor* poor."

Nor can be used with negative expressions. For example, "This is not how I normally dress, *nor* should you get the idea I have no taste in clothes."

The word *yet* sometimes functions as an adverb and has various meanings such as *in addition, even, still,* and *eventually*. It also functions as a coordinating conjunction with a meaning of *nevertheless* or *but*. For example, "Rosemary is an expert in computer programming, *yet* her real passion is poetry."

The word *for* is often used as a preposition, but it does sometimes act as a coordinating conjunction. When it is used as a coordinating conjunction it has a meaning of *because* or *since*. For example, "For he's a jolly good fellow."

The conjunction *so* can be used to connect two independent clauses along with a comma. It has the meaning of *as well* or *in addition*. Many writers would eliminate the *so* and use a semicolon between the two clauses.

✦ Subordinating Conjunctions

A subordinating conjunction comes at the beginning of a dependent clause and establishes the relationship between the clause and the rest of the sentence. For example, "He spoke Spanish *as if* he had been born in Mexico."

Many subordinating conjunctions also serve as prepositions (see Table 28-7). When they serve as subordinating conjunctions they introduce the dependent clause.

Correlative Conjunctions

Correlative conjunctions combine with other words to form grammatically equal pairs. The following is a list of correlative conjunctions.

- Both . . . and
- Not only . . . but also

TABLE 28-7	Common Subordinating Conjunctions	
After	If	Though
Although	If only	Till
As	In order that	Unless
As if	Now that	Until
As long as	Once	When
As though	Rather than	Whenever
Because	Since	Where
Before	So that	Whereas
Even if	Than	Wherever
Even though	That	While

- Also
- Not . . . but
- Either . . . or
- Neither . . . nor
- Whether . . . or
- As . . . as

Articles, Determiners, and Quantifiers

Articles, determiners, and **quantifiers** are little words that precede and modify nouns. For example, "*the* dog, *a* cat, *those* people, *whatever* purpose, *either* way, *your* choice." Sometimes these words tell you whether the subject is something specific or more general. Sometimes they tell you how much or how many.

The choice of the proper article or determiner is usually not a problem for the native English speaker. The following is a list of determiner categories:

- Articles—an, a, the

- Determiners—articles and other limiters such as: a, an, five, her, our, those, that, several, and some

- Possessive nouns—Kevin's, the worker's, my mother's

- Possessive pronouns—his, your, their, whose

- Numbers—one, two, three, etc.

- Demonstrative pronouns—this, that, these, those, such

Articles

The three articles *a, an,* and *the* are a type of adjective. *The* is called the **definite article** because it tends to name something specific. *A* and *an* are called **indefinite articles** because they refer to things in a less specific way.

The is used with specific nouns and is required when the noun refers to something that is unique. For example, "*The* earth orbits *the* sun." *The* is also used for abstract nouns. For example, "The City of Atlanta has encouraged *the* use of mass transit."

A is used before singular nouns that begin with consonants. For example, "*A* dog, *a* cat, *a* mountain." *An* is used before singular nouns that begin with vowels or vowel-like sounds. For example, "*An* apple, *an* eagle, *an* invitation."

Predeterminers

Predeterminers occur prior to other determiners and include multipliers (*double, twice, two/three times* etc.) fractional expressions (*one-half, one-third,* etc) the words *both, half,* and *all,* and the intensifiers *quite, rather,* and *such.*

Multipliers precede plural count and mass nouns and with singular count nouns denoting numbers or an amount. For example, "This classroom holds *three times* the students my old room did."

Fractional expressions have a similar construction as multipliers and optionally include *of.* For example, "*One-half of* the voters favored lower taxes.

Intensifiers occur primarily in casual speech and are more common in British English than in American English. For example, "This food is *rather* bland, isn't it? The voters made *quite a* fuss over the debate."

Quantifiers

Quantifiers are words that also precede and modify nouns. They are used to communicate how many or how much. Selecting the correct quantifier depends on whether they are used with a countable or non-countable noun. For example, the following quantifiers can be used with countable nouns: *many* people, a *few* people, *several* people, *a couple of* people, *none of the* people. The following quantifiers can be used with non-count nouns: *not much* eating, *a little* eating, *little* eating, *a bit of* eating, *a good deal of* eating, *a great deal of* eating, *no* eating.

Interjections

Interjections are words or phrases used to communicate excitement, orders, or protests. Sometimes they can be used by themselves, but often they are contained within more complex sentence structures. For example, "*Wow,* I can't believe it. *Oh,* I didn't realize you were here. *No,* you shouldn't have done that."

Most interjections are treated as parenthetical elements and are set apart from the rest of the sentence by commas or a set of commas. If the interjection is more forceful, it is followed with an exclamation point.

CHAPTER 29

Language Usage and Style

Sentence Subject

The **subject** of a sentence is the person, place, or thing that is the main focus of the sentence. To find the subject of a sentence, first locate the verb. Then answer the question, what or who is being "verbed?" For instance, in the sentence, "The monkeys in the treetops must be observed," the verb is *must be observed*. So, what must be observed? The answer is, *monkeys*. A **simple subject** is the subject without any modifiers. For example, the simple subject of the following sentence is *event*. "The upcoming event, stripped of all the hype, is nothing but a fundraiser."

Sometimes a simple subject can be more than one word or even an entire clause. Consider the following: "*What he had forgotten about the law* was amazing considering how many years he spent in law school." The simple subject is the entire clause written in italics.

Usually, when the subject of a sentence is *you* and the sentence is a suggestion, order, or command, the *you* is left out. For example, "Get out of the way!" *You* is understood to be the subject.

For sentence analysis, the person who initiates an action is called the **agent** of a sentence. When the active voice is used, the subject is the agent. For example, "The *class* failed the test." When the passive voice is used, the agent is not the subject. In fact, some passive sentences don't contain an agent.

Subject-Verb Inversion

Normally, a sentence contains a subject and then a verb in that order. This pattern is disturbed only in a few instances. Here are a few examples:

- In questions—"Have you read that book?"

- In expletive constructions—"Here is your book."

- To put focus on a particular word—"What's more important is his reluctance to find a job."

- When a sentence begins with an adverb, adverbial phrase, or clause—"Rarely have so many been eaten in just one meal."

- After the word "so"—"I believe him; so do the people."

Subject-Verb Agreement

The basic rule of subject-verb agreement is that a singular subject needs a singular verb. Likewise, plural subjects need plural verbs. For example, "My *brother is* a psychologist. My *brothers are* psychologists."

Indefinite pronouns like *anyone, everyone, someone, no one,* and *nobody* are singular subjects and, thus, require singular verbs. For example, "Everyone *is* studying hard."

Some indefinite pronouns, such as *all* and *some,* can be singular or plural depending on whether the thing they're referring to is countable or not. For example, "Some of the candy *is* missing. Some of the dogs *are* barking."

There is one indefinite pronoun, *none,* that can be either singular or plural, and it doesn't matter whether you use a singular or plural verb—that is, unless something in the sentence specifies its number. For example, "None of you *write* poetry. None of the cars *are* speeding."

Some indefinite pronouns like *everyone* and *everybody* sound like they are talking about more than one person. However, they are both singular. For example, "Everyone is working hard." The pronoun *each* is often followed by a prepositional phrase ending in a plural word, "Each of the monkeys." *Each,* however, is also singular. For example, "Each of the monkeys *is* eating a banana."

Don't confuse the word *and* with the phrases *together with, as well as,* and *along with.* They do not mean the same and do not create compound subjects the same way *and* does. For example, "The boy, as well as his brother, *is* going to school. The boy and his brother *are* going to school."

The pronouns *neither* and *either* are singular even though they appear to be referring to two things. For example, "Neither of the two computers is obsolete. Either is a good choice for a student." Sometimes *neither* and *either* take a plural verb when they are followed by a prepositional phrase that begins with *of.* For example, "*Have* either of you two kids seen my dog? *Are* either of you listening to me?"

When the conjunctions *or* and *nor* are used, the subject closest to the verb determines whether the verb is singular or plural. For example, "Neither the bear nor the monkeys *were* awake when we visited the zoo." It's also a good idea to put the plural subject closest to the verb since the following version of the same sentence would be incorrect: "Neither the monkeys nor the bear was awake when we visited the zoo."

The words *there* and *here* can never be subjects in a sentence. For example, "Here *are* my two books. There better *be* a good reason you have them." These are called expletive constructions, and the subject follows the verb and determines whether the verb is singular or plural.

Verbs for third-person, singular subjects like *he, she,* and *it* have s-endings. For example, "He loves to eat."

Sometimes modifiers will slip between a subject and a verb. When this happens, don't let them confuse the subject-verb agreement. For example, "The *workers,* who always seem to be standing around taking a break, gathered around in a circle like a football huddle, *are* being fired."

Sometimes nouns take peculiar forms that make it confusing to tell whether they are singular or plural. Words such as *glasses, gloves, pliers,* and *scissors* are thought of as plural unless they're preceded by the phrase *pair of*—in which case *pair* becomes the subject. For example, "My glasses *are* on the desk. The pair of glasses *is* on the desk."

Some words that end in *-s* seem to be plural but are really singular and thus require singular verbs. For example, "The evening news *is* full of disasters." There are other words that end in *-s* that refer to a single thing, but are actually plural and require a plural verb. For example, "His assets *were* totally wiped out by the bankruptcy."

Fractional expressions such as *half of* and *a percentage of* can be either singular or plural. The same is true when words like *some, all,* and *any* serve as subjects. For example, "One-half of the population *is* over sixty-five. One-quarter of the students *were* absent. Some of the houses *are* painted white. Some of the money *is* missing."

Finally, when you have a sentence that combines a positive and a negative subject, and one is plural and the other singular, the verb should agree with the positive subject. For example, "It's the teacher, not the students, who *decides* what to teach."

Predicates

Predicates are used to complete a sentence. The subject names the person, place, or thing that is doing something. A simple predicate consists of a verb, verb string, or a compound verb. For example, "The flower *bloomed.* The flowers *have been blooming.* The bulbs *opened, blossomed, and then closed for the night.*"

A **compound predicate** consists of two or more predicates connected. For example, "The mountain biker *began to ride down the trail* and *eventually entered one of the most beautiful valleys in the area.*"

A **complete predicate** consists of a transitive verb and all modifiers and other words that complete its meaning. For example, "The slowly moving thunderstorm *flashed lightning across the dark foreboding sky.*"

A **predicate adjective** follows a linking verb and describes the subject of the sentence. For example, "The minerals in the water taste *bad.*"

A **predicate nominative** follows a linking verb and describes what the subject is. For example, "Lucy Edson is *president* of the firm."

Objects

Objects are the part of a sentence that receive actions. For example, "He threw *the ball.*" In this example, *the ball* is a **direct object.**

An **object complement** renames or describes a direct object. For example, "He named his monkey Meep." In this example, *his monkey* is the direct object; *Meep* is the object complement.

An **indirect object** identifies to what or to whom the action of a verb is directed. For example, "He sold me his car." In this example, *me* is the indirect object, and *his car* is the direct object. The word *me*—along with other pronouns such as *him, us,* and *them*—is not always an indirect object; it can also serve as a direct object. For example, "Save me!"

✸ Complements

A **complement** is any word (or phrase) that completes a subject, object, or verb. A **subject complement** follows a linking verb and is used to rename or define the subject. For example, "A tarn is a small glacial *lake.*"

An **object complement** follows or modifies a direct object and can be a noun or adjective. For example, "The players named Logan *captain* to keep him *happy.*" In this example, the noun *captain* complements the direct object *Logan;* the adjective *happy* complements the direct object *him.*

A **verb complement** is either a direct or indirect object of a verb. For example, "Mark gave *Terry* (indirect object) all his old *albums* (direct object)."

✸ Modifier Placement

Modifiers are words that limit certain aspects of a sentence. Some modifiers—such as *only, just, nearly,* and *barely*—can easily end up in the wrong place in a sentence. Compare, "He only threw the ball ten feet," with "He threw the ball only ten feet." The best rule is to place these modifiers immediately before the word they modify. When a modifier improperly modifies something, it is called a **dangling modifier.** One common example is starting a sentence with a prepositional phrase.

If you have a sentence where a participial phrase is followed by an expletive construction, you will often have a **dangling participle.** For example, "Cleaning the windows every six months, there is a simple way to keep a building looking better." This example could be rewritten as, "If you clean the windows every six months, you can keep a building looking better."

Another situation where dangling participles can occur is when you have a participial phrase followed by a passive verb. This happens because the real actor in the sentence is disguised. For example, "Cleaning the windows every six months, the building was kept in beautiful condition." This example could be rewritten as, "Cleaning the windows every six months, they kept the building in beautiful condition."

Infinitive phrases can also end up as dangling modifiers. For example, "To keep the employees interested in their health, a fitness center was set up in the basement." In this example, the infinitive phrase, *To keep the employees interested in their health,* should probably modify the person who set up the fitness center. Thus, this example could be rewritten as, "To keep the employees interested in their heath, the manager set up a fitness center in the basement."

Finally, one additional misplaced modifier problem involves adverbs. Adverbs can be placed almost anywhere in a sentence, but their placement can sometimes obscure their meaning. For example, "The people who listen to public radio often like classical music." Does this mean that anyone who listens to public radio a lot likes classical music? By moving the placement of the adverb *often,* this example could be rewritten as, "The people who often listen to public radio like classical music."

Noun Phrases

A **phrase** is a group of related words that does not include a subject and verb. If a subject and verb are present, it is considered to be a **clause.** A noun phrase includes a noun and its modifiers. For example, "The tall dark man." The modifiers that are included in the noun phrase can be any of the following:

- Adjectives—"tall dark man"

- Participial phrase—"the bushes following the edge of the sidewalk"

- Infinitive phrase—"the first woman to fly around the world"

- Modifying clause—"the mistakes he had made the day before"

- Prepositional phrase—"the trail next to the lake, over by the dam"

Usually all the words in a noun phrase are together; however, occasionally they can be broken up into what is called a **discontinuous noun phrase.** For example, "*Several burglaries* have been reported *involving people who were gone for the weekend.*" There is nothing wrong with a discontinuous noun phrase. They are sometimes useful for balancing a subject and predicate. Otherwise we end up with a 10-word subject and a three-word verb.

One common problem to avoid involves a long string of compound noun phrases. This often happens when the string also involves a group of compound nouns, such as *student body, book cover,* or *meeting place*. If you put together a long string of these phrases, the result can be a very difficult sentence.

An addressed person's name or substitute name is called a **vocative.** These sometimes take the form of a noun phrase. A vocative is treated as a parenthetical element and is set apart from the rest of the sentence by a pair of commas if it appears within the flow of a sentence. For example, "Mike, stop the car." You do not need to add commas every time someone's name is mentioned in a sentence. Commas are only used when the name refers to someone who is being addressed in the sentence. Overall, there are four types of vocatives:

- Single names, with or without a title
- The personal pronoun *you*
- Appellatives of endearment, such as *darling, my dear, sweetheart,* and *sir*
- Nominal clauses, such as *"Whoever is singing,* stop it now."

Prepositional Phrase

A **prepositional phrase** consists of a preposition, a noun or pronoun that serves as the object of the preposition, and an adjective or two that modifies the object. Prepositional phrases usually tell us when or where something is happening. For example, "in a half hour."

A prepositional phrase used at the beginning of a sentence is called an **introductory modifier.** You can set apart an introductory modifier with a comma; however, it is optional unless the introductory modifier is long.

You have probably heard the rule regarding ending a sentence with a preposition. Although you can easily revise sentences that do this, sometimes the revision results in a very clumsy sentence.

Appositive Phrase

An **appositive phrase** involves re-naming or amplifying a word that immediately precedes it. For example, "My favorite professor, *a world famous author,* just won a prestigious literary award."

Absolute Phrase

An **absolute phrase** is a group of words consisting of a noun or pronoun, a participle, as well as any modifiers. Absolute phrases do not connect to or modify any other word in a sentence; instead, they modify the entire sentence. Absolute phrases are often treated as parenthetical elements set off from the rest of the sentence with a comma or pair of commas.

Infinitive Phrase

An **infinitive phrase** consists of a infinitive—the root verb preceded by *to*—along with modifiers or complements. Infinitive phrases can act as adjectives, adverbs, or nouns. Consider the following examples:

- His plan *to eliminate smoking* was widely popular. (*To eliminate smoking* serves as an adjective that modifies *plan.*)
- *To watch him eat ribs* is something you have to see. (*To watch him eat ribs* serves as the noun-subject of the sentence.)

- Eric went to college *to study to be an engineer.* (*To study to be an engineer* tells us why he went, so it's an adverb.)

Gerund Phrase

Gerund phrases consist of verbals that end in *-ing* and act as nouns, along with modifiers and complements. These phrases can do anything a noun can do. For example, "*Walking after dark* is not very safe."

Participial Phrase

Present participles (verbals ending in *-ing*) and past participles (verbals ending in *-ed* or other irregular past participles) can be combined with complements and modifiers to create a **participial phrase.** These always act as adjectives. When they begin a sentence, they are set apart by a comma just like an introductory modifier. If they appear within the middle of a sentence, they are set apart with a pair of commas. For example, "*Working around the clock,* the workers repaired the airport runway in less than a week. The concrete, *having been damaged by the crash landing of the airliner,* needed to be replaced."

Clauses

A **clause** is a group of words that contains a subject and a verb. As discussed earlier, a clause is different from a phrase because a phrase does not include a subject and a verb.

Independent Clauses

An **independent clause** could stand by itself as a sentence. But, if it did, it would be a sentence and not a clause. When an independent clause is included in a sentence, it is usually separated from the rest of the sentence by a comma. Being able to recognize when a clause is acting as an independent clause is essential to knowing when to use commas in avoiding sentence fragments and run-on sentences.

Two independent clauses can be combined into a single thought. For example, "Charlie didn't mean to run away, but he did it." In this example, two independent clauses are separated by a comma and a coordinating conjunction *but*. If the word *but* was missing, this example would be a comma splice.

Clauses can be combined three different ways:

- With coordination
- With subordination
- By using a semicolon

Coordination involves using coordinating conjunctions such as *and, but, or, nor, for, yet,* and sometimes *so.* By using a coordinating conjunction, you avoid monotony and what is often called "primer language"—simple sentence constructions. Your sentences are also balanced.

Subordination involves turning one of the independent clauses into a subordinate element using a subordinating conjunction or a relative pronoun. When the clause begins with a subordinating word, the clause is transformed into a dependent clause. For example, "Linda never liked to fly in airplanes, because she was afraid of heights."

Semicolons can be used to connect two independent clauses with or without the help of a conjunctive adverb. However, semicolons should only be used when the two independent clauses are very closely related and nicely balanced in length and content. For example, "Sheena is a very pretty girl; she looks like an angel."

Dependent Clauses

A **dependent clause** cannot stand by itself like an independent clause. It must be combined with an independent clause in order to become a sentence.

Dependent clauses can perform a variety of different functions within a sentence. They can be noun clauses, adverb clauses, or adjective clauses. Noun clauses can do anything a noun can do in a sentence. For example, *"What he knows about boxing* is not important to me." Adverb clauses tell us about what is going on in the independent clause: where, when, or why. For example, *"When the game is over,* we'll go get some burgers." Adjective clauses function just like multi-word adjectives to modify a noun. For example, "My wife, *who is a video producer,* has just completed an award-winning documentary about music."

Sentence Fragments

A **sentence fragment** fails to be a sentence because it cannot stand by itself. It does not contain at least one independent clause. There are several reasons why a group of words may appear to be a sentence but turn out to be a sentence fragment instead. The sentence fragment may contain a series of prepositional phrases without a proper subject-verb relationship. For example, "In Texas, sometime in early April, just before the bluebonnets appear." The sentence fragment may be a verbal phrase that wants to modify something, but that something is missing. For example, "Working deep into the night in an effort to get his taxes completed." Finally, the sentence fragment may have a subject-verb relationship, but it has been subordinated to another idea or word so it cannot stand by itself. For example, "Although he was taller than his older brother."

Sentence Variety

A **sentence** is a group of words containing a subject and a predicate. There are many different types of sentences, and the way they are used in your writing, the order they are used in, and the way they are combined and punctuated determines your writing style.

It is relatively easy to write short sentences. However, if you use only short sentences, your writing will appear to be primer style and give your reader a poor impression of your level of professionalism.

To write more complicated sentences, you have to create constructions of clauses and phrases. Long sentences and run-on sentences are not the same thing. Combining too long a series of clauses may cause the reader to get confused. However, many writers are afraid they'll create run-on sentences and tend to lean towards the shorter variety.

By coordinating the use of clauses and punctuation, you can allow the complexity of a sentence to develop after the verb, not before it. The key is to make the subject-verb connection and then allow the sentence to paint a picture of the world surrounding that subject and verb. As you allow a sentence to develop in the predicate, be careful to keep your structures in parallel form.

One issue that is difficult for many business writers is the need to repeat key terms in long sentences. It feels awkward. When properly handled, though, repeated phrases can create a rhythm that helps to emphasize the meaning of the sentence.

Another way to enhance sentence variety and complexity is to avoid clumsy "which clauses" and replace them with other dependent clauses. For example, "Atlanta continues to grow in every direction, which means that homes are rapidly replacing the fields and forests in outlying areas." An alternative would be, "Atlanta continues to grow in every direction, as homes are rapidly replacing the fields and forests in outlying areas."

When you use them sparingly, you can create an interesting twist to a sentence by ending it with a set of prepositional and participial phrases, each beginning with a present or past participle or a preposition. For example, "You'll find working with Videologies to be an excellent experience, one that will develop into a lasting relationship or partnership winning future business for us all."

Resumptive and Summative Modifiers

By adding modifying phrases to the end of a sentence, you take a sentence in an unexpected direction. A **resumptive modifier** takes a word from a sentence that appears to be ending and adds additional information. For example, "You'll find working with Videologies to be both enlightening and rewarding—enlightening due to the many innovations we'll introduce to your company, rewarding because of the enhancements to productivity your company will experience."

A **summative modifier** re-names or summarizes what has been going on earlier in the sentence and adds new information. For example, "The e-mail etiquette seminar promises to show employees how to write effective e-mails: e-mails that get results and e-mails that result in a positive image for your business—two benefits that can enhance the productivity of any business."

✦ Modifier Placement

You can add variety to your sentences by the way you place modifiers. The following are four different strategies for modifier placement.

Using Initial Modifiers

- Dependent clause: Although he was tired, Bob wrote the report.
- Infinitive phrase: To please his boss, Bob wrote the report.
- Adverb: Slowly and laboriously, Bob wrote the report.
- Participial phrase: Hoping to be promoted, Bob wrote the report.

Using Mid-Sentence Modifiers

- Appositive: Bob, an expert on regulations, wrote the report.
- Participial phrase: Bob, hoping to catch up on his work, worked late.

Using Terminal Modifiers

- Present participial phrase: Bob worked on the report, hoping to please his boss.
- Past participial phrase/Adjectival phrase: Bob worked on the report, pushed by ambition.

Combining Modifiers

- Slowly and laboriously, Bob, an expert on regulations, worked on the report, hoping to please his boss.

✦ Other Ideas on Sentence Variety

Remember to throw an occasional question, exclamation, or command into your writing. Questions can be useful at the beginning of a paragraph to summarize the content that follows. Commands provide direction and energy by telling your readers what to do.

Occasionally, try to begin sentences with something other than the normal subject-verb combination. Try starting with a modifying clause or participial phrase. Consider beginning a sentence with a coordinating conjunction (*and, but, nor, for, yet,* or *so*). Many people think they should never begin a sentence with *but.* Instead, it should be linked to the previous sentence into a compound structure. But, a sentence like this calls attention to itself and can be a useful device.

Sentence Types

There are a variety of basic sentence structures including:

- Simple—one independent clause

- Compound—more than one independent clause

- Complex—one independent clause and at least one dependent clause

- Compound Complex—more than one independent clause and at least one dependent clause

- Periodic—beginning with modifying phrases and clauses and ending with an independent clause

- Cumulative—beginning with an independent clause and ending with a series of modifying constructions

Compound Sentences

A **compound sentence** consists of two or more independent clauses. Thus, there are two thoughts within the sentence, and either can stand alone. The clauses of a compound sentence are either separated by a semicolon or by a comma and a coordinating conjunction. The most common coordinating conjunction is *and;* it simply links the two ideas. Other coordinating conjunctions such as *but, or, for, yet,* and *so,* establish a relationship between the two clauses.

Compounding Sentence Elements

You can combine various sentence elements to create compound sentences:

- Subjects—Two or more subjects doing parallel things can be combined as a compound subject. For example, "Working together, *IBM and Apple Computer* developed the Power PC processor."

- Objects—When the subjects are acting on two or more things in parallel, the objects can be combined. For example, "The company president believed *that* the partnership between the two companies might help them increase sales *and that* he could eventually force a merger."

- Verbs and Verbals—When the subjects are doing two things simultaneously, the elements can be combined by compounding verbs and verbals. For example, "He *studied* sentence structure and grammar *and learned* how to speak and write effectively.

- Modifiers—When appropriate, modifiers and prepositional phrases can be compounded. For example, "The company recruited their programmers *from universities across the country and various competing companies.*"

Transitions

As you compound sentences and vary your sentence structures to add variety to your writing, you will want to consider using transitions between ideas. Transitions help guide a reader from one idea to the next.

There are four general ways to add transitions between ideas:

- Using transitional expressions
- Repeating key words and phrases
- Using pronoun reference
- Using parallel forms

Transitional Expressions

In addition to coordinating conjunctions—*and, but, nor, for, yet, or,* and *so*—you can use conjunctive adverbs and transitional expressions such as *however, moreover,* and *nevertheless* to transition your sentences from one thought to the next.

The key is to avoid using the same transitional elements, as it becomes boring. The following is a list of some conjunctive adverbs that can add spice to your transitions.

- Addition—again, also, and, and then, besides, equally important, finally, first, further, furthermore, in addition, in the first place, last, moreover, next, second, still, too

- Comparison—also, in the same way, likewise, similarly

- Concession—granted, naturally, of course

- Contrast—although, and yet, at the same time, but at the same time, despite that, even so, even though, for all that, however, in contrast, in spite of, instead, nevertheless, on the contrary, on the other hand, otherwise, regardless, still, though, yet

- Emphasis—certainly, indeed, in fact

- Example—after all, as an illustration, even, for example, for instance, in conclusion, in short, it is true, namely, specifically, that is, to illustrate, thus

- Summary—all in all, altogether, as has been said, finally, in brief, in conclusion, in other words, in particular, in short, in simpler terms, in summary, on the whole, that is, therefore, to put it differently, to summarize

- Time sequence—after a while, afterward, again, also, and then, as long as, at last, at length, at that time, before, besides, earlier, eventually, finally, formerly, further, furthermore, in addition, in the first place, in the past, last, lately, meanwhile, moreover, next, now, presently, second, shortly, simultaneously, since, so far, soon, still, subsequently, then, thereafter, too, until, until now, when

Repeating Key Words

By repeating a key word or phrase, you can establish its importance in the mind of the reader.

Pronoun Reference

Pronouns can be used to refer the reader to something earlier in the text. A pronoun such as *this* causes the reader to summarize what has been said so far. For example, "There has been an increase in the number of earthquakes in California in the past 10 years. We know *this* to be true because we have geological records that go back almost 150 years, and *they* show a clear trend."

Parallelism

Parallel constructions are expressions with similar content and function. Their similarity enables the reader to more easily recognize the content and understand the message.

Articles such as *the, a,* and *an* must either be used only before the first term in a group or be repeated before each term. For example, "At the World's Fair we saw all the latest model automobiles, including the new Hondas, Toyotas, and Nissans. We left on Sunday for vacation with the Wilsons, the Wausons, and the Bruecks."

Correlative expressions (*both, and; not, but; not only, but also; either, or; first, second;*) should be followed by the same grammatical construction. For example, "It was not only the blowing wind but also the freezing temperatures that made travel so treacherous."

When making comparisons, the things compared should be in parallel form.

Avoiding Redundancies

While a well-rounded writing style includes compound and complex sentences, it is important to avoid redundancies. Avoid saying the same thing twice. The following is a list of some of the most common redundant phrases:

- 12 midnight
- 12 noon
- 1 a.m. in the morning
- Circle around
- Close proximity
- Completely unanimous
- Cooperate together
- Each and every
- Enclosed herewith
- End result
- Exactly the same
- Final completion

- Free gift
- In spite of the fact that
- In the field of
- In the event of
- New innovations
- One and the same
- Particular interest
- Period of X days
- Personally, I think
- Personal opinion
- Refer back
- Repeat again

- Return again
- Revert back
- Shorter in length
- Small in size
- Summarize briefly

- Surrounded on all sides
- The future to come
- There is no doubt but
- We are in receipt of

Phrases and Words to Omit

The following is a list of words that are usually not necessary in a sentence. They don't add anything and can be omitted without changing the meaning.

- Really
- Very
- Quite
- Extremely
- Severely
- All things considered
- As a matter of fact
- As far as I'm concerned
- At the present time
- Because of the fact that
- By means of
- By virtue of the fact
- Due to the fact
- For all intents and purposes
- For the most part

- For the purpose of
- Have a tendency to
- In a manner of speaking
- In a very real sense
- In my opinion
- In the case of
- In the final analysis
- In the event that
- In the nature of
- In the process of
- It seems that
- The point I am trying to make
- Type of
- What I mean to say is

Clichés

Clichés are overused expressions that have become trite and even annoying. The following is a list of clichés that should be avoided:

- Acid test
- At loose ends
- Babe in the woods
- Better late than never
- Brought back to reality
- Black as night
- Blind as a bat
- Bolt from the blue

- Busy as a bee (or beaver)
- Cat's meow
- Cool as a cucumber
- Cool, calm, and collected
- Crack of dawn
- Crushing blow
- Cry over split milk
- Dead as a doornail

- Dog-eat-dog world
- Don't count your chickens
- Dyed in the wool
- Easier said than done
- Easy as pie
- Feathered friends
- Face the music
- Flash in the pan
- Flat as a pancake
- Gentle as a lamb
- Go at it tooth and nail
- Good time was had by all
- Greased lightning
- Happy as a lark
- Head over heels
- Heavy as lead
- Horns of a dilemma
- Hour of need
- Keep a stiff upper lip
- Ladder of success
- Last but not least
- Looking a gift horse in the mouth
- Meaningful dialogue
- Moving experience
- Needle in a haystack
- Open-and-shut case
- Pain in the neck
- Point with pride
- Pretty as a picture
- Put it in a nutshell

- Quick as a flash (or wink)
- Rat race
- Ripe old age
- Ruled the roost
- Sad but true
- Sadder but wiser
- Set the world on fire
- Sick as a dog
- Sigh of relief
- Slow as molasses
- Smart as a whip
- Sneaking suspicion
- Spread like wildfire
- Straight as an arrow
- Straw that broke the camel's back
- Strong as an ox
- Take the bull by the horns
- Thin as a rail
- Through thick and thin
- Tired but happy
- To coin a phrase
- To make a long story short
- Trial and error
- Tried and true
- Under the weather
- White as a sheet
- Wise as an owl
- Work like a dog
- Worth its weight in gold

✦ Unbiased Language

Most gender problems can be avoided without the use of *he/she, he or she, him or her,* or *him/her* constructions. Plural pronouns such as *they* can be very helpful in this regard. An occasional he or she is okay, but after a while it becomes distracting. When a singular pronoun is necessary, use either he or she consistently to avoid confusion.

Sexist Language

There are a variety of words and phrases that make demeaning assumptions about gender role. However, in some cases people go out of their way to be politically correct and try awkward alternatives. Substitutes should be reasonable and appropriate. Try not to highlight the fact you are trying to avoid sexist language.

The following is a list of words to avoid and their alternatives:

- Actress—(actor)
- Anchorman—(anchor)
- Businessman—(businessperson)
- Chairman—(chairperson or chair)
- Coed—(student)
- Forefathers—(ancestors)
- Foreman—(supervisor)
- Freshman—(first-year student)
- Mailman—(mail carrier)
- Male nurse—(nurse)
- Man (meaning human being)—(person, people)
- Managers and their wives—(managers and their spouses)
- Mankind—(humanity, people)
- Poetess—(poet)
- Policeman—(police officer)
- Salesman—(sales representative)
- Stewardess—(flight attendant)
- Waiter/Waitress—(server)

Common English Usage Problems

✴ Language: Key to Your Success

Give careful attention to your use of the English language. The ability to write and speak correctly is so important to a business career that you'll find the following to be almost always true: As you improve your speech, you will also naturally improve your business success.

Words, phrases, and sentences that are outworn should not be used in a business letter. Stock phrases, like slang, give the impression that the writer has not thought the idea through and has not chosen the best language for expressing those ideas. It's necessary first to understand thoroughly what you want to say and then to say it forcefully with words as natural to you as those of a conversation. This will help you accomplish the purpose of communication.

To help yourself write naturally, consider how you would respond to a luncheon invitation from an acquaintance. Would you say, "In accordance with your request that I have lunch with you, I beg to advise that I shall be happy to do so"? No. You would be more likely to say, "Thanks. I'll be glad to have lunch with you."

✴ Verbose Expressions

You should be alert to everything you write. Beware of words that do not mean exactly what you want to say. Also beware of phrases that are careless, vague, or wordy. Table 30-1 gives examples of such pitfalls. After studying this list, protect yourself from similar mistakes. As a famous company once said in its ads, "The audience is listening!"

✴ Correct Usage

In addition to being verbose, many letter writers frequently misuse parts of speech. The following examples are given to alert you to these. Some of the examples are grammatically correct for colloquial use but not for formal speech and writing—which is the only kind you should use in business.

TABLE 30-1 Verbose Expressions	
Verbose Expressions	**What You Really Mean**
I beg to be advised	Please tell me
Thank you kindly	Thank you
I feel that you are able to appreciate	You can appreciate
Which you will remember is in connection with	Regarding
I am not at present in a position to	I am unable to
I would, therefore, ask that you kindly write	Please write
We would appreciate it if you would investigate the matter and inform us and report	Please check the matter
You have my permission to	You may
I am in receipt of the a complaint from John Smith	John Smith complains
You have not, I believe, favored us with a reply	You have not replied
I acknowledge receipt of your letter	I received your letter

Affect, Effect

Affect is most commonly used as a verb, meaning "to influence." It is used as a noun only as a psychological term, meaning "feeling or emotion." *Effect* is a verb meaning "to bring about." It is also used as a noun, meaning "a result or consequence, or a mental impression."

WRONG: The light effects my vision.

RIGHT: The light affects my vision.

WRONG: Can you affect a change in the operation?

RIGHT: Can you effect a change in the operation?

Already, All Ready

Already denotes time; *all ready* denotes preparation.

RIGHT: She had already arrived.

RIGHT: We are all ready to leave.

All Right

Always spell *all right* as two words, never one.

WRONG: It will be alright if you wish to go.

RIGHT: It will be all right if you wish to go.

Altogether, All Together

Altogether means "quite" or "in all." All *together* means "in one place."

RIGHT: She is altogether pleasant.

RIGHT: His bills came to fifty-seven dollars altogether.

RIGHT: The books were all together on one shelf.

Any, Either

Any refers to one of several. *Either* refers to one of two.

> RIGHT: **You may have any of the six books.**

> RIGHT: **Either of those two cars will be acceptable.**

Awful, Awfully

Never use as a synonym for *very*.

> WRONG: She performed an awful hard task.

> RIGHT: **She performed a very difficult task.**

> WRONG: Bill is awfully smart.

> RIGHT: **Bill is unusually smart.**

A While, Awhile

Awhile is an adverb and should never be used as the object of a preposition (which can only be a noun or pronoun).

> WRONG: Please come to my home for awhile before you start your journey.

> RIGHT: **Please come to my home for a while before you start your journey.**

> RIGHT: **Relax awhile before you begin the task.**

Badly

Badly is an adverb, but it is often mistakenly used as an adjective.

> RIGHT: **He wanted badly to go with them.**

> WRONG: She felt badly after her operation.

> RIGHT: **She did not feel well after her operation.**

Because

Because is not to be used in place of *that*.

> WRONG: The reason he did not attend the party is because he was in Chicago.

> RIGHT: **The reason he did not attend the party is that he was in Chicago.**

> RIGHT: **He did not attend the party because he was in Chicago.**

Between, Among

Between is used to differentiate two, and only two, objects. *Among* is used to differentiate more than two.

> RIGHT: **The dog was sitting between John and me.**

> RIGHT: **There were three good books among the many he gave me.**

Both, Alike

It's illogical to use the combination *both alike* since two items can't be alike if one is not.

WRONG: The cars are both alike.

RIGHT: **The two cars are alike. They are both of the latest model.**

Both, Each

Both is used to describe a condition that applies to two entities. *Each* is used to describe a single entity.

WRONG: There is a picture on both sides of the mantel.

RIGHT: **There is a picture on each side of the mantel.**

Bring, Take

Bring is used to denote movement toward someone or something, while *take* is used to denote movement from someone or something.

RIGHT: **Bring me the book.**

RIGHT: **Take the book from Jim.**

Bushel

Add an *s* when referring to more than one bushel.

WRONG: Eight bushel of oats.

RIGHT: **Eight bushels of oats.**

Business

Don't use *business* when you really mean *right*.

WRONG: What business is it of theirs to question my action?

RIGHT: **What right have they to question my action?**

Came By

Came by is a colloquial phrase.

WRONG: He came by to see me.

RIGHT: **He came to see me.**

Can't Seem

Seem is a verb that means look or appear. Using *can't* with seem is awkward.

WRONG: I can't seem to make the journey in an hour.

RIGHT: **It seems impossible for me to make the journey in one hour.**

Combination

Don't confuse *combine*—normally a verb unless referring to farm equipment—with *combination,* which is a noun referring to a group of entities.

WRONG: That combine will be a large one.

RIGHT: **That combination will be a large one.**

Cooperate

Cooperate is a verb that means to work together. Therefore, *cooperate together* is redundant.

> WRONG: If they cooperate together, their purpose will be accomplished.
>
> **RIGHT: If they cooperate, their purpose will be accomplished.**

Council, Counsel, Consul

A *council* is a group of persons convened for advisory purposes. *Counsel* is advice; the word sometimes means "attorney." A *consul* is an official appointed by a government to report on matters that the official observes while residing in a foreign land.

Credible, Credulous

Credible means "believable" or "worthy of being believed." *Credulous* means "inclined to believe too readily."

> **RIGHT: He related the incident in a credible manner.**
>
> **RIGHT: She is too credulous for her own good.**

Data

Data is always plural. *Datum* is the singular form.

> WRONG: This data proves that our business is growing.
>
> **RIGHT: These data prove that our business is growing.**

Deal

Deal should not be used informally to refer to a business agreement.

> WRONG: She made a deal to buy the house.
>
> **RIGHT: She made an agreement to buy the house.**

Different From, Different Than

Different from takes an object; *different than* is used to introduce a clause.

> WRONG: That coat is different than mine.
>
> **RIGHT: That coat is different from mine.**
>
> **RIGHT: He was different than I remembered.**

Don't, Doesn't

Don't means do not; *doesn't* means does not.

> WRONG: He don't care to go with us.
>
> **RIGHT: He doesn't care to go with us.**

Each, Their

Pronouns must agree in number and person with the words to which they refer.

> WRONG: Each drives their own car.
>
> **RIGHT: Each drives his own car.**
>
> **RIGHT: Each of the women listed her needs.** (The singular pronoun *each* is the subject.)

Either, Neither

Either and *neither* refer to two.

> WRONG: Neither of the four books suited him.
>
> **RIGHT: None of the four books suited him.**
>
> WRONG: Either of the three books is the one I want.
>
> **RIGHT: Either of the two books will do.**
>
> **RIGHT: Any of the three books will suit me.**

Enthuse, Enthusiastic

Enthuse is used only as a colloquialism. For the formal language needed for business writing, use *to be enthusiastic*.

> WRONG: He was enthused over winning the award.
>
> **RIGHT: He was enthusiastic about winning the award.**

Except, Unless

Except is a preposition used to introduce a prepositional phrase. *Unless* is an adverbial conjunction used to introduce a subordinate clause. They are not interchangeable. *Except* may be used as a conjunction only when it's followed by the word *that;* however, that construction, although correct, is often awkward, and *unless* is preferable.

> WRONG: The horse cannot be entered in the race except the judges permit.
>
> **RIGHT: The horse cannot be entered in the race unless the judges permit.**

Expect

Don't use *expect* to mean *think* or *suppose*.

> WRONG: I expect she was well received.
>
> **RIGHT: I suppose she was well received.**
>
> **RIGHT: I expect you to be there at 8 a.m.**

Farther, Further

Farther shows a specific, quantifiable distance. *Further* shows degree or extent.

> WRONG: I walked farther than he did.
>
> **RIGHT: He will go further with your help than without it.**

Fix

Fix means to repair. Don't use it to mean a bad situation.

> WRONG: She is in a desperate fix.
>
> **RIGHT: She is desperate because of her present situation.**

Foot, Feet

Foot is singular, *feet* is plural.

WRONG: The room is twelve foot long.

RIGHT: The room is twelve feet long.

Got

Don't use *got* when you could use *have, has, or must.*

WRONG: I have got a new car.

RIGHT: I have a new car.

RIGHT: He has a new job.

WRONG: I've got to stop at his house. (colloquial)

RIGHT: I must stop at his house OR I have to stop at his house.

Gotten

This is an obsolete term. Do not use; replace with *got.*

Guess

Don't use *guess* when you really mean *think.*

WRONG: I guess you are right.

RIGHT: I think you are right.

RIGHT: In the word game, Marcus was the first to guess correctly.

Inaugurate

Don't use *inaugurate* in place of *started or began.*

WRONG: The program was inaugurated on August 1.

RIGHT: The program was begun on August 1.

RIGHT: The President of the United States was inaugurated on January 4.

Inside Of, Within

In speaking of time, don't use *inside of* where you could use *within.*

WRONG: He will visit us inside of a week.

RIGHT: He will visit us within a week.

Invite

Don't confuse *invite* (a verb) with *invitation* (a noun).

WRONG: I have an invite to the party.

RIGHT: I have an invitation to the party.

Its, It's

Its (without an apostrophe) is a possessive pronoun. *It's* (with an apostrophe) is a contraction meaning "it is."

RIGHT: It's getting dark. (meaning "It is getting dark.")

RIGHT: The ship was flying its flag at half-mast.

Kind

Kind is singular; *kinds* is plural.

> WRONG: She asked for those kind of flowers.
>
> **RIGHT: She asked for those kinds of flowers.**
>
> **RIGHT: She asked for that kind of flower.**

Kind Of, Sort Of

Kind of and *sort of* are unclear. Be definite when speaking or writing.

> WRONG: He appeared to be kind of ill.
>
> **RIGHT: He appeared to be rather ill.**
>
> WRONG: She was sort of ill at ease.
>
> **RIGHT: She was somewhat ill at ease.**

Learn, Teach

Before you can *learn,* someone must first *teach* you.

> WRONG: She learned me how to type.
>
> **RIGHT: She taught me how to type.**
>
> **RIGHT: If I teach him correctly, he will learn quickly.**

Less, Fewer

Less refers to a smaller amount, degree, or value. *Fewer* refers to a quantifiable number.

> **RIGHT: This mine contains less gold than the Jackass Mine.**
>
> **RIGHT: This city has fewer people today than it had a year ago.**

Let, Leave

Let means "to permit." *Leave* means "to depart," to "bequeath," or "to allow, to remain."

> **RIGHT: Leave her alone.**
>
> **RIGHT: Let her go with us.**

Liable, Likely

Liable should be used when referring to legal responsibility.

> **RIGHT: The landlord is liable for damages.**
>
> **RIGHT: That horse is likely to win the race.**

Lie, Lay

Many people confuse the two because the word *lay* is both the present tense of *lay (lay, lay, laid)* and the past tense of *lie (lie, lay, lain)*. *Lie* means "to remain in position" or "to rest." It is intransitive, meaning no object ever accompanies it. *Lay* means "to place something somewhere." It is transitive, meaning an object always accompanies it.

> WRONG: He lays down after lunch every day.
>
> **RIGHT: He lies down after lunch every day.**

RIGHT: **Yesterday he lay on the couch for two hours.**

RIGHT: **Will you please lay the book on the table?**

RIGHT: **The pen lay on the desk all day.**

Like, As

Like is a preposition always followed by a noun or pronoun in the objective case. *As* is an adverbial conjunction used to introduce a subordinate clause.

WRONG: It appears like he isn't coming.

RIGHT: **It appears as if he isn't coming.**

RIGHT: **Though he was such a little boy, he marched like a major.**

Line

Line should not be used in place *of business.*

WRONG: He is in the jewelry line.

RIGHT: **He is in the jewelry business.**

Loan

A *loan* should be used as a noun to refer to an agreement to borrow. To allow someone to borrow is *to lend.*

WRONG: Loan me your pen.

RIGHT: **Lend me your pen.**

RIGHT: **He went to the bank to receive a loan.**

Lost

Don't use extra words—like *out*—that are not necessary for meaning.

WRONG: He lost out.

RIGHT: **He lost.**

Lots

Don't use *lots* when referring to an amount of something.

WRONG: She receives lots of fan mail.

RIGHT: **She receives a great deal of fan mail.**

Mad, Angry

Use *angry* rather than *mad.* Remember, dogs go mad, people get angry

WRONG: Mary was mad at Jane.

RIGHT: **Mary was angry with Jane.**

May, Can

May refers to permission. *Can* refers to ability.

WRONG: Can I help you?

RIGHT: **May I help you?**

RIGHT: **Can he drive a car?**

Might Of, Would Of, Could Of

This construction is the result of poor pronunciation. The correct phrases are *might have, would have, and could have.*

WRONG: If you could of arranged it, I would of gone.

RIGHT: **If you could have arranged it, I would have gone.**

Most, Almost

Most of all is a colloquial expression. Use *most of* or *almost* instead.

WRONG: We walked most of all the way.

RIGHT: **We walked most of the way.**

RIGHT: **We walked almost all the way.**

Never

Never means never; it does not refer to a limited period of time.

WRONG: We never saw your dog since yesterday.

RIGHT: **We have not seen your dog since yesterday.**

RIGHT: **We never saw your dog. What breed was he?**

Off

Off is always used alone and not with *of.*

WRONG: The ribbon was taken off of the package.

RIGHT: **The ribbon was taken off the package.**

Only

Be careful of where you place this adverb; position determines which word you modify.

RIGHT: **I could only get him to play one piece.** (modifying *get*)

RIGHT: **I could get him to play only one piece.** (modifying *one*)

Open

Open should be used without up.

WRONG: We open up the doors promptly at noon.

RIGHT: **We open the doors promptly at noon.**

Party

Party can be used to refer to a person in legal documents, but it is too formal for common use. A party can also be a celebration.

WRONG: The party I called was disturbed.

RIGHT: **The person I called was disturbed.**

RIGHT: **(In legal documents): The party of the second part hereby agrees . . .**

RIGHT: **He celebrated his birthday with a party.**

People

People refers to a large group of individuals. When referring to people of a particular organization or place, it's better to use *people* before the name.

WRONG: The General Motors people.

RIGHT: The people of General Motors; the people of Massachusetts.

Percent

This is one word following an amount, never *per cent*.

RIGHT: Six percent interest was charged.

Percentage

Use when no amount is given.

RIGHT: What percentage of interest was charged?

Posted, Informed

Don't use *posted* in place of *informed*.

WRONG: You are well posted on the subject.

RIGHT: You are well informed about Australia.

Raise, Rise

Raise is a transitive verb and must always take an object. *Rise is* transitive verb and never takes an object.

RIGHT: They raise the question at every meeting.

RIGHT: I rise to make a motion.

Real

Don't use *real* when you really mean *very*.

WRONG: He is real handsome.

RIGHT: He is very handsome.

Run

When referring to a business or organization, don't use *run* in place of *manage*.

WRONG: He runs the bakery.

RIGHT: He manages the bakery.

Same

Don't use *same* to refer to the subject of a sentence.

WRONG: Your letter arrived, and I acknowledge same with thanks.

RIGHT: Your letter arrived, and I acknowledge it with thanks.

Shape (meaning tangible form)

Don't use *shape* to refer to the status of something.

WRONG: The transaction was completed in good shape.

RIGHT: The transaction was completed to everyone's satisfaction.

Shall, Will

Use *shall* to express a simple expected action with the first person. Use *will* with second and third persons. However, to express determination or command, reverse the order; use *will* for the first person and *shall* for the second and third.

> RIGHT: **I shall go tomorrow.**

> RIGHT: **He will go, too.**

> RIGHT: **You will be at school by the time we arrive.**

> RIGHT: **I will go tomorrow, and no one can stop me.**

> RIGHT: **He shall go with me even if I must force him.**

> RIGHT: **You shall never do that again.**

Should, Would

Using *should* instead of *shall* and *will* expresses an expected action but implies a doubt that the action will take place. *Should* may also be used to show obligation. *Would* may be used to show habit or determination.

> RIGHT: **A child should love his parents.**

> RIGHT: **If I had enough money, I would buy a car.**

Sit, Set

Sit is an intransitive verb. *Set* is a transitive verb.

> RIGHT: **She sits near her husband at every meeting.**

> RIGHT: **He sets the plates on the table in an orderly manner.**

So

Avoid overuse of this adverbial conjunction. *Consequently, therefore,* and *inasmuch as* are good substitutes when you want to vary the style.

> AVOID: It had snowed over a foot that day; so we drove the jeep into town.

> RIGHT: **It had snowed over a foot that day; consequently we drove the jeep into town.**

Sometime, Some Time

Sometime means at some indefinite time. *Some time* means an amount of time.

> WRONG: I will go sometime this morning.

> RIGHT: **If I have some time this morning, I shall do the job for you.**

To, At

Do not use either with *where*.

> WRONG: Where are you at?

> RIGHT: **Where are you?**

WRONG: Where did he go to?

RIGHT: **Where did he go?**

Try And, Come And, Be Sure And

Don't use a word if it is not necessary to convey your meaning.

WRONG: Try and be here at noon.

RIGHT: **Try to be here at noon.**

WRONG: Come and see me tomorrow.

RIGHT: **Come to see me tomorrow.**

WRONG: Be sure and watch out as you cross the street.

RIGHT: **Be sure to watch out as you cross the street.**

Wait On

When *wait* refers to time, *on* is not needed. When it refers to the actions of a waiter or waitress, *wait on* is acceptable.

WRONG: Please do not wait on me if I am not at the station when you arrive.

RIGHT: **Please do not wait for me if I am not there when you arrive.**

RIGHT: **The headwaiter assigned the red-haired woman to wait on me.**

Where

Whether used as an adverb or a conjunction, *where* denotes position or place. It should never be used as a substitute for *that* when introducing a clause.

WRONG: Did you read in the paper where our mayor was honored at a banquet?

RIGHT: **Did you read in the paper that our mayor was honored at a banquet?**

Which

When used to introduce a clause, *which* must refer to a specific noun or pronoun and not to a whole situation.

WRONG: He did not arrive in time for the meeting, which caused the president embarrassment.

RIGHT: **His failure to arrive in time for the meeting caused the president embarrassment.**

RIGHT: **His failure to arrive, which caused the president embarrassment, was the reason for his dismissal.**

Who, Which, That

Who is used to refer to people. *Which* and *that* refer to objects.

RIGHT: **She is the woman who smiled at him.**

RIGHT: **She is the kind of person whom everyone likes.**

RIGHT: **I read the book, which I found fascinating.**

✦ Problem Pronouns

I, We, He, She, They

Pronouns in the nominative (also called subjective) case—*I, we, he, she, they*—serve as subjects of verbs but never objects of verbs or prepositions. You can often tell that the wrong case is being used because the sentence sounds odd. However, when compound subjects or compound objects are used, it may be difficult to hear the correct case.

To **TEST** such an instance, drop the other subject or object and repeat the sentence with only the pronoun in question.

I—nominative case, never an object

WRONG: This is just between you and I.

RIGHT: **This is just between you and me.**

WRONG: He asked that the money be given to you and I.

TEST: He asked that the money be given to I.

RIGHT: **He asked that the money be given to you and me.**

TEST: He asked that the money be given to me.

She, He—nominative case, never an object

WRONG: If you stay there, the ball will hit you and she.

TEST: If you stay there, the ball will hit she.

RIGHT: **If you stay there, the ball will hit you and her.**

TEST: If you stay there, the ball will hit her.

They—nominative case, never an object

WRONG: I will give the money to you and they.

TEST: I will give the money to they.

RIGHT: **I will give the money to you and them.**

TEST: I will give the money to them.

WRONG: You and them are welcome to come.

TEST: Them are welcome to come.

RIGHT: **You and they are welcome to come.**

TEST: They are welcome to come.

We—nominative case, never an object

WRONG: Us boys are ready to play the game.

TEST: Us are ready to play the game.

RIGHT: **We boys are ready to play the game.**

TEST: We are ready to play the game.

Me, Us, Her, Him, Them

Similarly, pronouns in the objective case—*me, us, her, him, them*—are always used as objects of either verbs or prepositions and never as subjects. With a compound subject, use the same way of testing as above, changing the number of the verb as needed.

Me, Us—objective case, never a subject

WRONG: Jim and me went to the movies.

TEST: Me went to the movies.

RIGHT: Jim and I went to the movies.

TEST: I went to the movies.

RIGHT: Jim went to the movies with me.

WRONG: Julie and us sat on the top bleacher.

TEST: Us sat on the top bleacher.

RIGHT: We and Julie sat on the top bleacher.

TEST: We sat on the top bleacher.

RIGHT: Julie sat on the top bleacher with us.

Her, Him, Them

Her, him, and *them* are in the objective case. *She, he,* and *they* are the subjective case.

WRONG: Tommy and her [him, them] argued every day.

TEST: Her [him, them] argued every day.

RIGHT: Tommy and she [he, they] argued every day.

My, your, her, his, and *their* are used to convey possession.

⭐ Dangling Participles

A dangling participle is a participle or participial phrase which modifies the wrong noun or pronoun. Since position determines the referent, how you construct the sentence determines the meaning.

WRONG: Walking down Main Street, the art museum is visible. (This implies the art museum is walking down Main Street.)

RIGHT: Walking down Main Street, you can see the art museum.

Spelling

With easy access to spelling checkers in word processing programs, is there really a need for an administrative assistant to be concerned with spelling? For some people, running spell check on their word processing document takes the place of a good proofread. Computerized spelling checkers are indeed useful to any writer. However, there are many words that may appear to be correctly spelled according to the word processor's spelling checker, when in reality they are incorrectly spelled for the particular context, or the wrong word has been used entirely. For example, a spelling checker cannot tell the usage differences between there, their, and they're.

Thus, there is a need for basic spelling skills. This chapter focuses on the most common spelling rules that any good administrative assistant should know.

 Dictionary Uses

The constant study of spelling and the exact meaning of words is an important aspect of every administrative assistant's career. Always keep a dictionary close at hand. Besides providing spelling and definitions, this invaluable aid also sets out such information as the following:

- Syllabication (useful when you want to split a word at the end of a typewritten line)
- Variant spellings, with the preferred spelling listed first
- Pronunciations, with the preferred form shown first
- Capitalization
- Hyphenation
- Italicization
- Part of speech
- Plural of nouns
- Cases of pronouns

- Verb tenses
- Comparative and superlative forms of irregular adverbs and adjectives
- Derivations of the word
- Synonyms and antonyms
- Status label (if a word is colloquial, obsolete, etc.)

Some words whose spelling frequently puzzles many of us are discussed in this chapter in order to sharpen your awareness of spelling in general.

Plurals

1. The general rule is to form the plural of a noun by adding *s*:
   - book—books
   - clock—clocks
   - pen—pens

2. A noun ending in *o* preceded by a vowel takes an *s* for the plural:
   - curio—curios
   - folio—folios
   - radio—radios
   - ratio—ratios
   - studio—studios

Some nouns ending in *o*, preceded by a consonant, take *es* to form the plural, while others take *s:*
   - banjo—banjos
   - buffalo—buffaloes
   - cargo—cargoes
   - Eskimo—Eskimos
   - hero—heroes
   - mosquito—mosquitoes
   - motto—mottoes
   - piano—pianos
   - potato—potatoes
   - soprano—sopranos
   - tomato—tomatoes

3. A singular noun ending in *ch, sh, s, x,* or *z* takes *es* for the plural:
   - bush—bushes
   - chintz—chintzes
   - dress—dresses
   - inch—inches
   - wax—waxes

4. A noun ending in *y* preceded by a consonant changes the *y* to *i* and adds *es* for the plural:
   - ability—abilities
   - auxiliary—auxiliaries
   - discrepancy—discrepancies
   - facility—facilities
   - industry—industries
   - lady—ladies
   - society—societies

31 ■ SPELLING

5. A noun ending in *y* preceded by a vowel takes only an *s* for the plural:

- attorney—attorneys
- monkey—monkeys
- galley—galleys
- turkey—turkeys
- kidney—kidneys

6. Some plurals end in *en:*

- child—children
- man—men
- ox—oxen

7. Some nouns ending in *f* or *fe* change the *f* or *fe* to *v* and add *es* for the plural:

- calf—calves
- life—lives
- knife—knives
- loaf—loaves
- leaf—leaves
- shelf—shelves

But there are some exceptions:

- bailiff—bailiffs
- gulf—gulfs
- belief—beliefs
- roof—roofs
- chief—chiefs

8. Some nouns require a vowel change for the plural:

- foot—feet
- mouse—mice
- goose—geese
- tooth—teeth

9. The plural of numerals, signs, and letters is shown by adding an *s* (or an apostrophe and an *s* to avoid confusion):

- COD—CODs
- one B—four B's

10. To proper names ending in *s* or in an *s* sound, add *es* for the plural:

- Brooks—the Brookses
- Burns—the Burnses
- Jones—the Joneses

11. A compound noun, when hyphenated or when consisting of two separate words, shows the plural form in the most important element:

- attorney-in-fact—attorneys-in-fact
- brigadier general—brigadier generals
- brother-in-law—brothers-in-law
- notary public—notaries public
- passerby—passersby

12. The plural of solid compounds (a compound noun written as one word) is formed at the end of the solid compound:

    - bookshelf—bookshelves
    - stepchild—stepchildren
    - cupful—cupfuls
    - stepdaughter—stepdaughters
    - lumberman—lumbermen

13. Some nouns have the same form for singular and plural:

    - Chinese
    - sheep
    - corps
    - vermin
    - deer
    - wheat
    - salmon

14. Some nouns are always treated as singular:

    - civics
    - molasses
    - mathematics
    - music
    - measles
    - milk
    - news
    - statistics

15. Some nouns are always treated as plural:

    - pants
    - scissors
    - proceeds
    - thanks
    - remains
    - trousers
    - riches
    - tweezers

✴ The Suffix

1. Words whose roots end with *ge* or *ce* generally retain the *e* when a suffix is added:

   - change—changeable
   - damage—damageable
   - disadvantage—disadvantageous
   - outrage—outrageous

2. A final silent *e* is usually dropped before a suffix that begins with a vowel:

   - argue—arguing
   - change—changing
   - conceive—conceivable

3. A final silent *e is* usually retained before a suffix that begins with a consonant:

   - achieve—achievement
   - definite—definitely

4. In words ending in *c*, add *k* before a suffix beginning with *e, i,* or *y,* so that the hard sound of the original *c* is retained:

- frolic—frolicked—frolicking
- mimic—mimicked—mimicking
- picnic—picnicked—picnicking

5. A word ending in *ie* changes the *ie* to *y* when adding a suffix:

- die—dying
- tie—tying
- lie—lying
- vie—vying

6. Words that end in y preceded by a vowel retain the y when adding the suffix:

- survey—surveying—surveyor

7. Words that end with *y* preceded by a consonant change *y* to *i* when adding a suffix, except when the suffix is *ing:*

- embody—embodying—embodied
- rely—relying—relied
- satisfy—satisfying—satisfied

8. A final consonant is usually doubled when it is preceded by a single vowel and takes a suffix:

- mop—mopping

9. A final consonant is doubled when it is followed by a suffix, and the last syllable is accented when the suffix is added:

- acquit—acquitted

10. The final consonant is not doubled when the accent is shifted to a preceding syllable when the suffix is added:

- refer—referring—reference

or when the final consonant is preceded by two vowels:

- fooled—fooling

Irregular Spelling

1. Irregular spellings to watch closely:

- acknowledgment
- ninth
- awful
- truly
- judgment
- wholly

2. While they may sound the same, there are three ways to spell words ending in *ceed, cede,* and *sede:*

- exceed
- intercede
- precede
- proceed
- recede
- secede
- succeed
- supersede

MEMORIZE: The only English word that ends in *sede* is *supersede.* The only English words that end in *ceed* are *exceed, proceed,* and *succeed.*

3. Watch for *ant* and *ent* endings:

- relevant
- correspondent
- eminent

4. Watch for *ance* and *ence* endings:

- occurrence
- perseverance

5. Watch for *able* and *ible* endings:

- deductible
- accessible
- compatible
- comfortable
- affordable

6. Don't omit silent letters:

- silhouette
- hemorrhage
- acquisition
- diaphragm
- abscess

7. Don't be confused over double consonants:

- accommodate
- commitment
- necessary
- occurrence

8. Some words are not spelled the way they are pronounced:

- asterisk
- separate
- auxiliary
- boundary
- prerogative

Capitalization

Proper nouns that denote the names of specific persons or places are capitalized, though names that are common to a group are not. Following are examples of words that are capitalized:

Acts of Congress

- Civil Rights Act
- Taft-Hartley Act
- Child Labor Amendment
- Eighteenth Amendment

Associations

- Society of Professional Engineers
- American Business Association
- Young Women's Christian Association
- American Heart Association

Book Titles and Their Subdivisions

- *The American Way,* Chapter VI
- *Remembrance of Things Past,* Volume 11
- *Bulletins and Periodical Titles*
- *New York Retail Bulletin, Wall Street Journal*

Cars of Railroads and Automobile Models

- Car 54, Train 93
- Plymouth
- Cadillac

Churches and Church Dignitaries

- Fifth Avenue Presbyterian Church
- the Archbishop of New York
- Bishop John Barnes

Cities

- Jefferson City, Missouri
- Los Angeles
- BUT—the city of Los Angeles

Clubs

- Possum Kingdom Club
- The Do-Gooders
- The Union League Club
- BUT—many Republican clubs in the West

Codes
- the Code of Building Maintenance
- BUT—the building code
- Code VI

Compass Points Designating a Specific Region
- the Northeast (*section of the country*), the Pacific Northwest
- BUT—just drive north
- the West
- BUT—west of town

Constitutions
- the Constitution of Texas
- the Constitution of the United States
- BUT—the constitution of any nation

Corporations
- American Brake Corporation
- Container Corporation of America
- BUT—The corporation was dissolved.

Courts
- the Criminal Court of Appeals
- BUT—a court of appeals
- the Supreme Court
- the Magistrate's Court
- BUT—a county court

Decorations
- Purple Heart
- Good Conduct Medal
- Croix de Guerre
- BUT—Soldiers are given decorations to signal their acts of heroism.

Degrees (academic)
- B.A.
- M.D.
- D.D.
- Ph.D.

Districts
- First Congressional District
- BUT—a congressional district

Educational Courses

- English 101
- Spanish Grammar
- Mathematics Made Easy
- BUT—He is studying physics and chemistry.

Epithets

- First Lady of the State
- Alexander the Great

Fleets

- the Third Fleet
- BUT—The ship was part of the fleet.

Foundations

- Carnegie Foundation
- Ford Foundation
- BUT—He established a foundation.

Geographic Divisions

- Lone Star State
- Sooner State
- BUT—There are fifty states in our country.
- Northern Hemisphere
- South Pole
- Old World, Near East

Government Divisions

- Federal Reserve Board
- the Boston Fire Department
- BUT—The department was headed by Mr. Charles Bleeker.

Historical Terms

- Dark Ages
- Renaissance
- Christian Era
- World War II
- Battle of the Bulge
- Declaration of Independence
- Magna Carta

Holidays

- Thanksgiving Day
- Passover
- Easter Sunday
- New Year's Eve

Libraries
- Carnegie Library
- Albany Public Library
- BUT—The library is a source of information.

Localities
- Western Europe
- East Africa
- Wheat Belt
- West Side
- Mississippi Delta

Military Services
- United States Navy
- Signal Corps
- Second Battalion
- Company B
- Squadron 28

Nobility and Royalty
- Queen of Belgium
- BUT—Many queens were honored here.
- Duke of Windsor
- BUT—She was proud to have met a duke.

Oceans and Continents
- Pacific Ocean
- BUT—He was glad to be crossing the ocean.

Parks, Peoples, and Tribes
- Greenleaf Park
- Lake Texoma State Park
- Yellowstone National Park
- BUT—The park was in a southern state.
- Jews
- Christians
- Malay
- Chickasaw

Personification
- He was recognized by the Chair and spoke briefly.
- He sang about Summer in all its glory.
- BUT—In summer the days are longer.

Planets and Other Heavenly Bodies
- Mars
- Venus
- Big Dipper
- EXCEPTIONS: moon, sun, stars

Rivers

- Mississippi River
- Wabash River
- BUT—The Mississippi and Wabash rivers were flooding after the torrential rains.

Sports Stadiums and Teams

- Dallas Cowboys
- Madison Square Garden
- Super Bowl
- Dodgers

Confusing Homonyms

Homonyms are words that are pronounced the same but have different meanings. For example, *brake* for *break,* or *there* for *their.* The following is a list of commonly confused homonyms:

- tick—tic
- piqued—peaked
- discrete—discreet
- born—bourn
- altar—alter
- caret—carrot
- yoke—yolk
- stationary—stationery
- advise—advice
- principal—principle
- cubicle—cubical
- rein—reign—rain
- dual—duel
- council—counsel
- vice—vise
- peace—piece
- tow—toe
- waved—waived
- compliment—complement
- role—roll
- ringer—wringer
- loath—loathe
- mettle—metal
- breach—breech
- deserts—desserts
- led—lead
- foreword—forward
- too—to—two

American English and British English Differences

There are differences between the way certain words are spelled in American English and the way they are spelled in British English. Table 31-1 lists words that have this peculiar treatment.

Compound Words and Hyphenation

Compound words are two or more words that are used to mean a single concept. Some compound words are written as two separate words with a space

TABLE 31-1	Words Spelled Differently in American English than British English
American English	**British English**
Humor	Humour
Honor	Honour
Endeavor	Endeavour
Center	Centre
Fiber	Fibre
Theater	Theatre
Analyze	Analyse
Paralyze	Paralyse
Burned	Burnt
Dreamed	Dreamt
Spoiled	Spoilt
Canceled	Cancelled
Worshiping	Worshipping
Acknowledgment	Acknowledgement
Aging	Ageing
Usable	Useable
Anesthetic	Anaesthetic
Fetus	Foetus
Maneuver	Manoeuvre
Encyclopedia	Encyclopaedia
Catalog	Catalogue
Dialog	Dialogue
Check	Cheque
Draft	Draught
Plow	Plough
Program	Programme

between them. These are called **open compounds.** Some compound words are combined into a single word, called **closed compounds.** Another variation is compound words that are separated by a hyphen. These are called **hyphenated compounds.**

Open Compounds

The following is a list of commonly used open compounds:

- drop in
- life cycle
- time frame
- stick up
- side effects
- half brother
- bed wetter
- under way
- more or less
- T square
- V neck
- ad hoc
- bona fide
- vice versa

Closed Compounds

The following is a list of commonly used closed compounds:

- backslide
- clearheaded
- deadpan
- handwrite
- lifeline
- longtime
- standstill
- twofold
- waterlogged
- stickhandle

- sidecar
- crossbreed
- coldcock
- layoffs
- makeup
- sendoff
- shortlist
- carryover
- ongoing

Hyphenated Compounds

The following is a list of commonly used hyphenated compounds:

- bed-wetting
- cold-shoulder
- cross-fertilize
- drop-kick
- time-out
- back-check
- dead-on
- off-color
- stand-in
- time-out
- self-esteem
- president-elect
- nuclear-free

- water-resistant
- anti-inflammatory
- non-native
- pre-engineered
- multi-item
- de-emphasize
- all-encompassing
- all-knowing
- ex-husband
- ex-employee
- co-worker
- self-doubts
- community-wide

Hyphenation With Numbers

You should include a hyphen when spelling out any two-word number or fraction:

- twenty-nine
- ninety-nine

When a fraction includes more than two numbers, you should only hyphenate the two-word number:

- twenty-nine
- one hundred seventy-five
- thirty-six

- two and three-quarters
- one twenty-fifth

✳ Negative Formations

Just as not all plurals are made by adding *s* to a word, not all negatives are made by adding *un* as a prefix. There are many other methods for creating negatives. The following is a list of common negative formation techniques.

A or An
A or *An* is often used before a vowel or words beginning with *h:*
- amoral
- asexual

Anti
Anti is added to a word to mean "the opposite of":
- antichrist
- antifreeze
- antimatter
- antibiotic

Counter
Counter is added to a word to mean "the opposite of or contrary to":
- counterculture
- counterclockwise

De
De is added to a word to mean "the reverse of":
- de-emphasize
- demagnetize
- decompose
- deforestation

Dis
Dis is added to a word to mean "the reverse of":
- disrespectful
- disarm
- discontented

Dys
Dys is added to a word to mean "abnormal or impaired":
- dysfunctional
- dyspeptic

Mal
Mal is added to mean "bad or incorrect":
- malformed
- malfunctioning

Mis
Mis is added to mean "bad or incorrect":
- misuse
- misinterpret
- misfortune

Non

Non is added to a word to reverse the meaning.

- nonexistent
- nonfattening
- nonintoxicating

Un, In, Il, Im, Ir

These are added to a word to reverse the meaning.

- undressed
- undrinkable
- incapable
- illegitimate
- imbalance
- implausible
- irrefutable
- irrevocable

Less

Less is added to the end of a word to mean "without":

- shoeless
- motionless
- helpless

Free

Free is added to a word to mean "without":

- caffeine-free
- sugar-free
- crime-free

✴ Commonly Misspelled Words

A

absence abundance accessible accidentally acclaim accommodate accomplish accordion accumulate achievement acquaintance acquire acquitted across address advertisement advice advise affect alleged amateur analysis analyze annual apartment apparatus apparent appearance arctic argument ascend atheist athletic attendance auxiliary

B

balloon barbecue bargain basically beggar beginning belief believe beneficial benefit biscuit boundaries business

C

calendar camouflage candidate Caribbean category cemetery challenge changeable changing characteristic chief choose chose cigarette climbed clothes clothing cloth collectible colonel column coming commission committee commitment comparative competent completely concede conceivable conceive condemn condescend conscience conscientious conscious consistent continuous controlled controversial controversy convenient correlate correspondence counselor courteous courtesy criticism criticize

D
deceive defendant deferred definitely definition dependent descend describe description desirable despair desperate develop dictionary difference dilemma dining disappearance disappoint disastrous discipline disease dispensable dissatisfied dominant drunkenness

E
easily ecstasy effect efficiency eighth either eligible eliminate embarrass emperor encouragement encouraging enemy entirely environment equipped equivalent especially exaggerate exceed excellence exhaust existence existent expense experience experiment explanation extremely exuberance

F
facsimile fallacious fallacy familiar fascinating feasible February fictitious fiery finally financially fluorescent forcibly foreign forfeit formerly foresee forty fourth fuelling fulfill fundamentally

G
gauge generally genius government governor grammar grievous guarantee guardian guerrilla guidance

H
handkerchief happily harass height heinous hemorrhage heroes hesitancy hindrance hoarse hoping humorous hygiene hypocrisy hypocrite

I
ideally idiosyncrasy ignorance imaginary immediately implement incidentally incredible independence independent indicted indispensable inevitable influential information inoculate insurance intelligence interference interrupt introduce irrelevant irresistible island

J
jealousy judicial

K
knowledge

L
laboratory laid later latter legitimate leisure length license lieutenant lightning likelihood likely loneliness loose lose losing lovely luxury

M

magazine maintain maintenance manageable maneuver manufacture marriage mathematics medicine millennium millionaire miniature minuscule minutes miscellaneous mischievous missile misspelled mortgage mosquito mosquitoes murmur muscle mysterious

N

narrative naturally necessary necessity neighbor neutron ninety ninth noticeable nowadays nuisance

O

obedience obstacle occasion occasionally occurred occurrence official omission omit omitted opinion opponent opportunity oppression optimism optimistic orchestra ordinarily origin outrageous overrun

P

pamphlets parallel particular pavilion peaceable peculiar penetrate perceive performance permanent permissible permitted perseverance persistence personal personnel perspiration physical physician piece pilgrimage pitiful planning pleasant portray possess possession possessive potato potatoes possibility possible practically prairie precede precedence preceding preference preferred prejudice preparation prescription prevalent primitive principal principle privilege probably procedure proceed profession professor prominent pronounce pronunciation propaganda psychology publicly pursue

Q

quantity quarantine questionnaire quizzes

R

realistically realize really recede receipt receive recognize recommend reference referring relevant relieving religious remembrance reminiscence repetition representative resemblance reservoir resistance restaurant rheumatism rhythm rhythmical ridiculous roommate

S

sacrilegious sacrifice safety salary satellite scary scenery schedule secede secretary seize sense sentence separate separation sergeant several severely shepherd shining siege similar simile simply simultaneous sincerely skiing sophomore souvenir specifically specimen sponsor spontaneous statistics stopped strategy strength strenuous stubbornness studying subordinate subtle succeed success succession sufficient supersede suppress surprise surround susceptible suspicious syllable symmetrical synonymous

T

tangible technical technique temperamental temperature tendency
themselves theories therefore thorough though through tomorrow
tournament towards tragedy transferring tries truly twelfth tyranny

U

unanimous undoubtedly unforgettable unique unnecessary until
useable usage usually utilization

V

vacuum valuable vengeance vigilant village villain violence visible
vision virtue volume

W

warrant warriors weather Wednesday weird wherever whether which
wholly withdrawal woman women worthwhile writing

Y

yacht yield young

Pronunciation

✸ Perfecting Your Speech

How you pronounce the words you choose to say can dramatically support—or undercut—the substance of what you're saying. Incorrect pronunciation or slurred enunciation reflects poorly on one's intelligence and ability. While this judgment may be unfair, it's reality: First impressions count. To make a favorable impression, try to perfect your speech.

Begin by carefully listening to the speech of others and comparing it with your own. What are the differences, especially between yourself and the people you most admire? Consult the dictionary when you hear differences to see whether you or the other person has made a mistake. This moment of truth will quickly improve your pronunciation and help you enlarge your vocabulary. It is one of the finest steps toward cultivation of improved speech patterns.

Following is a partial list of words often mispronounced; perhaps a vowel or a consonant sound is mispronounced, or a syllable is commonly dropped, added, or slurred. Sometimes letters that should be silent are sounded, or vice versa. Study the correct pronunciation carefully. You may be accustomed to pronouncing several of these words differently, but remember: Colloquial pronunciation is not preferable for business standards. Words followed by a double asterisk (**) denote that word is among the most mispronounced in the English language.

✸ Word List

abject (ab' jekt)
absolutely (ab' so lute lee)
abstemious (ab stee' mee us)
absurd (ab serd')
accede (ak seed')
accept (ak sept')
accession (ak sesh' un)
accessories (ak sess' o reez)

accidentally (ak si den' tal e)
acclimate (a kly' mut)**
address (a dress'; both noun and
    verb)**
admirable (ad' ma ra bl)**
adult (a dult'; NOT add' ult)
aerial (air' ree al)
ally (verb: al ly'—noun: al' ly)

applicable (ap' pli ka bl)**
architect (ar' ki tekt)
arctic (ark' tik)
area (air' ee a)
attacked (a takt')
attitude (at' i tyud)
attorney (a ter' nee)**
autopsy (aw' top see)**
avenue (av' a nyu)
aviation (ay vi ay' shun)
battery (bat' er e; NOT bat' tree)
being (pronounce the *g*)
beneficent (be neff' i sent)
bicycle (by' sik l)
biography (by og' ra fee)
breadth (bredth; pronounce the d)
casualty (cazh' ul tee)
champion (cham' pee un)
chastisement (chass tyze' ment)
chauffeur (show' ferr)**
chestnut (chess' nut)
chocolate (chock' o lut)
clique (klik)**
comment (com' ment)
compromise (com' pro myze)
concave (con cayv')
concentrate (con' sen trayt)
concierge (con se erzh')**
condolence (con doe' lens)
conversant (con ver' sunt)**
convex (con vex')
corps (kor)
creek (kreek; NOT krik)
cruel (kroo' el)
data (day' tah)**
deaf (def)
decade (deck' ayd)
decisive (dee sy' siv)
defect (de fekt)
deficit (def' i sit)
demonstrable (de mon' stra bl)
depot (dee' po)
depths (pronounce the *th*)
dessert (de zert')
detour (dee' toor)
diamond (dy' a mund)**
distribute (dis trib' yute)

divide (di vyd')
doing (doo' ing; pronounce the *g*)
drowned (drownd; one syllable,
    NOT drownded)
duly (dyu' lee)
duty (dyu' tee)
edition (eh dish' un)
educate (edd' yu kate)
elm (as written; NOT elum)
envelop (verb: en vell' up)
envelope (noun: en' va lowp)
epitome (ee pitt' o mee)
equitable (ek' wi ta bl)**
era (ihr' a)
err (urr; rhymes with fur)**
etiquette (ett' i kett)
every (ev' a ree)
exigency (eks' i jen see)
exponent (eks po' nent)
exquisite (eks' kwi zit)**
extant (eks' tent)
extraordinary (eks tror' di ner ee)
fact (pronounce the t)
family (fam' a lee)
fasten (fass' en)
favorite (fay' vo ritt)
figure (fig' yur)
film (as written; NOT fill um)
finance (verb: fi nans')**
finance (noun: fi' nans)
financial (fin nan' shul)
financier (fin nan seer')
forehead (for' id)
forte (for' tay)
formidable (for' mi da bl)**
fragmentary (frag' men ter ee)
friendship (frend' ship; pronounce
    the *d*)
genuine (jenn' yu inn)
gingham (ghing' um)
glisten (gliss' en)
gondola (gonn' do la)
government (guv' ern ment;
    pronounce both n's)
grievous (gree' vuss)
guardian (gar' dee un)
hasten (hayss' en)

height (hyt; does NOT end in *th*)

heinous (hay' nuss)**

herculean (herk yu lee' un)

heroism (her' o izm)

homeopathy (ho mee opp' a thee)

horizon (ho ryz' un)

hostile (hoss' til)**

hundred (as written; NOT hunnerd)

idea (eye dee' a)

ignoramus (ig no ray' muss)

immediate (im mee' dee ut)

impious (im' pee uss)

incognito (in cog nee' toe)

incomparable (in com' pa ra bl)

indictment (in dyt' ment)

industry (in' dus tree)**

inexorable (in eks' o ra bl)

inexplicable (in eks' pli ka bl)

infamous (in' fa muss)

inquiry (in kwy' ree)**

Iowa (I' o wah)

irrevocable (ir rev' o ka bl)**

Italian (Itt al' yun)

italics (ih tal' iks)

judiciary (joo dish' a ree)

just (as written; NOT jest)

knew (nyu)

lapel (la pel')

large (larj; No *d* sound)

latent (lay' tent)

length (pronounce the g; NOT lenth)

library (as written; NOT ly' bay ree)

lieu (lyu)

lightning (lyt' ning; NOT
    lyt' en ning)

long-lived (long' lyvd')**

longevity (lon jev' i tee)

luxury (luk' shu ree; NOT
    lug' shu ree)**

lyceum (ly see' um)

manufacture (manyu fakt' chyur)

maturity (ma tyu' rit tee)

memorable (mem' uh ra bl)

mischievous (miss' cha vuss)**

municipal (myu niss' i pul)

museum (myu zee' um)

new (nyu)

oblique (o bleek')

office (off' fiss; NOT aw' fuss)

often (off' en)

on (as written; NOT awn)

ordeal (or deel')

osteopath (oss' tee o path)

osteopathy (oss tee opp' a thee)

overalls (as written; NOT over halls)

parade (pa rayd'; NOT prayd)

partner (as written; NOT pard' ner)

patron (pay' trun)

pecan (pe kon')

pecuniary (pee kyu' nee er ee)**

peremptory (per emp' te ree)

piano (pee an' o)

picture (pik' tyur)

pique (peek)

plumber (plum' er)

positively (poz' it tiv lee)

possess (po zess')

precedence (pre see' dens)**

preface (pref' iss)

preferable (pref' er a bl)

prescription (pre scrip' shun)

presentation (prez en tay' shun)

radiator (ray' dee ay tor)

radio (ray' dee o)

rambling (as written; NOT
    ram' bol ing)

realm (as written; NOT rellum)

recognize (rek' og nyz)

recourse (ree' cors)

refutable (re fyut' a bl)

reputable (rep' yut a bl)

research (re serch')

resources (ree sors' ez)

respite (res' pit)**

revocable (rev' o ka bl)**

robust (ro bust')*'

romance (ro mans')

Roosevelt (Ro' za velt; NEVER
    Roose' a velt)**

route (root)

sagacious (sa gay' shuss)

schism (si' zem)

simultaneous (sy mul tay' nee uss)

short-lived (short' lyvde')**

slippery (as written; NOT slip' ree)
solace (sol' uss)**
solder (sod' er)
sphere (sfeer)**
status (stay' tuss)*
strictly (as written; NOT strick' li)
subpoena (sup pee' na)
subtle (sut' tl)
suit (sute)
superfluous (soo per' floo uss)
surprise (ser pryz')
telegrapher (tell egg' ra fer)
temperament (as written; NOT
    tem' per ment)**
tenet (ten' ett)
theater (thee' a ter)**
tract (as written; NOT track)**
trembling (as written; NOT
    trem' bol ing)
tremendous (tre men' dus)

tribune (trib' yun)
tube (tyub)
Tuesday (tyuz' day)**
tumult (tyu' mult)
umbrella (as written; NOT
    um ba rel' lah)**
usurp (yu serp')
Utica (yu' tik a)
vagary (va gair' ee)**
vehement (vee' a ment)**
vehicle (vee' ih kel)**
verbose (ver bowss')
was (wahz)
water (wa' ter)**
what (hwot; NOT wot)**
wheel (hweel; NOT weel)**
whether (hweth' er)**
white (hwyt)**
wrestle (res' l)

Punctuation

Purpose of Punctuation

The sole purpose of punctuation is to make the text clear. If a mark of punctuation does not clarify the text, it should be omitted. Of course, you'll follow your boss's preference if he or she instructs you, for example, to insert more commas or semicolons than today's magazines and newspapers typically use. When public changes occur, not every person immediately approves. But if a matter is left to your discretion, remember that the old tried-and-true comma rule also applies for many other marks of punctuation: "When in doubt, leave it out."

Nevertheless, there are still standards and formalities in punctuation that you must fully grasp, not only to satisfy your boss but also to help promote your own career. Once it leaves the office, your work speaks for itself. You want it to be a source of pride for both your employer and you.

Following is a list of punctuation marks with usage rules and examples for each.

The Period

A period is used at the end of a declarative sentence to denote a full pause:

- I am going to town.
- You may go with me if you wish.

Use a period, not a question mark, when the sentence contains an indirect question:

- He could not understand why she was leaving.

Also use a period for a request phrased as a question:

- Will you please return the diskette when you are finished.

The period is used in decimals to separate a whole number from a decimal fraction:

- 5.6 percent
- $19.50

It is also used in abbreviations:

- Mrs.
- Ph.D.
- etc.

The Comma

The presence of a comma, or its absence, can cause different interpretations of a written sentence. It is thus of vast importance, particularly in legal documents. The comma tells the reader to pause. Some writers can tell where commas belong by reading their sentences aloud and inserting commas where there seems to be a natural pause. This only works, however, if you read a sentence carefully and accurately.

Series

Commas are used to separate nouns in a series or adjectives in a series of the same rank modifying the same noun:

- The workers picked cherries, peaches, and plums.
- We swam in cool, clear, fresh water.

Some bosses may prefer to omit the comma before the *and* in such sentences unless it's needed for clarity. The same applies to *but* and *or*. Many writers believe these words take the place of the final comma in a series.

Sometimes a term consisting of years, months, and days is considered not a series but a single unit of time. No commas are used:

- Interest will be computed for 6 years 3 months and 2 days.

Compound and Complex Sentences

Two sentences are often connected with a comma and conjunction, such as *and* or *but*. A comma is used between the clauses of a compound sentence:

- John went to the theater, but he left before the play ended.

Do not confuse this with a compound predicate, which takes no comma:

- John went to the theater but left before the play ended.

An adverbial clause usually follows the independent clause, and no comma is used. But for emphasis, the order of the clauses is sometimes transposed. Then a comma is used.

- USUAL ORDER: John was met by a large delegation when he came home.
- TRANSPOSED ORDER: When John came home, he was met by a large delegation.

Introductory Expressions

Introductory expressions, such as transitional words and phrases, mild exclamations, and other independent expressions, are set off by a comma when they occur alone at the beginning of a sentence:

- Yes, I will go.
- Well, perhaps she is right.
- Nevertheless, I wish he had waited for me.
- To tell the truth, I think you should go.
- As a rule, he arrives very early.

A few introductory expressions are more emphatic without punctuation, however, and need not be followed by a comma:

- Doubtless she just couldn't be here.
- At least you tried.
- Undoubtedly the plane's engines both failed.
- Indeed you may bring your friends with you.

    To distinguish between the two, ask whether you naturally pause after the word or words in question. A comma is used to signal the natural pause.

Other Transitional Words

A comma is used to set off the transitional words *however, therefore,* and *moreover* when used within the sentence or as the first or last word of the sentence:

- Jean may not arrive until noon, however.
- Her problem, therefore, must be solved at once.
- I will be there, moreover, as soon as I can.

Sometimes *though* is used to mean *however* and should be set off with commas:

- I will be there, though, if at all possible.

Prepositional Phrases

No comma is used for prepositional phrases within a sentence unless the phrase comes between the subject and the predicate of the clause:

- I am sure that because of your generosity we will be able to build the new dormitory.
- The bag, in addition to a hatbox, will be sent to you today.

Contrasting Phrases

Contrasting expressions within a sentence are set off by commas:

- The lion, not the tiger, growled.
- We walk slowly, never quickly, to the garage.
- This letter was meant for you, not for me.
- BUT—This letter was meant for you but not for me.

Nonrestrictive Modifiers

Nonrestrictive modifiers are phrases or clauses that could be omitted without affecting the meaning of the main clause. These should be set off from the rest of the sentence by a comma or by parenthetical commas:

- John, my favorite friend, is visiting me.
- That car is, I believe, a new model.
- Mary Brown, who lives next door, is in the third grade.
- BUT—That is the girl who lives next door.

Infinitive Phrases

An infinitive phrase used independently is set off by commas:

- The color is too dark, to list one fault.

If the phrase is used as a modifier, it is not punctuated:

- The piano is too large to fit in the room.

Dialogue

A comma is used to separate a dialogue quotation from the main sentence:

- "Please go with me," the boy said.
- "What do you think," Mr. Bleeker asked, "the Mayor will do next?"

Commas also separate the name of the person addressed in dialogue from the remainder of the sentence:

- "Will you come with me, John?"
- "But, Jane, how do you know that the plane is late?"

A confirming question within a sentence is set off by commas:

- "He left, did he not, on the noon plane?"

Repeated Words

A comma is used for clarity and to avoid confusion when the same word is repeated:

- Whoever goes, goes without my consent.

Omission

When words are omitted in one part of a sentence because they were used in a previous part, a comma is used to show where the words were omitted:

- Sam's first car was a Cadillac, and mine, a Ford.

Transposed Adjective Order

An adjective normally precedes the noun it modifies. When an adjective follows a noun, the adjective is set off by commas; when an adjective precedes a noun but also precedes the article before the noun, a comma follows the adjective:

- The physician, dignified and competent, told them the bad news.
- Dignified and competent, the physician told them the bad news.

Numbers

A comma is used in writing large numbers, separating the thousands digits from the hundreds, the millions digits from the thousands, and so forth:

- 249,586
- 1,345,000

A comma is used to separate two or more unrelated numbers:

- On August 1, 1992, 437 people visited the museum.
- Out of eighty, twenty were discarded.

Do not forget the second comma when the date occurs in the middle of the sentence:

- She left for England on June 22, 2003, and returned a month later.

However, it is acceptable if your boss prefers no commas at all:

- She left for England on June 22 2003 and returned a month later.

Addresses

Elements of an address are set off by commas:

- He lives at 410 Hawthorne Street, Chicago, Illinois, near the University of Chicago campus.

On an envelope address, there is no comma between the state and the zip code.

Titles

A comma is used to separate a name and a title:

- The letter was from Mrs. Masterson, our President, and contained a list of instructions.

Set off Jr. and Sr. from a proper name by a comma. A Roman numeral is not set off by a comma:

- Philip W. Thompson, Sr.
- Philip W. Thompson III

Degrees are also set off by a comma:

- Jennifer Galt, M.D.

But descriptive titles are not:

■ Attila the Hun

Company Names
Company names consisting of a series of names omit the last comma in the series:

■ Pate, Tate and Waite

When *and Company* completes a series of names, the last comma is also omitted:

■ Pate, Tate, Waite and Company

Set off *Incorporated* from the name of a company by a comma:

■ Johnson Brothers, Incorporated

 ## The Question Mark

A question mark closes a question:

■ What time is it?

A question mark is used to express a doubt:

■ He is older (?) than she.

If the question is indirect, no question mark is used:

■ I wonder whether he will be here.

When a question is asked in the middle of a sentence, the question is enclosed by commas and the sentence ends with a question mark:

■ They are arriving, aren't they, on the noon train?

When the question is enclosed in parentheses, the question mark is inside the parentheses, not at the end of the sentence:

■ The magazine (did you see it?) describes the city in great detail.

If the question mark is part of a quotation, it is placed inside the closing quotation mark; if it is not a part of the quotation, it is placed outside the closing quotation mark:

■ The statement ended, "And is that all?"
■ What did she mean by "jobless years"?

If the last word in a question is an abbreviation and thus contains a period, the question mark is also used:

■ Do you think he will arrive by 4 p.m.?

When it is desired to make a question of a statement, the question mark is used:

- He is arriving today?
- Really?

The Exclamation Point

An exclamation point is used when making extravagant claims or to express deep feeling:

- Here is the finest car on the market!
- The announcement was unbelievable!

An exclamation point is used after a word or phrase charged with emotion:

- Quick! We don't want to be late.

It is also used for double emphasis:

- Did you catch that innuendo!

CAUTION: Some people get into the habit of using exclamation points far too often to express strong emotion, and they end up blunting the very purpose of the punctuation. For effective writing, show emotion through the choice of words instead and reserve exclamation points for only the strongest of feelings.

The Semicolon

A semicolon is used when the conjunction is omitted between parts of a compound sentence:

- I went with them; I should have stayed at home.

A semicolon precedes words such as *however, moreover,* or *otherwise* when they introduce the second of two connected full sentences:

- She is arriving at noon; however, she will not stay long.

If parts of a series contain inner punctuation such as a comma, the parts are separated by a semicolon:

- He came to see his mother, who was ill; his sister, who lived in the next town; and his old schoolmate.

The Colon

The colon generally follows a sentence introducing a tabulation or a long quotation.

- The following quotation is from the *Detroit Free* Press: "Regardless of what may be accomplished, the company will still be involved."

- During your first year, you will study such subjects as these: algebra, physics, chemistry, and psychology.

EXCEPTION: When the tabulated list is the object of a verb or a preposition, a colon is never used:

- During your first year, you will study algebra, physics, chemistry, and psychology.

Emphasis or Anticipation

The colon is also used to stress a word, phrase, or clause that follows it or when a sentence creates anticipation for what immediately follows:

- The newspaper published a startling statement: the city had been completely destroyed by fire.

Time

The colon is used to separate hours and minutes in expressions of time:

- 4:15 A.M. CST

Titles

The colon is used to separate a title from a subtitle:

- *Gone With the Wind: A Story of the Old South*

Quotation Marks

Double quotation marks are used to set off any material quoted within a sentence or paragraph. If the quoted material consists of several paragraphs, the opening quotation mark is used at the beginning of the quotation and at the beginning of each paragraph within the quotation; a closing quotation mark, however, is used only at the conclusion of the quotation. It is not used at the end of each paragraph within the quotation, as many people mistakenly think. For example:

> The passage he read aloud was from the first chapter: "The discovery of this energy brings us to the problem of how to allow it to be used. The use of atomic power throws us back to the Greek legend of Prometheus and the age-old question of whether force should be exerted against law.
>
> "The man of today must decide whether he will use this power for destruction or for peaceful purposes." When he had finished the reading, there was loud applause.

Quotations within Quotations

Single quotation marks indicate a quotation within the quotation:

- He said, "Did you hear John make the statement, 'I will not go with her,' or were you not present at the time he spoke?"

Titles

In printed text, the titles of essays, articles, poems, stories, or chapters are set off within quotation marks; titles of plays, books, and periodical publications are italicized:

- The name of the article is "I Believe."
- The title of the book is *Journey Into Night*.
- It was first published in *Harper's Magazine*.

Quotation Marks and Punctuation

Place quotation marks outside the comma and the period:

- "Don't stop now," he said, "when you have so little left to finish."

Place quotation marks inside the colon and the semicolon:

- He called her a "little witch"; that was right after she broke his model plane.

Place quotation marks outside an exclamation point or a question mark when the quoted material alone is an exclamation or a question:

- "I passed my test!"

Place quotation marks inside an exclamation point or a question mark when the quoted material alone is not an exclamation or a question:

- Didn't he claim to be "too tired"?

Italics

Italics are sometimes used for emphasis:

- Notice where you are, not where you *have been*.

But the best writing avoids italics for this purpose, depending on choice of language to bring out the emphasis.

As mentioned earlier, italics are used for the names of books, pamphlets, and periodicals:

- *Saturday Evening Post*
- *Black Beauty*
- *Washington Daily News*

The names of ships are italicized but not abbreviations in front of them.

- *Sea Witch*
- USS *Heinz*

NOTE: When using a typewriter and not a word processor or computer, indicate italics by underlining:

- <u>Sea Witch</u>
- <u>USS Heinz</u>
- <u>Washington Daily News</u>

The Apostrophe

As a mark of omission, the apostrophe may denote that a word has been contracted intentionally:

- It's time to go.
- Haven't you finished the task?

Possession

To show possession, use an apostrophe followed by an *s* after a singular noun:

- the city's founder

Use it alone after plural nouns ending in *s:*

- the books' titles

Plural nouns not ending in *s* form the possessive by adding an apostrophe and an *s:*

- men's clubs
- sheep's clothing

The plural of compound nouns and joint possessive nouns is formed by adding an apostrophe followed by an *s* to the second word only:

- the Secretary-Treasurer's decision
- Mary and John's cassette player

But if the items are separately owned, the compound nouns each add an apostrophe followed by an *s:*

- Mary's and John's coats

No apostrophe is used with possessive pronouns:

- his
- hers
- its
- yours
- ours
- theirs

The apostrophe is used to express duration of time:

- a day's traveling time
- twelve months' duration

For a proper name ending in *s,* use an apostrophe followed by an *s:*

- Lewis's hat
- Miss Bliss's book

Two proper names are traditionally observed as exceptions:

- Moses' robe
- Jesus' parable

For plural proper names ending in *s,* use an apostrophe only:

- The Joneses' boots were left in the hall.

The Dash

The dash (in typing, indicated by two hyphens) is used to introduce an added thought:

- I shall go with you—you don't mind, do you?

The dash also breaks the continuity of a thought as a digression:

- "The Scherzo Sonata" by Tolstoy is a sad story—but the writing is magnificent.

It is sometimes used before and after a parenthetical expression in place of commas:

- Henry Higgins—bareheaded and without a coat—left the house and ran down the road.

Sometimes you can think of a dash as a super comma. When a sentence already contains a series separated by commas, a dash is a good tool for separating a clause that might otherwise look like it was part of the series. Consider the following:

- The Mississippi river weaves between Tennessee, Arkansas, and Louisiana—a state famous for its French culture—before emptying into the Gulf of Mexico.

Ellipses

To show omission of words in quoted material, three spaced dots (ellipses) are used if material is deleted within the sentence. When the last part of a quoted sentence is omitted, it is followed by three spaced dots plus its punctuation. At the end of the quotation, only the punctuation is used:

- "Five hundred firemen . . . attended the ball. . . .
- Mr. Brown went on to say: "The shoe department functions smoothly . . . many salespeople have won prizes for efficiency."

Ellipsis dots may also be used to mark a thought expressed hesitantly:

- He said, "If . . . if I do go with you, will you return early?"

Parentheses

Parentheses are used to enclose matter that is introduced by way of explanation:

- If the lessor (the person owning the property) agrees, the lessee (the person renting the property) may have a dog on the premises.

Parentheses are used to enclose figures that enumerate items:

- The book contained chapters on (1) capitalization, (2) spelling rules, (3) troublesome verbs, and (4) punctuation.

They are also used to enclose citations of authority:

- The definition of action is "the process or state of being active *(American College Dictionary)*."

And they are used to enclose figures repeated for clarity, as in legal documents:

- He was willed five thousand dollars ($5,000) by his uncle.
- You will be paid twenty (20) percent interest.

Brackets

Brackets and parentheses are sometimes used interchangeably, however brackets have two common uses:

- They identify changes to quoted material
- They enclose digressions within parentheses

Changes to Quoted Material

If you are quoting someone, but make a change to the quote in order to clarify something, you should put your change within brackets. Consider the following:

- Original Quote—"Everyone knew it was about to break any day now."
- Revised Quote—"Everyone knew it [the dam] was about to break any day now."

Digressions within Parentheses

Sometimes you will find situations where you need an extra set of parentheses nested within a previous pair. Consider the following:

- The computer's memory (Random Access Memory [RAM] and Read Only Memory [ROM]) is where software is loaded.

The Hyphen

Hyphens are used both in spelling and in punctuation. When it is used as punctuation, it is not part of a word or phrase. There are four general ways the hyphen can be used as punctuation:

- Breaking a word at the end of a line
- Combining words that form a compound adjective
- Acting as a substitute for a repeated word
- Indicating special pronunciations

Line Breaks

Most word processing programs, such as Microsoft Word, have a built-in hyphenation feature that you can turn on and off. This feature will automatically add hyphens to long words that won't fit on the end of a line. Sometimes the computer's idea of where to put a hyphen can cause the hyphenated word to look ridiculous. Therefore, it's important for you to know the general rules regarding line break hyphenation. Here are some of those rules:

- Don't break one syllable words.
- Don't break a word if just one letter is left on a line.
- Break hyphenated compound words at the hyphen.
- Break closed compound words between the words.

Compound Adjectives

Compound adjectives are groups of words or phrases used in a sentence to describe a noun. Consider the following:

- It was a once-in-a-lifetime opportunity.
- I wouldn't touch that line with a ten-foot pole.
- The computer's processor has a 512 single-byte bus.
- Eight-month-old kittens were given away.
- Eight month-old kittens were given away.

Do not use hyphens when the first word of a compound adjective ends in *-ly*. The following examples are INCORRECT:

- It was a highly-motivated student body.
- It was a beautifully-made sweater.

Hyphens as Substitute Words

If a word repeats with a different modifier in a sentence, it can make the sentence sound long and difficult. One way to solve this problem is to use a hyphen. Consider the following examples:

- We both over- and underestimated the amount of driving time for the trip.
- The Dallas Cowboys used a three-, four-, and five-man line.
- Most computers today have either a 32- or 64-bit processor.

Hyphens for Pronunciation

You can use hyphens when writing dialogue in order to achieve a particular pronunciation in the reader's mind.

- "S-s-s-s," said the snake.
- "Mr. S-s-smith," he stuttered, "May I p-p-please have some w-w-water?"

Slash

The slash is often used as shorthand or when the choice between outcomes is nebulous. Since the slash is often ambiguous, it should be used with caution.

The slash is used for the following:

- With and/or combinations
- To indicate other relationships between words

And/Or Combinations

The slash can be used to indicate options that are available, equal possibilities, or to show that something has more than one function. For example:

- The potter worked alone in the cold garage/studio.
- Dear Sir/Madam:
- The ingredients of the drink are: ice, rum, lime/lemon, and cola.

Indicating Other Relationships

The slash can be used to separate elements that are being compared, to separate origins and destinations, to separate the numerals in a date, to indicate a period that spans two or more calendar years, in place of the word "per," and to write fractions.

- The Redskins/Cowboys rivalry has a long history.
- The Dallas/Atlanta flight was canceled.
- 12/31/2005
- For the 2004/05 school year, the eighth graders will be taking technology education for the first time.
- 1,000 km/hour
- $1/2 = 1/4 + 1/4$

Numerals

Words or Figures?

Your main concern with numbers is whether to spell them out in words or to express them in figures. As so often happens with matters of English usage, there are many times when both forms are correct, and you will regularly come across variations not covered in a book of rules, so use your discretion. Clarity is always your strongest guideline.

Printed Text and Prose Text

Generally, in prose text, numbers under 101 are spelled out, and numbers over 101 are shown in figures. The more formal the text is, the greater is the tendency to express the number in words.

In printed text, a number used for comparison with other numbers in the same section should be in numerical form.

- An excavation of 500 feet can be finished as rapidly as one of 200 feet if the right equipment is used.

At the Beginning of a Sentence

A number appearing at the beginning of a sentence, if it can be expressed in one or two words, should be spelled out:

- Sixteen new cars were delivered.
- Thirty or forty bushels were needed.
- NOT: 2,746,892 copies were purchased.

The last example should be rewritten so that the figure appears later in the sentence:

- The company purchased 2,746,892 copies.

Legal Documents

In legal documents, numbers are written in both words and figures to prevent misunderstanding, and the same is true in papers that transfer land title:

- The west thirty (30) feet of Lot Nine (9) in Block Four (4) . . .

Round Numbers

Approximate round numbers are spelled out:

- The station is about fifty blocks away.
- He found nearly two thousand dollars.

Sets of Numbers

To differentiate two sets of numbers occurring in the same sentence, use words for one and figures for the other:

- Three of the men drove 2,000 miles each; four drove 3,000 miles each; and only one drove the complete 3,000 miles.

If the sentence cannot be rewritten, use a comma or dash to separate the numbers:

- During the year 1992, 20 million people visited the park.
- We received 1,213—113 of which ...

Large Numbers

As a general rule, write out numbers up to and including one hundred and use figures for numbers over one hundred. But for large numbers, if a number can be written as one or two words, do so:

- four hundred
- five million
- two billion

Use the short form for writing numbers over a thousand not pertaining to money:

- fourteen hundred
- NOT: one thousand four hundred

Large, even amounts may combine figures and words:

- production of 37 million paper clips and a budget of $146 billion

If a figure or the word several precedes *hundred, thousand, million, billion,* and so on, the singular form is used. After *many,* the plural form is used:

- six hundred pages
- several million years
- many hundreds of pages

Separating Digits

All numbers above 999 are written with commas to separate every group of three digits, counting from the units place:

- 1,001
- 123,000
- 1,436,936

EXCEPTIONS: Commas are omitted in long decimal fractions, page numbers, addresses, telephone numbers, room numbers, and form numbers:

- .10356
- 201-555-9088
- Page 3487
- Room 2630
- 1467 Wilshire Boulevard
- Form 2317-A

Commas are also omitted in four-digit year numbers, but they are added for years with five or more digits:

- The company began in 1992.
- The pottery shards were dated at about 14,000 B.C.
- This science fiction novel takes place in the year 27,345 A.D.

Patent numbers are written with commas:

- Patent No. 3,436,987

Serial numbers are written without commas:

- Motor Number 245889954
- Policy Number 894566

✴ Dollars and Cents

Use figures for money:

- 1 cent
- 20 cents
- 20,000 dollars OR $20,000

However, as with other numbers, amounts of money are always written out when beginning a sentence:

- One cent was contributed by each child.
- NOT: 1 cent was contributed by each child.

A series of prices is written in figures only:

- These shoes were priced at $50, $60, and $85.

Dollar and Cent Signs

Use the dollar sign before the number, not the word *dollar or dollars* after the number.

- The duplex rents for $700 per month.

If a large dollar amount combines figures and words, use the dollar sign before the figure:

- The budget calls for $850 billion.
- NOT: The budget calls for 850 billion dollars.

Repeat the dollar sign with successive numbers:

■ The bonds could be purchased in denominations of $10,000, $12,000, $15,000, and $20,000.

EXCEPTION: Omit all but the first dollar sign when numbers are in tabulated form:

■ The bonds could be purchased in denominations of the following amounts:

$10,000

12,000

15,000

20,000

The dollar sign is not used when the figure given is in cents alone. Use the cent sign ¢ after amounts less than one dollar, but never use the cent sign with a decimal point:

■ 25¢   ■ NOT: .25¢, for that would mean one-fourth of a cent

EXCEPTION: The only time the dollar sign is used when the figure is in cents alone is in statistical work when the part of the dollar is carried out to more than two decimal places:

■ $0.3564

Decimal Points

Decimal points are another way of writing fractions, especially large fractions. When a decimal occurs with no unit before it, use a cipher (a zero) for quick interpretation:

■ a 0.75-yard measurement   ■ rainfall of 0.356 inch

Sometimes the fraction is part of a dollar. When the amount of dollars given is not followed by cents, omit the decimal point and the ciphers:

■ $3

■ $1,200

■ BUT: $17.75

The decimal point and ciphers are not used with even amounts of money unless in tabulated form. If tabulated, and some amounts contain cents and some do not, the even amounts should contain ciphers:

$19.36

5.00

2.14

37.00

1.23

.19

.02

Time

When a figure and a word come together as an adjective to express time, connect the two with a hyphen:

- a 24-hour day
- BUT: a day of 24 hours
- two 2-year 12-percent notes
- BUT: two notes for two years at 12 percent

Hours, minutes, and seconds are separated by a colon:

- 10:05:02 a.m.

Never use "this a.m.." instead of "this morning." With *a.m.* or *p.m.* the word *o'clock* should not be used:

- I will meet you at 4 p.m.
- I will meet you at four o'clock this afternoon.

Ciphers after the number of the hour are unnecessary. For exact noon and midnight, it is correct to use the words:

- I will meet you at noon.
- The horn blew at midnight.

Dates

The day is written in numerals, without *th, st,* or *d,* unless the day is written before the name of the month:

- May 1, 1995
- NOT: May 1st, 1995
- BUT: On the 2d of June 1994
- In the August 21 and September 3 editions (NOT 21st or 3d)

In legal documents, dates are spelled out:

- the twelfth day of May, A.D. Nineteen Hundred and Ninety-Five

The Hyphen

Written-out numbers below one hundred are hyphenated:

- thirty-three
- ninety-nine
- twenty-seven

Hundreds and thousands are not hyphenated:

- six hundred thousand
- three hundred million

When modifying a noun, numbers are hyphenated, as are any compound adjectives:

- five-thousand-foot mountain
- three-foot rule

Fractions of less than one are hyphenated:

- one-third
- three-quarters
- BUT: one twenty-third

Mixed numbers are not hyphenated between the whole number and the fraction, both when written as words and figures:

- one and one-half
- 1 1/2

Do not write one part of the fraction as a numeral and the other as a word:

- one-fourth-inch bolt
- NOT: 1 fourth-inch bolt

When a mixed number is the subject of a sentence, the noun is plural. However, the verb is singular because the quantity is considered as a single unit:

- 1 5/8 inches is needed.
- 2 1/4 miles is the length of the track.

✸ Age

Use the general rule in giving the age of a person or a period of time (write out up to and including one hundred; use figures over one hundred):

- She is twelve years old.
- He has held the same position for twenty-six years.
- She is now 105 years of age.
- The company has been in this city for 102 years.

In compound adjectives denoting age, the words designating time may be used before *old*, but in that event the words *year* and *day* must appear in the singular:

- 12-day-old baby elephant
- 200-year-old building
- 6-month-old pony
- 3-day-old kitten

✸ Dimensions

The signs reserved for technical writing are ′ for feet, ″ for inches, and × for by.

- 9′ × 12″ (9 feet by 12 feet)
- 8″ × 10″ (8 inches by 10 inches)

In regular prose text, write out the word by for ×.

Ciphers can be used to indicate exact measurement if they improve clarity:

- 9′0″ × 12′0″ × 20′6″

Weights and Measures

Abbreviations are used without capitalization:

- 6 lb. 3 oz.
- OR 6 pounds 3 ounces
- 192 lbs.
- OR 192 pounds

In a compound adjective showing a weight or a measure, the numeral is hyphenated to a singular noun:

- 600-mile-an-hour speed
- BUT: speed of 600 miles an hour
- a 40-hour workweek
- BUT: a workweek of 40 hours

Percentages

The numeral is retained whether or not a percentage sign is used:

- 5% price reduction
- loss of 10 percent
- almost 30 percent of the population

For percentages in succession, use the sign after each numeral:

- 30% to 50%
- 6%, 8%, and 10%

Page Numbering

For all page numbering, use figures to show the numbers. Commas are not used in page numbers greater than 999.

Page Number Formats

On legal documents, a page number is centered at the bottom of each page; on other papers, it is usually shown at the top. Manuscripts and briefs are numbered in the upper right corner; papers that are to be bound at the left are numbered in the lower right corner. In each case, all numbers should appear at exactly the same place on all pages. Title pages are not numbered. A first page of a work or of a chapter is not marked with a number, although the numbering of the following pages takes into consideration the number of the first page.

It is acceptable to use a short dash before and after the page number, -3- for example, without a period. Never use quotation marks, and never type the word *page* before the number. Frequently, the number stands alone—2—without a period.

★ The Abbreviation for *Number*

The abbreviation for *number, no.,* or the number sign—#—is usually omitted:

- Building 38
- NOT: Building No. 38
- Invoice 3457
- NOT: Invoice #3457

- Page 92
- NOT: page no. 92

In text, however, it may be convenient to use the abbreviation:

- When he came to No. 16, he halted.
- The only houses to be painted this year are Nos. 16, 17, and 18.

★ Plurals of Numbers

Form the plural of a numeral or other character by adding *s* or *es* to the word. If the number is a figure, use *s* or *'s* as your boss prefers:

- 5s and 6s OR 5's and 6's OR fives and sixes
- the 1990s OR the 1990's
- MD88s OR MD88's

★ Roman Numerals

Roman numerals are often used in outlines and some dates. Table 34-1 lists the most commonly used Roman numerals. Use the forms listed in Table 34-2 for dates.

TABLE 34-1	**Most Commonly Used Roman Numerals**				
Arabic	**Roman**	**Arabic**	**Roman**	**Arabic**	**Roman**
1	I	15	XV	150	CL
2	II	16	XVI	200	CC
3	III	17	XVII	300	CCC
4	IV	18	XVIII	400	CD
5	V	19	IX	500	D
6	VI	20	XX	600	DC
7	VII	30	XXX	700	DCC
8	VIII	40	XL	800	DCCC
9	IX	50	L	900	CM
10	X	60	LX	1,000	M
11	XI	70	LXX	1,500	MD
12	XII	80	LXXX	2,000	MM
13	XIII	90	XC	3,000	MMM
14	XIV	100	C		

TABLE 34-2	Roman Numeral Dates				
1900	MCM	1960	MCMLX	2020	MMMXX
1910	MCMX	1970	MCMLXX	2030	MMMXXX
1920	MCMXX	1980	MCMLXXX	2040	MMMXL
1930	MCMXXX	1990	MCMXC	2050	MMML
1940	MCMXL	2000	MM		
1950	MCML	2010	MMMX		

FINANCIAL ACTIVITIES

SECTION FIVE

An administrative
assistant uses a PC to
store financial records.
Photo by Kevin Wilson.

Bookkeeping and Accounting

Financial Record Keeping

Bookkeeping and accounting are fields requiring special training. Smaller companies may assign these duties to the administrative assistant, especially with today's new computerized accounting programs. Larger companies typically have an in-house accounting department or contract for the services of an accountant to prepare tax statements and other important records. Even so, it's useful to familiarize yourself with the simple mechanics of bookkeeping and accounting no matter what size company you work for. The more informed you are, the more valuable you are to the company.

Assets

Property owned by a business organization and used in its operation is known as **assets.** The proprietor or owner of the business may be one person, two persons (in a partnership), half a dozen persons, or numerous persons operating a corporation. The interest of the owner or proprietor in the assets of the business is called proprietorship, net worth, or capital. If the business is free of claims against these assets, except for those of the proprietor, then assets equals proprietorship. For example, if John King purchased a stationery store for $10,000, his financial condition would be expressed in this way: Assets $10,000 equal proprietorship $10,000.

Liabilities

A business owner may obtain additional property by borrowing money to purchase the property needed or by purchasing the property with a promise to pay for that property at some future date. Those from whom business owners borrow are known as creditors. The creditor has a claim on the property until the proprietor pays in accordance with an agreement. These claims are known as the **liabilities** of the business.

For example, Mary Brown borrows $5,000 from a bank to enlarge the building used for her dry cleaning establishment. The bank thus becomes her creditor. This $5,000 increase in Brown's assets is accompanied by the bank's corresponding claim on her assets until the borrowed $5,000 is repaid. To fill the newly enlarged building, Brown purchases additional equipment and merchandise from the American Dry Cleaning Equipment Company amounting to $5,000; the American Dry Cleaning Company thus becomes another creditor. If Brown fails to pay this $5,000, the company can enforce its claim by legal action; this potential claim of the company on Brown's assets is another liability.

Assets of a business are, therefore, subject to two kinds of claims: (1) those arising from the rights of creditors and (2) those arising from the rights of the proprietor. The sum of these rights is equal to the value of the assets. Thus, assets equal liabilities plus proprietorship.

Effect of Business Transactions

The proprietor must know the effect of all business transactions on his or her assets, liabilities, and proprietorship in order to make decisions regarding future operations. Accounts furnish the proprietor with a record for this purpose, which is why it's critical that accounts be concrete, precise, and accurate.

For example, if the proprietor is considering hiring additional sales associates, he or she should know the results of the existing sales force to be able to estimate the probable results of hiring additional personnel. If the proprietor is considering purchasing additional merchandise, equipment, or space, attention should be given to the results from existing facilities.

The efficient proprietor is always seeking information concerning the effect of past operations in order to plan future operations. Such plans are known as budgets. Therefore, the primary purpose of accounting records is to give the proprietor information concerning the nature of his or her liabilities and proprietorship, as well as to furnish a concrete record of the effect of the business operation on these.

The purposes of accounting are to (1) record, (2) analyze and classify, and (3) summarize the activities of the business and their effects on each enterprise. Accounting simply reduces to writing the activities of a business.

Accounting Statements

Accounting statements (1) list a description of and amounts of property, together with ownership rights, and (2) report the effects of the operations on the owner's equity.

The first statement is known as the **balance sheet** (Figure 35-1). The balance sheet shows the assets, together with the rights of the creditors and the rights of the proprietor. The second statement is known as the **income statement** or **profit and loss statement** (Figure 35-2). It shows income and costs of operation, with the resulting increase or decrease in proprietorship. The bal-

Balance Sheet
November 30, 2005

Current Assests

Cash on hand and in the bank	$4000	
Merchandise inventory	90,000	
Accounts receivable	6,000	
Total Current Assets		$100,000

Fixed Assets

Real Estate—Land		18,000
Real Estate—Building		
Original Cost	$64,000	
Less Depreciation	3,000	61,000
Furniture, fixtures and equipment—		
original cost	$12,000	
Less Depreciation	600	11,400

Total Assets		$190,400

Current Liabilities

Accounts Payable	$32,000	
Notes Payable	16,000	

Total Current Liabilities		$48,000
Long-term Debt		22,000
Capital		120,400
Total Liabilities & Capital		$190,400

FIGURE 35-1. A balance sheet.

ance sheet shows the financial condition of the business at a given time; the income statement covers the periods between any two balance sheets.

These summaries are interesting to persons other than the proprietor. When the owner of the business wishes to borrow money from a bank, the bank officers, in order to judge the owner's ability to repay the loan, ask for information concerning the assets and liabilities and the profits earned in previous periods. Creditors request the same information before selling merchandise on account. The Internal Revenue Service (IRS) also requires a similar statement, to be assured that the income tax for the coming year is being estimated properly.

A large business has hundreds and even thousands of assets to list; these are classified as current assets, fixed assets, and deferred charges to expenses.

Current assets appear in the form of cash or items that may reasonably be expected to be converted into cash in the near future by the regular operation

Profit and Loss Statement
November 39, 2005

Sales		$200,000
Cost of Sales		140,000
Gross Income		60,000
Selling Expenses	$25,000	
General Expenses	10,000	
Operating Expenses		35,000
Operating Income		25,000
Interest Expense		1,200
Net Income Before Taxes		23,800
Income Taxes		6,600
Net Income		$17,200

FIGURE 35-2. Profit and loss statement.

of the business. This includes stocks, bonds, mutual funds, and other nego-tiable financial instruments. When listed on the balance sheet, these assets are arranged in the order in which they will be converted. Columns are also pro-vided to show the quantity, description, price, and extensions. When all these sheets are extended and totaled, their sum is entered on the balance sheet as merchandise inventory.

Fixed assets are those of a permanent (or fixed) nature that will not be con-verted into cash as long as they serve the needs of the business. They are not intended for resale but are expected to wear out in the course of the business. They include store equipment, office equipment, delivery equipment, buildings, and land.

Deferred charges to expenses are assets purchased for use in the business that will be consumed in the near future—for example, store supplies, office supplies, and prepaid insurance.

The classification system commonly used for liabilities is similar to that for assets: current liabilities, fixed liabilities, and deferred credits to income.

Current liabilities are those that will be due within a short time. For ex-ample, if John King purchases equipment on account with the agreement that he will pay for it within thirty days, this transaction results in a current liabil-ity. A liability is considered to be a current one if it comes due within one year after the balance sheet date. Under this heading are notes payable, accounts payable, and accrued liabilities.

Notes payable are promises given by the proprietor to someone to whom he or she owes money. The proprietor may give these to a creditor from whom he or she has purchased equipment or merchandise or to a bank when bor-rowing money.

Accounts payable are the financial obligations of a business, usually arising from a purchase on account, when the buyer has given his or her promise to pay at some future time for the goods received.

Accrued liabilities are amounts owed to the government on taxes, to employees on wages, or to creditors on interest. If one of these is unusually high, it may be set up singly under some designation such as "taxes payable," "wages payable," and so forth.

Fixed liabilities are those that will not be due for a comparatively long time after they are contracted. They usually arise in the purchase of fixed assets and include liabilities that will not be liquidated within one year from the date of the balance sheet—for example, mortgages payable or bonds payable.

A **mortgage payable** represents a debt owed by a business for which the creditor possesses a mortgage on a particular asset.

Bonds payable are long-term obligations of corporations commonly evidenced by bonds; a debt to be paid more than one year hence.

Deferred credits to income are the unearned portion of a payment when a business is paid in advance for a service. For example, an insurance company receives in one fiscal period a payment for insurance that extends over a future fiscal period. The unearned portion of the premium is a deferred credit to income and would usually be listed as unearned premium income.

The Balance Sheet

Usually the purpose of any business is to increase its proprietorship—that is, to make money. The amount of profit or loss incurred during a given period is the most important single fact.

A **balance sheet** (see Figure 35-1) shows the proprietor the amount of his or her proprietorship to help determine whether the proprietorship is increasing or decreasing; it does not, however, show the cause of the increase or decrease.

The Income Statement

At various intervals, the proprietor has to plan to increase profit and eliminate future losses. For this, a report is needed to show the amount of sales, the cost of procuring and selling the goods that are sold, and the difference between the two, which is the profit or loss. The **income statement** (see Figure 35-2) gives such information, as well as the gross profit on sales, operating expenses, and depreciation. The period it covers is known as the **fiscal** period.

Income Statement Terms

There are a variety of important terms included on an income statement that need some explanation.

■ **Sales**—The gross return from operations. Different businesses use different terms for their sales, depending on whether the business sells commodities or services. For example, sales in a mercantile business are the total amount of money customers have paid or agreed to pay for merchandise sold to them. Airlines have passenger revenue or freight revenue, whereas professional men and women have fees. Investment trusts have interest income and dividend income.

- **Cost of goods sold**—The purchase price paid by a business for the goods it has sold, as distinguished from the sales price. Cost of goods sold is made up of (1) the price charged by the seller as shown on the invoice of sale and (2) the shipping and handling charged for the delivery of the goods.

- **Gross profit on sales**—Derived by subtracting the cost of merchandise sold from the total sales, representing the profit that would be made if no expenses were incurred in conducting the business. Because expenses are always incurred, they must be considered in determining profit. The expenses of operating the business must be deducted to obtain the net profit.

- **Operating expenses**—Includes all commodities and services expended in the operation of a business: services of personnel, paper, electricity, fuel, postage, and so forth.

- **Depreciation**—The cost arising from the decrease in value of the fixed assets. Not only are supplies and services used to operate a business, but fixed assets, such as office equipment and store equipment, are gradually worn out through use.

The income statement shows the result of the operations of a specific business during a particular period of time. It lists the income from sales and subtracts from this the expenses of the business in making such sales. The last figure is the net profit from operations.

The Account

Each time a business performs a transaction, a change is made in one or more elements of the equation "assets equal liabilities plus proprietorship." Regardless of the number of transactions, the results of all changes must be ascertained in order to prepare an accurate balance sheet and an accurate income statement at the end of the fiscal period. To accomplish this, each transaction must be recorded as it occurs. The **account** is the method used to record these individual transactions, and it is from this word that the subject of accounting receives its name.

The Account Record

The account is the record of each item entered on the balance sheet and on the income statement—that is, the increases and decreases that occur. In its simplest form, the account provides (1) the name of the customer, (2) transactions decreasing the amount of proprietorship, and (3) transactions increasing the amount of the same item.

The Ledger

The **ledger** is a book containing a group of accounts. It contains a page for each account or several pages if the account is large. A separate account is maintained for each entry on the balance sheet and the income statement. Accounts are arranged in the ledger in the same order in which they are listed on the accounting statements. Current asset accounts precede fixed asset accounts, and all asset accounts come before liability accounts. Proprietorship accounts are listed last. Loose-leaf ledgers should be used, so that new accounts may be inserted alphabetically.

Trial Balance

If the bookkeeper has correctly recorded each transaction, the total of all the debits in all the accounts will equal the total of the credits in all the accounts. A test is made at intervals, usually at the end of the month, to check whether the debits do equal the credits; this test, known as a **trial balance,** summarizes the ledger information. If the sum of the debits does not equal the sum of the credits, an error has been made, and then the bookkeeper has the job of reconciling.

Mixed Accounts

If all transactions recorded in the accounts coincide with the accounting period as shown on the balance sheet and the income statement, the trial balance is a satisfactory check. But it is impossible to arrange transactions so that there will be no carry-overs between accounting periods. A means must therefore be provided to meet this condition; this is called a mixed account: an account with a balance that is partly a balance sheet amount and partly an income statement amount.

For example, the trial balance amount for the account called Office Supplies summarizes all office supplies purchased plus those on hand at the beginning of the period covered. To find out how many office supplies have been used during the accounting period, an inventory of office supplies is taken. The office supplies on hand are a balance sheet entry; the office supplies used are an income statement entry. Therefore the account Office Supplies is a mixed account.

The adjustment of mixed accounts must determine the correct balance sheet amount and the correct income statement amount for any trial balance entry that is mixed. For example, a typewriter is recorded as an asset at the time of purchase and appears in the trial balance. The depreciation of the typewriter is not recorded each day and must, instead, be recorded by an adjustment at the end of the accounting period.

Other types of business operations continually affect accounts, for example, as insurance expires and wages and salaries accrue. It's necessary to record all such mixed accounts. A purchase of office supplies is debited to the asset account Office Supplies, or it can be debited to the expense account Office Supplies Used. By means of an account for Office Supplies Used or Expired Insurance, the adjustment can be made. This is an asset adjustment. A liability adjustment is made similarly.

Adjusted Trial Balance

The **trial balance** summarizes only transactions during the accounting period. Insurance has expired, supplies have been used in operating the business, office and other salaries are incomplete, and equipment has depreciated. The adjustments must be combined with trial balance amounts by means of an adjusted trial balance.

Payroll

A good bookkeeping system must provide accurate information concerning the **payroll** (Figure 35-3). Because of Social Security laws, income-tax-withholding laws, and other state and federal regulations, any and all of this information must be instantly available. Therefore, an individual payroll record book should be maintained. The following information is needed for accurate and complete payroll accounting:

- Name of employee, with address and personal data
- Social Security number
- Company number (if any)
- Department number (if any)
- Date employment began and ended (and reason for separation)
- Dates worked, rate of pay, hours per day worked, regular and overtime status
- Regular salaries paid if not on hourly basis
- Deductions (federal withholding tax, Social Security taxes, state and local taxes, medical insurance premiums, union dues, retirement plan contributions, etc.)
- Totals by month, quarter, and year

Travel and Entertainment and Auto-Expense Records

If your boss travels as part of the job, he or she may ask your help in maintaining a record of travel and entertainment expenses. If the boss uses his or her personal vehicle for business travel, you'll need to maintain a vehicle expense record as well. The IRS requires detailed records with documentary evidence for each, especially for expenses over the "standard amounts" it specifies. Such records should be accurate.

Travel and Entertainment Expenses

Records for all travel and entertainment expenses should show:

- Expenditure amount
- Date of departure and date of return for every trip
- Number of days spent on business versus days spent on pleasure

Monthly Payroll Summary

Company Name: *Videologies, Inc.*   Month: *June 2006*

Employee Name: *Kevin Wilson*

Social Security Number: *123-12-1234*   Address: *2200 Main Street*

City: *Atlanta*   State: *Georgia 30234*

WK	Date Paid	Regular Wages	O.T. TIPS	Total Wages	S.S.	Med	FED TAX	ST. TAX	OTHER	NET WAGES
1	6-15	2500	0	2500	155	36.25	298.10	143.75	0	1867
2										
3										
4										
5										
Total	6-15	2500	0	2500	155	36.25	298.10	143.75	0	1867

FIGURE 35-3. Sample payroll form.

■ Business purpose of the expenditure

■ Place of travel or place of entertainment (if clients were entertained)

■ Relationship to the business of the person or persons being entertained by the taxpayer

Evidence for these expenses is required, such as credit card charge copies and receipts of all bills paid for lodging and meals while traveling. In addition, travel expense report forms are useful to keep track of out-of-pocket expenses, such as tolls, taxies, tips and telephone calls. These forms are obtainable from any office supply store.

Figures 35-4 and 35-5 show samples of expense report forms that can be created using the Task Wizard in Microsoft Works.

Automobile Expenses

Anyone who uses a personal automobile for business purposes (other than commuting) is entitled by the IRS to deduct such expenses on his or her income tax return. If the personal vehicle is used entirely for business, all expenses can be deducted; if the vehicle has both business and personal use, its expenses may be deducted in part. A printed form, Record of Automobile Expenses, is obtainable in most office supply stores. So is a pocket-size booklet that can be handily kept in a briefcase or automobile glove compartment.

You can also use a Personal Data Assistant (PDA) to record automobile mileage and expenses. A sample of an automobile expense record that can be created using one of the Task Wizards available in Microsoft Works is available in Figure 35-6.

If the boss does not want to keep detailed records of automobile expenses, an optional deduction method is allowed. Instead of deducting a vehicle's ac-

Travel Budget

Destination of trip:	Dallas
Goal of trip:	Rest and relaxation
Dates of trip:	7/1-7/5
Number of nights:	4
Number of days:	5
Total trip allowance:	$1,000.00
Per day allowance:	$200.00

Breakdown of expenses	Per day	Total
Hotel	$75.00	$300.00
Air fare		$175.00
Car rental	$20.00	$100.00
Bus/Taxi	$5.00	$25.00
Entertainment	$25.00	$125.00
Gifts and souvenirs	$20.00	$100.00
Meals	$35.00	$175.00
Other		
Other		
Other		
Other		
TOTAL	$180.00	$1,000.00

FIGURE 35-4. Sample travel expense record.

Screen shot reprinted by permission from Microsoft Corporation.

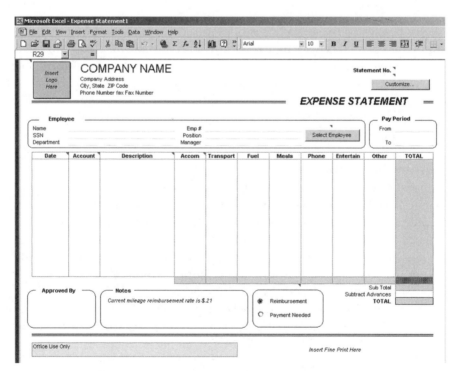

FIGURE 35-5. Sample expense report.

Screen shot reprinted by permission from Microsoft Corporation.

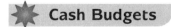

Microsoft Works

File Edit View Insert Format Tools Window Help

H62

Spreadsheet 3

	A	B	C	D	E	F	G	H	I
1				**Road Trip Log**					
2							*Last Modified:* February 15, 2003		
3									
4	Things to check before you leave								
5	q Fuel level				q Washer fluid level				
6	q Brake and clutch fluid levels				q Tire pressure				
7	q Engine coolant level				q Other _____				
8	q Engine oil level				q Other _____				
9									
10	Fuel Consumption				Initial odometer reading			5,800.0	
11									
12	Date	Location	Octane	Number of Gallons	Cost per Gallon	Odometer Reading	Number of Miles	Total Cost	
13	#####	Seattle, WA	89	6.0	$1.45	5,800.0	0	$8.70	
14	#####	Spokane, WA	89	8.0	$1.39	6,100.0	300	$11.12	
15								$0.00	
16								$0.00	
17								$0.00	
18								$0.00	
19								$0.00	
20								$0.00	
21								$0.00	
22								$0.00	
23								$0.00	
24								$0.00	
25								$0.00	
26								$0.00	
27								$0.00	
28								$0.00	
30							Total fuel expense	$19.82	
31							Total number of gallons	14.00	
32							Average miles per gallon	21.43	

Zoom 100%

FIGURE 35-6. Sample automobile expense record in Microsoft Works.

Screen shot reprinted by permission from Microsoft Corporation.

tual fixed and operating expenses with a separate deduction for depreciation (for an individual), the boss could deduct a standard mileage rate for annual business miles traveled. State and local taxes (not including gasoline tax) and interest payments on loans to purchase business vehicles are deductible as well.

These laws change frequently, and it would be wise for you or your employer to secure up-to-date IRS booklets for rules on required record maintenance and reporting to make sure you're keeping adequate records. But even with these booklets, your employer should also utilize the services of a competent accountant.

Cash Budgets

A **cash budget** is an estimate of expected cash receipts and expenditures. It is necessary for any business, especially a small business where every dime

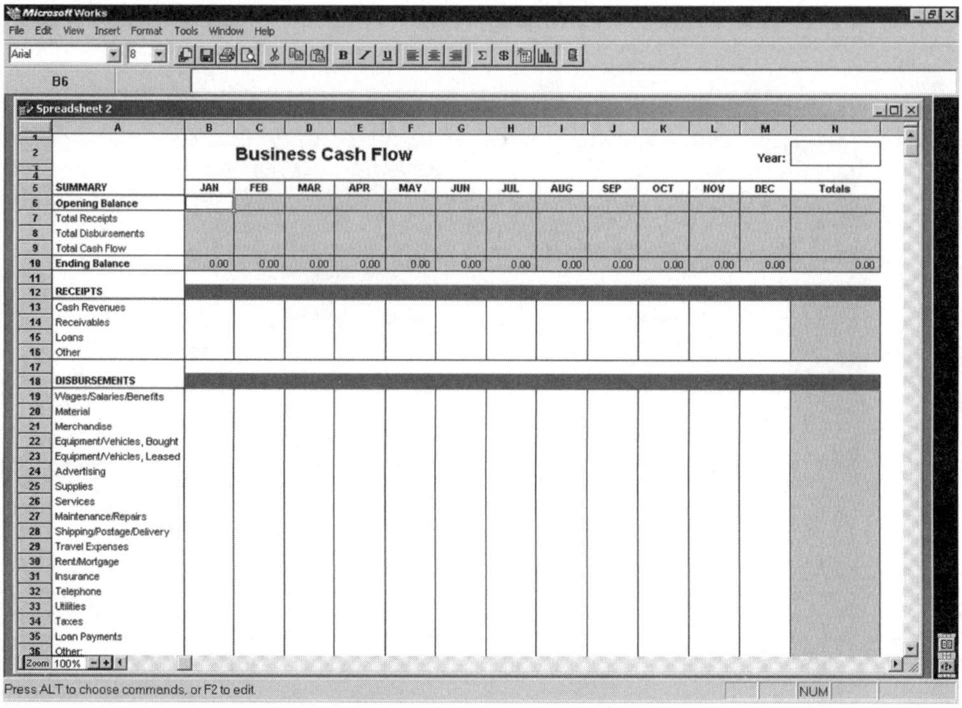

FIGURE 35-7. Cash flow statement.

Screen shot reprinted by permission from Microsoft Corporation.

counts. Cash budgets should be prepared six months ahead or, if possible, twelve months ahead with revision as needed.

When you help your boss develop a cash budget, it must be a realistic estimate. A cash budget is completely useless unless it is based on realistic, sober judgment springing entirely from experience.

Figure 35-7 shows a cash flow statement that can be created using one of the many Task Wizards available in Microsoft Works software.

Records for Lenders

If your employer is just starting a business, a lender is likely to request a specific list and total estimate of the business's start-up costs. Table 35-1 shows a sample. You might help your employer gather the necessary information.

As with a start-up estimate, a lender is likely also to request an estimate of probable monthly expenses, which when multiplied by twelve will be an estimate of first-year expenses. Table 35-2 shows a suggested form to use.

TABLE 35-1	An Estimate of Start-up Costs for a Retail Shop

STARTUP COSTS

Description	Cost
Inventory	$50,000
Fixtures and Equipment	7,000
Decoration	9,000
Legal and Professional Fees	2,000
Utility Deposits	100
Pre-opening Promotions	1,800
Cash Contingency Fund	2,000
Insurance	500
Supplies and Equipment	1,500
Security	2,000
Miscellaneous	500
Total	$76,400

TABLE 35-2	An Estimate of Monthly Expenses for a Retail Shop

MONTHLY EXPENSES

Description	Cost
Salaries	$2,000
Rental	800
Utilities and Telephone	200
Inventory Replenishment	4,000
Advertising	100
Supplies and Postage	200
Insurance	125
Maintenance	70
Professional Fees	100
Delivery Expense	250
Interest on Loan	80
Subscriptions and Dues	40
Miscellaneous	250
Monthly Total	$8,215

Business Taxes

✴ The Secretary's Role

Although your duties may not include filling out tax forms, it can be important to know what taxes are payable when and what forms are required. If you work for a small business, your chance is greater of being asked to help in this area. But if in no way else, you can help by keeping a list of tax forms and due dates and by reminding your employer a few weeks in advance of each deadline.

✴ Business Taxes

If the business that employs you is a corporation, a corporate tax form is due each year. This is Form 1120, and it's due March 15 of each calendar year, one month prior to the due date for personal returns. Throughout the year, estimated tax payments are also due; these are payable January 15, April 15, June 15, and September 15. To pay estimated taxes, a tax coupon book must be obtained from the Internal Revenue Service (IRS). This coupon book is used to make payments for a variety of different taxes. When filled out correctly, the coupon shows the type of tax (in this case 1120), along with the particular quarter of the year for which the payment is being made. Rather than send these payments directly to the IRS, you may pay them at the bank where the company maintains its checking account.

✴ EFTPS

The Electronic Federal Tax Payment System (EFTPS) is one of the most successful federal government programs undertaken in recent years. Millions of businesses are already enrolled in this system. It saves time and money, since there are no more last minute trips to the bank or Post Office, lost checks, or missed deadlines.

Here's how it works. By 8:00 p.m. Eastern Time—at least one calendar day prior to your tax due date—you log on, enter your tax payment report, review the information, and click **Submit** to initiate the payment. Per your instructions, EFTPS will automatically debit your indicated bank or credit union account and will transfer the funds to the U.S. Treasury on the date you indicate. Your tax records will be updated with the IRS.

In order to use EFTPS, you must enroll online at www.EFTPS.gov. After enrolling, you will receive a PIN and password.

State Taxes

If your state charges an income tax (and most do), the corporation must also pay estimated state taxes. You must obtain a state coupon book and make quarterly payments. However, in most cases these payments are made directly to the state by sending them in the mail.

Franchise Tax

The franchise tax is an annual tax on corporations payable to the Secretary of State's office in order to keep the corporation's status current. Usually the state sends the company a bill.

Sales Tax

If your employer is involved in the sale of goods or provides certain services, he or she may be liable to collect and pay sales tax. Sales tax amounts vary across the country, and forms sent by the state and county will explain how much to collect. Periodically, usually once each month, sales tax reports are sent out to each business. These must be filled out and returned with a check for the sales tax collected.

Employment Taxes

A variety of employment taxes must be filed and paid. For example, the federal and state taxes, Social Security tax, and Medicare fees that are withheld from employee paychecks must be paid periodically to the IRS and the state taxing authority. Federal and state guides for employers are available to explain how much to withhold from an employee's check and when payments are due. These withholding tax payments must be made promptly. In some cases the deadline is as fast as three days following the pay date. Form 941 must be filled out each quarter for federal tax reporting. Payments are made by using the tax coupon books at your local bank.

Another withholding tax is the unemployment tax, levied against businesses by your local state government throughout the year. If the company files with the state department of labor and the U.S. Department of Labor, it will receive reporting forms a few weeks before the filing deadlines. State taxes and report forms are sent to the state through the mail along with the payment. On the federal level, this tax requires filling out Form 940 once each year and using the coupon book to make the payment at the company's local bank.

Self-Employment Tax

If your boss does business as a partnership or a sole proprietor, he or she receives profits directly from the company. No Social Security tax is withheld from these profits. Therefore, when it comes time to file annual tax returns, your employer must pay a self-employment tax and file a Schedule SE. At the same time, any non-incorporated business owner must also file a Schedule C to report his or her business income just as employees on a payroll must pay their taxes throughout the year through withholding, so anyone owing self-employment tax must make estimated tax payments throughout the year. This can be done using 1040ES forms available from the IRS and sending payments into the IRS office for the particular IRS estimated tax region.

Employee or Independent Contractor?

What about you? Are you self-employed? If you are a part-time secretary and do not have "employee" status, your employer may consider you an **independent contractor.** This means that the employer will not withhold taxes from your check, and like a business owner, you are then liable for paying your own taxes. Depending on how much you earn, you may be required to make estimated tax payments throughout the year.

Determining Your Status

Whether you are an employee or a contractor is a difficult question to answer. The Department of Labor and IRS usually state that if you work at the company's place of business, use its tools, and work specific hours set by the company, then you are an employee. If you work at home, use your own computer, and come and go when you please, then you might be considered a contractor.

Effects of Status

The difference in your status can determine whether your employer is liable to pay half of your Social Security taxes (rather than you being solely responsible for self-employment taxes). In addition, an employer may pay unemployment tax and workers compensation.

Workers compensation, sometimes called **workers comp** is a state-funded insurance policy for employees who become injured or disabled while on the job. If you are injured, the insurance policy will pay for some of your medical bills, as well as a portion of your wages while you are off the job. Workers compensation is required in many states but varies depending on the business size.

Property and Net Worth Taxes

In most states, businesses pay local county and state governments a tax on inventory and on real property such as land or buildings. This tax is filed once each year. Land property tax bills are usually mailed each year, just like those that are sent to you if you own a home.

Net worth taxes are usually reported and paid at the same time the annual tax return is filled out. It requires that taxes be paid on business assets as well as cash and investments.

Business Licenses

All partnerships and sole proprietors along with some corporations are required to obtain a business license from the city and sometimes from the county where they are located and conduct business. To obtain a business license, the business owner must fill out paperwork and pay an annual fee. Business licenses can be renewed each year by paying an annual fee.

Tax Assistance

Many tax-planning aids are available from the IRS and your state department of revenue. Check your telephone book for the correct numbers, and call to ask for employers' guides and needed forms. Keep these on hand so your boss will always have them available in order to meet a deadline.

Banking

The Company's Bank

One important relationship every business must establish is with a bank. Many of the resulting financial details—whether from a checking account, business loan, or credit card—will be handled by the company's administrative assistant. The smaller the company is, the greater will be your involvement with your company's banking.

What if the bank gave away money, and you did not get in line? That's essentially what can happen if you don't understand a bank's full spectrum of financial products and services and use the correct ones when available. To save your company the most in fees while helping it nail down the most in interest, you need to know exactly what a bank can do for you.

Checking Accounts

The most basic account that every business needs is a checking account. There are several different types available, ranging from the basic checking account with a monthly fee to the money market account. Knowing which account the business qualifies for can help you reduce its monthly fees and even earn interest on its deposit. This is important information to pass on to your employer.

Basic Checking Account

A basic checking account is a convenient way to spend money without making frequent trips to the bank. It also allows you to pay bills through the mail without sending cash; cash should never be sent through the mail. In addition, a basic checking account provides you with a monthly record of the company's transactions, which helps you track income and expenses more easily. Most financial institutions do not pay interest on the money a business keeps in a basic checking account; instead, the banks charge a monthly fee. However, there is usually no minimum balance required to maintain this account.

NOW Account

A variation of the basic checking account is the NOW account, as it is known in the banking industry. This checking account has all the features of the basic checking account and pays interest on money in the account. NOW accounts require a minimum balance to be maintained. If the company's balance falls below that minimum, the account will be charged a monthly fee just like a basic checking account.

Super NOW Account

Like the NOW account, the Super NOW is a checking account that bears interest. However, it pays a higher rate of interest than a NOW, a rate which can fluctuate from month to month. The minimum balance required to maintain this account is usually $2,500.

Money Market Account

A money market account is similar to a Super NOW since it pays interest at the market rate, but the number of monthly transactions is limited by law. Like the Super NOW, a minimum balance is required to earn market interest rates, but only six transfers of funds such as checks, withdrawals, or wire transfers may be made each month. A money market account may substitute for a regular savings account for businesses that wish to invest on a short-term basis and still have quick access to their money.

Petty Cash

Most businesses keep a small amount of cash on hand to pay for cash items and to make change for customers. This cash must be accounted for with receipts for each expenditure. You can obtain petty cash by writing a check payable to "cash" or to a particular employee. In either case, whoever cashes the check will be responsible for making sure that accurate records are kept of expenditures.

Savings Accounts

If your employer's business has excess cash available, a variety of accounts can help save those funds for the future: a regular savings account, certificates of deposit (CDs), jumbo CDs, individual retirement accounts, savings bonds, automatic savings plans, and other retirement accounts.

A savings account is an ideal place to deposit cash or checks, providing a safe way to save for any purpose. In addition, excess funds earn interest while in the account. Unlimited withdrawals are permitted, but no checks may be written against the account. Interest rates may vary from one period to the next; the compounding of interest also varies among financial institutions.

Certificates of Deposit

Certificates of deposit (CDs) provide an investment option that pays a higher rate of interest than a savings account. A CD's interest rate and minimum deposit may vary depending on the term, such as six months or one year; however, once a CD is purchased, the interest rate is fixed. There are substantial penalties if the company needs to withdraw its funds before the term of the CD expires.

Another type of CD is the jumbo CD, so-called because it requires a minimum of $100,000 to open. The rate of interest is higher than that of a regular CD and varies depending on the term. Usually the longer the term is, the higher the interest rate. Like a regular CD, there is a substantial penalty for early withdrawal.

Savings Bonds

The purchase of government-backed U.S. savings bonds is another safe way to invest and save money. Series double E government bonds are available in denominations from $50 to $10,000 and carry a competitive interest rate. Earned interest is not subject to state or local taxes, and federal tax may be deferred until the bonds are redeemed and the interest is received.

Trust Services

One benefit offered by many large corporations is a retirement plan. Even small businesses may have retirement plans for some or all employees. Some retirement plans are offered by banks, and others can be set up through a mutual fund. The basic choices are a profit-sharing pension plan, a money-purchase pension plan, a 401k plan, a Keogh, and an individual retirement account.

Simplified Employee Pension Plan

A simplified employee pension plan can be adopted by small corporations. It usually consists of either a profit-sharing pension plan or a money-purchase pension plan or both. These plans can be set up by using fill-in-the-blank forms to determine the specifics for your business. With a simplified employee pension plan (SEP), the business contributes a percentage of the employee's annual salary into a pension account. This account is tax deferred and cannot be withdrawn by the employee until retirement age. With a profit-sharing plan, the contribution percentage is determined each year; the percentage can vary from year to year. It is not necessarily based on profits, and the business may have to contribute to the retirement fund even if there is a loss. With a money-purchase plan, the business must make a predetermined percentage contribution each year regardless of the business performance.

401(k) Plan

With a 401k plan, funds are deducted from the employee's salary and are deposited into the retirement account. The funds are tax deferred, and the interest earned on the account is also tax deferred. Sometimes the business may match the contribution of the employee up to a predetermined percentage and dollar amount limit determined by law.

Keogh Plan

If your boss is a self-employed individual in a small business, he or she may be interested in a special retirement plan called a Keogh, which provides a basic qualifying self-employment retirement plan for unincorporated business owners and their employees. Keogh participants may contribute up to 25 percent of their salaries and earned income into the retirement account, up to a certain dollar limit. Both the yearly contribution and interest earned on the account are tax deferred.

Individual Retirement Account

If the company does not offer its employees a retirement plan, and your individual income falls within certain limits, you may qualify for an Individual Retirement Account (IRA). The money that you deposit into an IRA can be deducted from your income before paying taxes. The interest earned by the account is tax deferred until you reach retirement age.

✹ Other Banking Services

Your boss and the company may be able to benefit from some of the other miscellaneous convenience services offered by financial institutions.

ATM Cards

ATM stands for "automated teller machine," a convenient way to get cash twenty-four hours a day. Besides providing you with petty cash for the office, the card allows you to check account balances, make deposits, and perform many other routine banking activities at your convenience. To use an ATM, the customer must be issued an ATM card, which is sometimes called a debit card. By using a secret password the customer is protected, and every transaction is conducted in private.

Safe Deposit Boxes

Many financial institutions have spaces within their vaults that are available for rental. These safe deposit boxes are a safe and fireproof way to store valuable documents and other small items of value. Only the owner of the box can access it using a special two-key system. Usually safe deposit boxes are available in several different sizes for a nominal annual rental fee.

Bill Paying by Telephone

Many banks allow you to pay routine bills such as utilities with just a telephone call, a boon for overworked secretaries. The organizations that your company must pay have prearranged code numbers. Use a touch-tone telephone to arrange payment from your company's account, and the financial institution makes sure your bill is paid immediately. A monthly statement of each transaction may be available to record expenditures.

Online Banking

With online or Web-based banking services, you can check balances, move funds between accounts, and automate your bill-paying process. Web-banking services can be accessed using a standard Web browser such as Microsoft Internet Explorer or Netscape Navigator. You must register to use your bank's Web-based banking services. A user name and password are required to access the bank's secure Web site.

To automate the bill-paying process, you must first enter information about each payee. This includes their name, address, phone number, and account number. Afterwards, the payees appear in a list. You can then enter a payment amount to schedule an electronic payment. You can also automate certain recurring bills such as rent and mortgage payments. One-time payees can also be entered. If the payee does not accept electronic payments, the bank will send them a bank check.

Online banking services are usually provided for a nominal monthly service fee. Depending on the type of account you have at the bank and the balance you keep, your bank may waive the fee.

Banking by Mail

If you do not want to or cannot visit a financial institution in person, you can use a bank-by-mail service. Primarily this service is for making deposits. Users are provided with preaddressed envelopes and deposit tickets to mail checks for deposit into their accounts.

Wire Transfers

If you need to send money quickly from one account to another, a wire transfer is the fastest way. It moves funds by telephone and electronic bookkeeping into another bank account in any part of the country or world.

It's important that you have some type of written authorization between the two parties involved, since once the funds have been transferred, they cannot be returned. To complete the transaction you need to know the names of the two account holders, the financial institutions involved, the American Banking Association numbers (a reference number that designates a particular bank), and the account numbers. You should get a receipt when the transaction is completed. A small transaction fee is required for the transfer, but the method is a safe and convenient way to transfer funds in a flash.

Foreign Currency Exchange

Foreign currency exchange can be a big help to a business in the import/export trade. The user of this service can convert money from one country to that of another at the current exchange rate. For businesspeople going abroad, changing currency in advance is much more convenient than waiting until they arrive at their destination. Later, after the business trip, the leftover foreign currency can be exchanged back into U.S. funds. Since the financial institution can adjust the exchange rate, there is usually a built-in fee for this service.

Bank Checks

When a business check or cash is not appropriate—such as transactions involving large dollar amounts—there are a variety of bank checks available, widely accepted as a safe, guaranteed substitutes for cash. Cashier's checks are issued by the bank and guarantee that funds are available. Money orders serve the same purpose but are usually issued in smaller amounts. Traveler's checks are sold in denominations such as $10, $20, $50, or $100 and can be refunded if lost or stolen.

Notary Service

Another useful business service offered by many banks is a notary service. Notaries verify the identity of individuals who need to sign certain official and legal documents. A notary can witness the signature and seal the signatures with a special stamp. Sometimes there is a small fee for this service, but many banks provide it free to customers who have an active account.

✳ Checks and Deposits

One of the most fundamental activities of any small business is the exchange of products and services for something else of value, normally money. This is called a **transaction.** Selling a product to a customer who pays cash is a typical transaction. But what about customers who pay by check? There are many transactions that do not involve cash, such as writing a check, accepting a check, making deposits or withdrawals at the bank, or transferring funds. It's important to understand the details of these transactions to protect your boss and the company from fraud and theft.

The most common transaction you will be involved in concerns checks, either personal or business. There are many different types and styles of checks, from the plain to the colorful. Yet all checks have some common basic elements such as numbers and names, and there is a specific set of requirements necessary before a check can be negotiable or cashable.

The first step in learning to negotiate a check is knowing the significance of each of its parts. There are two general areas to focus on: the preprinted information and the information filled in by the check writer. (See Figure 37-1.)

Looking at the preprinted information first, you will find the following:

■ In the upper left corner is the *name of the maker*—the person or persons who own the account. The maker is also sometimes called the *drawer*.

■ The *name and location of the financial institution* should also be printed on the check, usually just below the name of the maker. Often the bank includes its logo here.

■ The *sequential number of the check* is printed in the upper right corner.

■ Below the check number to the right of the date line is a fraction. This is called the American Banker's Association routing number and is referred to as the *ABA routing number.* When decoded, this number tells where the

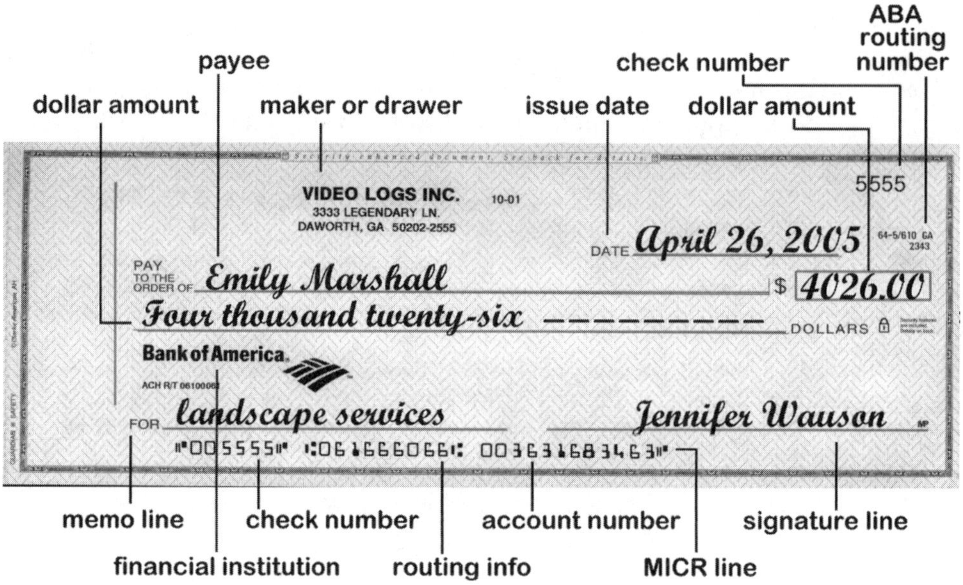

FIGURE 37-1. Parts of a check.

bank is located, the city, the specific bank branch, and the Federal Reserve bank serving this financial institution.

■ The *MICR line*, printed along the bottom of the check, contains the account number and the check number. MICR means magnetic ink character recognition; it is a number that can be read by a computer.

The parts of a check that most concern you are those filled in by the maker.

■ The *date line* provides space for the date the check was written.

■ The *pay-to-the-order-of* line indicates whom the maker intends to pay. This person or business is called the *payee*.

■ A line for the *dollar amount* to be written in figures is next to the payee line.

■ Underneath the payee line is a line for the maker to write the *dollar amount in words*.

■ A *for* or *memo line* is provided on the bottom left corner for the maker to note what the check is for.

■ The maker's signature goes on the *signature line* along the bottom right edge of the check.

Just as a bank examines a check you want to cash, you too should learn what to look for to make sure the checks you accept are legally negotiable:

■ There must be a date written on the date line of the check.

■ The pay-to-the-order-of line must be filled in. Checks written to the company cannot be cashed; they can only be deposited.

- The dollar amount must be filled in, both in numbers and in words, and the two amounts must match.

- The check must be signed by the maker, that is, the person listed on the printed part of the check. Look to see if two or more people must sign the check to make it legal. You'll know because there will be two signature lines on it and often the printed words "two signatures required" as well.

- The name and location of the financial institution must be printed on the check.

Examine the check for alterations. Scratch-throughs, white-outs, or any other indication that the check has been altered may make it unacceptable by the bank.

One of the goals of most financial institutions is to receive and retain deposits. Money taken into customer accounts through deposits provides the primary source of funds for the institution to loan and invest. If the company you work for is successful, you may make many routine deposits. There are two different types you can make: demand deposits and time deposits.

Demand deposits are made into checking and regular savings accounts where the money is readily available. The company can make a withdrawal at any time. On the other hand, with a **time deposit** such as a certificate of deposit, the company's money may be tied up for a period of time.

Making Deposits

You cannot walk into any bank on the street and deposit a check someone has given you or the company. Checks received by a business and made payable to the business name can be deposited only at a bank where the business has an established account. You cannot, for instance, go to the bank of the person who wrote the check and try to cash it there.

Another area of making deposits that confuses many people is something the banks classify as "on us" and "not-on-us" checks. An **on-us** check is one that is written and then deposited or cashed at the same bank. A **not-on-us** check is just what the name says: a check deposited at a bank that does not hold the account from which funds will be drawn. In most cases, there will be a longer delay in getting funds transferred when a transaction involves a not-on-us check. The delay can be longer if the transaction involves an out-of-state or a foreign bank. When there is a delay, most often, a hold will be placed on the deposit for a specified period of days. This means that the funds are not available as actual cash until the hold has expired and the funds have been transferred into the company's bank account.

When you make a deposit, you are giving the bank access to company funds. The deposit slip gives the bank permission to put money into the company's account or to collect funds from checks the company has received. It's your responsibility to make sure you have followed the correct procedures making the deposit, and that you get a receipt to ensure the company receives proper credit for the transaction. Therefore it is important that you understand what is involved in making a deposit.

THE DEPOSIT TRANSACTION

Generally a deposit transaction requires a deposit slip, items to be deposited, processing of the deposit by the bank teller, and issuing a receipt and/or cash back from the deposit. The transaction begins with the deposit slip. This key instrument of negotiation tells who is making the deposit, into what account the deposit is being made, and what amount is being deposited from what items.

DEPOSIT SLIP

A deposit slip must have the name and address of the account owner, either preprinted on the slip or written by hand. There must also be a date. In addition, there must be an MICR encoded account number to ensure proper crediting to your account. Most important, there should be a list of the items being deposited. These items must be listed in the form of currency, coins, and checks. Each check must be listed separately by amount. Additional space is usually provided on the back of the slip when depositing numerous checks. The subtotal of any checks deposited must be listed on the back and must also be filled in on the front part of the slip. Then all of the amounts for currency, coins, and checks should be totaled.

All checks deposited must be endorsed on the back. You must include the name of the company, its account number, and the words "for deposit only."

PROCESSING BY THE BANK TELLER

Bank tellers are trained to check and double-check every transaction. Therefore you should expect the teller to add up your deposit and to double-check your totals on the deposit slip. The teller should also verify the company's account number and make sure that all checks have been endorsed.

One important area to note concerns depositing cash items. Cash items are not just cash but any items that are accepted for deposit and credited to the company's account. They include all currency, coins, and many types of checks. Non-cash or collection items are accepted for handling but are not immediately credited to the account. These include checks that are not MICR encoded, foreign checks, promissory notes, and other items with documents or special instructions attached.

The important thing to remember is that, depending on whether you deposit cash or non-cash items, the company may not have instant access to the funds in its account for a specified period of time. If these banking details are your responsibility, it's up to you to find out when funds will be available. In this way the boss will not accidentally write a check with insufficient funds.

Withdrawals

Along with writing checks and making deposits, there may be times when you will be asked to make a withdrawal of cash from the company's checking or savings account. Withdrawing money from a checking account requires that you write a check on the company's account payable to yourself or to "cash." Some savings accounts also have checks that may be written to make a withdrawal. However, in some cases, when you do not have checks available, you can use a withdrawal slip.

A withdrawal slip must include the following information: the date, the amount of the withdrawal, the account number, and the signature of someone who has been approved to make withdrawals. If anything is missing or incorrect, the bank teller will ask you to correct your mistake or submit a new withdrawal slip.

If the withdrawal slip is correct, the teller will verify the signature with the one on file with the account. You should also be asked for proper identification. The teller must then check to make sure the company has funds available to cover the withdrawal. If it does, you will be given the cash and a receipt.

When withdrawing money from a business account, it's important to keep a few accounting and tax procedures in mind. All transactions must be accounted for. When you take cash from a business account, you must note the purpose. Usually the purpose will be to fund a petty cash account so you can pay for business supplies, stamps, or other incidentals. You must account for all cash you spend by getting receipts for your purchases. And before taking additional cash out of the business account, you should account for any previous withdrawals.

Special Situations

In addition to understanding normal business banking transactions, it's important that you understand what to do in some special circumstances. For instance, what if the boss accidentally writes or receives in payment an insufficient or "hot" check? Or what if you're asked to withdraw $10,000 or more in cash from the business account?

Returned Checks

A check may be returned to the company for any number of reasons such as a missing signature, closed account, or insufficient funds. If you receive a returned check, your best bet is to contact the person who gave the company the check and try to collect cash instead. If the person is not cooperative, you or the boss should contact local law enforcement authorities since theft of goods or services by check is against the law. If the company inadvertently should give someone a check that is returned, be prepared to pay cash and possibly to pay a special fee. You should make every effort to settle this matter amicably and at once. The company can be held legally responsible for the returned check; at the least it could suffer a damaging blow to its reputation.

Large Transactions

Transactions involving $10,000 or more in cash require special attention. The U.S. Treasury Department requires all financial institutions to provide the Internal Revenue Service (IRS) with information on large currency transactions. This information helps the IRS's criminal tax and regulatory investigations by discouraging the use of cash in illegal transactions. Some customers, such as retail businesses, may be exempted by this reporting. However, unless the company has been previously exempted, you must fill out the large currency transaction form. This can usually be done with the help of a teller or customer service representative.

Since carrying large amounts of cash is unsafe, if you are involved with withdrawals exceeding $10,000 what can you do instead? Let's say the boss is purchasing a car for the business. Many car dealers will not accept a check from the company account and allow the boss to drive away in the new car. Instead, he or she must provide the seller with something that is as good as cash.

Cashier's or Certified Check

A cashier's check or a certified check could be used to pay for the car since they verify that funds are available. A cashier's check is issued by a financial institution and is paid for at the time it is issued. A certified check is from the company account, and it has been officially certified by the bank that funds are available and have been set aside to pay this particular check. Both checks are as good as cash and allow the boss to complete the purchase.

Money Order

Money orders are often used by people who don't have checking accounts. They are sold for specific amounts by financial institutions and retail stores. They are made payable to the order of a particular business or individual when they are purchased; therefore they are as good as cash if you receive one from someone else. They also provide a receipt that can be used to prove payment or to get a refund in the case of theft or loss.

Traveler's Checks

Traveler's checks are also commonly used in many business transactions instead of cash. These special checks are issued by a financial institution in common denominations just like currency. When you purchase a traveler's check, you must endorse the check once before you leave the bank. When you get ready to pay for a transaction with a traveler's check, you then endorse the check a second time. If you accept a traveler's check as payment for goods or services, you should make sure both signatures are the same. This double-signature feature protects the purchaser of the checks in case they are lost or stolen. Receipts are also provided for this same purpose. Usually some form of identification is required when using traveler's checks.

Credit Cards

Depending on what type of business you work for, you may also be involved in transactions involving credit cards. Credit cards are often used as payment in transactions and are widely accepted all over the world for purchases of goods and services.

Credit cards are issued by a financial institution just like a loan. Each card has a unique account number, which can be verified electronically or by checking the list of accounts published by the card company. A credit card purchase slip is required to complete a transaction. It must include a stamp of the card, the account number, the name of the card holder, and the expiration date. The purchase slip must also include the amount of the purchase and be signed by the card holder. In some cases, such as mail order purchases, this information can be obtained over the telephone and filled in by hand.

Reconciling Bank Statements

Each month the bank will provide a statement for the previous month that lists company checks that have cleared and deposits made. The statement will also list any special fees or charges for items such as printing new checks, covering returned checks, renting safe deposit boxes, and so forth. Along with the statement the bank will provide copies of the canceled checks written against the account.

As soon as bank statements come in, they should be double-checked against the company's checkbook records for mistakes and possible fraud. This process is called **reconciling** or **balancing the checkbook.** If the duty falls to you, follow these guidelines:

■ Put the checks returned with the statement into numerical order.

■ Make sure each check is for the same amount that is listed in the company checkbook, and note in the checkbook that it has cleared.

■ Look at the bank statement to make sure each check is listed correctly there.

■ Follow the same procedures to verify deposits. Make sure the bank has credited the account for the same amount that you have listed in the company checkbook.

Usually checks that were written or deposits made at the end of a reporting period will not appear on the statement, and sometimes recipients of checks fail to deposit them promptly; all of these checks will be missing from the bank statement. Because of this, there will usually be a difference between the bank balance shown on the statement and the balance shown in the checkbook. Follow the simple guidelines for reconciling usually printed on the back of the statement. These guidelines will take into account missing checks and deposits made after the cut-off date, items that won't show up until next month's statement.

Although you're busy with many other duties, it's usually a good idea to reconcile the company's bank records as soon as they come in each month. Allowing them to pile up may result in account balance errors and eventual bank charges for returned checks. Also, there are time limits for correcting a mistake if you believe the bank is at fault. To protect your company's rights, its financial security, and its reputation, reconcile the statements as quickly as possible.

Once you've reconciled the statements, keep them in a safe place, where they are available only to people authorized by the business owners. These statements are often needed in the event of tax audits and when applying for business loans. Duplicates of missing statements may be obtained by writing or calling the company's bank.

Special Business and Financial Information for the Small Business Administrative Assistant

Frequently Asked Questions

Many administrative assistants work in what are considered to be "small businesses" (though under certain definitions, companies with as many 1,500 employees are considered to be small!). If you're such an assistant, you may perform different roles from those of an administrative assistant in a larger office. In a small business there's often no payroll department, no accounting department, no purchasing department, no human resources; there's only you. Because of this, you may find yourself with enormous responsibility, privy to the boss's most private concerns about the business.

As the boss's right hand, you'll be the first person he or she turns to with questions. Here, in a brief format, are answers to some of the most frequently asked questions your boss may have about the company.

How does the boss go about registering the company's name? Contact the county clerk in the county where the business is or will be located.

How can the boss incorporate the business? In most states, this can be done either with or without an attorney. Write to your state's Secretary of State in the state's capital city for information.

How can the boss obtain a copyright? Write for information from:

Copyright Information
Library of Congress
Washington, DC 20559
(202) 479-0700

How can the boss obtain a patent or a trademark? Write for information from:

Commissioner of Patents and Trademarks
Washington, DC 20231
(703) 557-3158 or (703) 557-3881

How can the boss receive patent, trademark, search, and technology assistance? Technical Applications Centers or Technology and Transfer Centers are located throughout the nation. Write to the Commissioner of Patents at the address above for the location nearest the company.

Where can the boss receive business tax information? To obtain a State Resale Tax Permit, write to the Comptroller of Public Accounts, State Capitol Building, in your state's capital city. To obtain a Federal Employee Tax Number for the boss, write the Internal Revenue Service (IRS) at a district office near you or at Washington, D.C. Or the boss can attend a workshop conducted by the IRS in your area. Call the nearest office of the IRS for details and dates.

Where can the boss receive import and export information? For importing information, contact your nearest U.S. Customs Department District Office. For information about exporting the company's products, contact an International Assistance Center; these are located throughout the nation and can supply you with an abundance of information concerning exports. A local Small Business Association Office can give you the location of a center near you.

Trading with Other Countries

Most small businesses strive to become large businesses and, in doing so, may seek world markets for their products and services. If your employer is among that group, he or she should ask the International Trade Administration (ITA) of the U.S. Department of Commerce for assistance. The ITA functions to help citizens benefit from foreign trade. The agency explains how to begin exporting the company's products and how to locate buyers and distributors for those products and services. The ITA publishes *A Basic Guide to Exporting*. For information on ordering a copy, write to:

Superintendent of Documents
U.S. Government Printing Office
Washington, DC 20402

This excellent publication is invaluable to business owners who wish to enter international markets. Also of assistance is the U.S. Department of State. Using Country Desk Officers, the Department of State advises representatives of American companies about the economic climate and political situation of the country each officer represents. For further information, write directly to:

Office of Commercial Affairs
EBIOCA
U.S. Department of State
Washington, DC 20520

Because of language barriers, it might be wise for the small business owner just beginning to enter foreign markets to start with countries where English is the spoken language. Chapter 5 contains a list of the languages spoken in nations around the world. You will note that there are many countries where English is the spoken language. But regardless of language, the boss might consider such questions as these:

■ What is the standard of living in each country?

■ What is the level of education prevailing in each country?

■ What is the anticipated market for the company's product or service? What information can be discovered about competitive products or services now offered in that country?

■ What is the price structure prevailing for similar products or services?

Another important agency is the Export-Import Bank of the United States. This independent organization of the U.S. government helps finance America's exports by offering loans to foreign purchasers of American goods and services. The agency works with commercial banks in this country and overseas to provide financial arrangements, which helps U.S. exporters offer credit assistance to their foreign buyers. For details and assistance, write to:

Export-Import Bank of the United States
811 Vermont Avenue, NW
Washington, DC 20571

✸ Sources of Financing

Some of the following sources provide money for all kinds of businesses, small and large. As you will notice by their titles, certain sources concern themselves with groups singled out by Congress for special financial aid. Others supply money to get certain kinds of things done by businesses:

■ Area Development Administration

■ Bureau of Commercial Fisheries

■ Bureau of Indian Affairs

■ Commodity Credit Corporation

■ Environmental Protection Administration

■ Federal Housing Authority

■ Federal Reserve System

■ Small-business investment companies

■ State and local development companies

■ Treasury Department

■ Veterans Administration

✦ Small Business Administration

What is the U.S. Small Business Administration? How can that agency be of assistance to your boss if he or she is a small business owner? The answer to this question is so lengthy the rest of the chapter has been devoted to it.

The Small Business Administration (SBA) helps build America's future by being at the forefront of developing this vital sector of the economy. Following is some general information about the SBA. This fundamental knowledge will be useful if the boss asks you to find out what the SBA can do for the company, or, later, if the boss asks that agency for information, advice, and assistance, or applies for an SBA loan.

What Is a Small Business?

There's nothing small about small business! The estimated 20 million small businesses in America today account for over 40 percent of the gross national product, employ half of America's workforce, and generate 53.5 percent of all sales.

Since it was established in 1953, the SBA has delivered more than 9 million loans, contracts, counseling sessions, and other forms of assistance—an average of 180,000 in every state—to businesses across the nation. The agency has 110 offices covering every state, the District of Columbia, Guam, Puerto Rico, and the Virgin Islands. With loan authorization of $4 billion, it is the government's most flexible and innovative economic development agency.

All SBA programs and services are extended on a nondiscriminatory basis. These programs and services stimulate capital formation, economic growth, and job creation. They address finance, marketing, production, procurement, and human resources management. Credit programs boost the availability of capital and build the confidence of both lenders and borrowers. Credit programs rely on guarantees of loans made by private lenders, so the cost to taxpayers is minimal.

SBA's General Loan Program

The SBA's prime financial assistance activity is the bank guarantee loan program. The SBA generally does not make loans itself, nor does it have a grant program for starting a small business. Rather, it assists small businesses by guaranteeing commercial loans made by local lenders, generally banks, up to $750,000. There is no theoretical minimum; however, most lenders are reluctant to process commercial loans of less than $25,000.

To obtain an SBA loan, each applicant first obtains a participating lender (bank, savings and loan, or regulated non-bank lender). The SBA loan application is then sent in by this lender. The SBA's guarantee is designed for long-term financial needs (five to twenty-five years, depending on use). Eligible small businesses must be independently owned and operated and engaged in non-investment, non-speculative, legal activities. Loans generally can be used for equipment, fixtures, construction, leasehold improvements, inventory, and working capital.

This general loan program represents 90 percent of the agency's total loan effort. It promotes small business formation and growth by guaranteeing up to 90 percent of the amount provided by commercial lenders. A recent study by Price Waterhouse reports that businesses that get these loan guarantees show higher growth than comparable businesses.

Seminars titled "How to Apply for a Business Loan Using the SBA's Loan Guarantee" are presented from time to time in your area. Contact your nearest SBA office for details and dates to pass along to the boss.

How Does the Loan Program Work?

The prospective borrower will be required to provide a capital contribution, normally 30 percent to 50 percent of the total capitalization of the business.

An existing business will be required to provide financial statements showing the business is a profit-making concern, does not have delinquent taxes, and after the loan is made, will have a debt-to-worth ratio not to exceed 3:1 or the industry average.

The SBA charges the tender (usually a bank) a 2 percent guarantee fee on the guaranteed portion of the loan. SBA policy allows the lender (the bank) to pass this guarantee fee on to the borrower (the business owner).

The SBA guaranteed loan maturity (length of loan) is based on the following schedule:

■ Working capital loans: five to seven years.

■ Fixed asset loans: seven to ten years.

■ Real estate and building: up to a maximum of twenty-five years.

The general size standards for SBA-guaranteed business loans are based on the average number of employees for the preceding twelve months or on the sales volume averaged over a three-year period according to the following schedule:

■ Manufacturing: varies from 500 to 1,500 employees

■ Wholesaling: no more than 100 employees

■ Services: from $3.5 million to $14.5 million

■ Retailing: from $3.5 million to $13.5 million

■ Construction: from $9.5 million to $17 million

■ Special trade construction: not to exceed $7 million

■ Agriculture: from $0.5 million to $3.5 million

Your boss should prepare for an appointment with a lender by having ready answers for the lender's questions. An even better way to prepare is to put all the information into a formal business plan; you can help by gathering and assembling the data. Be sure to include the items listed below:

■ Projected profit-and-loss statement

■ Cash flow projections

■ Market analysis

- Marketing strategy
- Description of the business
- Product or services advantage
- Management ability (resumes of the key staff)
- Financial information (both personal and business)
- Cash requirements

Not all business proposals are eligible for the SBA's guaranteed loan program. The following are ineligible:

- Partial purchase of a business
- Lending institutions
- Real estate held for speculation, investment, or rental
- Opinion molders (magazines, newspapers, trade journals, TV, radio, live entertainment, schools, etc.)
- Religious organizations and their affiliates

The Application Process

After a formal business plan that includes the information suggested above is developed, schedule an appointment for your boss with a local banker to discuss the plan and loan request. (The SBA can furnish a listing of your area's most active SBA lenders). If the boss's plan is acceptable, the bank will provide a loan application package for completion. If professional assistance is needed to complete the application, the lender may be able to refer the boss to several qualified loan packagers.

After the loan application package is complete, return it to the lender. If it's acceptable, the lender will forward the loan application along with the lender's credit analysis to the SBA. After SBA approval, the lender closes the loan and disburses the funds.

Other SBA Loan Programs

Following is a description of other SBA loan programs:

- *Development Company Loan Program.* Uses public/private partnerships to finance fixed assets. It has produced over $5 billion in investments and more than 300,000 jobs since its beginning in 1980.

- *Small Business Investment Company (SBIC) Program.* Made up of privately owned and operated investment companies licensed by the SBA to provide equity or venture capital and long-term loans to small firms to help them operate, grow, and modernize. Investment companies normally take an actual or potential ownership position in the small business firm to which they provide financing. SBIC's have invested nearly $11 billion in more than 70,000 small businesses.

- *Microloan Program.* Helps entrepreneurs in inner city and rural areas form small, often home-based enterprises.

- *Export Finance.* Offers normal and specialized loan guarantees of working capital and longer-term financing to promote exporting.

- *Disaster Loans.* Provides low-interest loans to help individuals, homeowners, and businesses rebuild after a disaster.

- *8(a) Program.* Targets socially and economically disadvantaged individuals interested in government contracting. An applicant must be a 51 percent owner and manager of an existing business that has been viable for the past two years. For more information, interested individuals should attend monthly seminars conducted by their nearest SBA office.

- *Procurement Assistance.* Ensures maximum competition by encouraging contracts for small businesses.

- *Surety Bond Guarantee Program.* Has provided more than 236,000 surety guarantees for billions in contracts since 1976, helping businesses win government construction contracts. If the boss needs bid or performance bonds for his or her contracting business, the SBA Surety Bond Guarantee Program is administered by your regional Office of the SBA. Contact it by telephone for information.

SBA Business Development Programs

Separate from the loan programs are other programs that provide marketing and training information, serving as a catalyst for small business development and growth. Programs focus on management training, international trade, veterans' affairs, women's initiatives, and resource partnerships. Here are the basic programs.

BUSINESS INITIATIVES, EDUCATION AND TRAINING PROGRAM

This produces a broad range of management and technical assistance publications and audiovisual materials. Each year the SBA distributes more than 3 million SBA publications and videotapes.

INTERNATIONAL TRADE

Information, advice, and export financing help prepare businesses to take advantage of the new world market, particularly in Mexico, the Pacific Rim, Canada, and Europe.

VETERANS' AFFAIRS

This program provides business management, technical training, and counseling. Every year about 1,200 training conferences are held for prospective and established business owners who were veterans.

WOMEN'S BUSINESS OWNERSHIP ASSISTANCE

This program was developed by the SBA for emerging and expanding women businesses through the Women's Business Ownership Act of 1988, to provide long-term training and counseling for women, mentoring programs, and training/counseling centers for women nationwide. Each year more than 100,000 women are counseled, and more than 180,000 are trained. For more information, contact the Center for Women's Business Enterprise at the regional SBA office nearest you.

SMALL BUSINESS INNOVATION RESEARCH (SBIR) PROGRAM
The SBA is the focal point in helping small businesses gain access to federally funded research and development activities. Any for-profit small business concern may apply directly for competitive research contracts and grants from eleven federal agencies. To obtain a quarterly Pre-Solicitation Announcement containing information on the SBIR solicitations of participating federal agencies, call your nearest SBA office.

SERVICE CORPS OF RETIRED EXECUTIVES (SCORE)
SCORE counselors are experienced former business owners and executives who, free of charge, assist small businesses with problems and prospective owners with counseling and direction. If your boss would like to talk to someone who can and will help his or her business with related questions, you might contact SCORE. There may be SCORE volunteers in your community. Major service activities are located throughout the nation.

SCORE volunteers sponsor and present monthly "Going into Business" seminars at a minimal cost to attendees. From time to time they also present a workshop "How to Start and Manage a Small Business." For a listing of SCORE chapters near you, contact your nearest SBA office.

SMALL BUSINESS INSTITUTE (SBI) PROGRAM
The SBI program offers small businesses individual help with site location, marketing studies, industry research, industry trends, and many other business challenges through area colleges and universities. Call your nearest SBI office for a list of local participating colleges and universities.

SMALL BUSINESS DEVELOPMENT CENTER (SBDC)
If the boss needs assistance in preparing a business plan, evaluating business prospects, seeking capital, obtaining specific information on international trade, technical problems, or opportunities in selling to the government, your local SBDC may be the answer. SBDC's are located in many areas, not necessarily only in the city where an SBA regional office is located. The SBDC program provides in-depth training and counseling assistance to small businesses. Call your nearest SBA office for details and locations of a Small Business Development Center near you.

In all, SCORE, SBI, and SBDC handle more than 800,000 counseling and training cases each year.

Selling to the Federal Government

If your employer would like to sell the company's services or products to the federal government, the Small Business Development Center can help through its Center for Government Contracting. A fee may be charged for this help.

You should also contact government contracting agencies such as the Department of Defense in a regional office near you or in Washington, D.C.; the General Services Administration (GSA) in a regional office or in Washington, D.C.; the Regional SBA Procurement Division in a regional office; or the Procurement Automated Source System (PASS) program, which is a computer directory describing the profile of a company interested in competing for federal procurement. Call your SBA office for complete details.

Weights and Measures

 U.S. Weights and Measures

The following tables (39-1 through 39-7) list standard U.S. weights and measurements.

TABLE 39-1	Linear Measure

1 inch = .0083 foot
12 inches (in) = 1 foot (ft)
3 feet = 1 yard (yd)
5 1/2 yards = 1 rod (rd), pole, or perch =16 1/2 ft
40 rods = 1 furlong (fur) = 220 yds = 660 ft
8 furlongs = 1 statute mile (mi) = 1,760 yds = 5,280 ft
3 land miles = 1 league
5,280 feet = 1 statute or land mile
6,076.11549 feet = 1 international nautical mile

TABLE 39-2	Area Measure

144 square inches = 1 sq ft
9 square feet = 1 sq yd = 1,296 sq in
30 1/4 square yards = 1 sq rd = 272 1/4 sq ft
160 square rods = 1 acre = 4,840 sq yds = 43,560 sq ft
640 acres = 1 square mile
1 mile square = 1 section (of land)
6 miles square = 1 township = 36 sections = 36 square miles

TABLE 39-3 Cubic Measure

1,728 cubic inches (cu in) = 1 cu ft
27 cubic feet = 1 cu yd

TABLE 39-4 Liquid Measure

1 gill (gi) = 4 ounces (oz)
4 gills = 1 pint (pt) = 28.875 cu in
2 pints = 1 quart (qt) = 57.75 cu in
4 quarts = 1 gallon (gal) = 231 cu in = 8 pts = 32 gills

TABLE 39-5 Dry Measure

2 pints = 1 qt = 67.2006 cu in
8 quarts = 1 peck (pk) = 537.605 cu in = 16 pts
4 pecks = 1 bushel (bu) = 2,150.42 cu in = 32 qts

TABLE 39-6 Units of Circular Measure

Second (") = —
Minute (') = 60 seconds
Degree (°) = 60 minutes
Right angle = 90 degrees
Straight angle = 180 degrees
Circle = 360 degrees

TABLE 39-7 Troy Weight

24 grains = 1 pennyweight (pwt)
20 pennyweights = 1 ounce troy (oz t) = 480 grains
12 ounces troy = 1 pound troy (lb t)
= 240 pennyweights
= 5,760 grains

✳ The International System (Metric)

The following tables (39-8 through 39-12) list various metric measurements.

TABLE 39-8	Linear Measure (Metric)

10 millimeters (mm) = 1 centimeter (cm)
10 centimeters = 1 decimeter (dm) = 100 millimeters
10 decimeters = 1 meter (m) = 1,000 millimeters
10 meters = 1 dekameter (dam)
10 dekameters = 1 hectometer (hm) = 100 meters
10 hectometers = 1 kilometer (km) = 1,000 meters

TABLE 39-9	Area Measure (Metric)

100 square millimeters (mm^2) = 1 sq centimeter (cm^2)
10,000 square centimeters = 1 sq meter (m^2) = 1,000,000 sq millimeters
100 square meters = 1 are (a)
100 ares = 1 hectare (ha) = 10,000 sq meters
100 hectares = 1 sq kilometer (km^2) = 1,000,000 sq meters

TABLE 39-10	Volume Measure (Metric)

10 milliliters (ml) = 1 centiliter (cl)
10 centiliters = 1 deciliter (dl) = 100 milliliters
10 deciliters = 1 liter (l) = 1,000 milliliters
10 liters = 1 dekaliter (dal)
10 dekaliters = 1 hectoliter (hl) = 100 liters
10 hectoliters = 1 kiloliter (kl) = 1,000 liters

TABLE 39-11	Cubic Measure (Metric)

1,000 cubic millimeters (mm^3) = 1 cu centimeter (cm^3)
1,000 cubic centimeters = 1 cu decimeter (dm^3) = 1,000,000 cu millimeters
1,000 cubic decimeters = 1 cu meter (m^3) =
1 stere = 1,000,000 cu centimeters =
1,000,000,000 cu millimeters

TABLE 39-12	Weight Measure (Metric)

10 milligrams (mg) = 1 centigram (cg)

10 centigrams = 1 decigram (dg) = 100 milligrams

10 decigrams = 1 gram (g) = 1,000 milligrams

10 grams = 1 dekagram (dag)

10 dekagrams = 1 hectogram (hg) = 100 grams

10 hectograms = 1 kilogram (kg) = 1,000 grams

1,000 kilograms = 1 metric ton (t)

Conversion Table

The following table (39-13) can be used to convert various U.S. measurements into metric. In the table, × means multiply, / means divide, and # means the value is exact. All other values are approximate.

TABLE 39-13	Conversion Table	
From	**To**	**Formula**
acres	hectares	× 0.4047
acres	square kilometers	/ 247
acres	square meters	× 4047
acres	square miles	/ 640
barrels (oil)	cubic meters	/ 6.29
barrels (oil)	gallons (UK)	× 34.97
barrels (oil)	gallons (US)	× 42
barrels (oil)	liters	× 159
centimeters	feet	/ 30.48
centimeters	inches	/ 2.54
centimeters	meters	/ 100
centimeters	millimeters	× 10
cubic cm	cubic inches	× 0.06102
cubic cm	liters	/ 1000
cubic cm	milliliters	× 1
cubic feet	cubic inches	× 1728
cubic feet	cubic meters	× 0.0283
cubic feet	cubic yards	/ 27
cubic feet	gallons (UK)	× 6.229
cubic feet	gallons (US)	× 7.481
cubic feet	liters	× 28.32
cubic inches	cubic cm	× 16.39
cubic inches	liters	× 0.01639
feet	centimeters	× 30.48
feet	meters	× 0.3048
feet	yards	/ 3
fluid ounces (UK)	fluid ounces (US)	× 0.961
fluid ounces (UK)	milliliters	× 28.41

From	To	Formula
fluid ounces (US)	fluid ounces (UK)	× 1.041
fluid ounces (US)	milliliters	× 29.57
gallons	pints	× 8 #
gallons (UK)	cubic feet	× 0.1605
gallons (UK)	gallons (US)	× 1.2009
gallons (UK)	liters	× 4.54609
gallons (US)	cubic feet	× 0.1337
gallons (US)	gallons (UK)	× 0.8327
gallons (US)	liters	× 3.785
grams	kilograms	/ 1000
grams	ounces	/ 28.35
hectares	acres	× 2.471
hectares	square km	/ 100
hectares	square meters	× 10000
hectares	square miles	/ 259
hectares	square yards	× 11 960
inches	centimeters	× 2.54
inches	feet	/ 12
kilograms	ounces	× 35.3
kilograms	pounds	× 2.2046
kilograms	tonnes	/ 1000
kilograms	tons (UK/long)	/ 1016
kilograms	tons (US/short)	/ 907
kilometers	meters	× 1000
kilometers	miles	× 0.6214
liters	cubic inches	× 61.02
liters	gallons (UK)	× 0.2200
liters	gallons (US)	× 0.2642
liters	pints (UK)	× 1.760
liters	pints (US liquid)	× 2.113
meters	yards	/ 0.9144
meters	centimeters	× 100
miles	kilometers	× 1.609
millimeters	inches	/ 25.4
ounces	grams	× 28.35
pints (UK)	liters	× 0.5683
pints (UK)	pints (US liquid)	× 1.201
pints (US liquid)	liters	× 0.4732
pints (US liquid)	pints (UK)	× 0.8327
pounds	kilograms	× 0.4536
pounds	ounces	× 16
square feet	square inches	× 144
square feet	square meters	× 0.0929
square inches	square cm	× 6.4516
square inches	square feet	/ 144
square km	acres	× 247
square km	hectares	× 100
square km	square miles	× 0.3861

(continued)

From	To	Formula
square meters	acres	/ 4047
square meters	hectares	/ 10 000
square meters	square feet	× 10.76
square meters	square yards	× 1.196
square miles	acres	× 640
square miles	hectares	× 259
square miles	square km	× 2.590
square yards	square meters	/ 1.196
tonnes	kilograms	× 1000
tonnes	tons (UK/long)	× 0.9842
tonnes	tons (US/short)	× 1.1023
tons (UK/long)	kilograms	× 1016
tons (UK/long)	tonnes	× 1.016
tons (US/short)	kilograms	× 907.2
tons (US/short)	tonnes	× 0.9072
yards	meters	× 0.9144

CAREER ADVANCEMENT

SECTION SIX

There are many opportunities for advancement for dedicated administrative assistants who care about the quality of their work.

Photo by Jennifer Wauson. Digital photography courtesy of Kyocera Optics.

Your Future

Growing as the Company Grows

As you begin or continue your career, you have numerous choices regarding type and size of companies. Which is better to work for: a large or a small one? You'll find as many answers as there are administrative assistants. A large company often offers the best available salary and benefits, as well as steady advancement within its corporate structure. Yet small companies, too, offer growth potential. They may not always be able to afford as generous a salary or benefit package but often provide a wider range of experience that would otherwise be impossible to get. And when a small company successfully expands, the administrative assistant has the excitement of getting in on the ground floor and growing with the business. In many instances the small business administrative assistant can inherit as much responsibility as he or she wants.

Learn About the Business

It's important that no matter what type of business you work for, what size it is, or where it's located, you should do your best to learn as much about it as possible. In Chapter 1 we discussed learning about the business to make a favorable impression during your job interview. This learning process should never stop. Even if your duties are strictly defined and fairly routine, you should do your best to discover how the business is managed, how customers or clients are obtained, and how the products or services provided are produced. Although you may see no immediate need for this knowledge, it can be invaluable in a later emergency, as you advance, or if you seek work with a different company.

Upgrade Your Skills

No matter what type or size company you work for, focus on acquiring essential business skills, whether or not you need any one of them now. Make sure your skills are top-notch in such office-related areas as keyboarding, maintaining a filing system, handling incoming and outgoing mail, setting appointments, answering telephones, taking dictation, and using office machines. Try to acquire proficiency in correspondence, research, customer service, purchasing, budgeting, bookkeeping, invoicing, training new employees, and supervising an office staff. You should learn how to write and speak effectively and be able to plan and organize your work. And finally, you must be computer literate. Having all these skills will give you the most flexible preparation to meet any challenge you face—either an on-the-job crisis or a career opportunity.

As proof of the level of quality of your skills, you may want to investigate being certified by the National Secretaries Association as a Certified Professional Secretary (CPS). This certification is granted only upon the successful completion of examinations in various aspects of secretarial procedures and skills. Serious secretaries and administrative assistants may find it worthwhile to inquire about the activities of this outstanding association. Being certified can be a tremendous boost to your career.

✴ Recognizing a Time for Change

One of the trends in modern business is the changing nature of administrative work. Today in businesses of all sizes, more managers are doing work on their own desktop computer systems that in the past would have been handled by a secretary. As these trends continue, there will be fewer and fewer secretaries and more office and information specialists. It's up to you to create a place for yourself in this changing world.

Learning new skills and improving your old ones is the best professional insurance you can acquire, and it can put you in the position of being a better secretary than your current position demands. If you cannot expand your current role but are capable of much more than you're doing, your dissatisfaction may lead you to want to change your direction in life and seek out a new job. Your new skills will help you get the best possible situation.

These skills will also prove invaluable if change is forced upon you. Gone are the days when a secretary might work forty-five years for the same company, many of those years for the same boss. This is true of both large and small companies. A large company used to provide stability, but no longer. Corporate restructurings, which have affected hundreds of thousands of people over the past years, have been a mixed blessing for administrative assistants. In the wake of restructuring, some assistants have to leave their position when their boss leaves, but others are asked to take on greater responsibility, to "take up the slack" as middle managers are phased out. Either situation could be professionally devastating if it was not what the administrative assistant would have chosen himself or herself.

On the other hand, small businesses have their own dangers, particularly in the first eighteen months of operation, though knowing that doesn't make it easier for the secretary who faces possible job loss. Rather than restructure, a small business may just fold completely, perhaps without giving you adequate notice, perhaps even without giving you a final paycheck.

Always be alert to conditions or changes that could affect your job, no matter what size company you work for. In a large company, be wary if your boss is excluded from meetings he or she used to attend, is dropped from routing lists, or is told to cut back on budget and staff. Do people who used to lunch or chat with your boss still do so? These warning signs can also signal that your own position might be in jeopardy.

In a small business where you work directly for the owner, pay attention to details. Has business been slipping lately? Is it just a temporary slump or something more serious? Has the boss paid vendors and other creditors, or are you starting to receive dunning letters and telephone calls? Of critical importance to you is whether the boss has paid payroll taxes and health insurance premiums. If your boss has not, and the business folds, the Internal Revenue Service will look to the individual to pay the overdue taxes even though the money was already withheld from earlier paychecks. The individual may have no health care coverage even though deductions for premiums may have been taken. And the individual might not even be able to collect unemployment benefits though taxes for that were deducted too.

What should you do if something like this should happen to you? Your best bet is to consult an attorney; however, be advised that though you might file and win a lawsuit against your former employer, collecting your judgment may prove to be difficult and costly.

The better advice is to be aware of the financial health of your employer so you can take action before it's forced on you. These events are the exception, but it's better to be employed and equipped with this knowledge than to experience it naively when you can least afford it.

Finding a Job

When, for whatever reason, you feel the need to find a new job, explore all possible ways. Don't simply look in the paper or sign up at an employment agency for a position as a secretary, administrative assistant, or office manager. A more aggressive search can find you a more satisfying position.

Start by researching companies you might want to work for or areas where you might like to work. With newspapers and trade journals in hand, you might read about companies that were voted "family friendly" or had instituted company-wide training programs in computers or second languages or had a strong policy of promoting from within. One company might be known for its laid-back atmosphere and flexible hours. Another might be known for its hard-driving excellence. Which interests you more? Which do you need more? These are the companies to target.

Locally, drive around office or industrial parks or anywhere else businesses are located. Stop in and talk and ask questions. Find out what the business does and if there are any job openings. These cold-call in-person visits are not as difficult as they might sound. If you are friendly and don't take up too much time, you can gain much valuable information.

You can also conduct research by looking through directories available in larger public libraries. The Better Business Bureau and the chamber of commerce of the town or city you're interested in will give you lists of local businesses. Both organizations are also good sources for checking the reputation of a particular business you may be interested in.

Tap your network of relatives, friends, neighbors, and professional associates for information. That insurance agent who calls, that vendor you talk to so frequently, that secretary you met at an office skills conference: these are just some of the people to tell when you're looking for a new position.

Also check job postings on Internet job sites such as Monster.com and HotJobs.com. You can conduct searches by key word, city, or date. These Web sites also allow you to post your resumé for prospective employers.

Finally, don't overlook temporary placement services. One benefit is that many agencies provide free training on new equipment and software packages, which can make you more desirable to a prospective employer. A second benefit is that temporary work allows you to experience different companies as an insider; once you find a company you like, apply for full-time work. Yet another benefit is that temporary work allows you maximum flexibility in scheduling your personal time.

✦ Your Resumé

No matter which path you take to look for a new job, you will need a professional looking resumé, the document describing your work history and skills to a potential employer. There are two basic formats to follow. One focuses on a history of where you've worked (Figure 40-1), and the other on particular skills you have (Figure 40-2). All resumés should include:

- Your name, address, and telephone number
- Your educational background (schools attended; degrees, diplomas, or certificates awarded; special training received or courses attended)
- A listing of all previous employment
- Your current job

One mistake many people make on a resumé is attempting to explain why they left one job and moved on to another. This is not the place to discuss it. You may be asked this question in an interview, so be prepared with an answer, but don't volunteer it in your resumé.

It can be very useful to prepare several versions of a resumé, adapting the basic facts to emphasize the different skills required for different jobs. Suppose the administrative assistant were applying for a position in a sales department. She might want to rewrite the skills-format version of her resumé, putting her sales experience as the first item and enlarging upon it wherever possible. Did she work with sales representatives? Did she handle objections or close calls herself? Did she find new prospects for the salespeople? Emphasizing this side of her experience could make her more attractive to the interviewer.

Evelyn Flo Boyd
12345 Heartside Dr.
Western Branch, GA 31234
404-555-1234

Experience
1999–Present   Lyon's Still Photography
Acworth, Georgia

Office manager and assistant to business owner
Maintained files and records, accounts receivable, and customer database.
Assisted photographer with photo subjects, as well as sales of proofs and
prints. Handled scheduling of business activities, all correspondence, and
travel arrangements.

1997–1999   Third Coast Video, Inc
Austin, Texas

Office assistant
Scheduled clients and facilities for video production and postproduction
facility. Scheduled freelance crews and equipment rentals. Arranged for
shipping of equipment and travel for crews. Also handled invoicing and
correspondence.

Education
1993–1997   B.A.-English
University of Texas
Austin, Texas

References furnished upon request.

FIGURE 40-1. Sample resumé in a chronological format.

This in no way means you should make up qualifications. If you do, it could
prove disastrous if you are called on to perform a task you claim to be experienced at doing.

The Cover Letter

Along with your resumé, you should also include an application or cover letter
that states your interest in a particular job, briefly lists your qualifications, and
explains why you might like to work for this particular employer (Figure 40-3).

Evelyn Flo Boyd
12345 Heartside Dr.
Western Branch, GA 31234
404-555-1234

Experience

ADMINISTRATION — Maintained files and records, accounts receivable, and customer database. Handled scheduling of business activities all correspondence, and travel arrangements.

SALES — Worked with customers to set appointments and to sell photography services.

VIDEO PRODUCTION — Coordinated scheduling of crews and facilities. Hired freelance crews and outline equipment rentals.

TECHNICAL SKILLS — Complete understanding of IBM-compatible software including: Windows, Word for Windows, Excel, and WordPerfect. Also, some understanding of Apple Macintosh computers including Microsoft Word and Excel. Good typing skills, 50 wpm. Working knowledge of most office equipment, copiers, fax machines, and typewriters.

Work History

1999–Present
Office Manager and Assistant to Business Owner
Lycon's Still Photography
Acworth, Georgia

1997–1999
Office Assistant
Third Coast Video, Inc.
Austin, Texas

*Education*1993–1997 B.A.-English
University of Texas
Austin, Texas

References furnished upon request.

FIGURE 40-2. Sample resumé in a skills format.

12345 Heartside Dr.
Western Branch, GA 31234
December 2, 2004

Mr. Kevin Wilson
President
Videologies, Inc.
10 North Main St.
Atlanta, GA 30303

Dear Mr. Wilson,

I am very interested in applying for the job of office assistant listed in the *Atlanta Constitution* on December 1.

As you can see from my enclosed resumé, I have worked for both a still photographer and a small video production company. I enjoyed working at both of these companies, and I feel this past experience qualifies me for the position described in your advertisement.

I have a good understanding of the visual medium and the many details you must handle in your work. I believe I can help take responsibility for some of these details with little additional training.

I would appreciate the opportunity for a personal interview. You can reach me at 555-1234.

Thank you for your consideration.

Sincerely yours,

Evelyn Boyd

FIGURE 40-3. Job application cover letter.

The Interview

If your resumé and letter are successful, your next step will be an interview with the prospective employer. There are several ways you can prepare and techniques you can use for conducting yourself during it:

■ Examine your image. How do you look to the outside world? Consider the way you dress, the way you talk, even the way you stand. Can you talk to someone and look that person in the eye, rather than glance around or stare at your feet?

■ How about your skills? Can you do anything that someone would want to hire you to do?

■ What about experience? Have you ever practiced these skills in an employment situation?

■ How much money do you want? What are employers in your area willing to pay for your skills? Find this out before you go to the interview by asking people and checking resources at the library, Chamber of Commerce, or Better Business Bureau.

■ What do you know about the company where you're going to interview? How does it make money? What does its success depend on?

If you can find out this information, you'll be prepared to show how you can help make the business better. And that's what an employer wants to hear.

The Plus Element

The ending of this book can be brief because the most important instruction of all must come from your own heart and character. You must enlarge on every possibility to keep in rhythm with your employer, work with graceful efficiency, and anticipate the needs of the office. Then with your own pride and pleasure in the work you've done, you'll also see your employer's great satisfaction in having at last found the "right hand" he or she has always needed.

Index